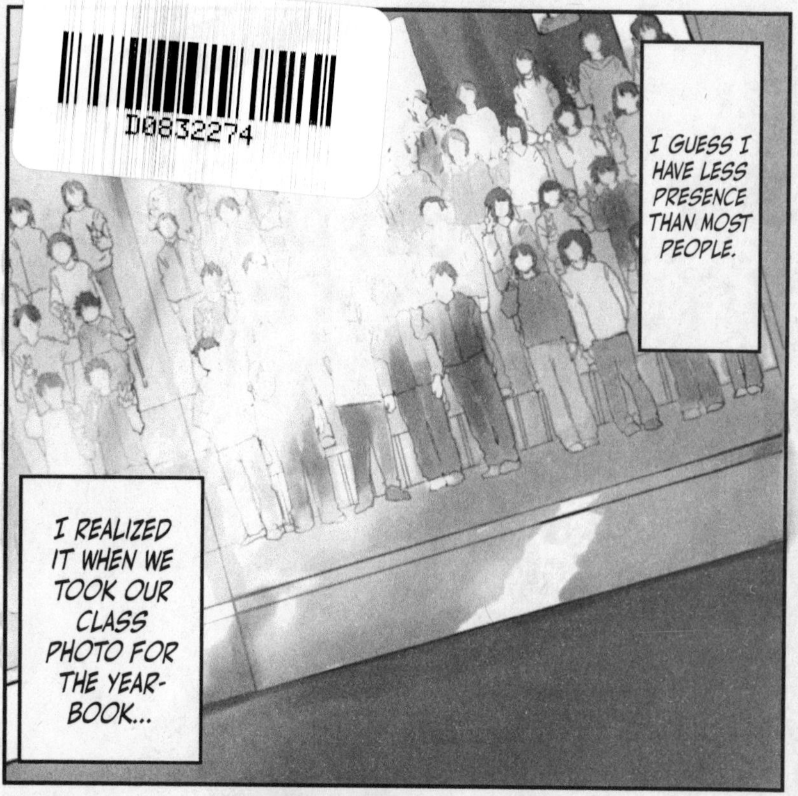
I GUESS I HAVE LESS PRESENCE THAN MOST PEOPLE.
I REALIZED IT WHEN WE TOOK OUR CLASS PHOTO FOR THE YEAR-BOOK...

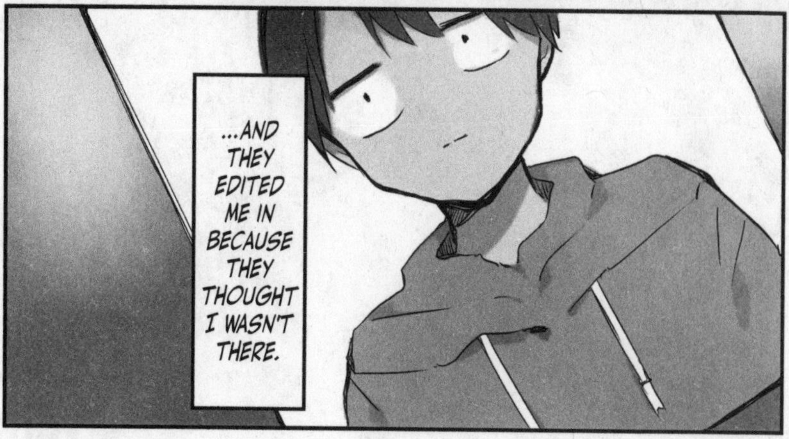
...AND THEY EDITED ME IN BECAUSE THEY THOUGHT I WASN'T THERE.

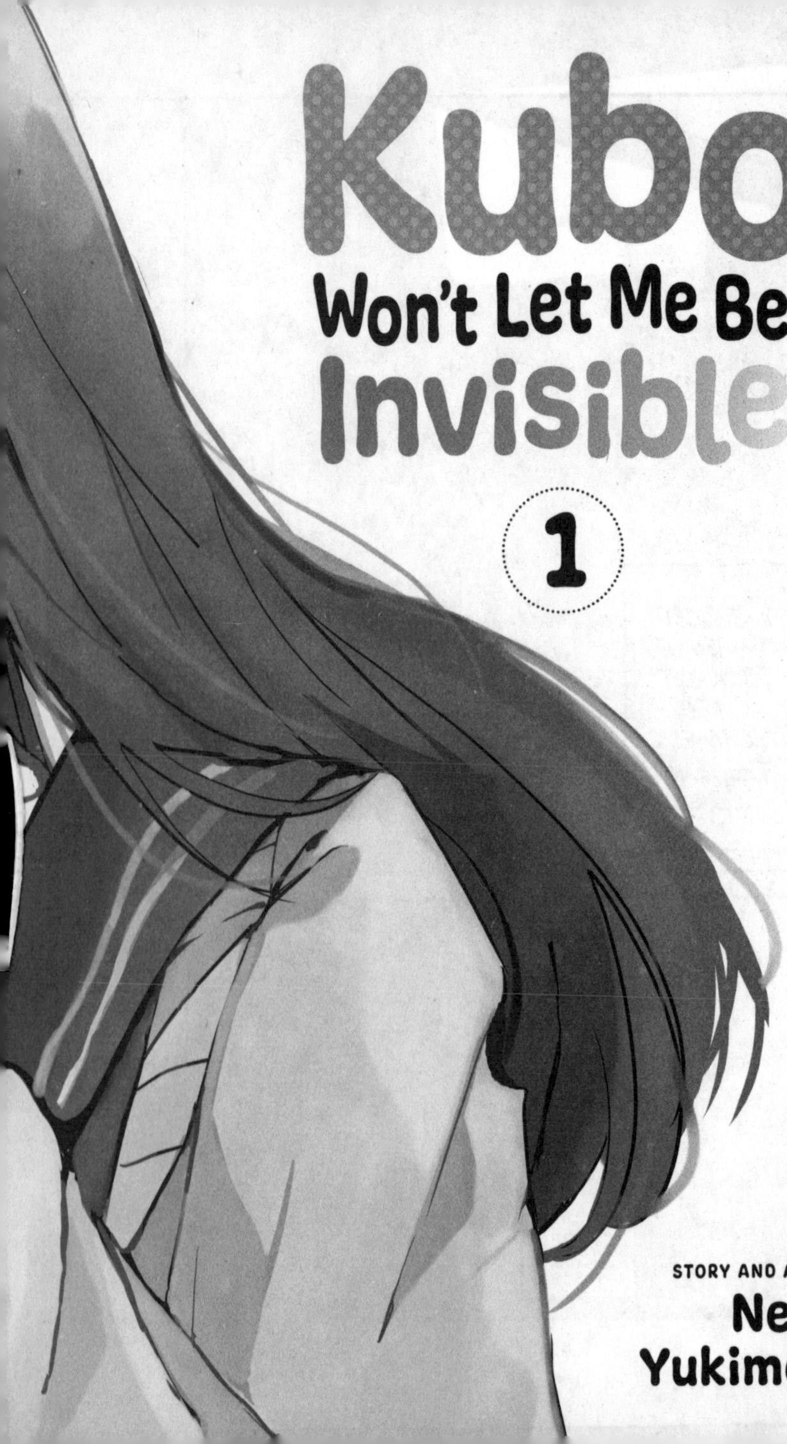

Kubo Won't Let Me Be Invisible

1

STORY AND ART BY

Nene Yukimori

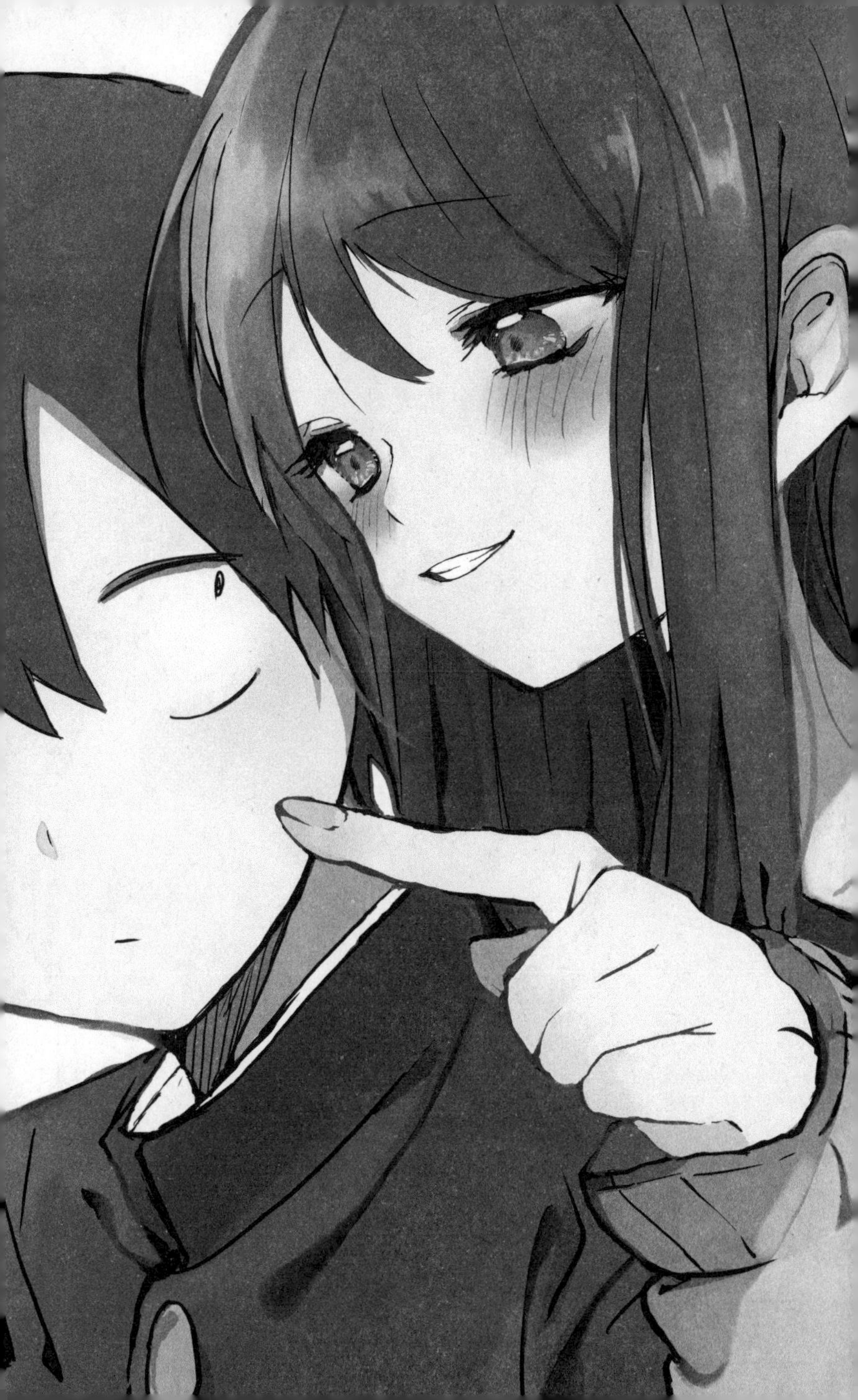

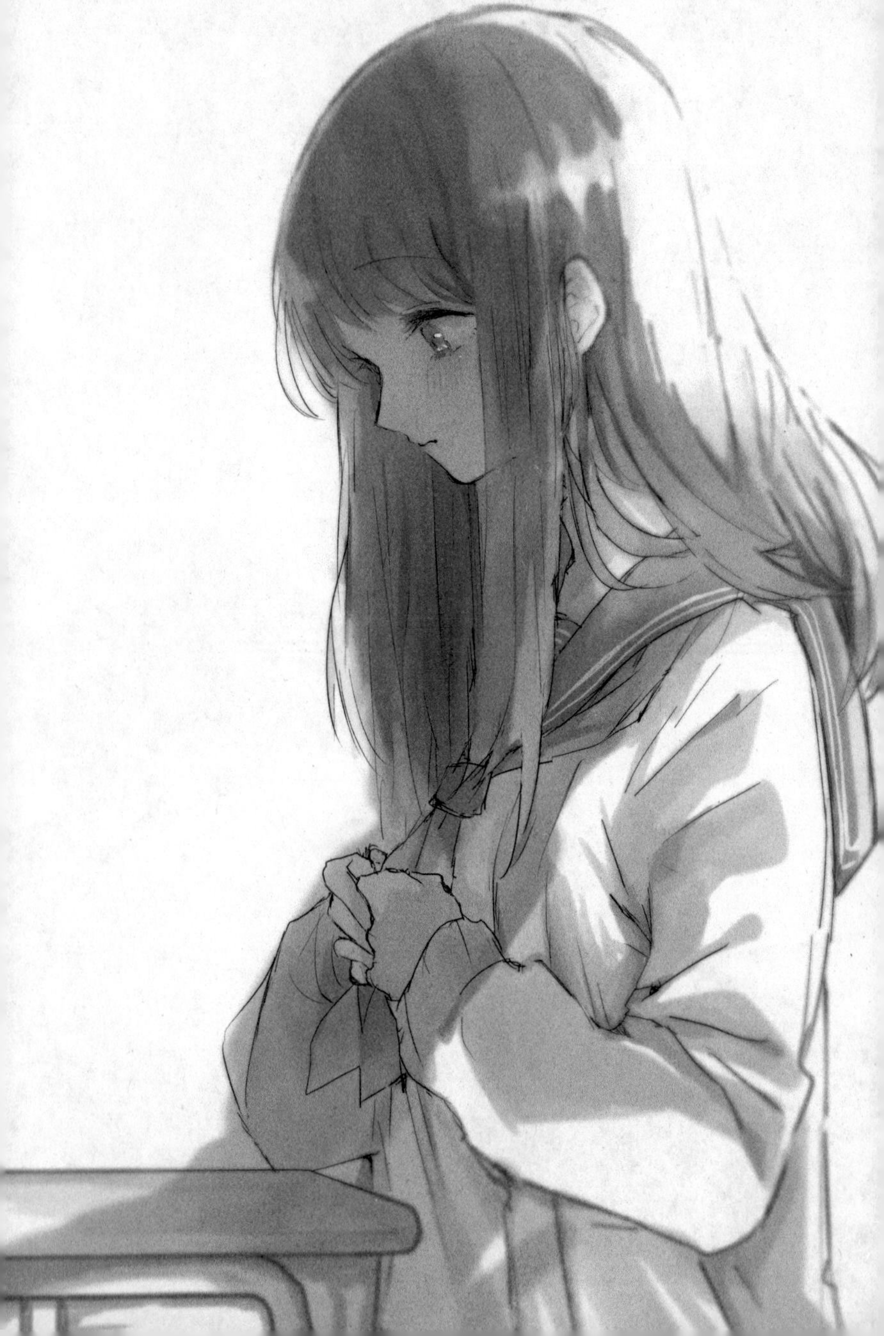

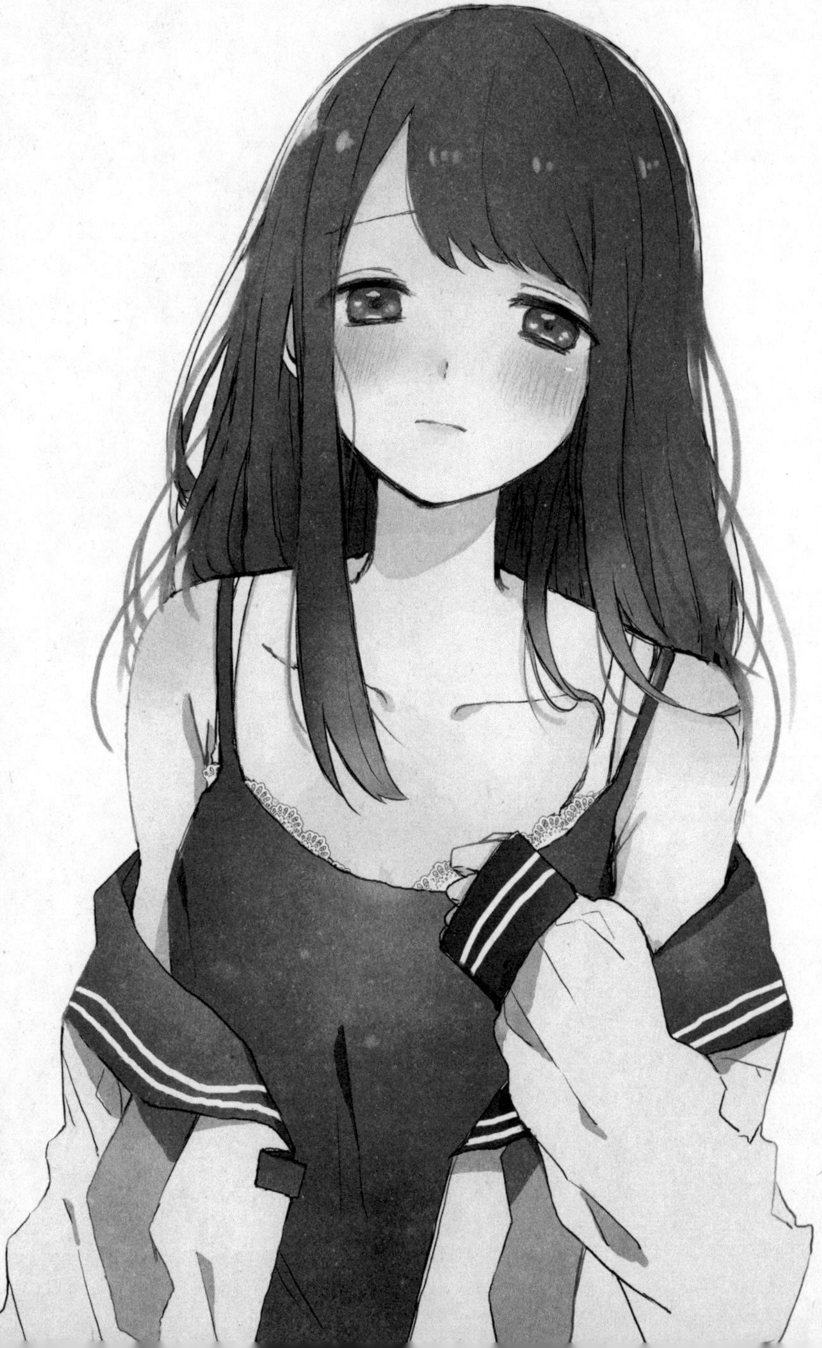

CONTENTS

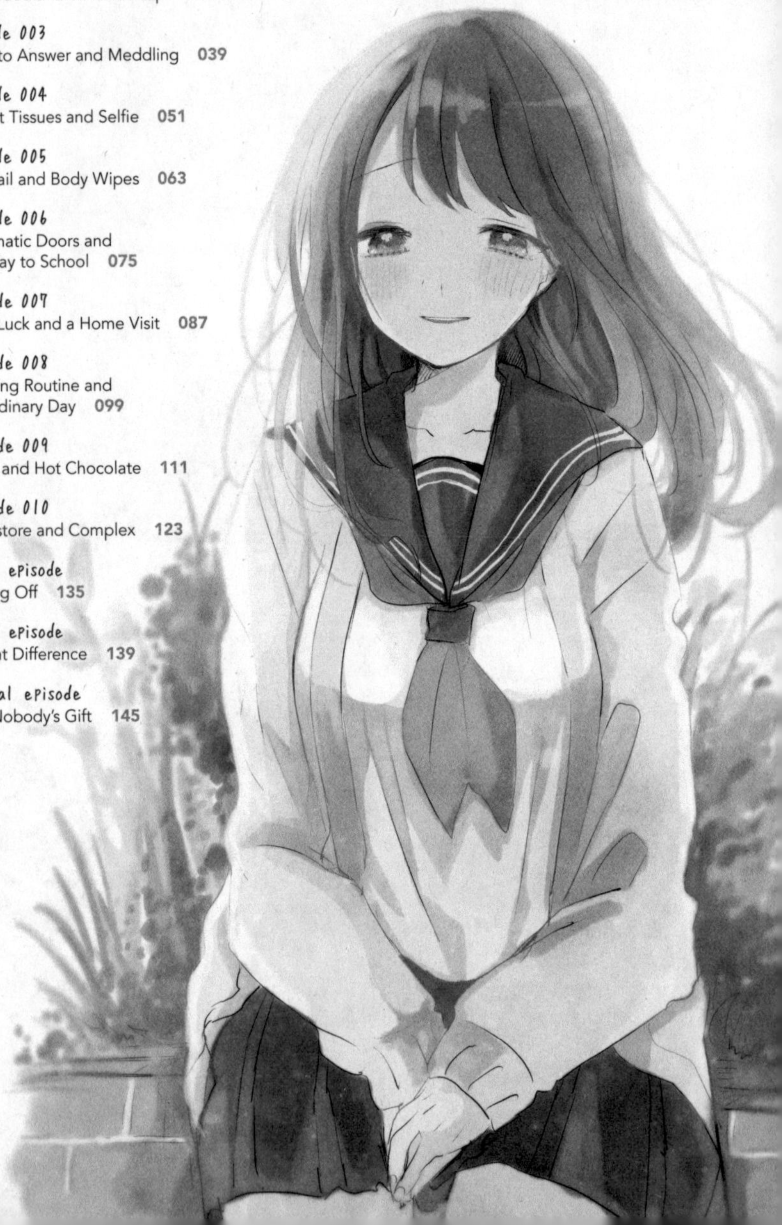

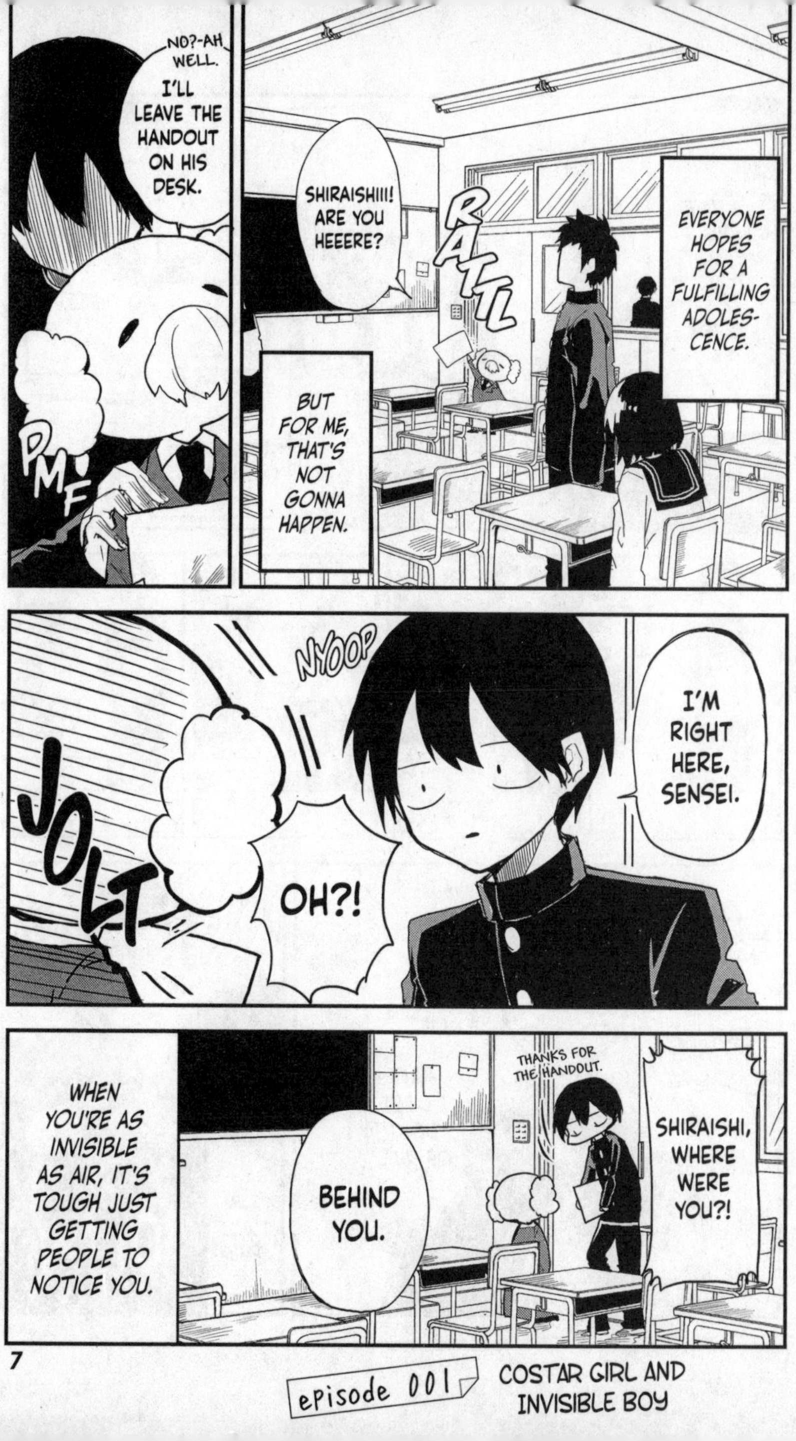
EVERYONE HOPES FOR A FULFILLING ADOLES-CENCE.
RATTL
SHIRAISHIII! ARE YOU HEEERE?
BUT FOR ME, THAT'S NOT GONNA HAPPEN.
NO?-AH WELL. I'LL LEAVE THE HANDOUT ON HIS DESK.
PMF
I'M RIGHT HERE, SENSEI.
NYOOP
OH?!
JOLT
SHIRAISHI, WHERE WERE YOU?!
THANKS FOR THE HANDOUT.
BEHIND YOU.
WHEN YOU'RE AS INVISIBLE AS AIR, IT'S TOUGH JUST GETTING PEOPLE TO NOTICE YOU.

episode 001 COSTAR GIRL AND INVISIBLE BOY

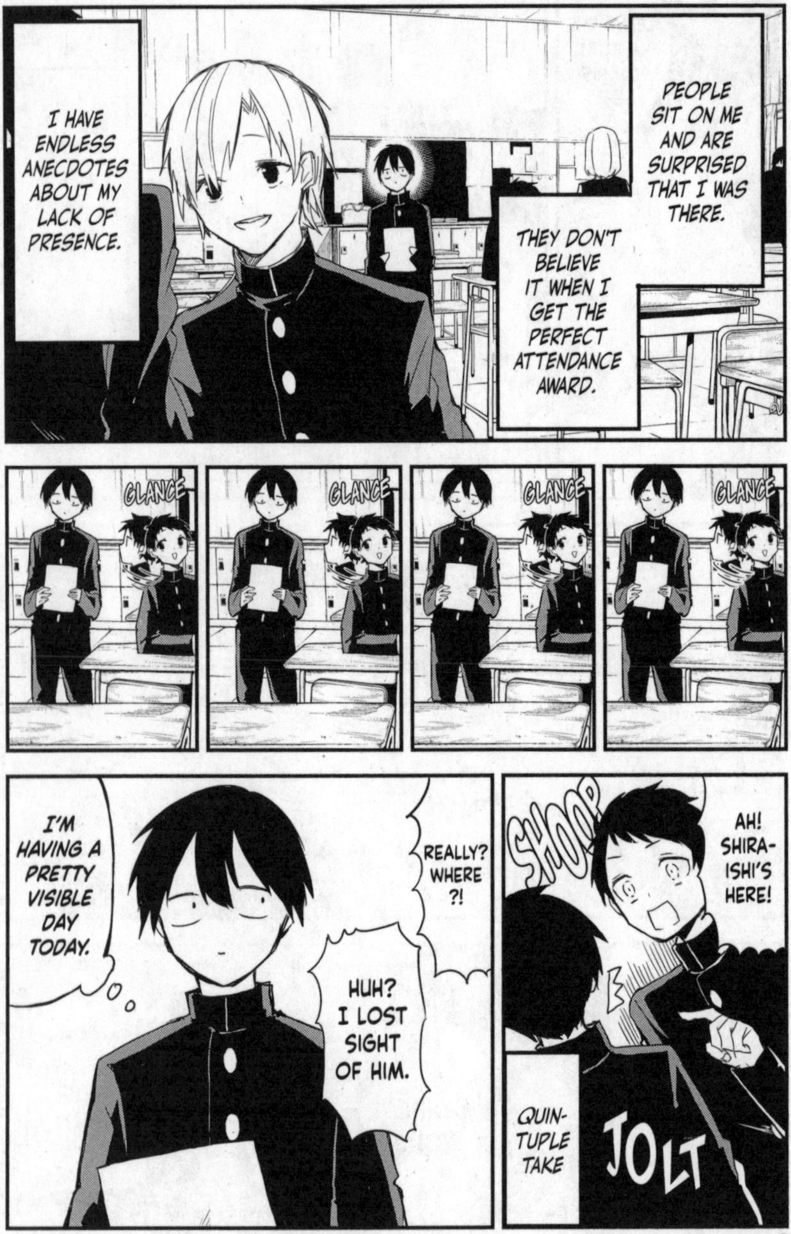
PEOPLE SIT ON ME AND ARE SURPRISED THAT I WAS THERE.
THEY DON'T BELIEVE IT WHEN I GET THE PERFECT ATTENDANCE AWARD.
I HAVE ENDLESS ANECDOTES ABOUT MY LACK OF PRESENCE.
GLANCE
GLANCE
GLANCE
GLANCE
SHOOP
AH! SHIRA-ISHI'S HERE!
JOLT
QUIN-TUPLE TAKE
REALLY? WHERE ?!
HUH? I LOST SIGHT OF HIM.
I'M HAVING A PRETTY VISIBLE DAY TODAY.

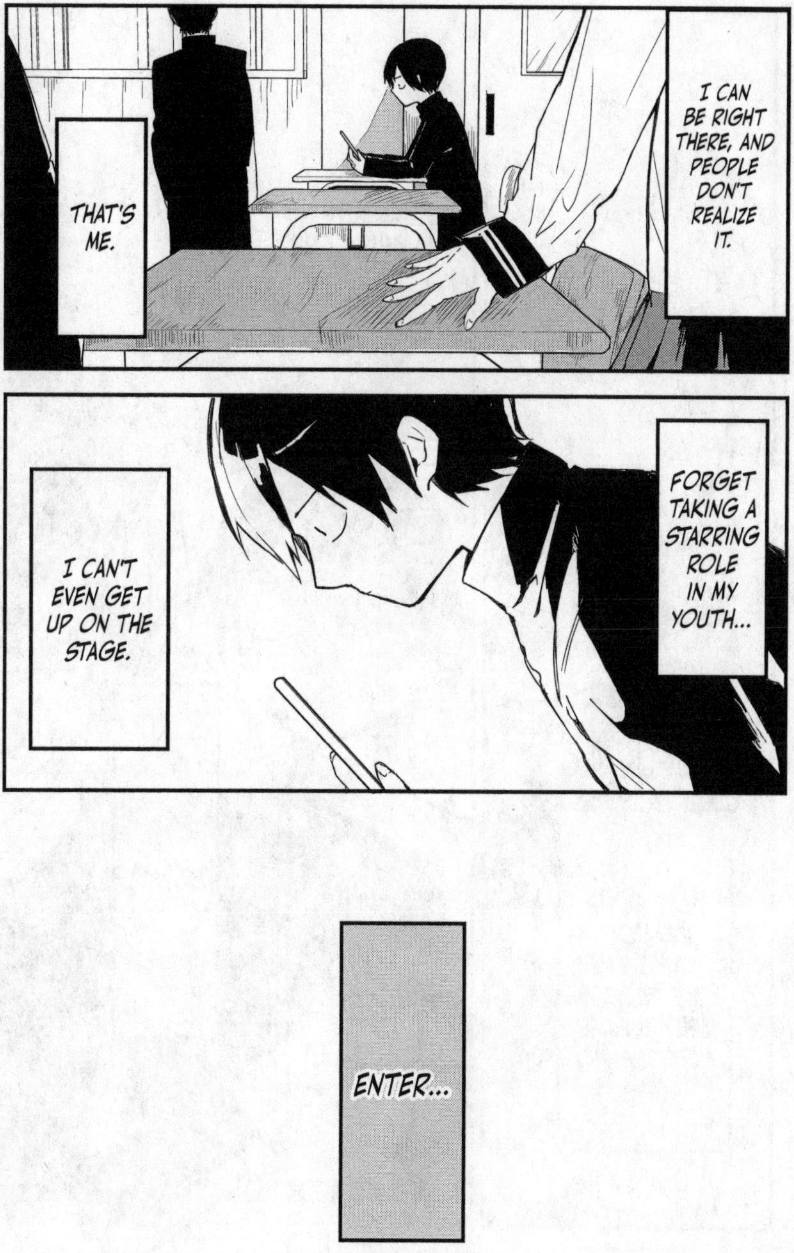
I CAN BE RIGHT THERE, AND PEOPLE DON'T REALIZE IT.
THAT'S ME.
FORGET TAKING A STARRING ROLE IN MY YOUTH...
I CAN'T EVEN GET UP ON THE STAGE.
ENTER...

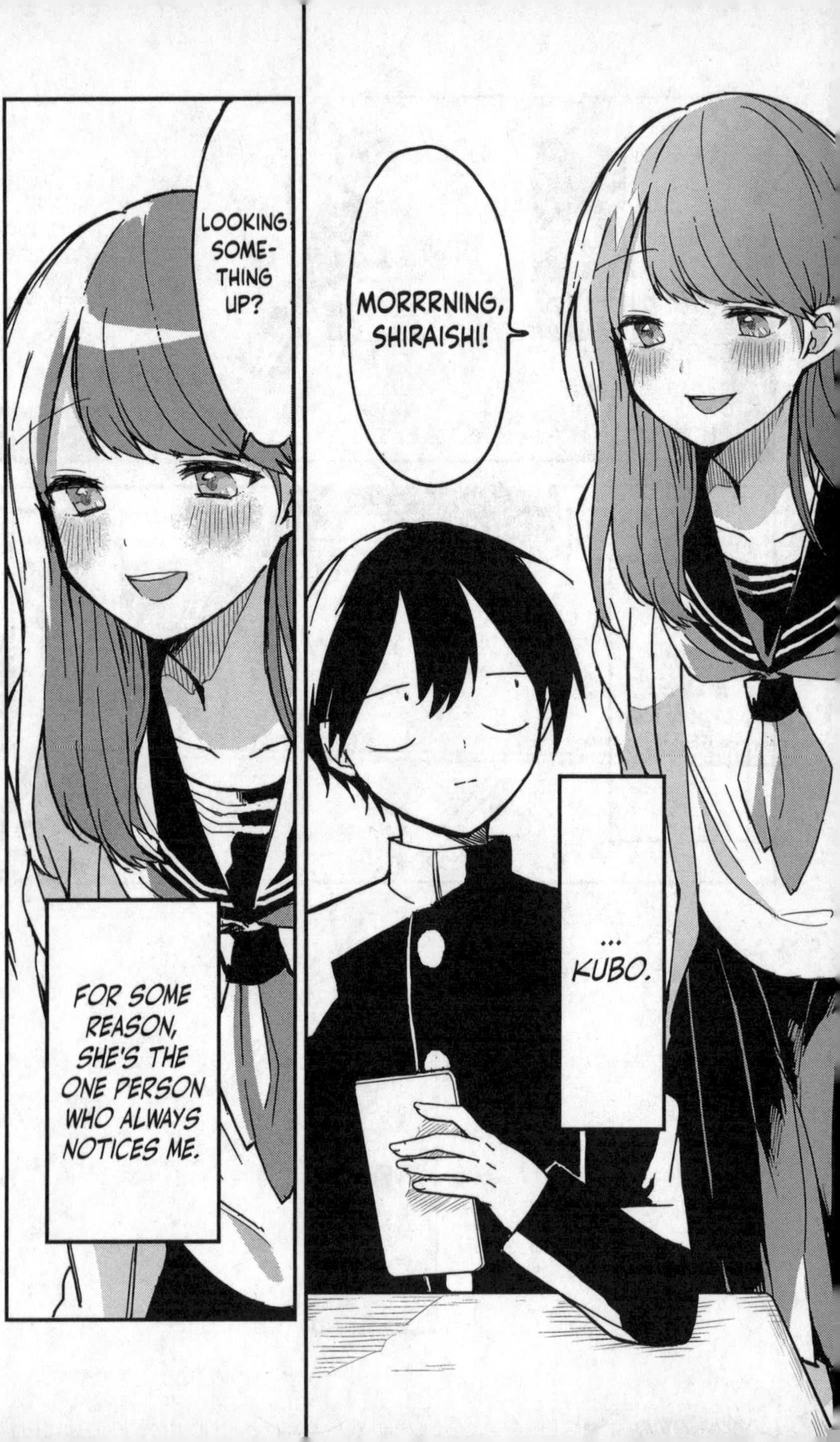
MORRRNING, SHIRAISHI!
...KUBO.
LOOKING SOMETHING UP?
FOR SOME REASON, SHE'S THE ONE PERSON WHO ALWAYS NOTICES ME.

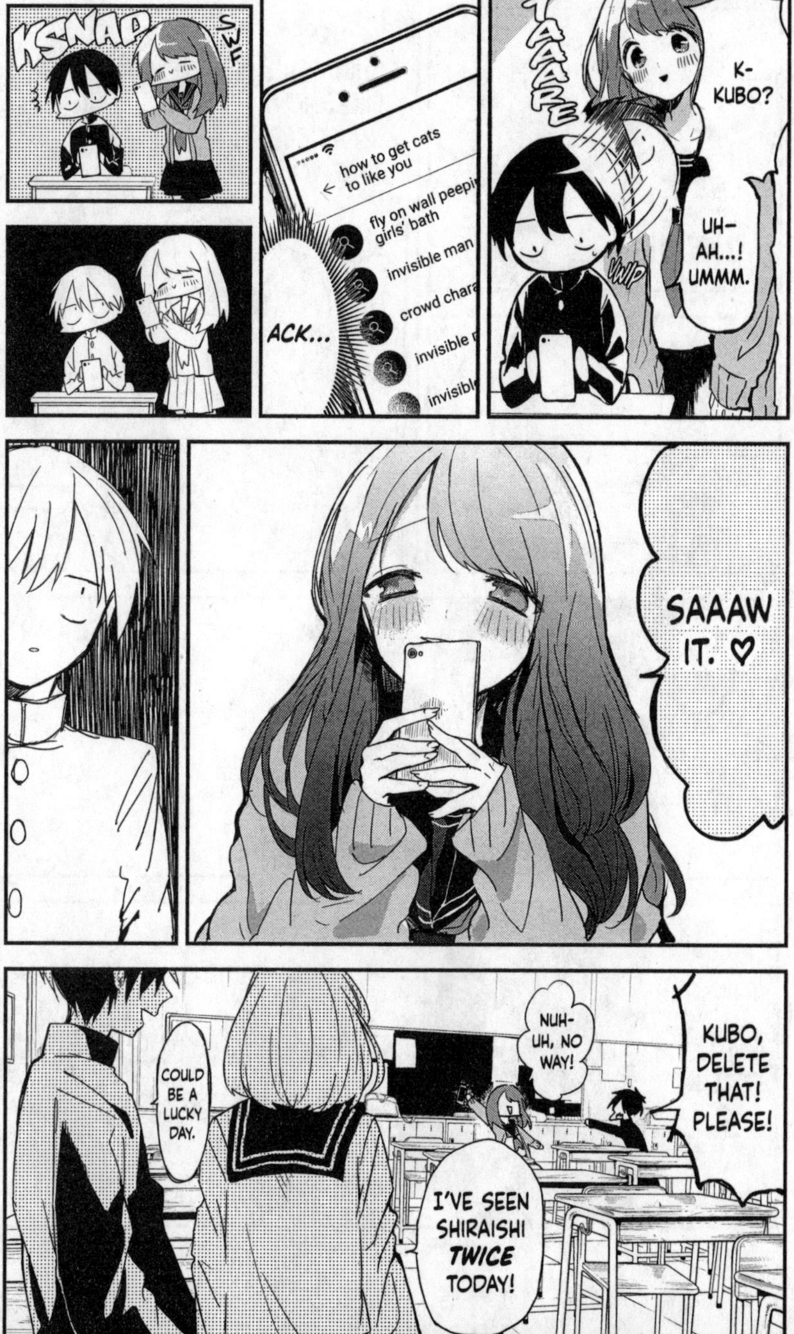

K-KUBO?
STAAARE
UH-AH...! UMMM.
VWIP
how to get cats to like you
fly on wall peepi girls' bath
invisible man
crowd chara
invisible
invisible
ACK...
KSNAP
SWF
SAAAW IT. ♡
KUBO, DELETE THAT! PLEASE!
NUH-UH, NO WAY!
I'VE SEEN SHIRAISHI *TWICE* TODAY!
COULD BE A LUCKY DAY.

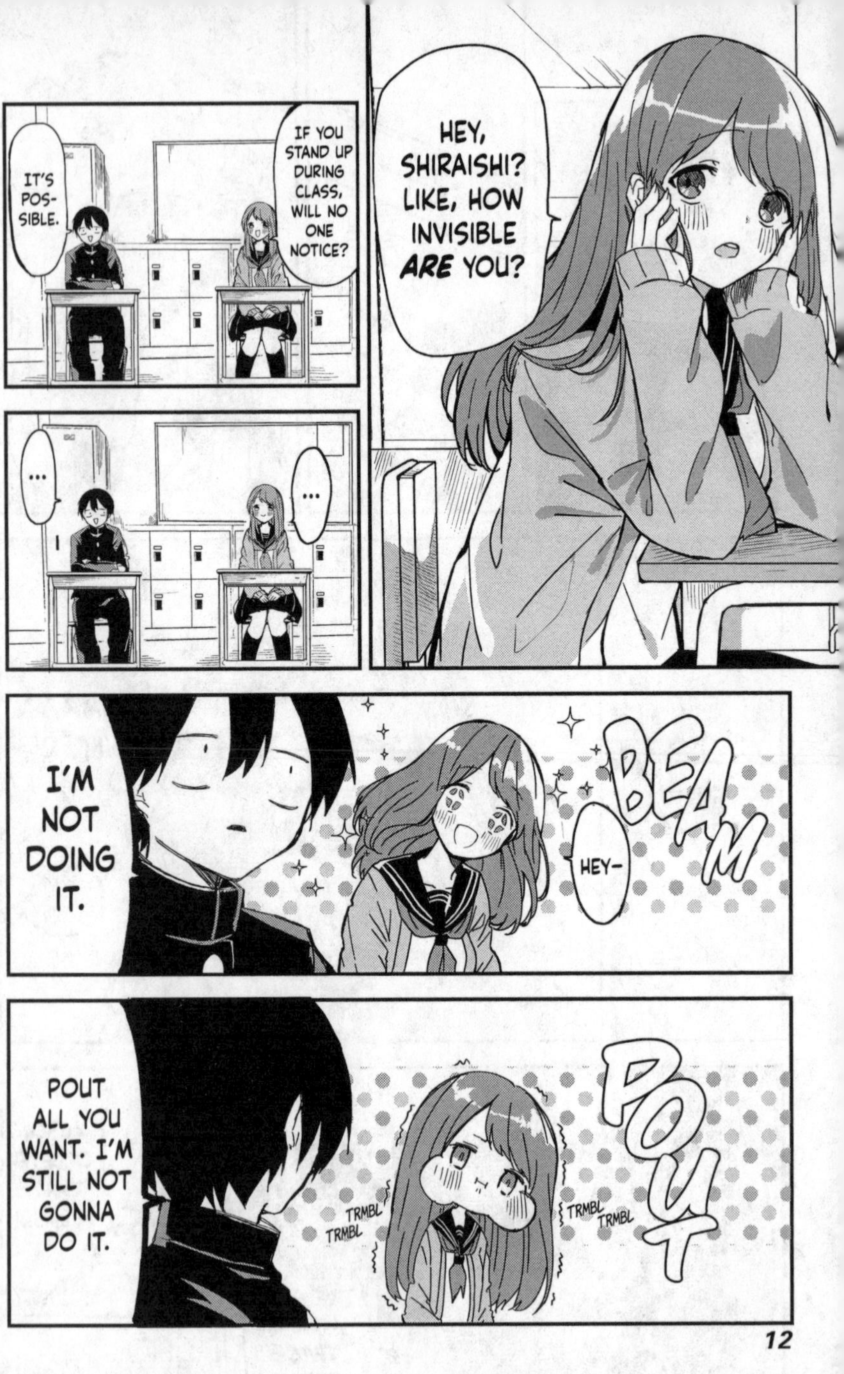
HEY, SHIRAISHI? LIKE, HOW INVISIBLE ARE YOU?
IF YOU STAND UP DURING CLASS, WILL NO ONE NOTICE?
IT'S POS-SIBLE.
...
...
BEAM
HEY-
I'M NOT DOING IT.
POUT
TRMBL TRMBL
TRMBL TRMBL
POUT ALL YOU WANT. I'M STILL NOT GONNA DO IT.

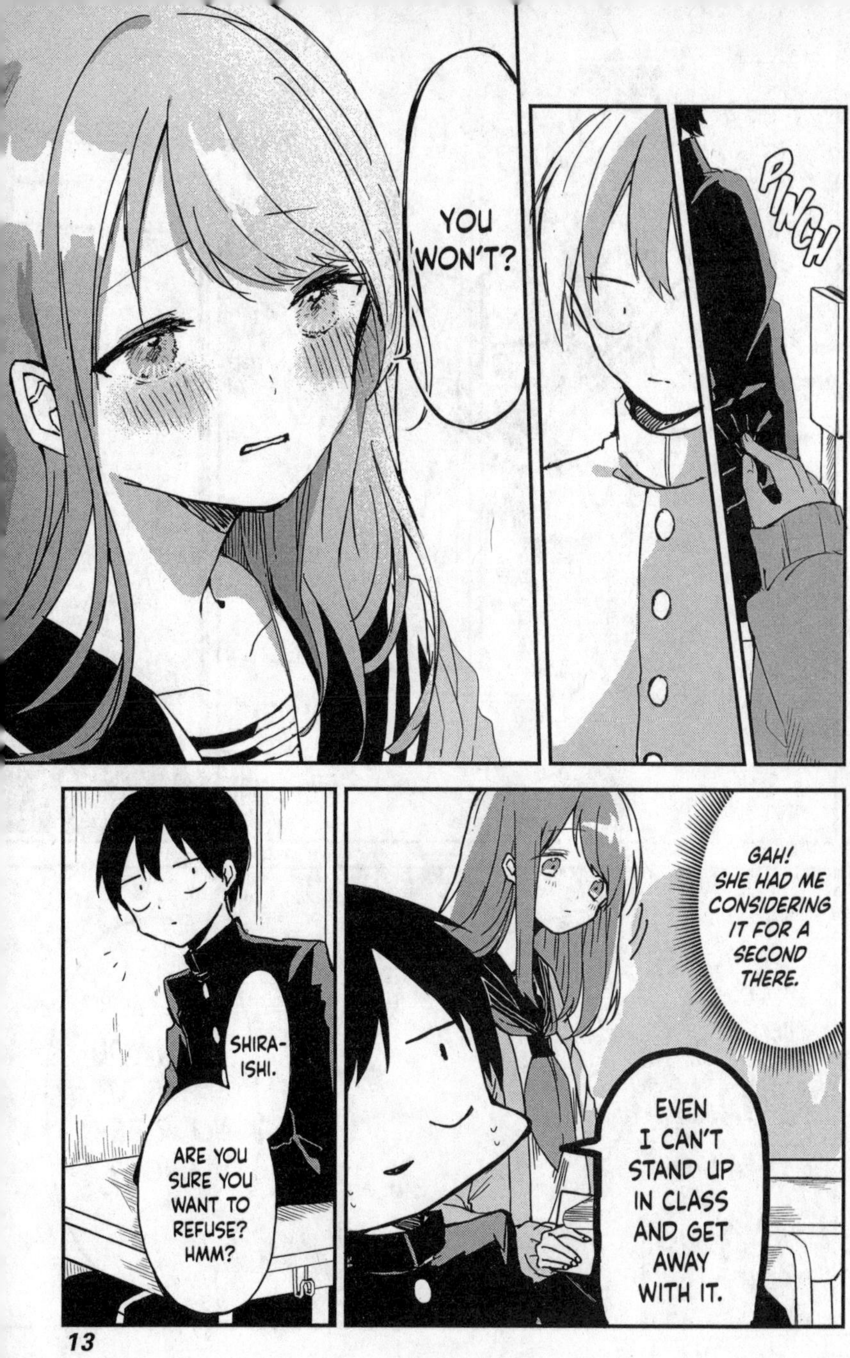
PINCH
YOU WON'T?
GAH! SHE HAD ME CONSIDERING IT FOR A SECOND THERE.
EVEN I CAN'T STAND UP IN CLASS AND GET AWAY WITH IT.
SHIRA-ISHI.
ARE YOU SURE YOU WANT TO REFUSE? HMM?

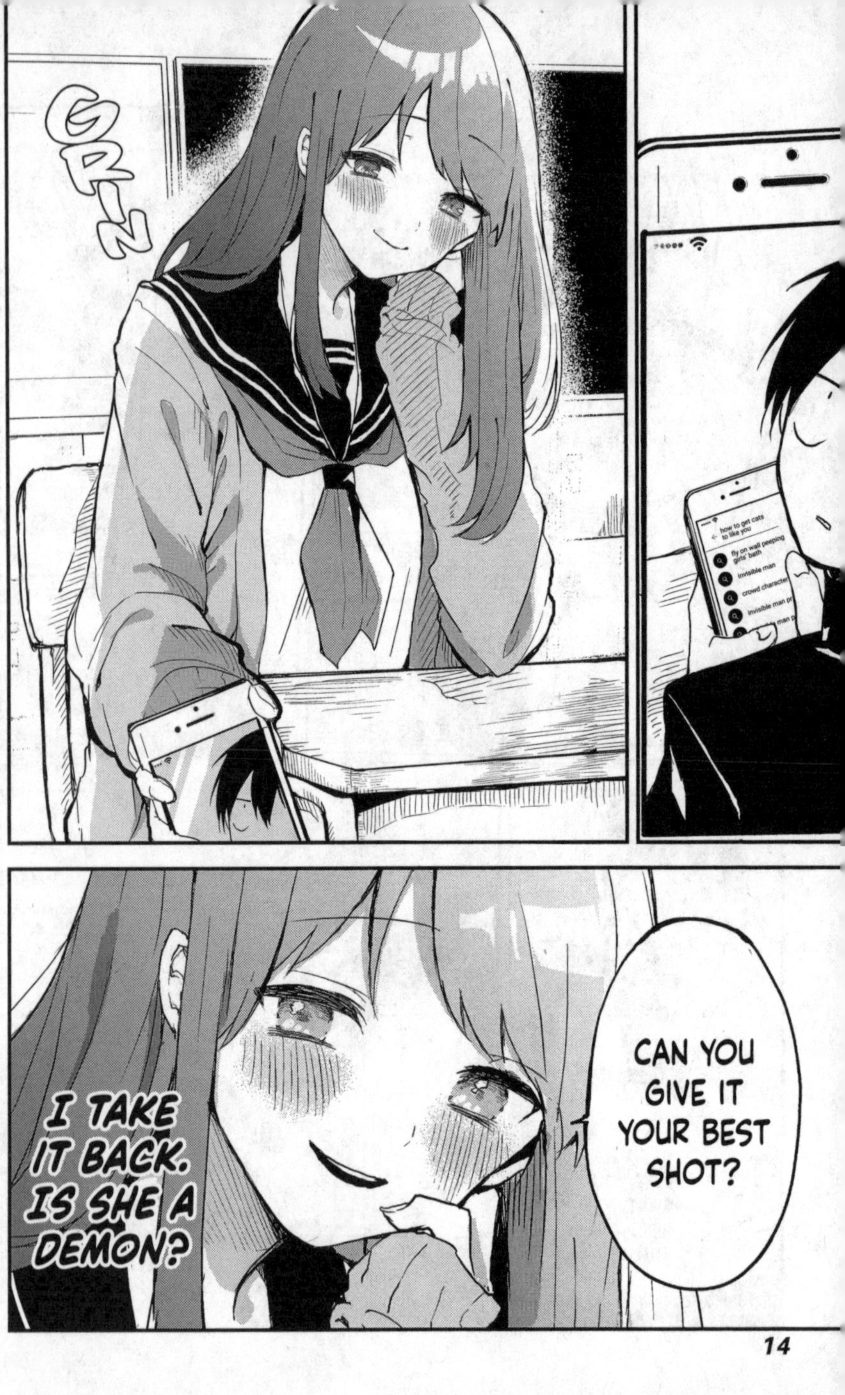
how to get cats to like you
fly on wall peeping girls' bath
invisible man
crowd character
invisible man pr
GRIN
CAN YOU GIVE IT YOUR BEST SHOT?
I TAKE IT BACK. IS SHE A DEMON?

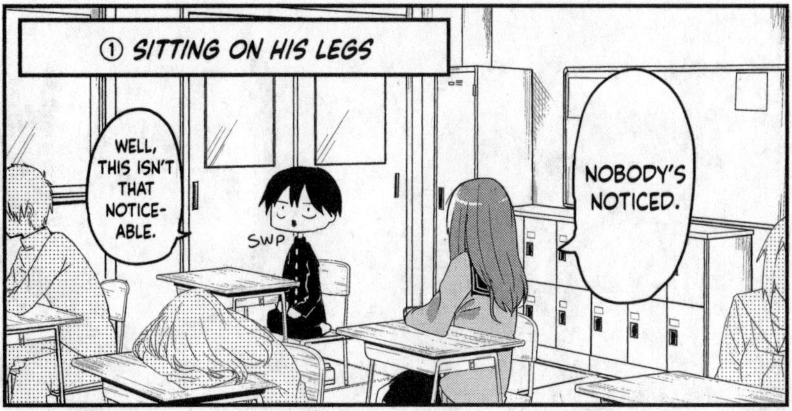
① SITTING ON HIS LEGS
NOBODY'S NOTICED.
WELL, THIS ISN'T THAT NOTICE-ABLE.
SWP

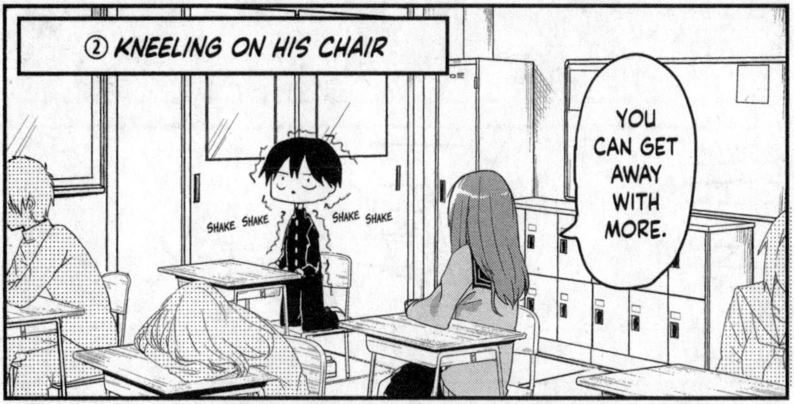
② KNEELING ON HIS CHAIR
YOU CAN GET AWAY WITH MORE.
SHAKE SHAKE
SHAKE SHAKE

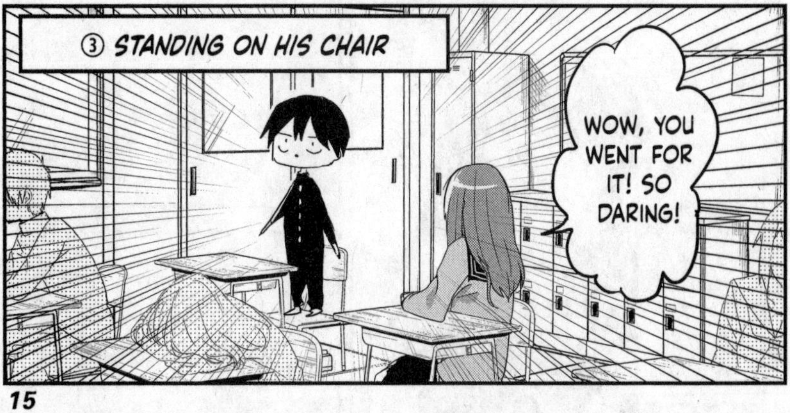
③ STANDING ON HIS CHAIR
WOW, YOU WENT FOR IT! SO DARING!

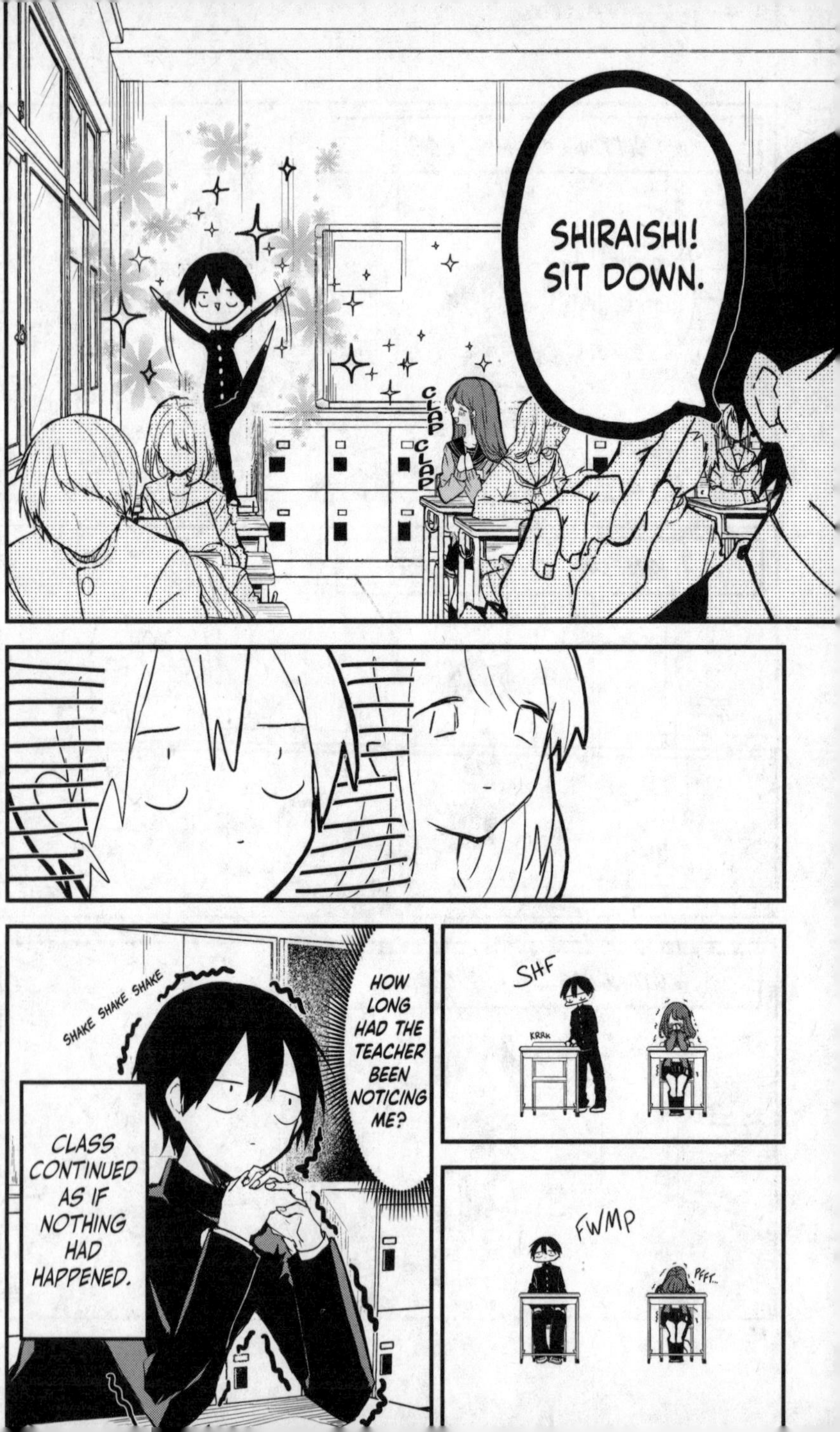
SHIRAISHI! SIT DOWN.
CLAP CLAP
SHF
KRRK
FWMP
PFFT...
HOW LONG HAD THE TEACHER BEEN NOTICING ME?
SHAKE SHAKE SHAKE
CLASS CONTINUED AS IF NOTHING HAD HAPPENED.

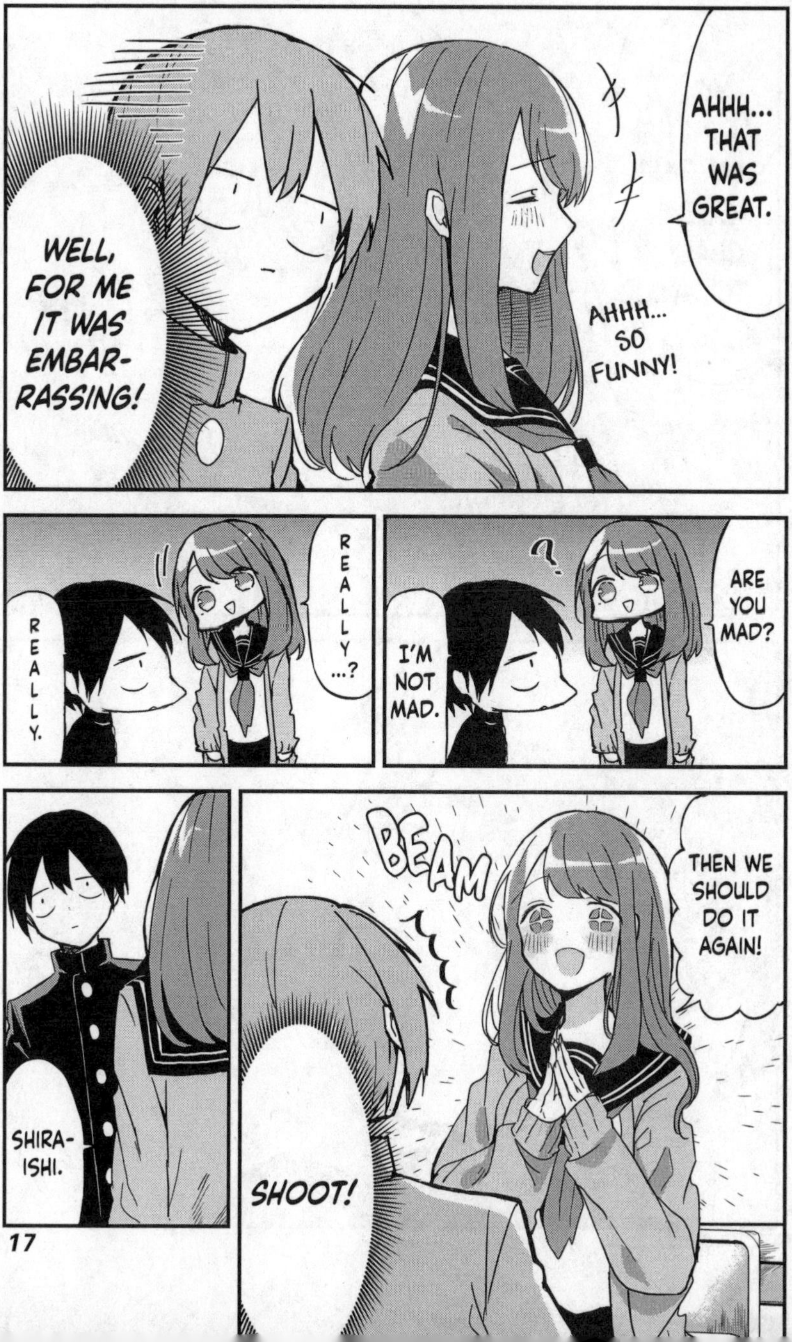
AHHH... THAT WAS GREAT.
AHHH... SO FUNNY!
WELL, FOR ME IT WAS EMBARRASSING!
ARE YOU MAD?
I'M NOT MAD.
REALLY...?
REALLY.
THEN WE SHOULD DO IT AGAIN!
BEAM
SHOOT!
SHIRAISHI.

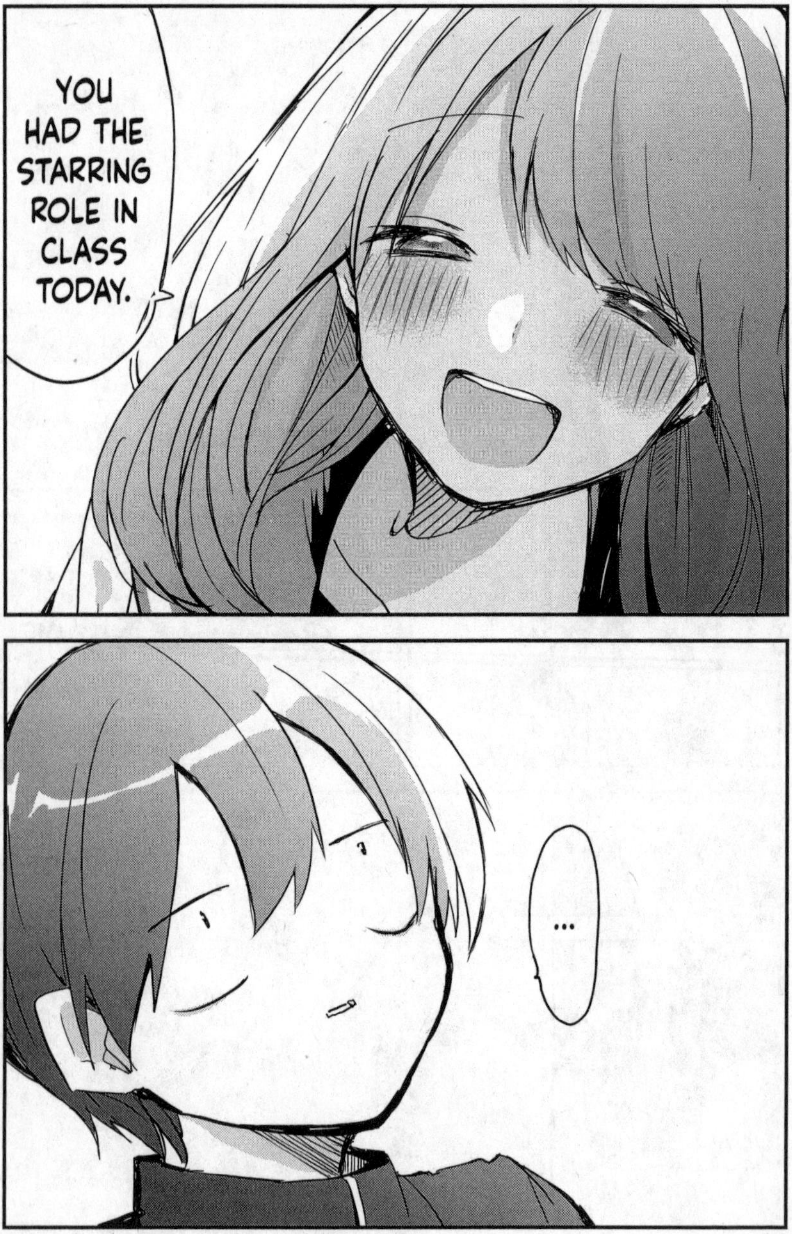
YOU HAD THE STARRING ROLE IN CLASS TODAY.
...

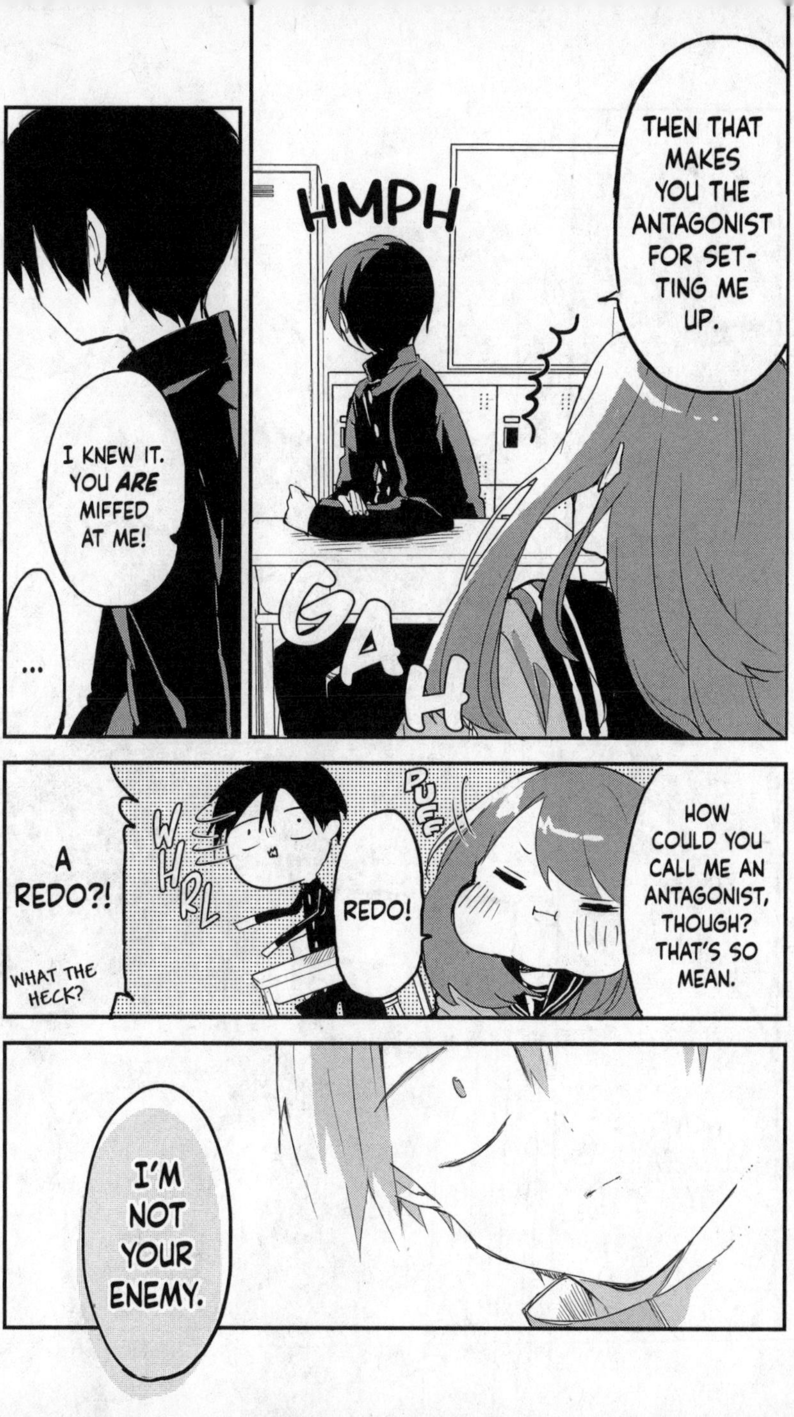
THEN THAT MAKES YOU THE ANTAGONIST FOR SET-TING ME UP.
HMPH
GAH
I KNEW IT. YOU ARE MIFFED AT ME!
...
HOW COULD YOU CALL ME AN ANTAGONIST, THOUGH? THAT'S SO MEAN.
PUFF
REDO!
WHRL
A REDO?!
WHAT THE HECK?
I'M NOT YOUR ENEMY.

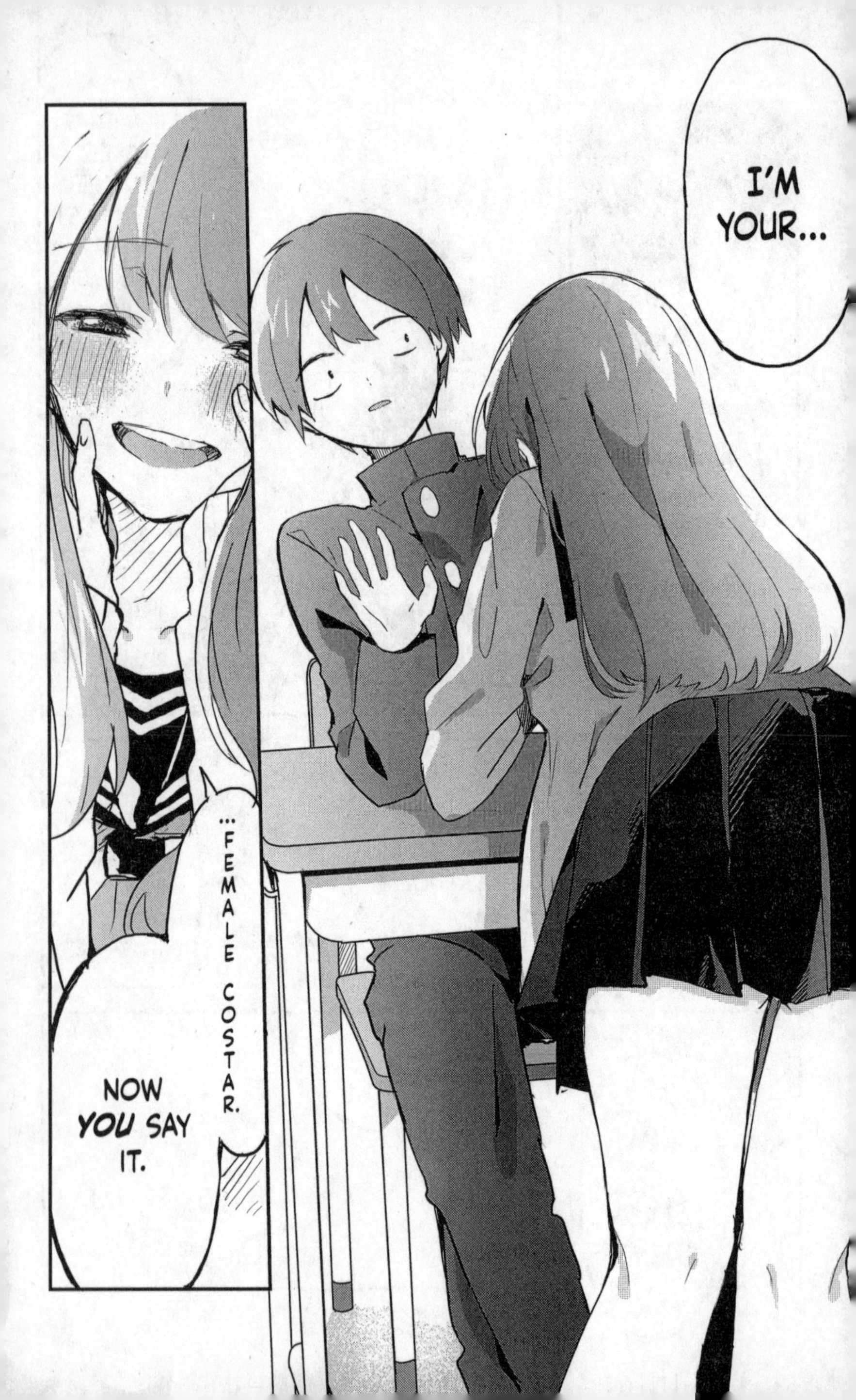
I'M YOUR...
...FEMALE COSTAR.
NOW *YOU* SAY IT.

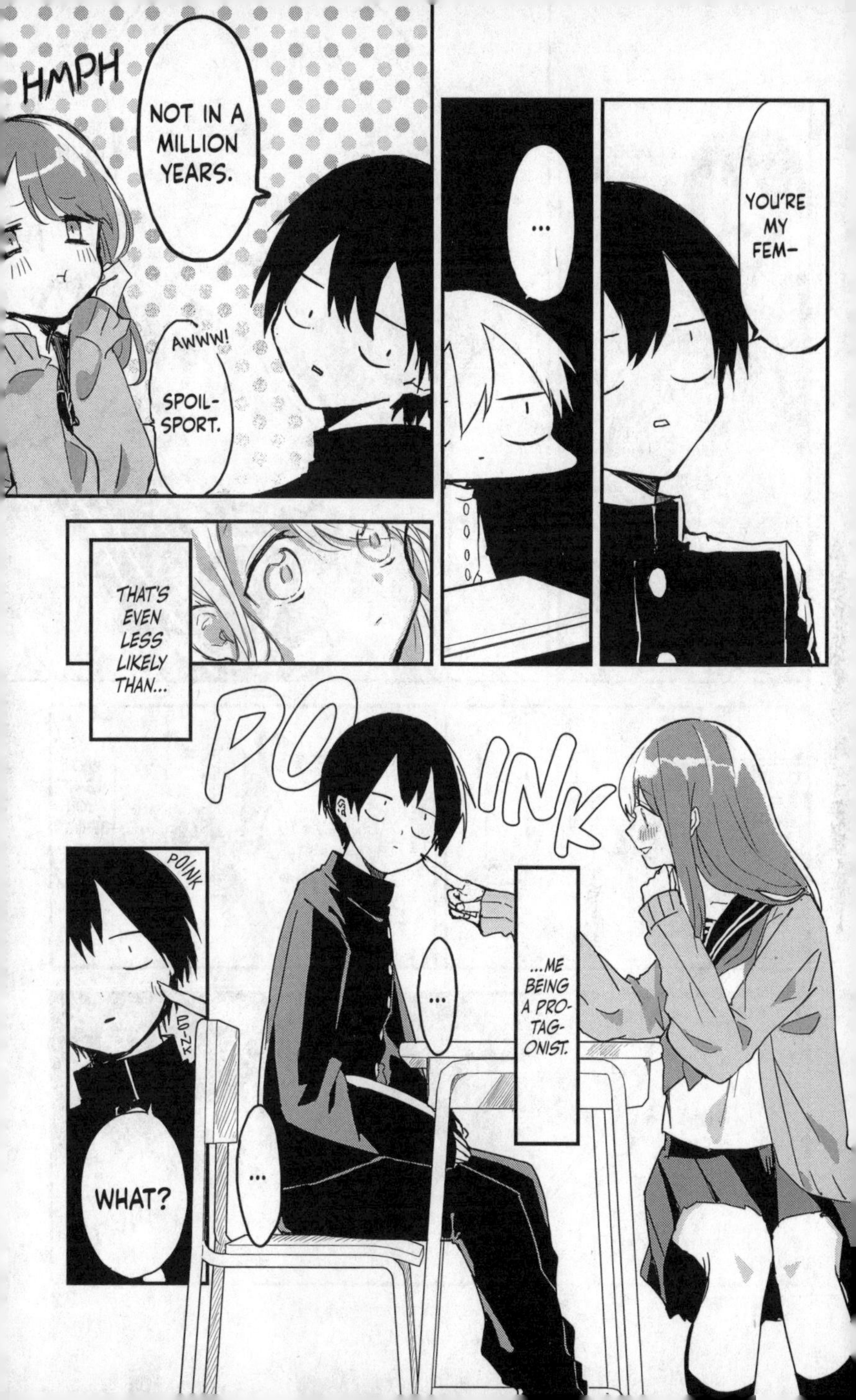
HMPH
NOT IN A MILLION YEARS.
AWWW!
SPOIL-SPORT.
YOU'RE MY FEM-
...
THAT'S EVEN LESS LIKELY THAN...
POINK
...ME BEING A PRO-TAG-ONIST.
...
POINK
POINK
WHAT?
...

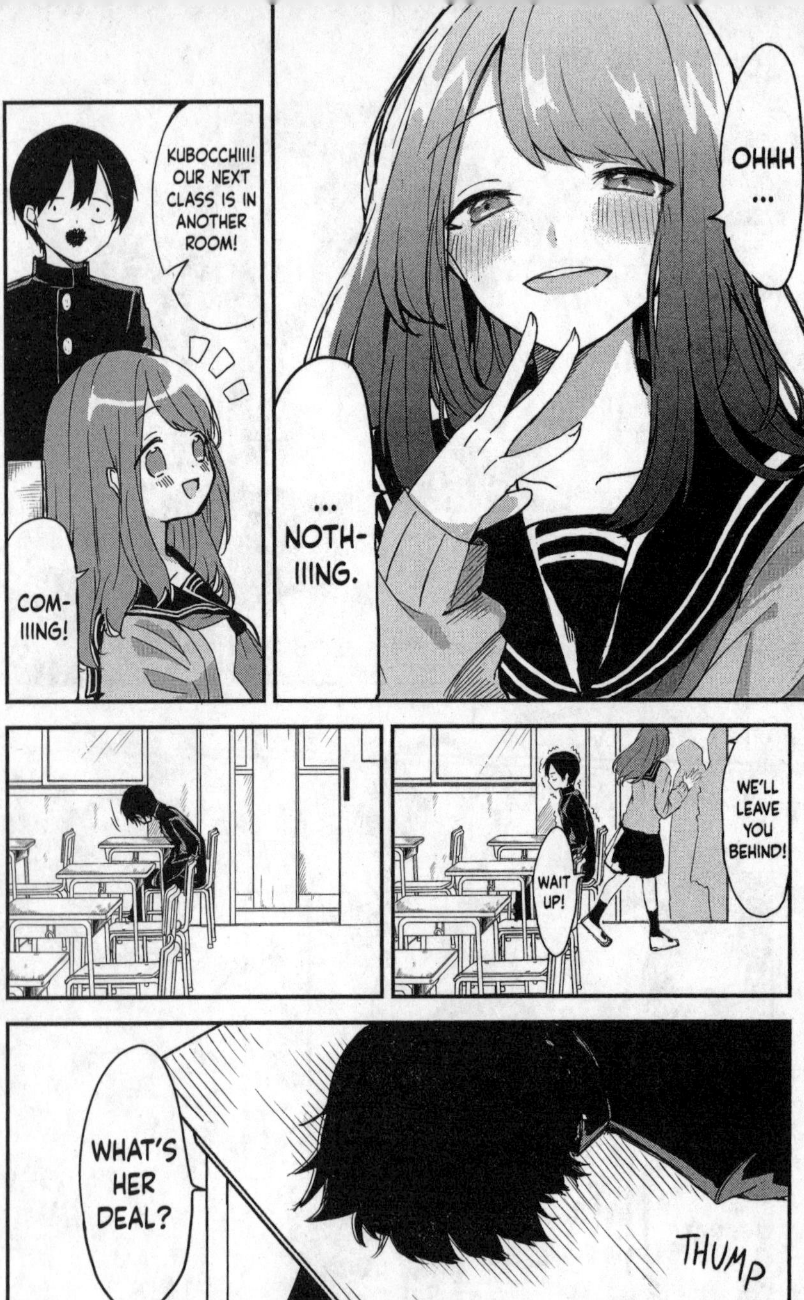
OHHH ...
... NOTH-IIING.
KUBOCCHIII! OUR NEXT CLASS IS IN ANOTHER ROOM!
COM-IIING!
WE'LL LEAVE YOU BEHIND!
WAIT UP!
THUMP
WHAT'S HER DEAL?

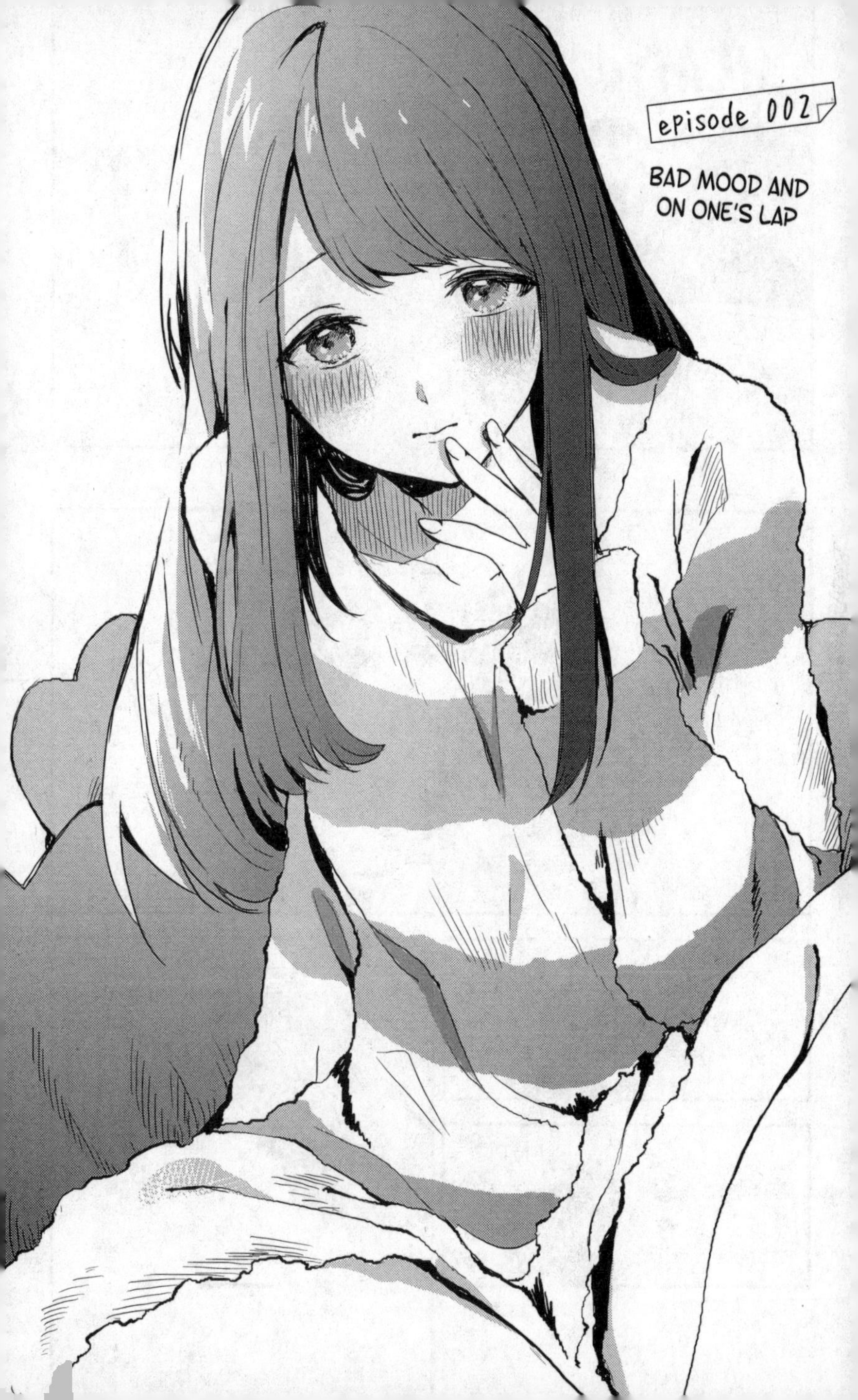
episode 002
BAD MOOD AND ON ONE'S LAP

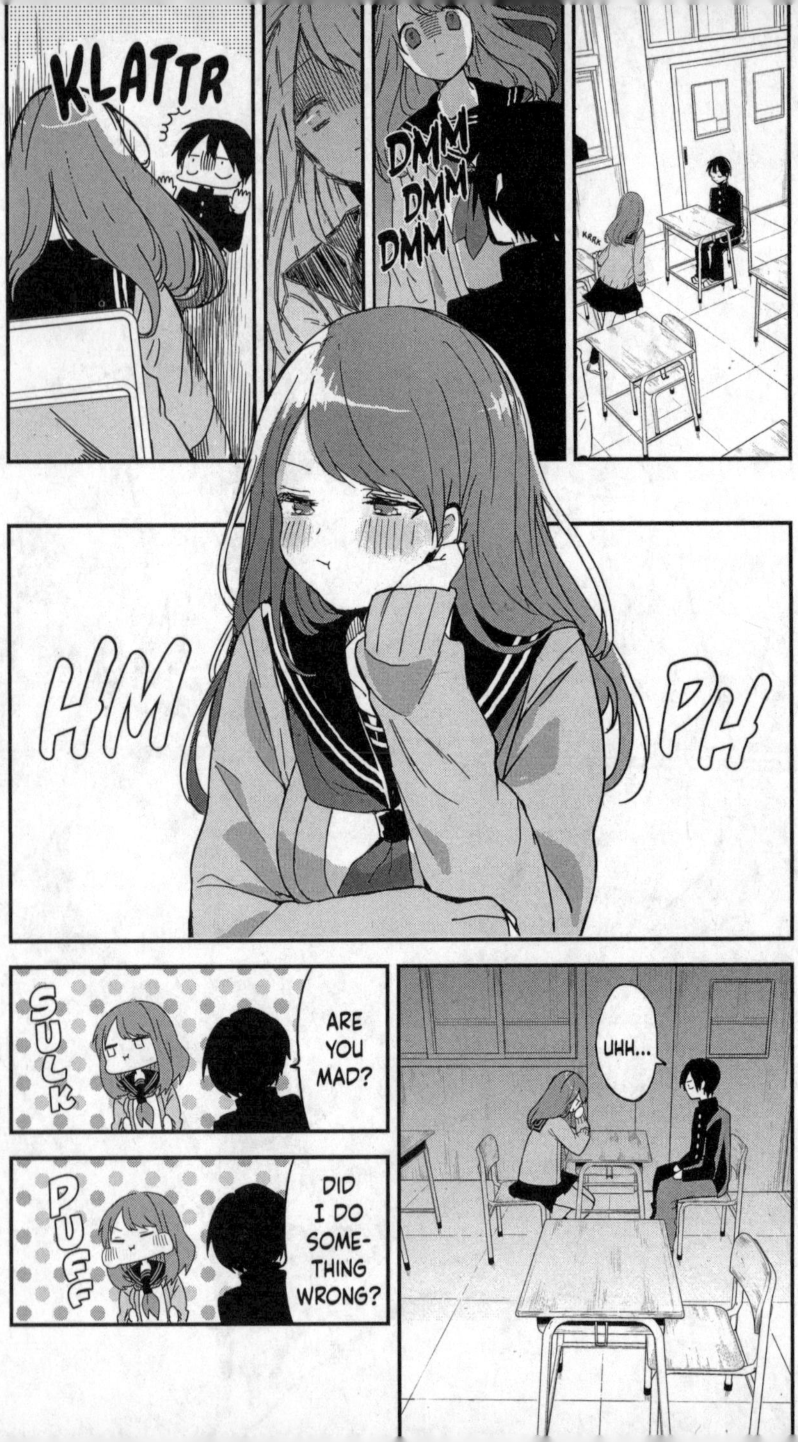
KRRK
DMM
DMM
DMM
KLATTR
HM
PH
UHH...
ARE YOU MAD?
SULK
DID I DO SOME-THING WRONG?
PUFF

ANY-THING COME TO MIND?

MRF

HONESTLY? I HAVE NO CLUE.

TAKE IT.

DUN

CALCIUM IS GOOD FOR REDUCING ANGER!

HOMETOWN MILK

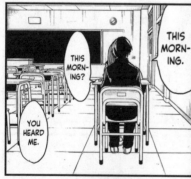

THIS MORN-ING?

THIS MORN-ING.

YOU HEARD ME.

DMM DMM DMM DMM DMM

WHAT WAS THAT FOR?

I'M VERY SORRY.

UMMM...

THINK VERRRY HARD.

x

25

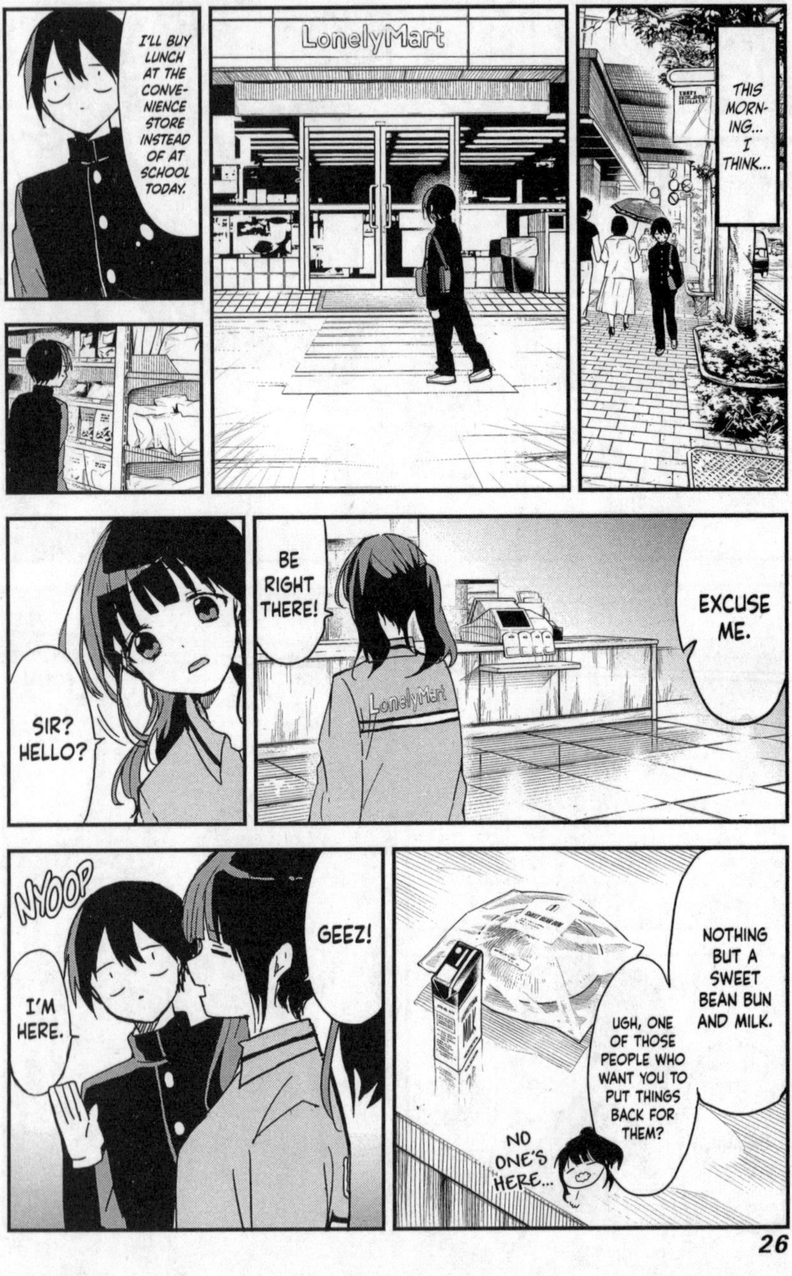

THIS MORNING... I THINK...
LonelyMart
I'LL BUY LUNCH AT THE CONVENIENCE STORE INSTEAD OF AT SCHOOL TODAY.
EXCUSE ME.
BE RIGHT THERE!
LonelyMart
SIR? HELLO?
NOTHING BUT A SWEET BEAN BUN AND MILK.
UGH, ONE OF THOSE PEOPLE WHO WANT YOU TO PUT THINGS BACK FOR THEM?
NO ONE'S HERE...
GEEZ!
NYOOP
I'M HERE.

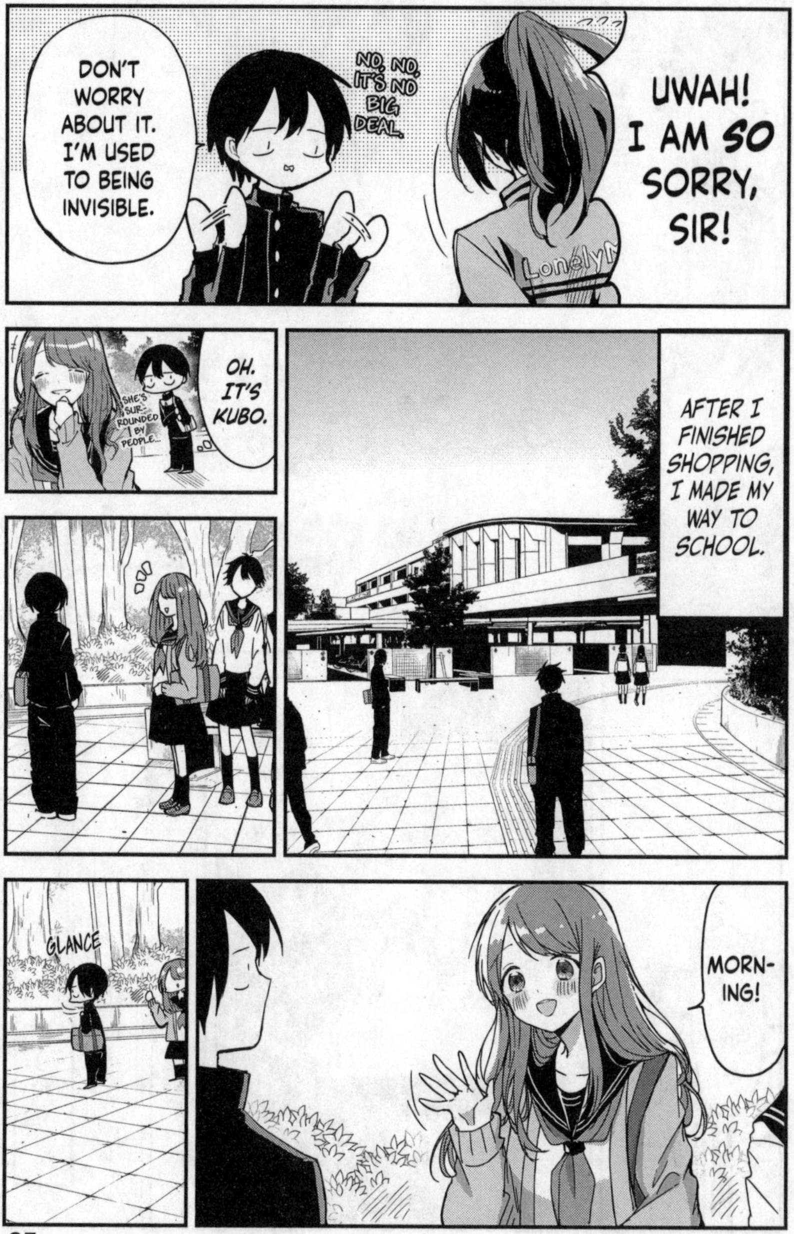
UWAH! I AM SO SORRY, SIR!
NO, NO, IT'S NO BIG DEAL.
DON'T WORRY ABOUT IT. I'M USED TO BEING INVISIBLE.
AFTER I FINISHED SHOPPING, I MADE MY WAY TO SCHOOL.
OH. IT'S KUBO.
SHE'S SUR-ROUNDED BY PEOPLE...
MORN-ING!
GLANCE

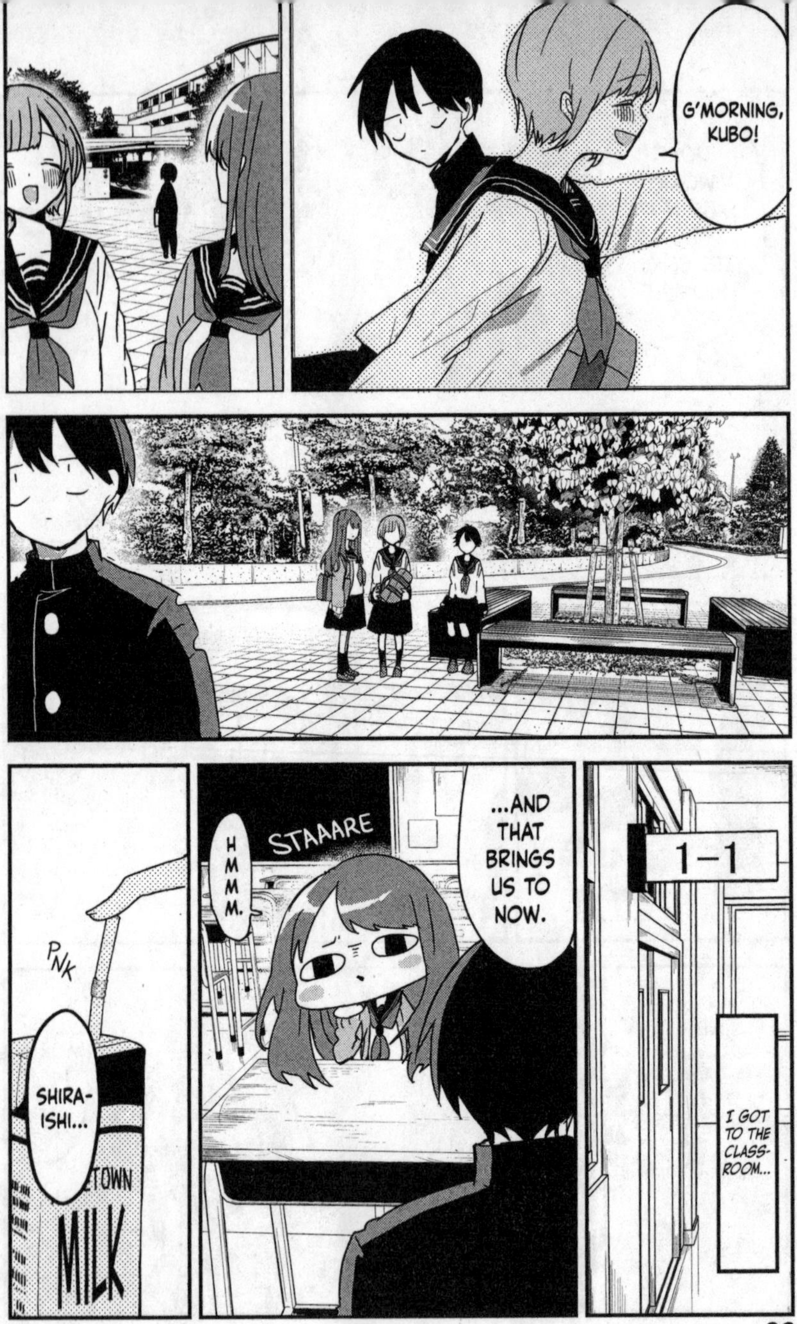
G'MORNING, KUBO!
I GOT TO THE CLASSROOM...
...AND THAT BRINGS US TO NOW.
STAAARE
HMMM.
PNK
SHIRA-ISHI...
MILK

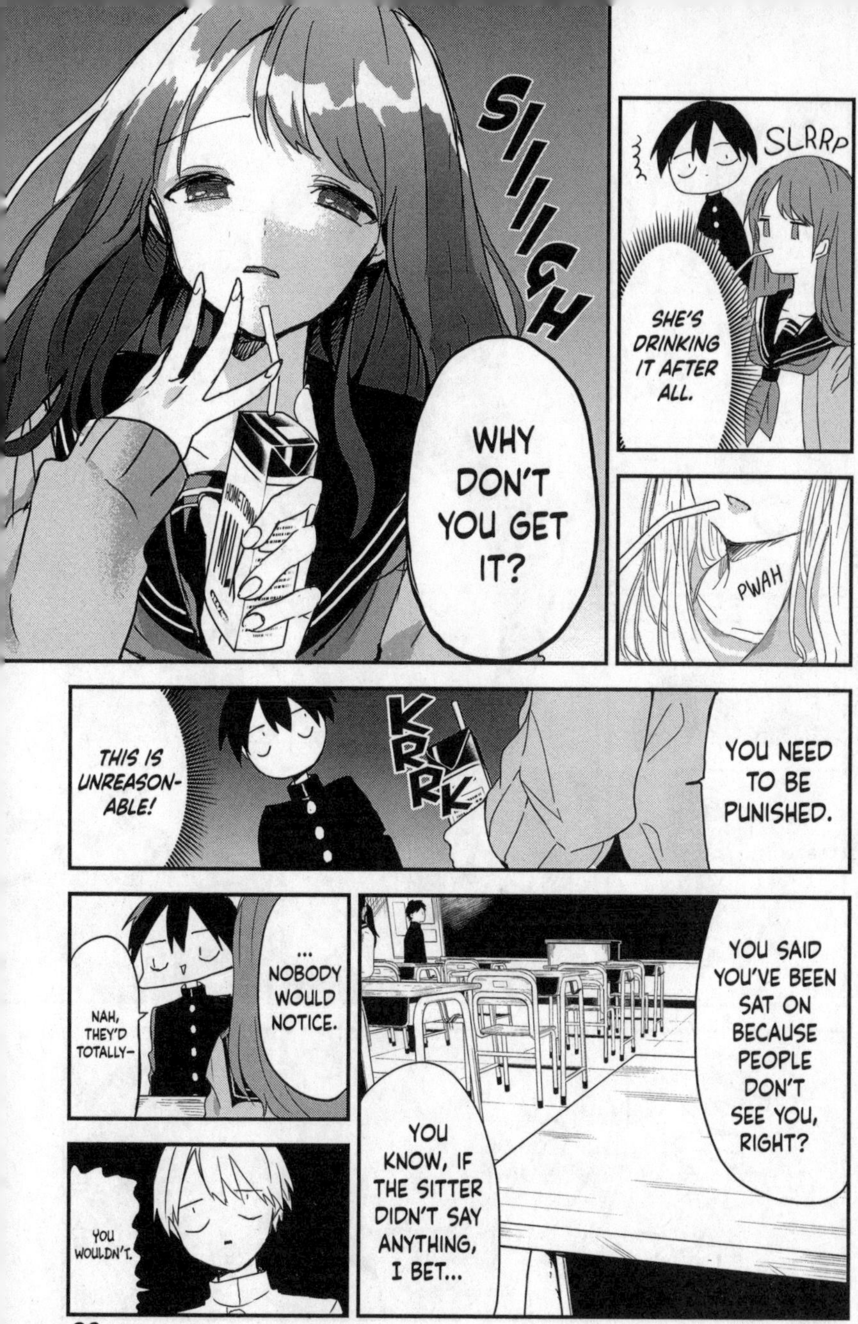
SLRRP
SHE'S DRINKING IT AFTER ALL.
PWAH
SIIIIGH
WHY DON'T YOU GET IT?
HOMETOWN MILK
YOU NEED TO BE PUNISHED.
KRRK
THIS IS UNREASON-ABLE!
YOU SAID YOU'VE BEEN SAT ON BECAUSE PEOPLE DON'T SEE YOU, RIGHT?
YOU KNOW, IF THE SITTER DIDN'T SAY ANYTHING, I BET...
... NOBODY WOULD NOTICE.
NAH, THEY'D TOTALLY—
YOU WOULDN'T.

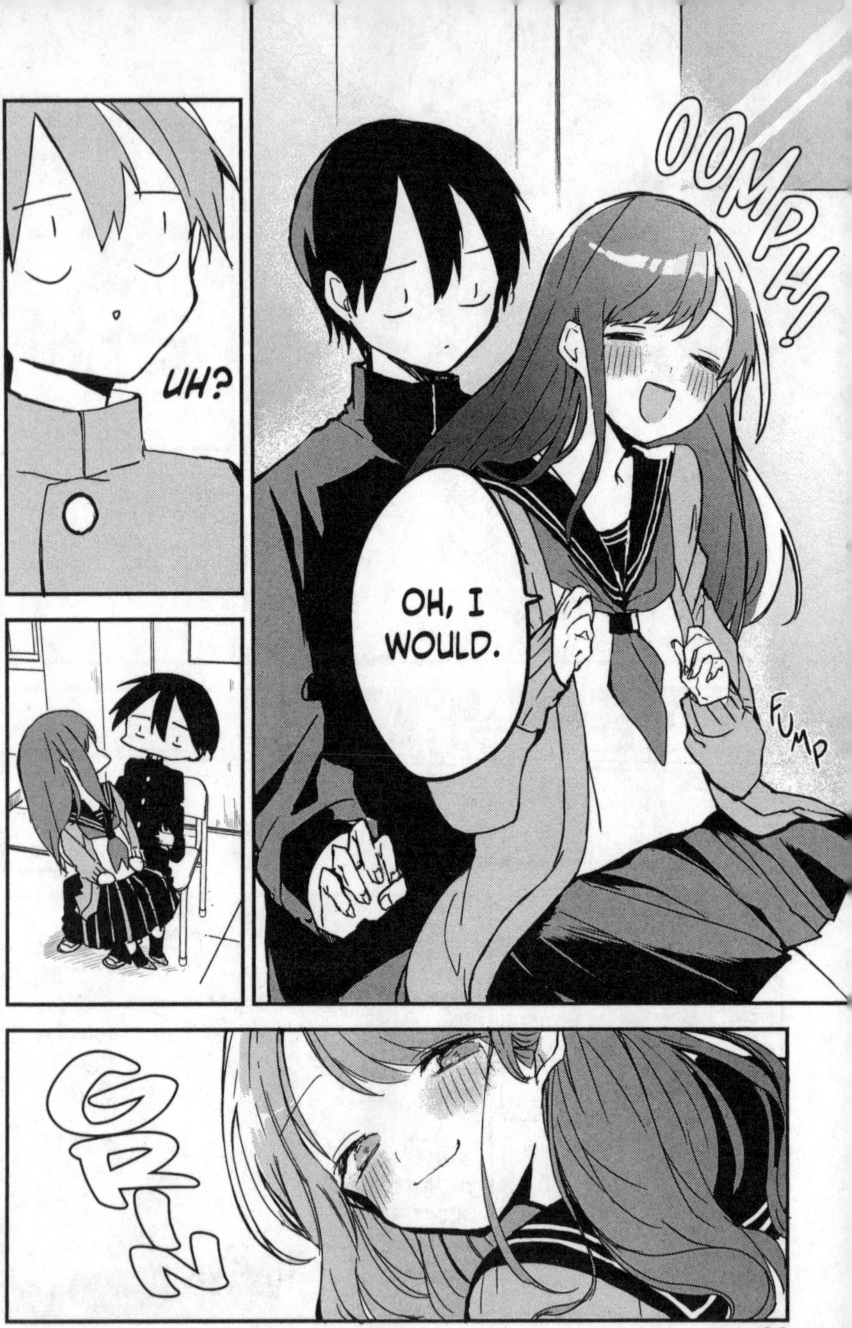
OOMPH!
OH, I WOULD.
FUMP
UH?
GRIN

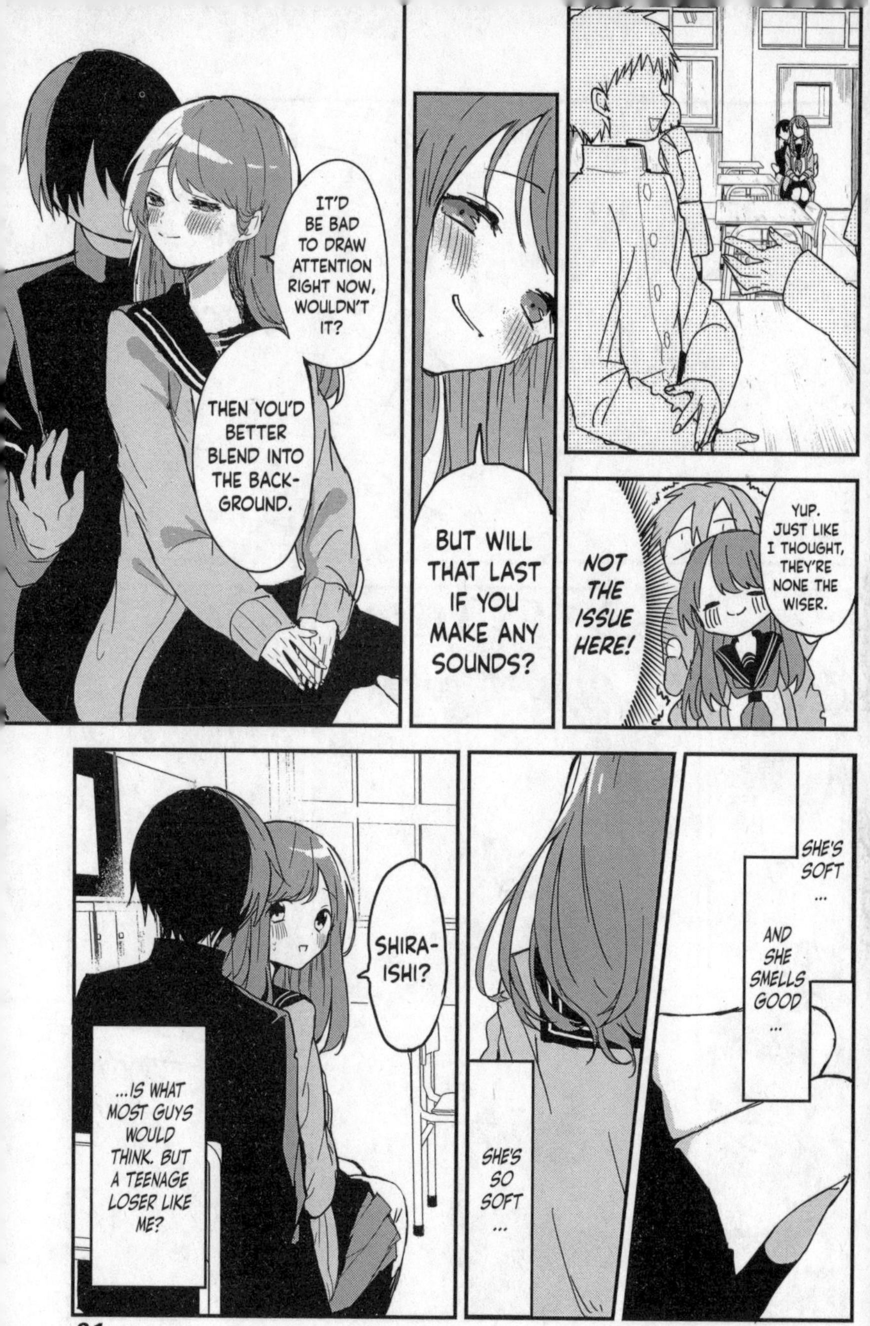
YUP. JUST LIKE I THOUGHT, THEY'RE NONE THE WISER.
NOT THE ISSUE HERE!
BUT WILL THAT LAST IF YOU MAKE ANY SOUNDS?
IT'D BE BAD TO DRAW ATTENTION RIGHT NOW, WOULDN'T IT?
THEN YOU'D BETTER BLEND INTO THE BACK-GROUND.
SHE'S SOFT ...
AND SHE SMELLS GOOD ...
SHE'S SO SOFT ...
SHIRA-ISHI?
...IS WHAT MOST GUYS WOULD THINK. BUT A TEENAGE LOSER LIKE ME?

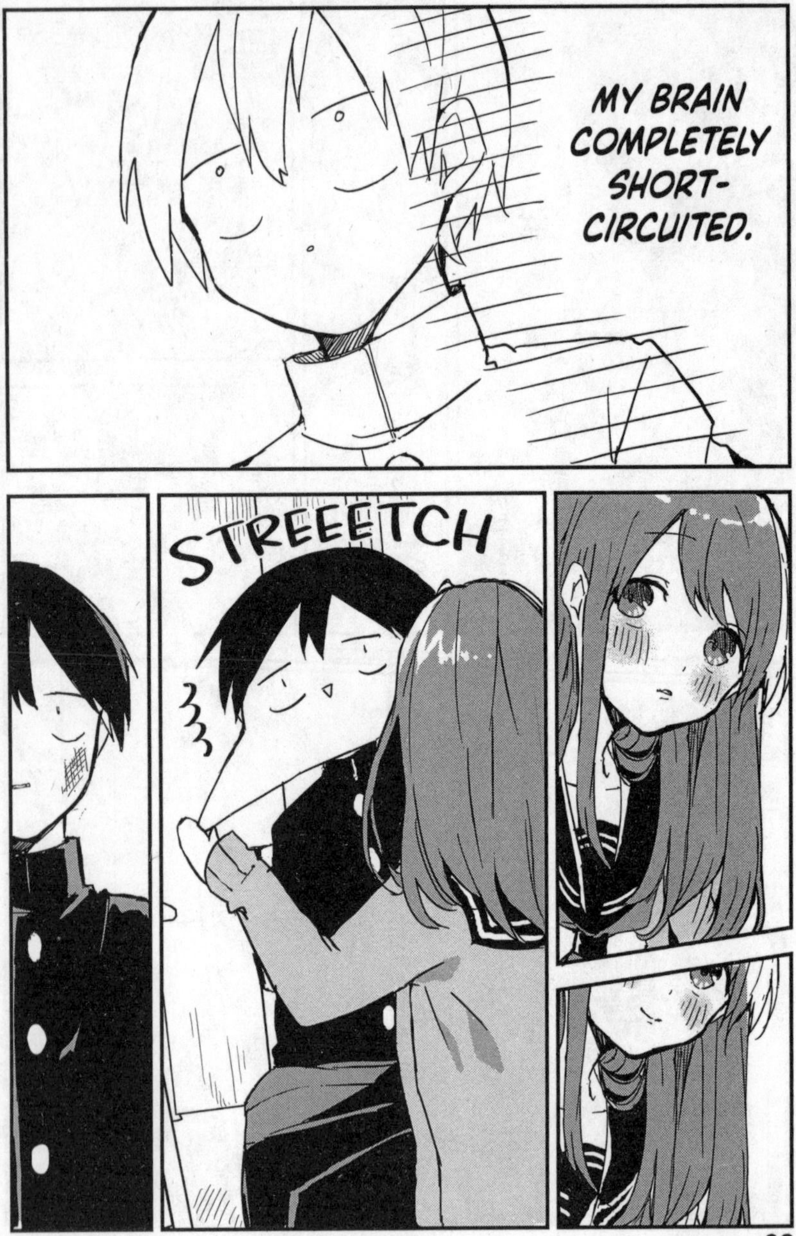
MY BRAIN COMPLETELY SHORT-CIRCUITED.
STREEEETCH

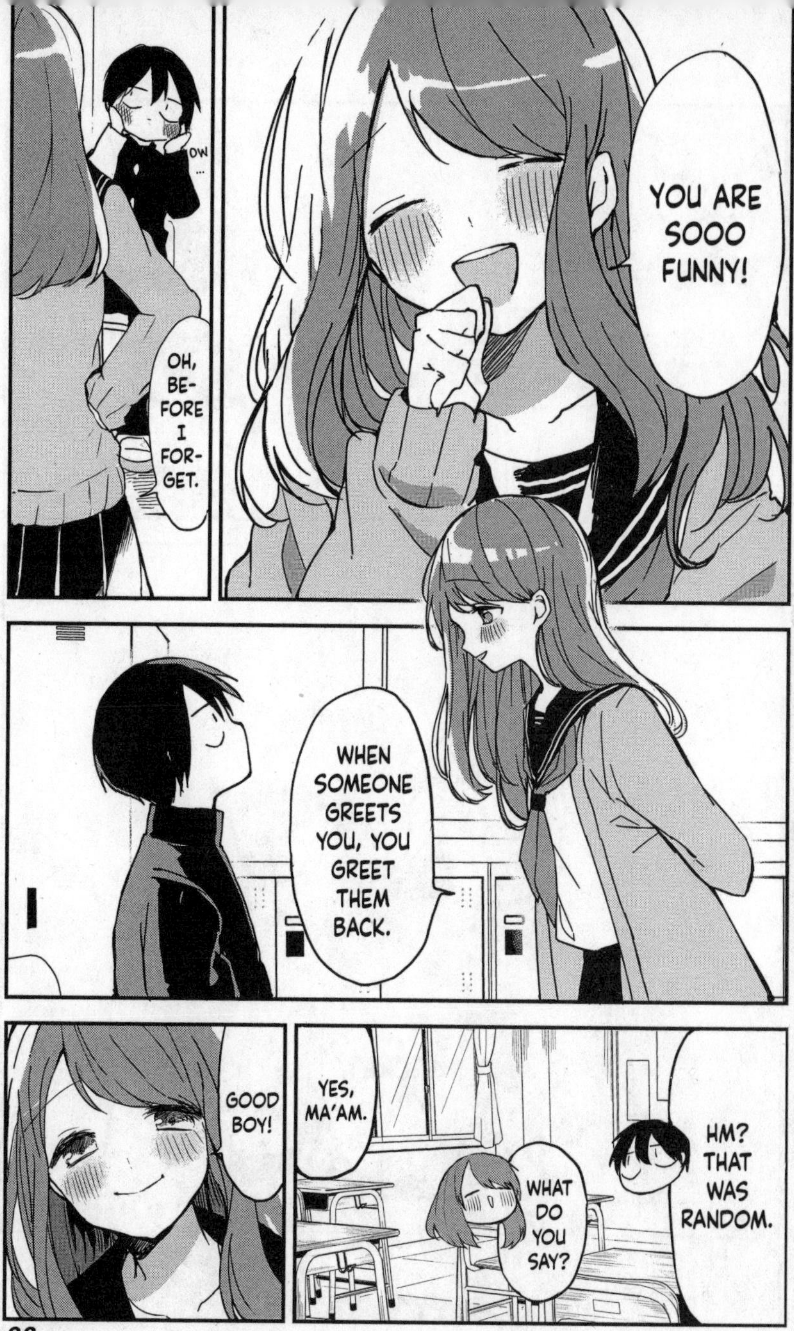
YOU ARE SOOO FUNNY!
OW ...
OH, BE-FORE I FOR-GET.
WHEN SOMEONE GREETS YOU, YOU GREET THEM BACK.
HM? THAT WAS RANDOM.
WHAT DO YOU SAY?
YES, MA'AM.
GOOD BOY!

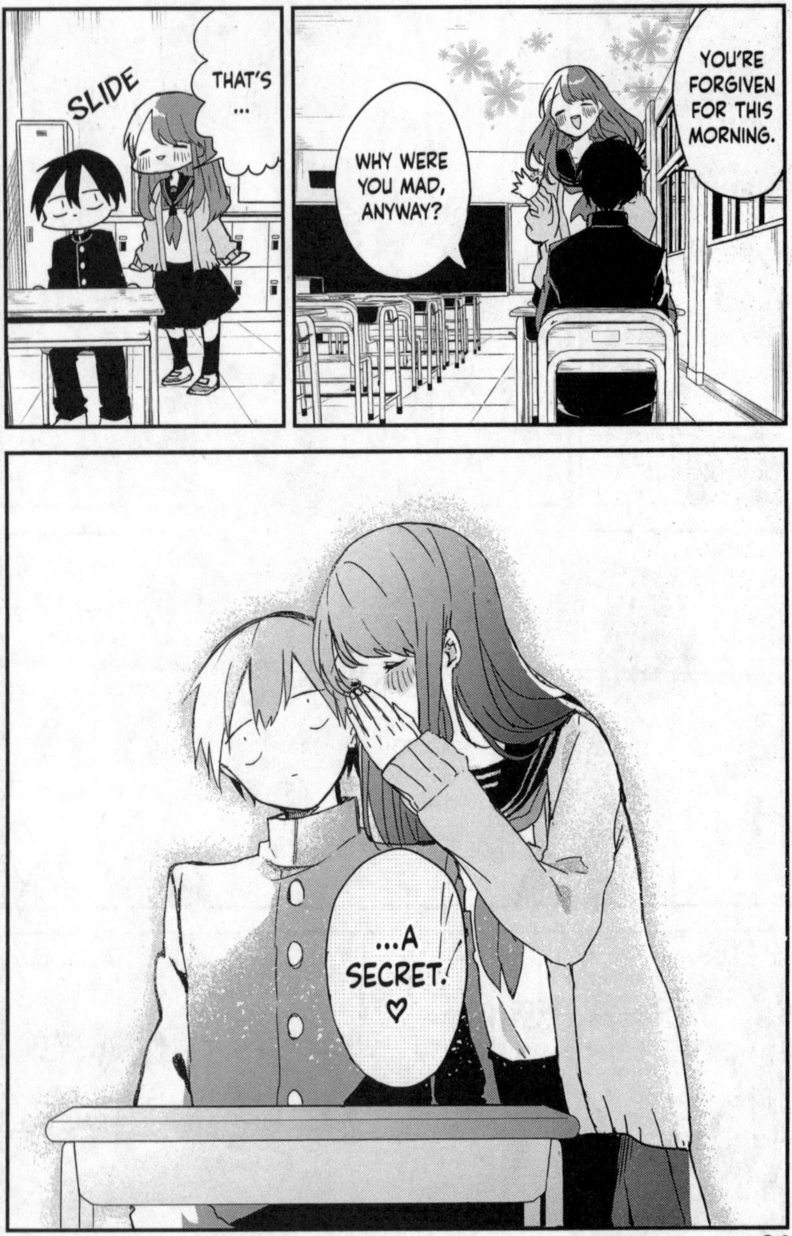
YOU'RE FORGIVEN FOR THIS MORNING.
WHY WERE YOU MAD, ANYWAY?
THAT'S ...
SLIDE
...A SECRET. ♡

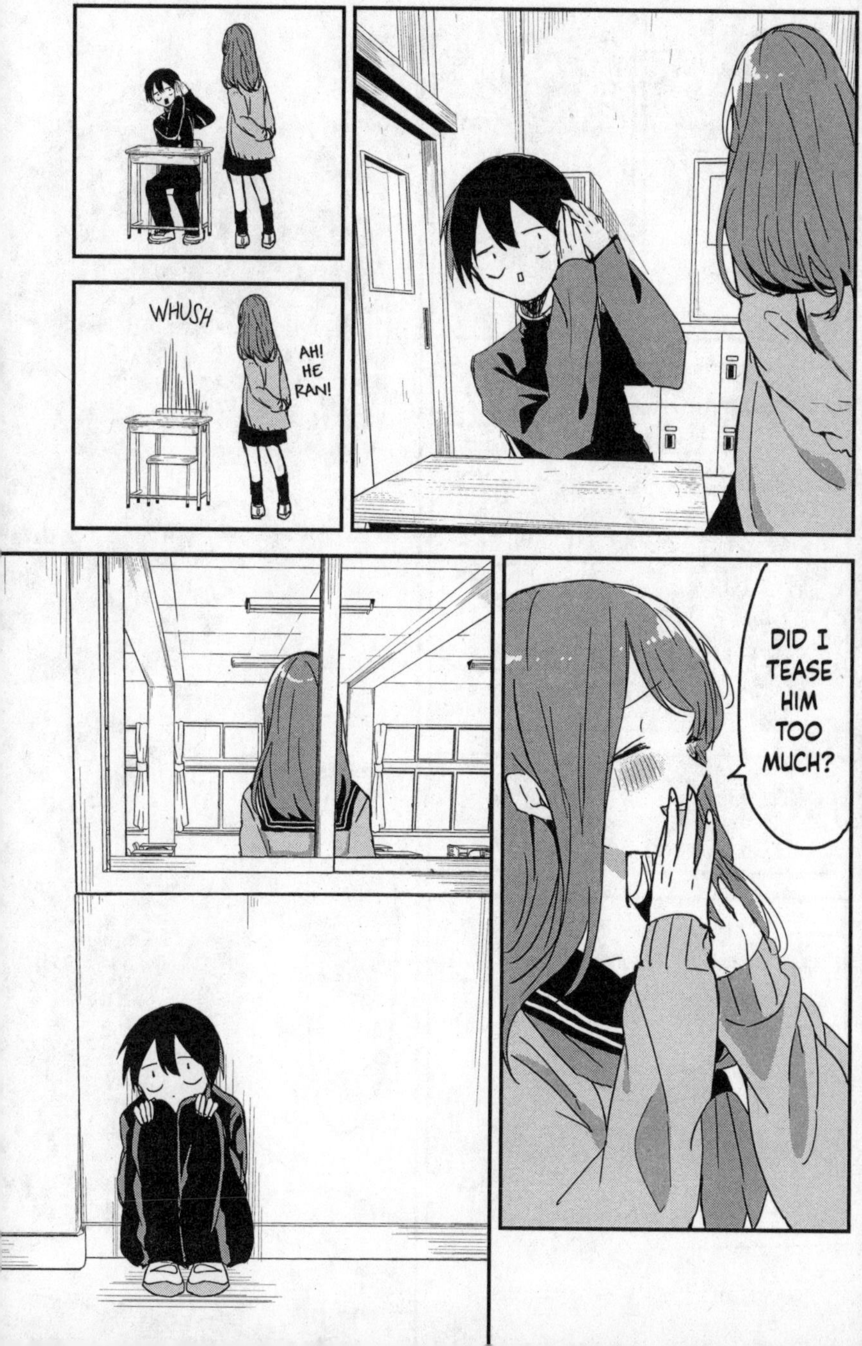
WHUSH
AH! HE RAN!
DID I TEASE HIM TOO MUCH?

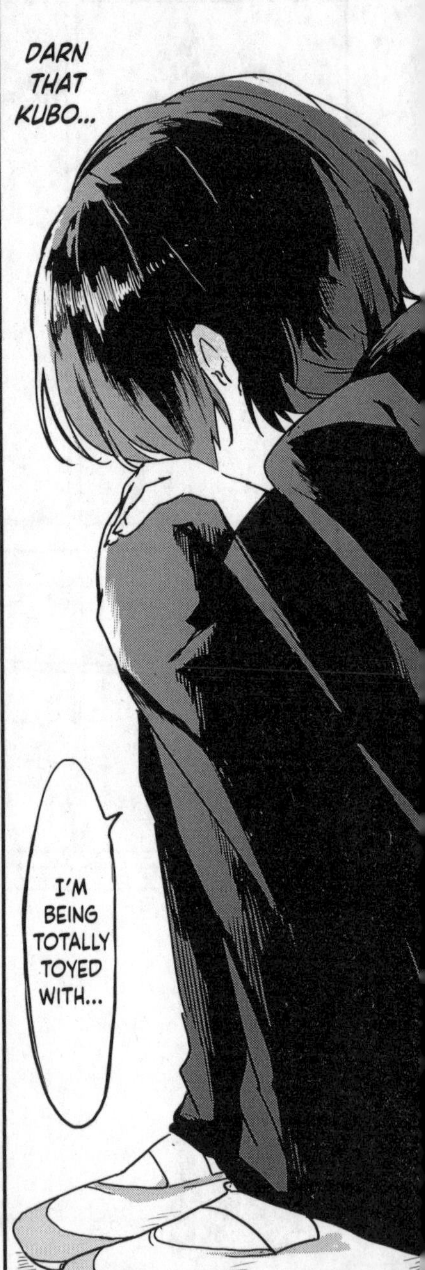
DARN THAT KUBO...
I'M BEING TOTALLY TOYED WITH...

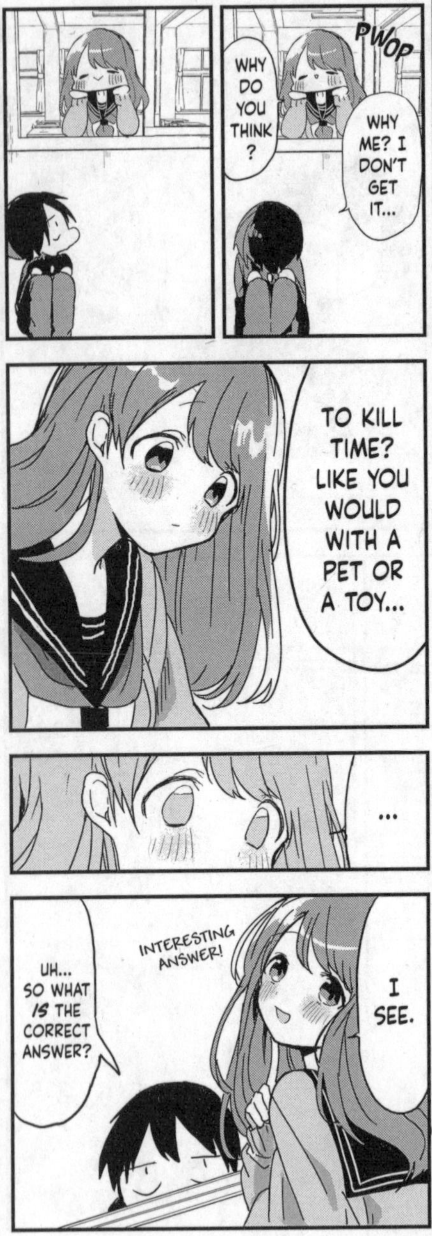
PWOP
WHY ME? I DON'T GET IT...
WHY DO YOU THINK?
TO KILL TIME? LIKE YOU WOULD WITH A PET OR A TOY...
...
I SEE.
INTERESTING ANSWER!
UH... SO WHAT *IS* THE CORRECT ANSWER?

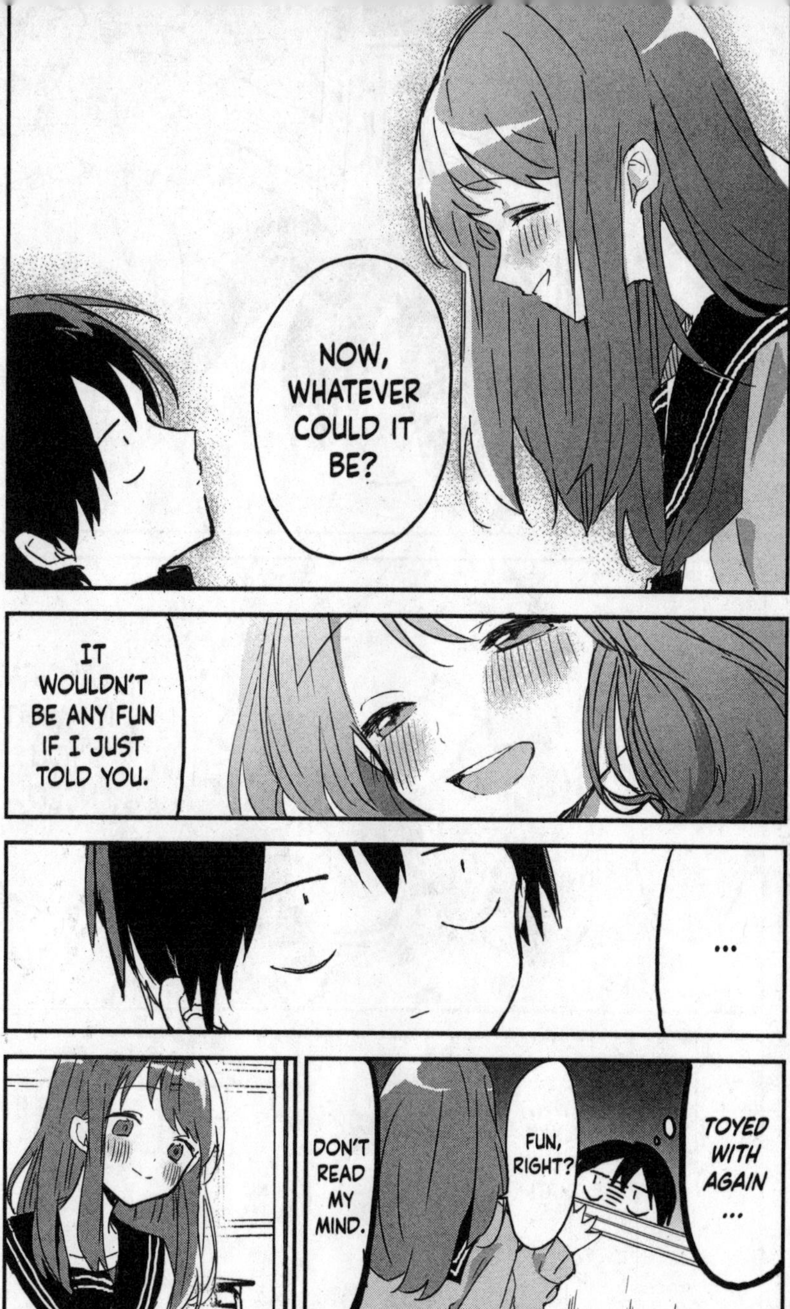
NOW, WHATEVER COULD IT BE?
IT WOULDN'T BE ANY FUN IF I JUST TOLD YOU.
...
TOYED WITH AGAIN ...
FUN, RIGHT?
DON'T READ MY MIND.

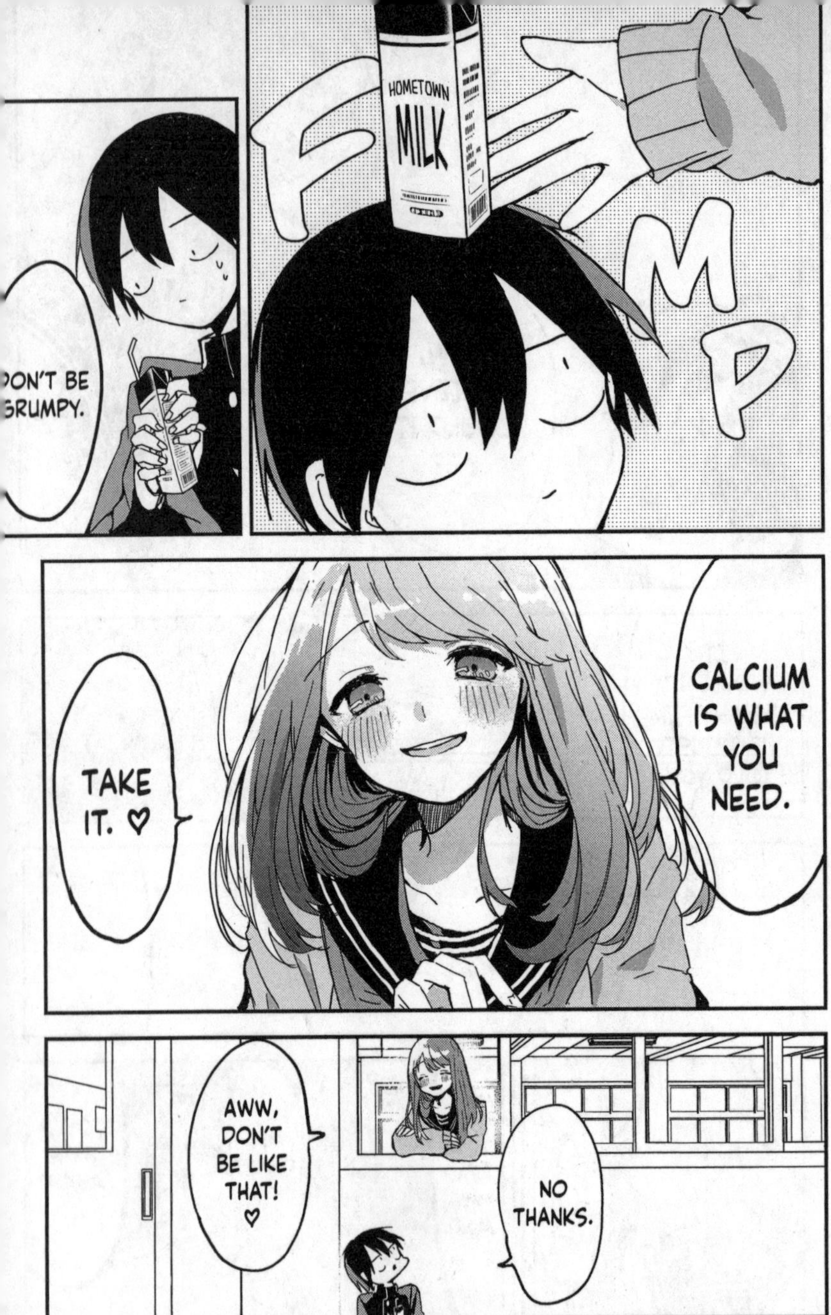
HOMETOWN MILK
FUMP
DON'T BE GRUMPY.
CALCIUM IS WHAT YOU NEED.
TAKE IT. ♡
NO THANKS.
AWW, DON'T BE LIKE THAT! ♡

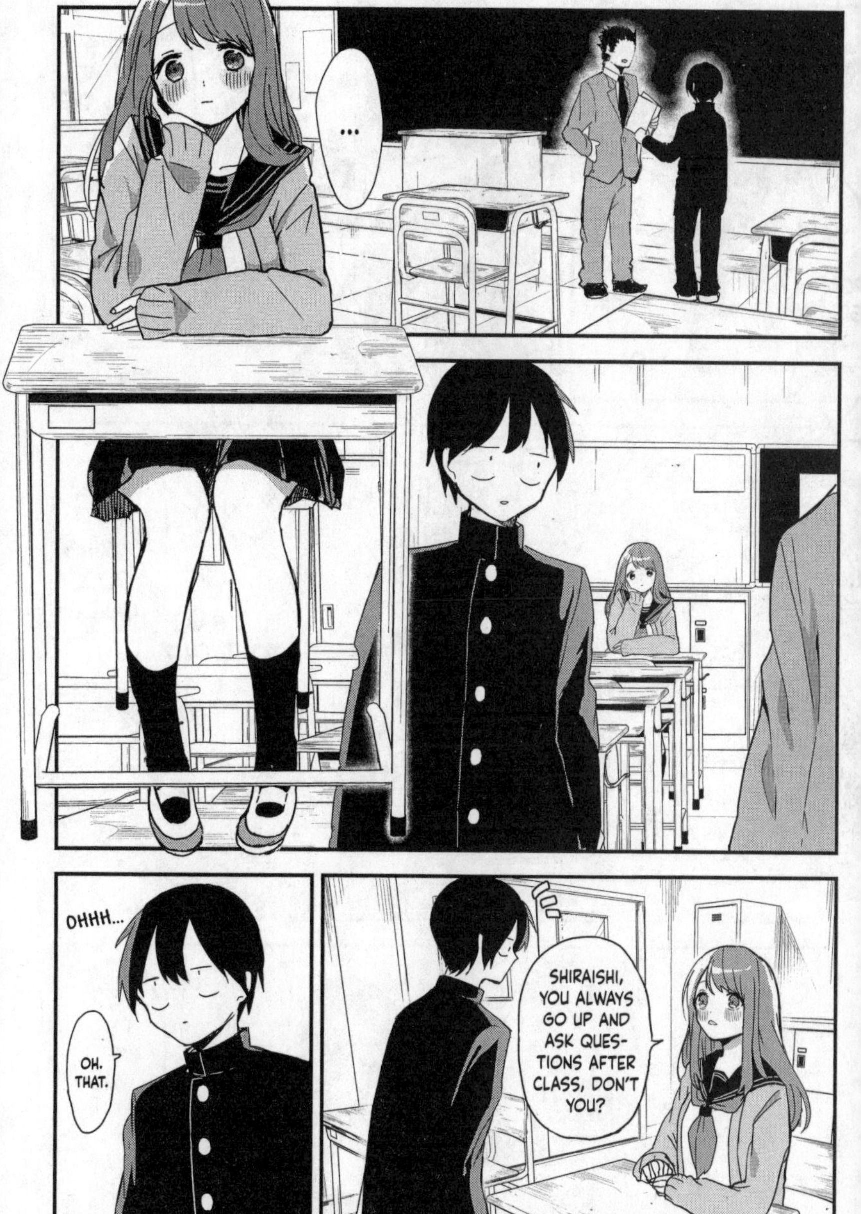
...
SHIRAISHI, YOU ALWAYS GO UP AND ASK QUES-TIONS AFTER CLASS, DON'T YOU?
OHHH...
OH. THAT.

episode 003 RIGHT TO ANSWER AND MEDDLING

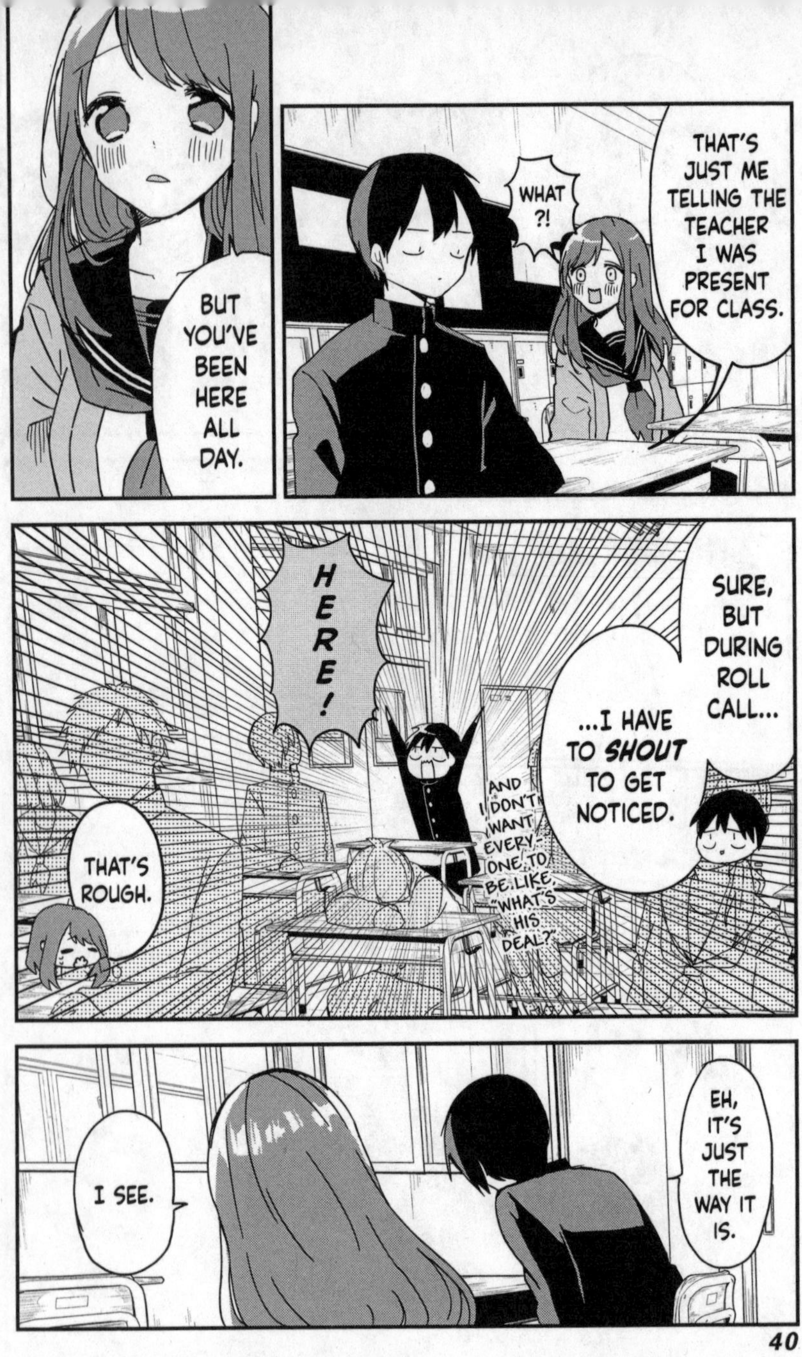
THAT'S JUST ME TELLING THE TEACHER I WAS PRESENT FOR CLASS.
WHAT ?!
BUT YOU'VE BEEN HERE ALL DAY.
SURE, BUT DURING ROLL CALL...
...I HAVE TO SHOUT TO GET NOTICED.
HERE!
AND I DON'T WANT EVERYONE TO BE LIKE "WHAT'S HIS DEAL?"
THAT'S ROUGH.
EH, IT'S JUST THE WAY IT IS.
I SEE.

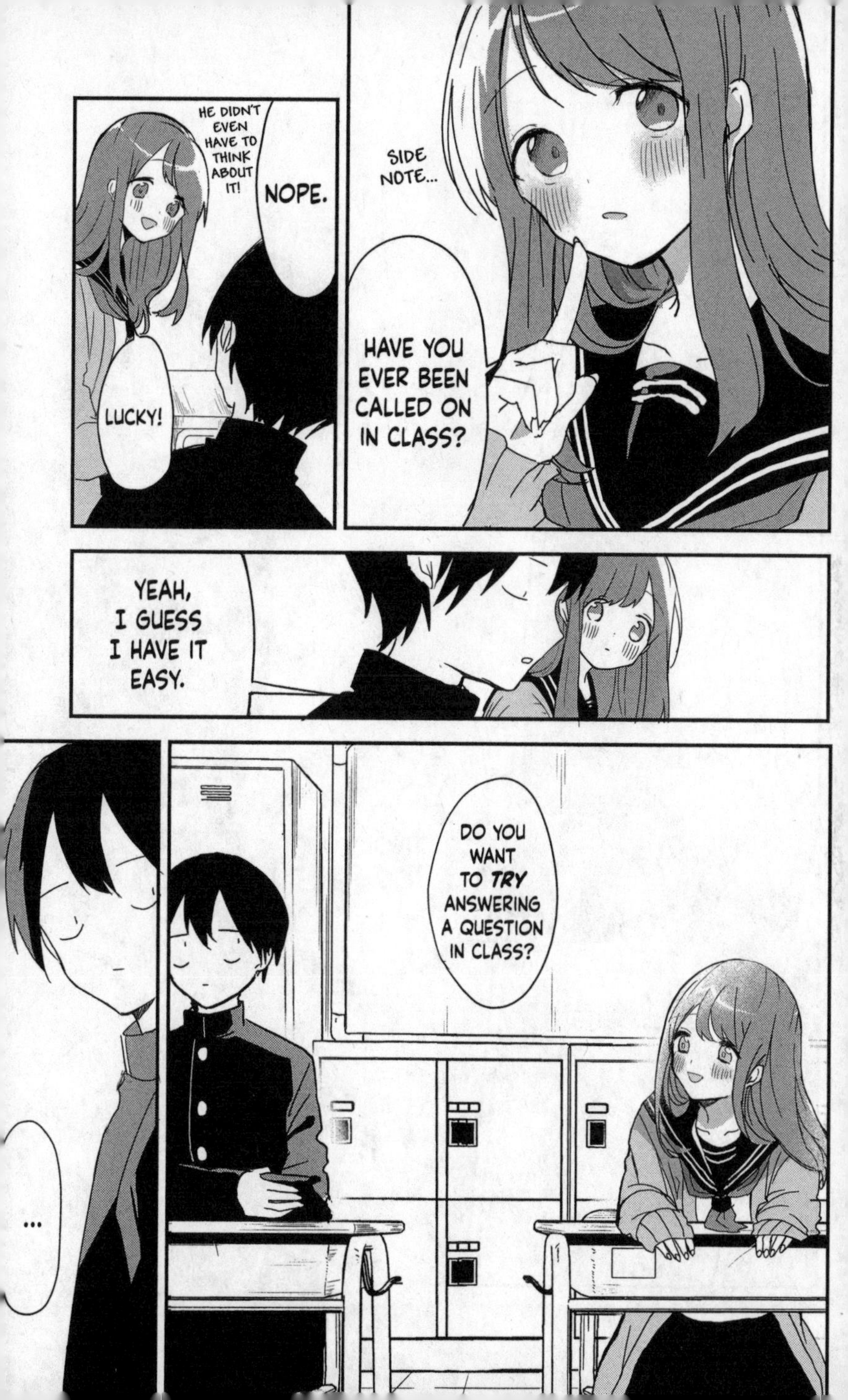
SIDE NOTE...
HAVE YOU EVER BEEN CALLED ON IN CLASS?
NOPE.
HE DIDN'T EVEN HAVE TO THINK ABOUT IT!
LUCKY!
YEAH, I GUESS I HAVE IT EASY.
DO YOU WANT TO *TRY* ANSWERING A QUESTION IN CLASS?
...

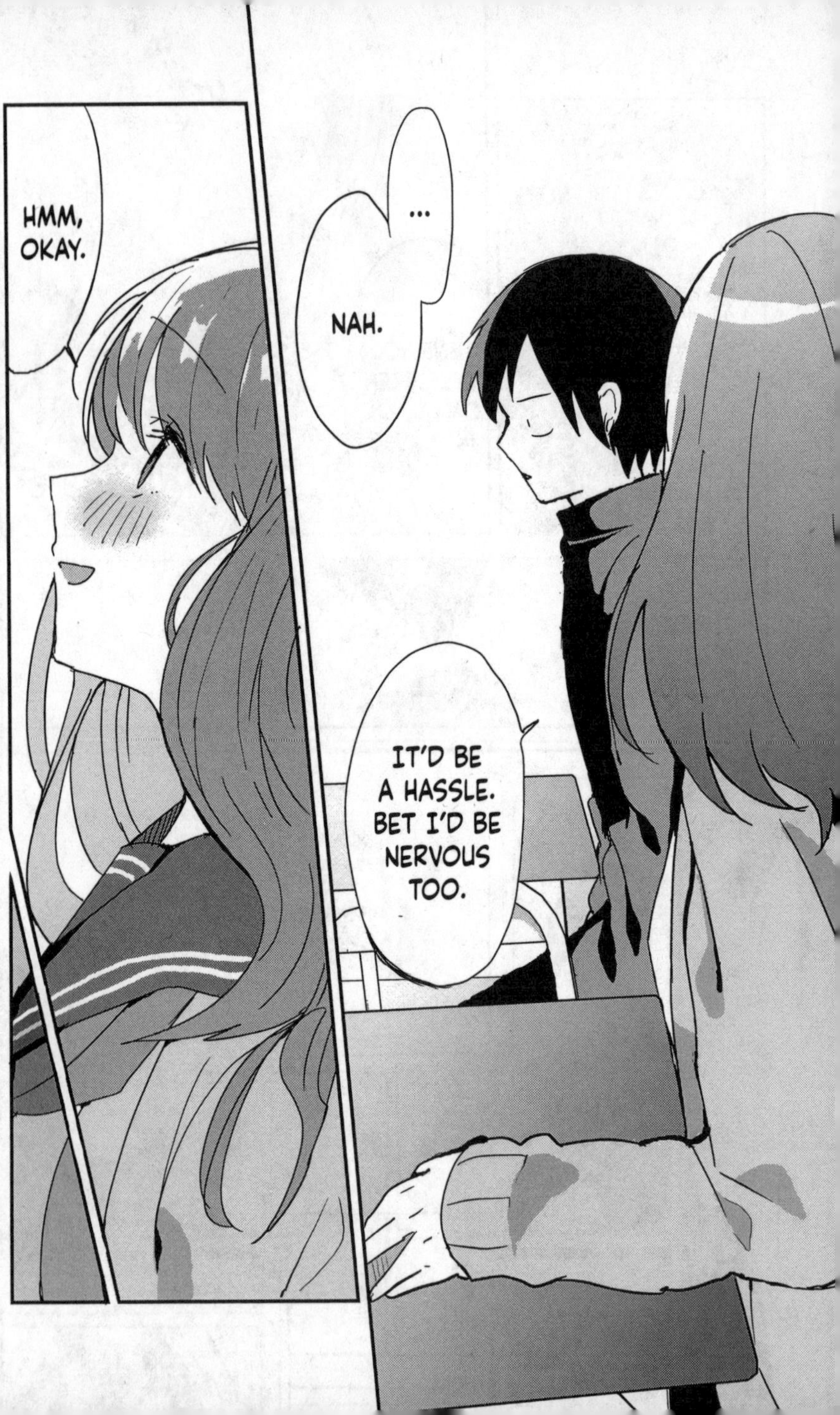
... NAH.
IT'D BE A HASSLE. BET I'D BE NERVOUS TOO.
HMM, OKAY.

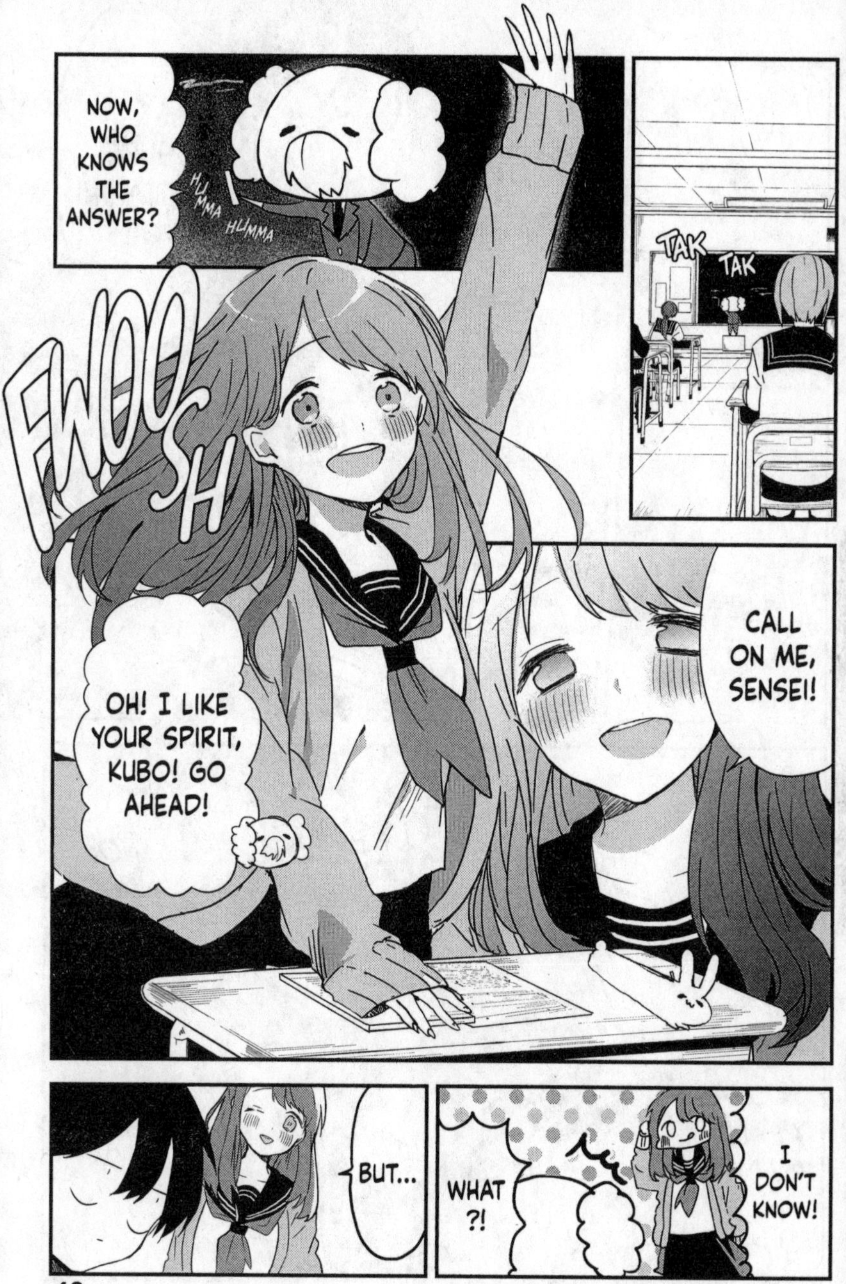
TAK
TAK
NOW, WHO KNOWS THE ANSWER?
HUMMA
HUMMA
FWOOSH
CALL ON ME, SENSEI!
OH! I LIKE YOUR SPIRIT, KUBO! GO AHEAD!
I DON'T KNOW!
WHAT?!
BUT...

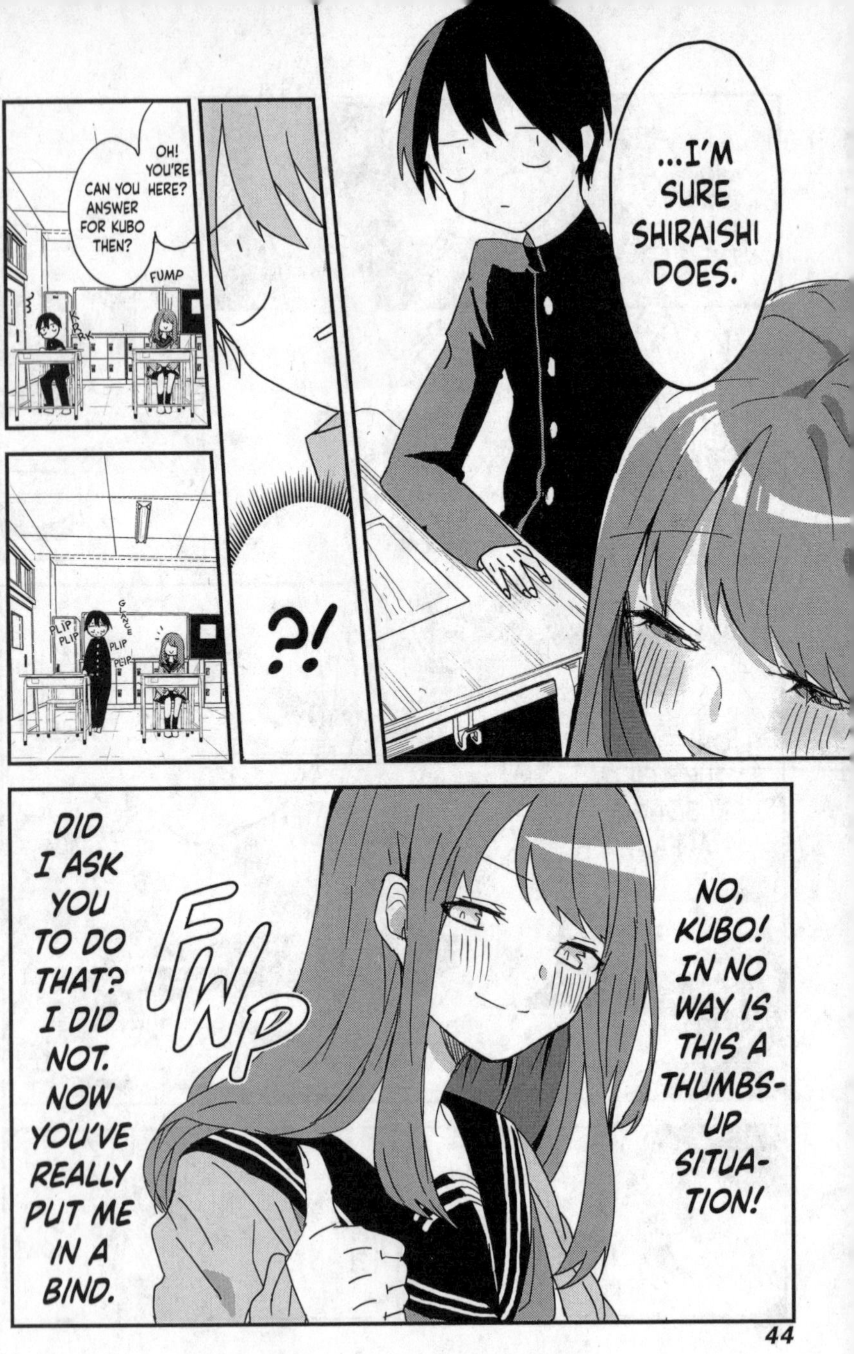
...I'M SURE SHIRAISHI DOES.
?!
OH! YOU'RE HERE?
CAN YOU ANSWER FOR KUBO THEN?
FUMP
KRRK
PLIP PLIP
GLANCE
PLIP PLIP
NO, KUBO! IN NO WAY IS THIS A THUMBS-UP SITUATION!
FWP
DID I ASK YOU TO DO THAT? I DID NOT. NOW YOU'VE REALLY PUT ME IN A BIND.

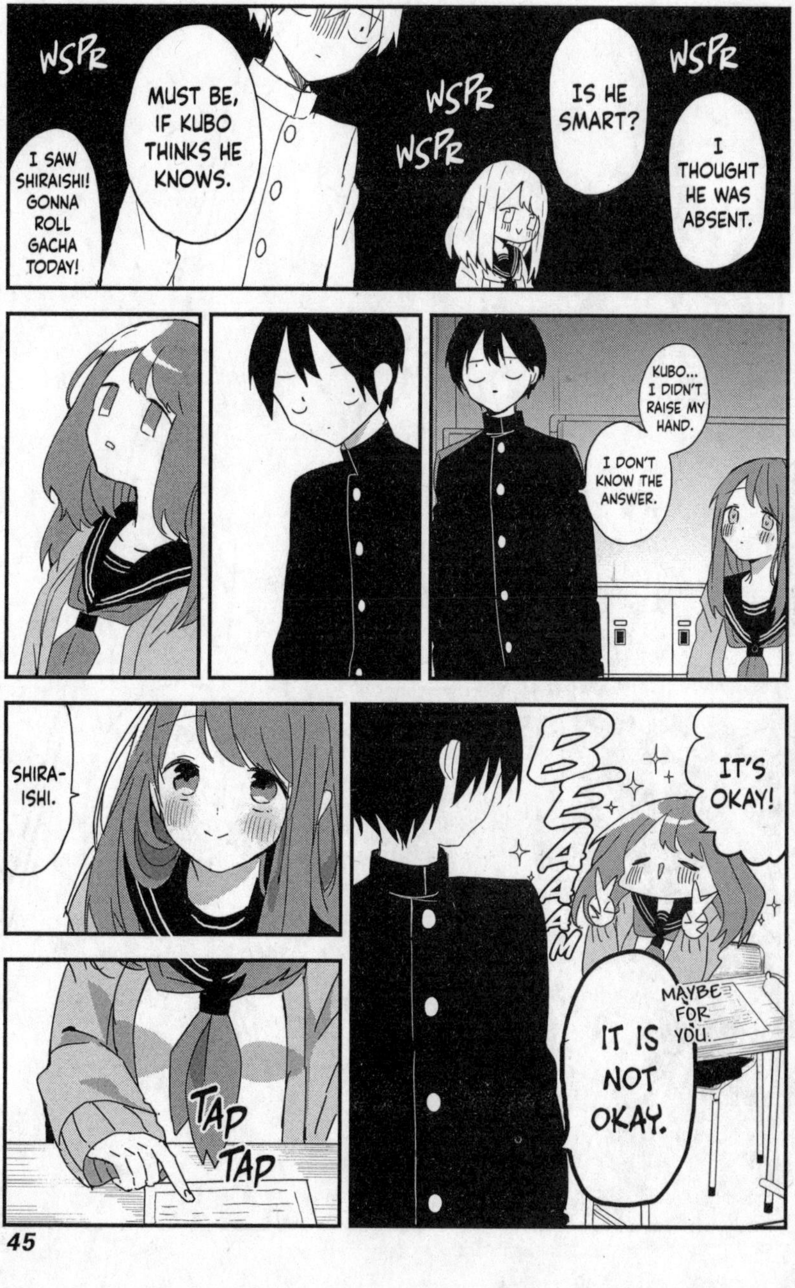
WSPR
I THOUGHT HE WAS ABSENT.
WSPR
IS HE SMART?
WSPR
WSPR
MUST BE, IF KUBO THINKS HE KNOWS.
WSPR
I SAW SHIRAISHI! GONNA ROLL GACHA TODAY!
KUBO... I DIDN'T RAISE MY HAND.
I DON'T KNOW THE ANSWER.
IT'S OKAY!
BEAAAM
MAYBE FOR YOU.
IT IS NOT OKAY.
SHIRA-ISHI.
TAP TAP

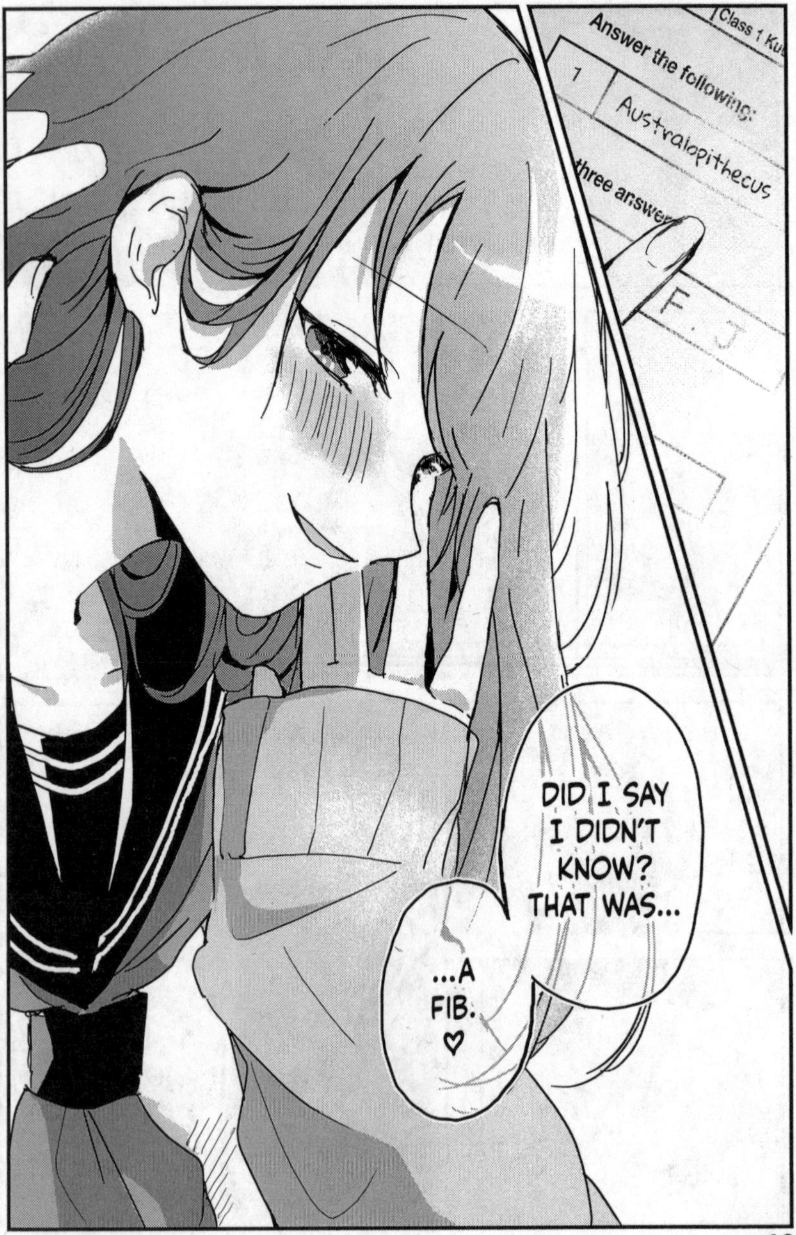
Class 1 Ku
Answer the following:
1
Australopithecus
three answer
F. J
DID I SAY I DIDN'T KNOW? THAT WAS...
...A FIB. ♡

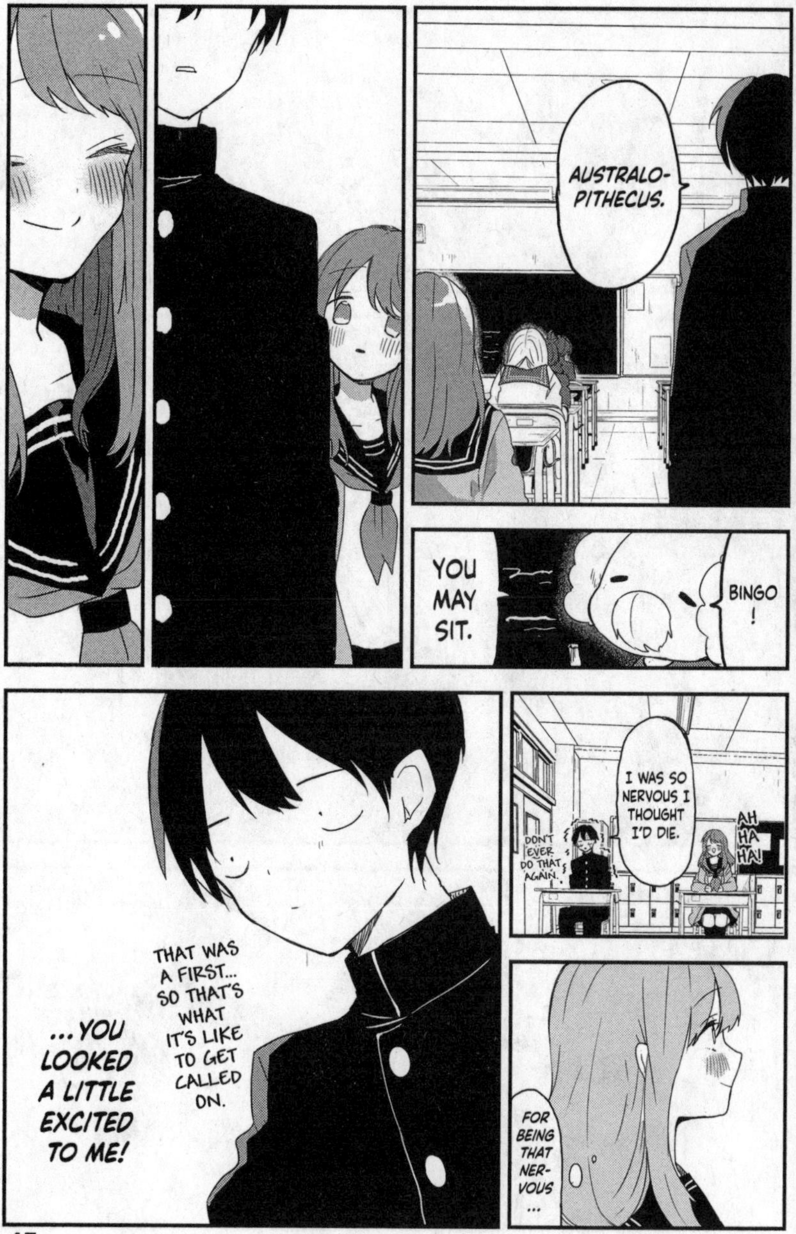
AUSTRALO-PITHECUS.
BINGO!
YOU MAY SIT.
I WAS SO NERVOUS I THOUGHT I'D DIE.
AH HA HA!
DON'T EVER DO THAT AGAIN.
FOR BEING THAT NERVOUS...
THAT WAS A FIRST... SO THAT'S WHAT IT'S LIKE TO GET CALLED ON.
...YOU LOOKED A LITTLE EXCITED TO ME!

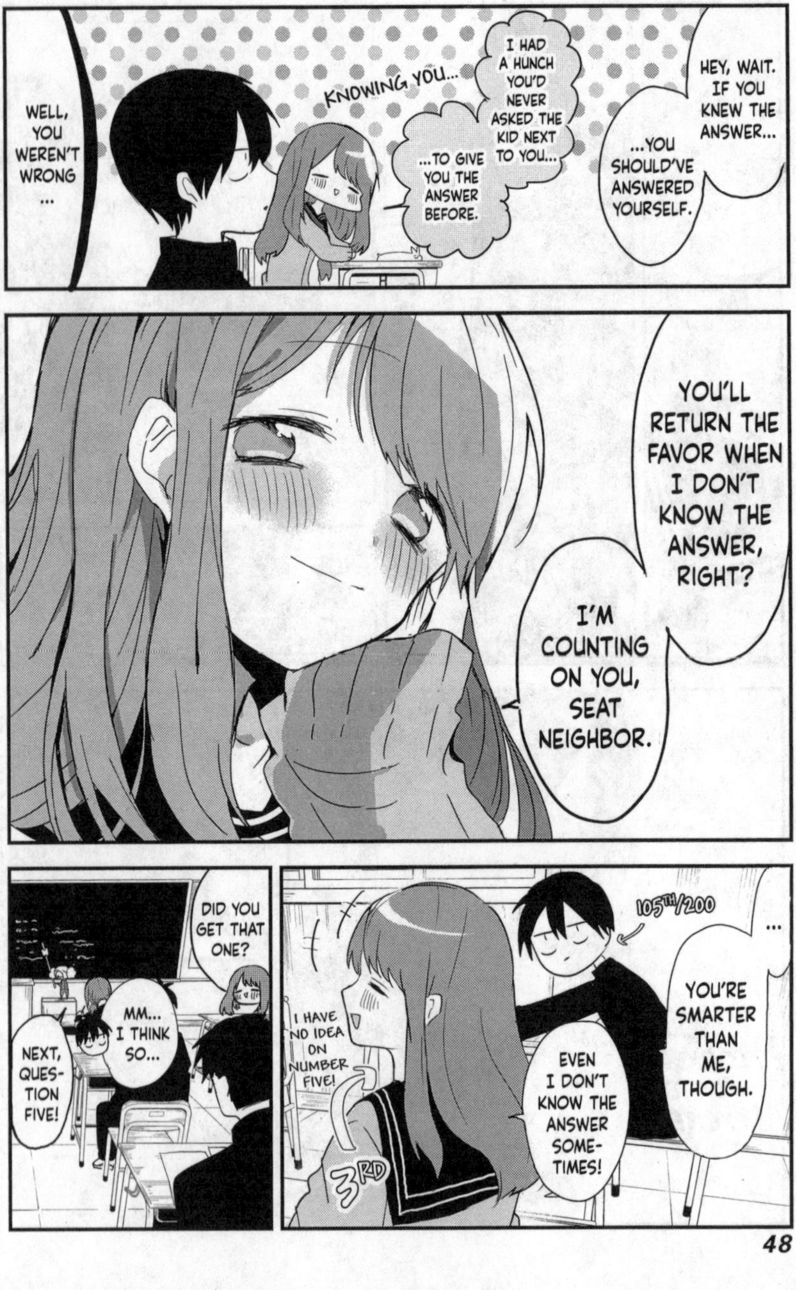
HEY, WAIT. IF YOU KNEW THE ANSWER...
...YOU SHOULD'VE ANSWERED YOURSELF.
I HAD A HUNCH YOU'D NEVER ASKED THE KID NEXT TO YOU...
KNOWING YOU...
...TO GIVE YOU THE ANSWER BEFORE.
WELL, YOU WEREN'T WRONG ...
YOU'LL RETURN THE FAVOR WHEN I DON'T KNOW THE ANSWER, RIGHT?
I'M COUNTING ON YOU, SEAT NEIGHBOR.
...
YOU'RE SMARTER THAN ME, THOUGH.
105TH/200
EVEN I DON'T KNOW THE ANSWER SOME-TIMES!
I HAVE NO IDEA ON NUMBER FIVE!
3RD
DID YOU GET THAT ONE?
MM... I THINK SO...
NEXT, QUES-TION FIVE!

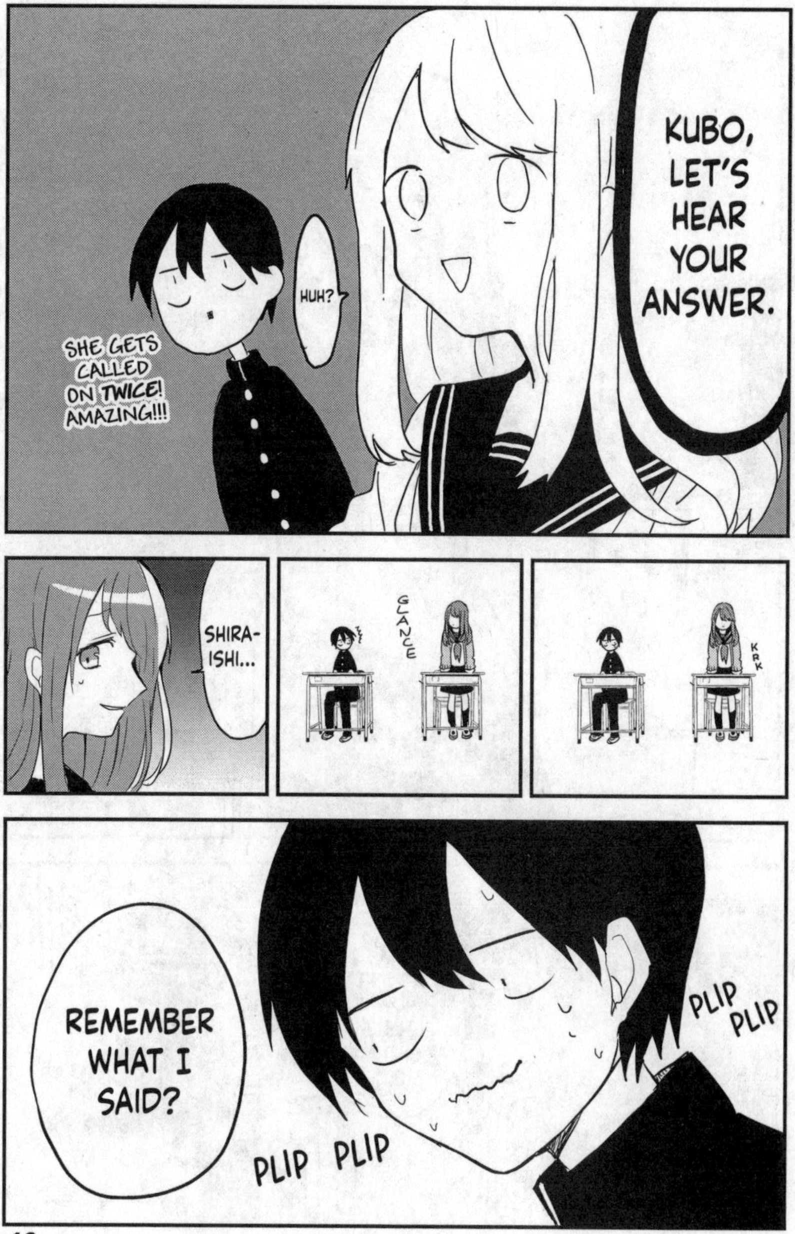
KUBO, LET'S HEAR YOUR ANSWER.
HUH?
SHE GETS CALLED ON TWICE! AMAZING!!!
KRK
GLANCE
SHIRA-ISHI...
PLIP PLIP
REMEMBER WHAT I SAID?
PLIP PLIP

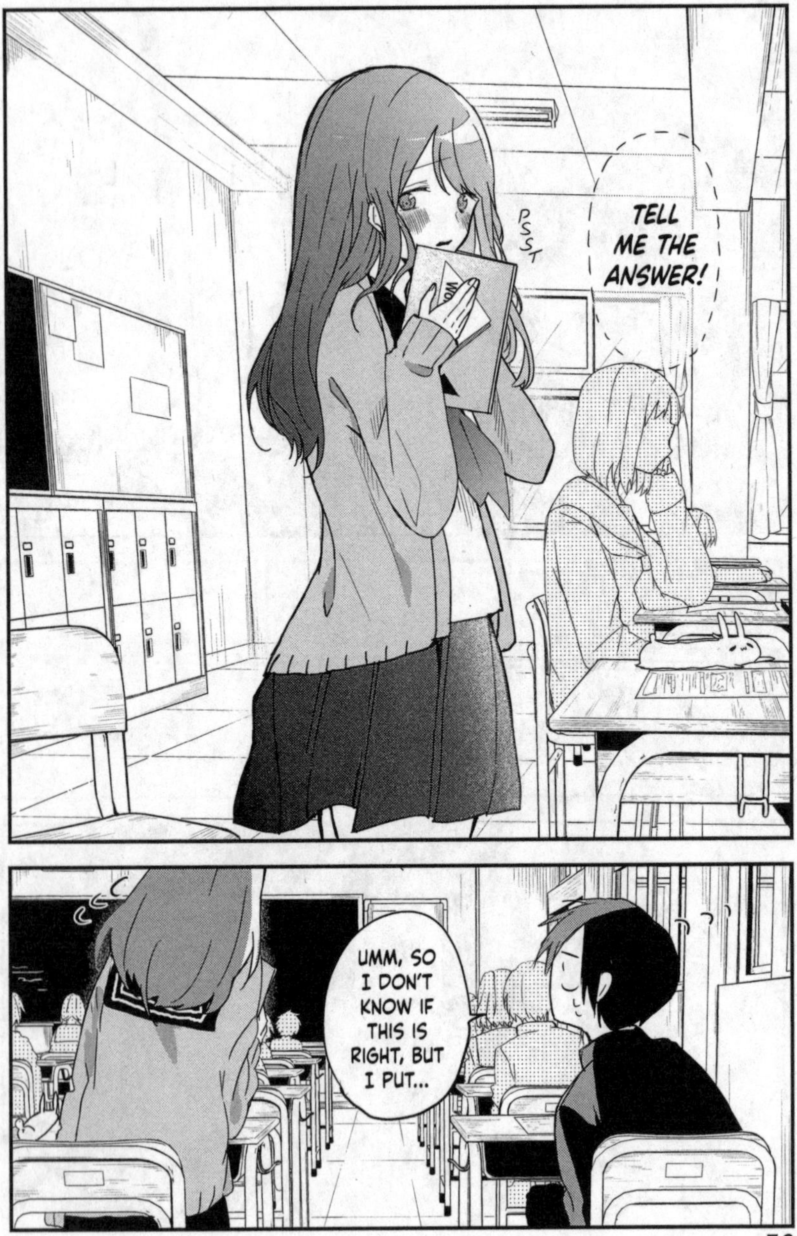
TELL ME THE ANSWER!
PSST
UMM, SO I DON'T KNOW IF THIS IS RIGHT, BUT I PUT...

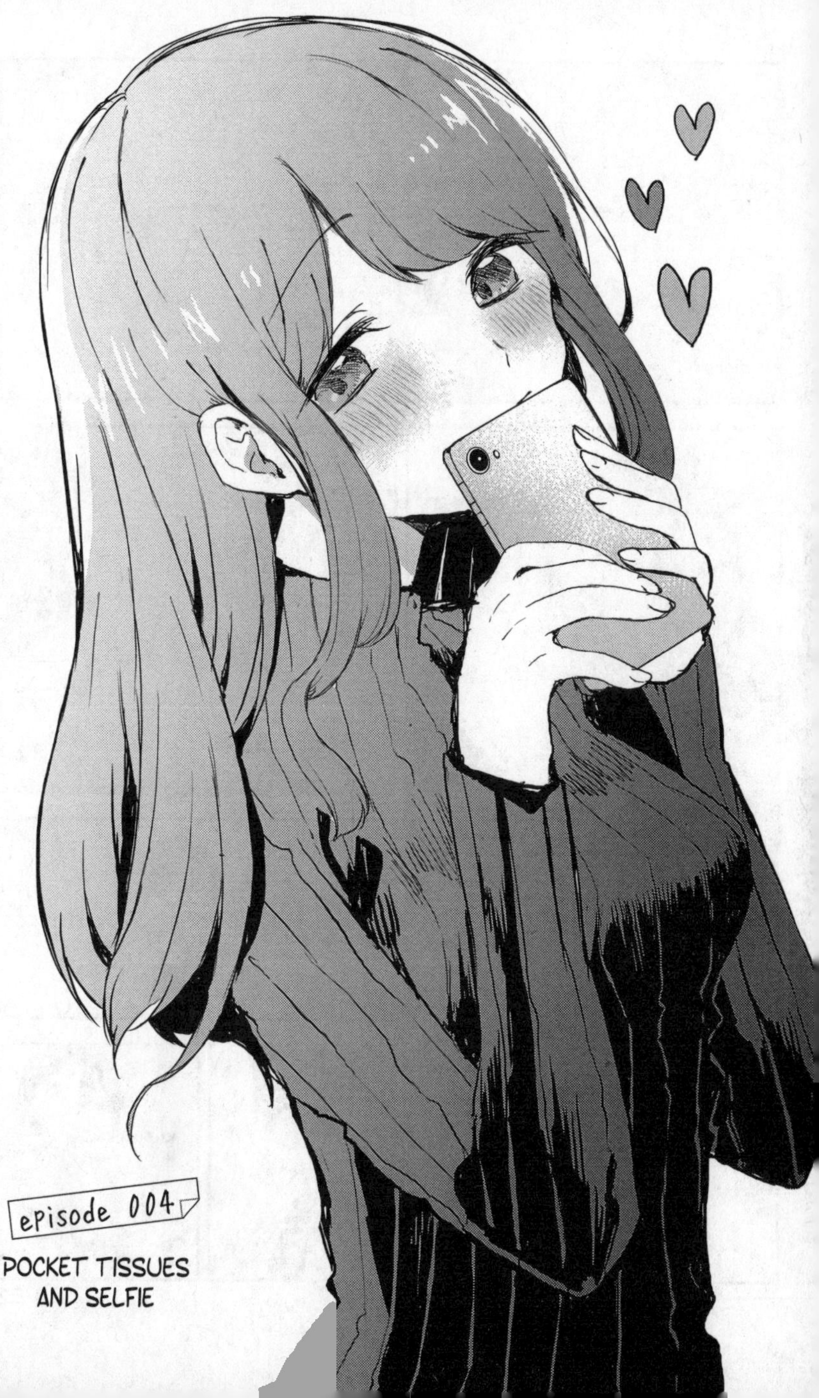
episode 004
POCKET TISSUES AND SELFIE

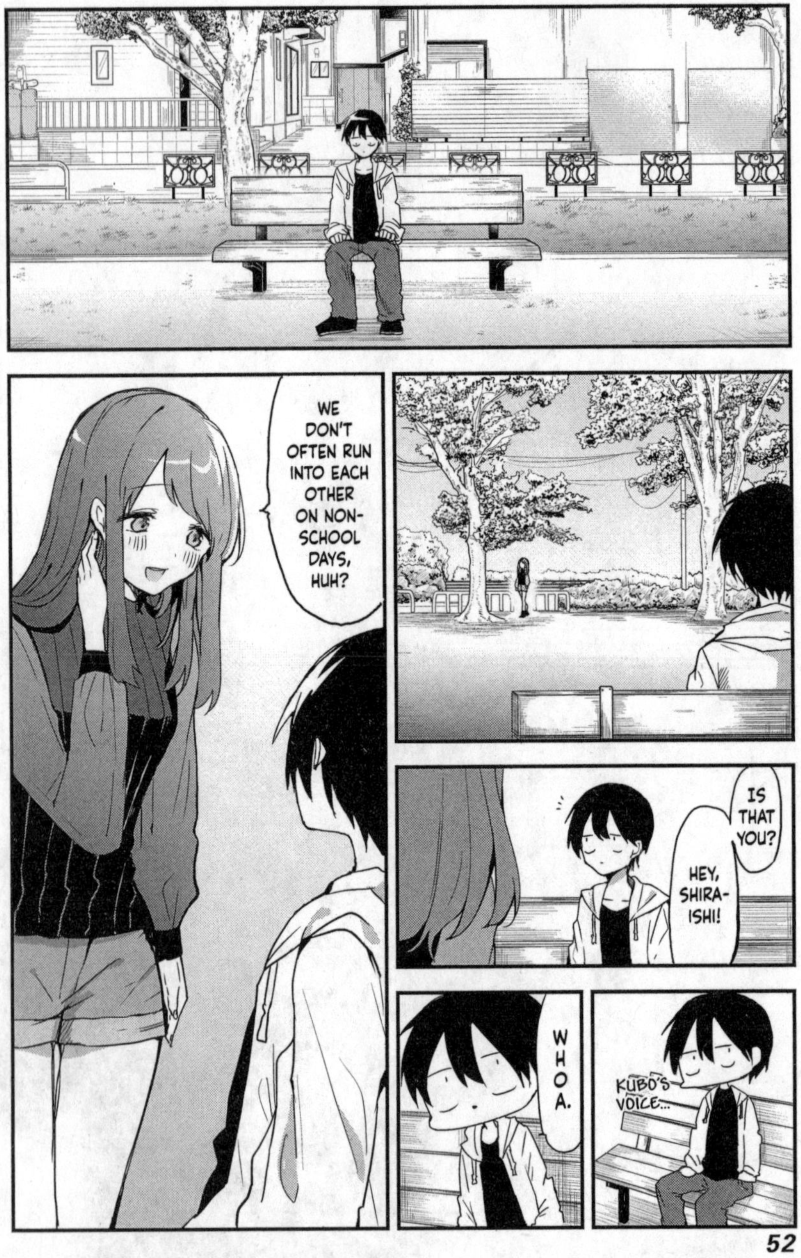
IS THAT YOU?
HEY, SHIRA-ISHI!
KUBO'S VOICE...
WHOA.
WE DON'T OFTEN RUN INTO EACH OTHER ON NON-SCHOOL DAYS, HUH?

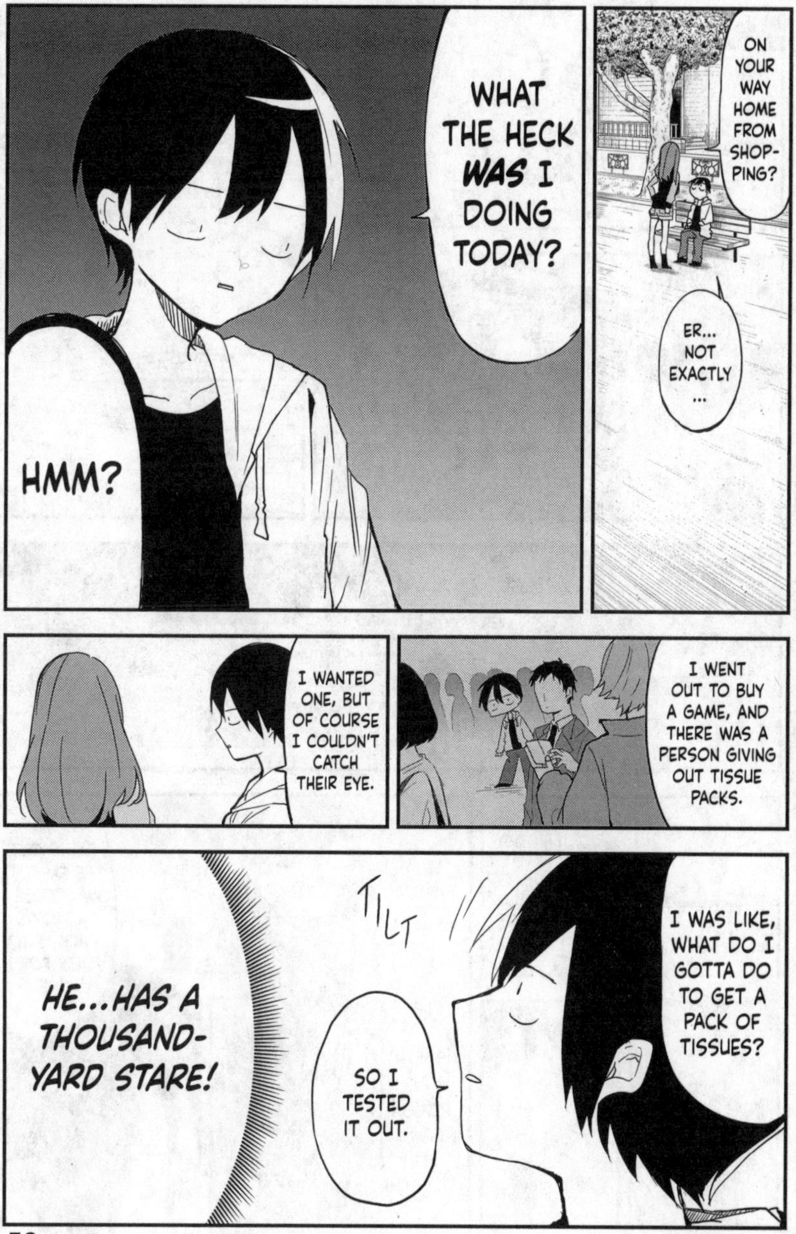
ON YOUR WAY HOME FROM SHOP-PING?
ER... NOT EXACTLY...
WHAT THE HECK *WAS* I DOING TODAY?
HMM?
I WENT OUT TO BUY A GAME, AND THERE WAS A PERSON GIVING OUT TISSUE PACKS.
I WANTED ONE, BUT OF COURSE I COULDN'T CATCH THEIR EYE.
I WAS LIKE, WHAT DO I GOTTA DO TO GET A PACK OF TISSUES?
TILT
SO I TESTED IT OUT.
HE...HAS A THOUSAND-YARD STARE!

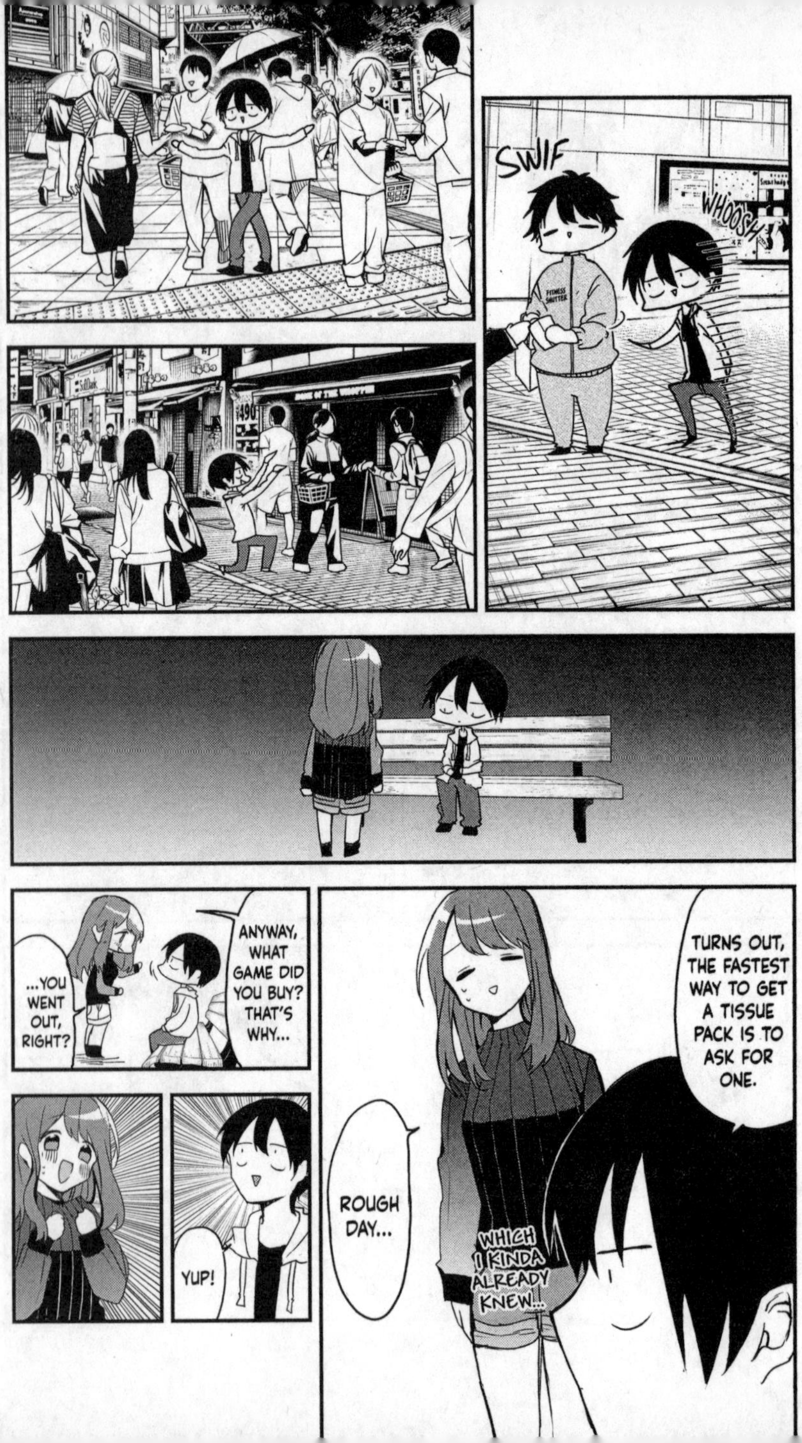
SWIF
WHOOSH
FITNESS SHUTTER
$490
TURNS OUT, THE FASTEST WAY TO GET A TISSUE PACK IS TO ASK FOR ONE.
ROUGH DAY...
WHICH I KINDA ALREADY KNEW...
ANYWAY, WHAT GAME DID YOU BUY? THAT'S WHY...
...YOU WENT OUT, RIGHT?
YUP!

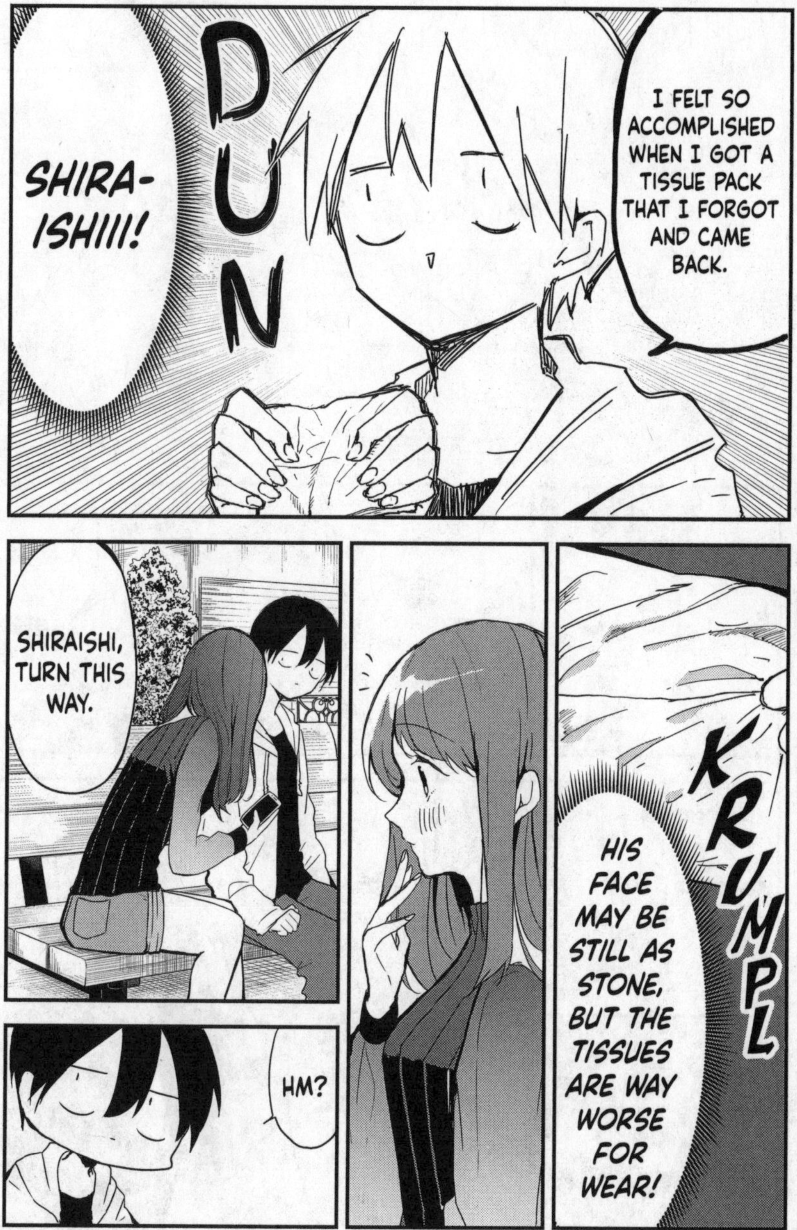
I FELT SO ACCOMPLISHED WHEN I GOT A TISSUE PACK THAT I FORGOT AND CAME BACK.
DUN
SHIRA-ISHIII!
KRUMPL
HIS FACE MAY BE STILL AS STONE, BUT THE TISSUES ARE WAY WORSE FOR WEAR!
SHIRAISHI, TURN THIS WAY.
HM?

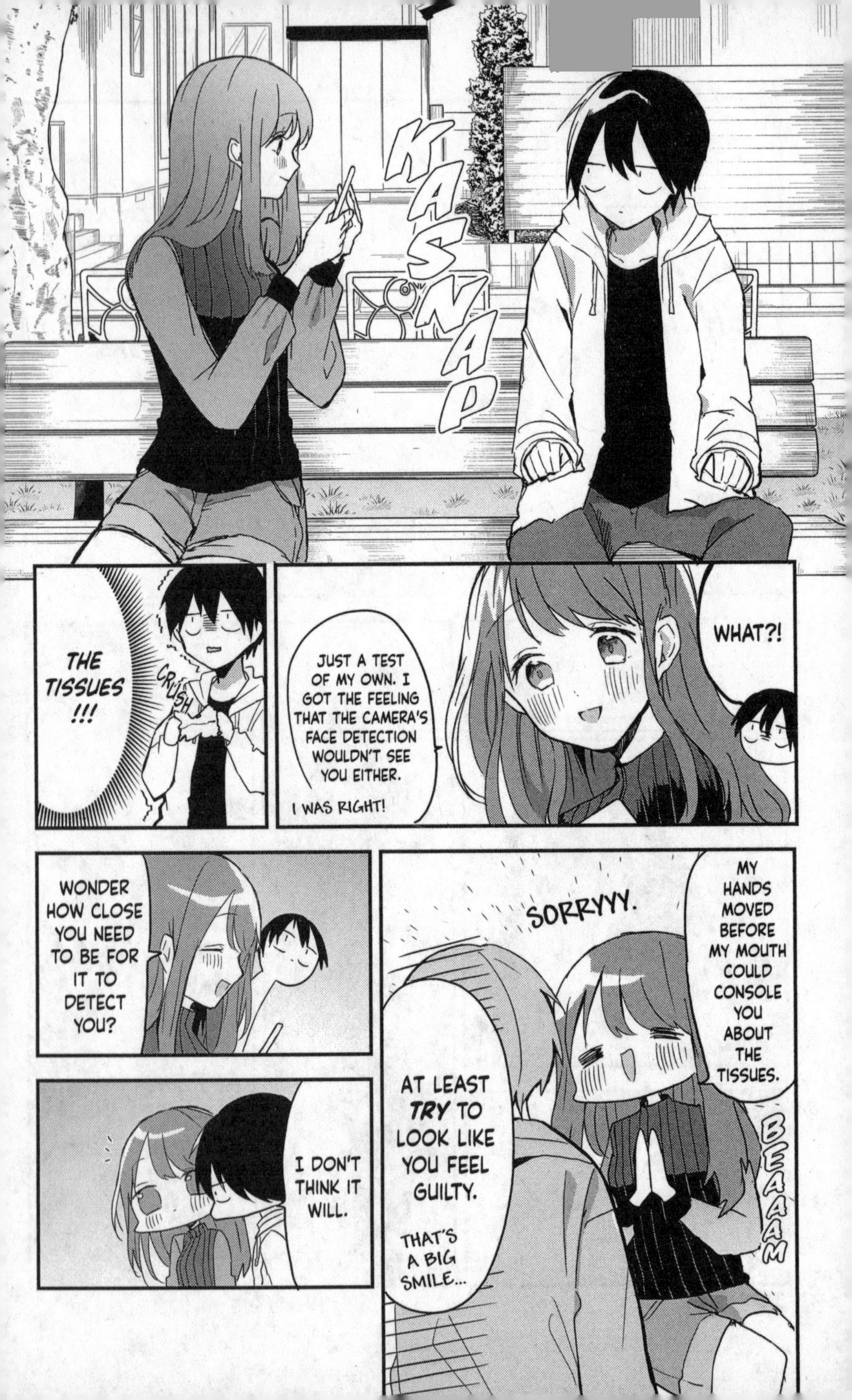
KASNAP
WHAT?!
JUST A TEST OF MY OWN. I GOT THE FEELING THAT THE CAMERA'S FACE DETECTION WOULDN'T SEE YOU EITHER.
I WAS RIGHT!
THE TISSUES!!!
CRUSH
MY HANDS MOVED BEFORE MY MOUTH COULD CONSOLE YOU ABOUT THE TISSUES.
SORRYYY.
BEAAAM
AT LEAST TRY TO LOOK LIKE YOU FEEL GUILTY.
THAT'S A BIG SMILE...
WONDER HOW CLOSE YOU NEED TO BE FOR IT TO DETECT YOU?
I DON'T THINK IT WILL.

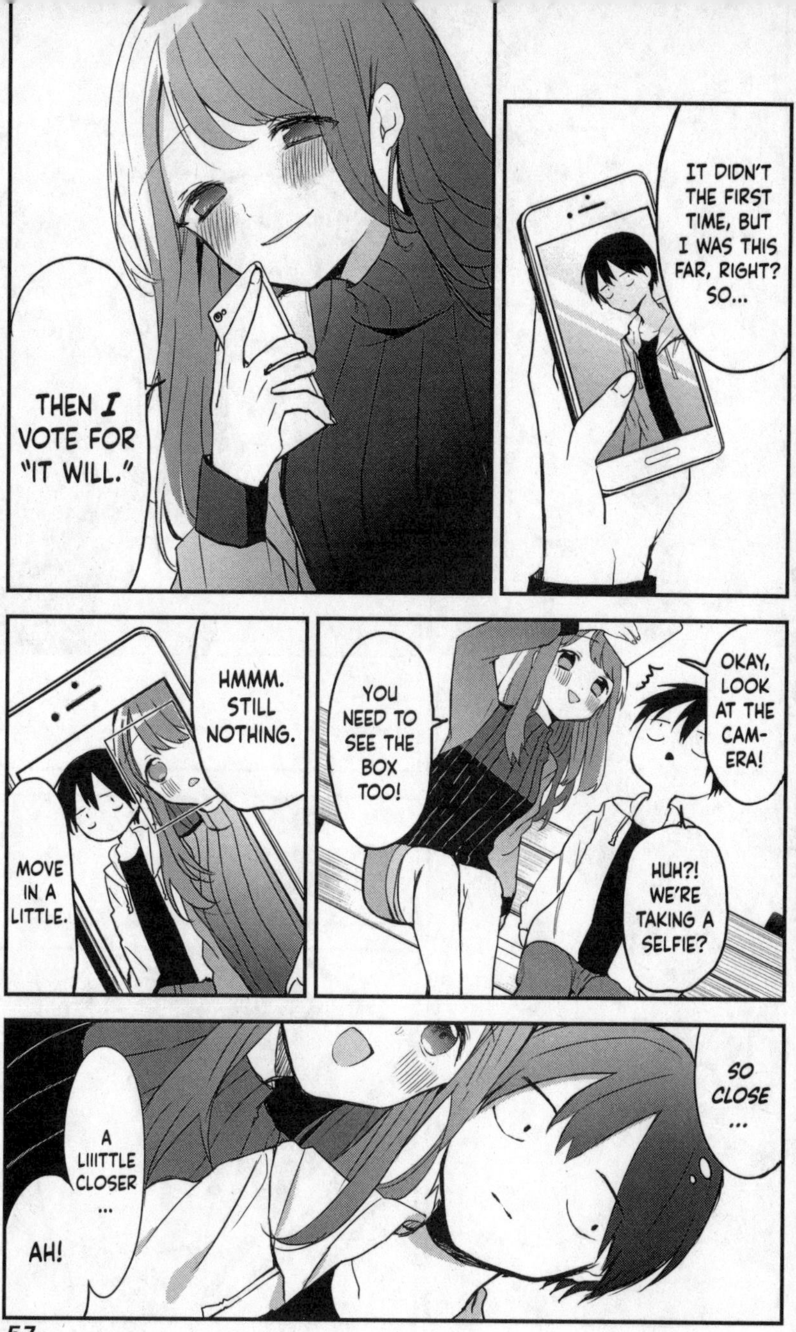
IT DIDN'T THE FIRST TIME, BUT I WAS THIS FAR, RIGHT? SO...
THEN *I* VOTE FOR "IT WILL."
OKAY, LOOK AT THE CAM-ERA!
HUH?! WE'RE TAKING A SELFIE?
YOU NEED TO SEE THE BOX TOO!
HMMM. STILL NOTHING.
MOVE IN A LITTLE.
SO CLOSE ...
A LIIITTLE CLOSER ...
AH!

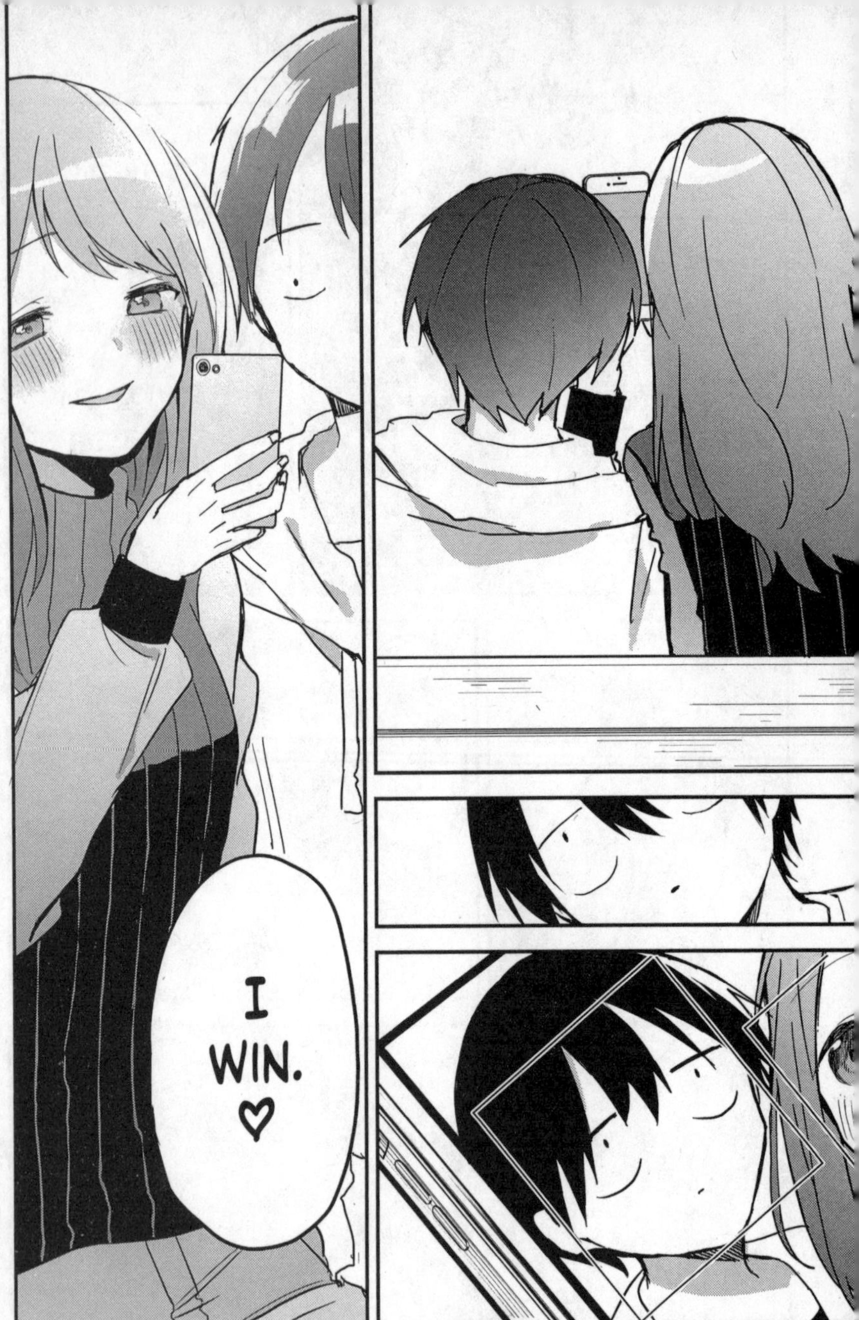
I WIN. ♡

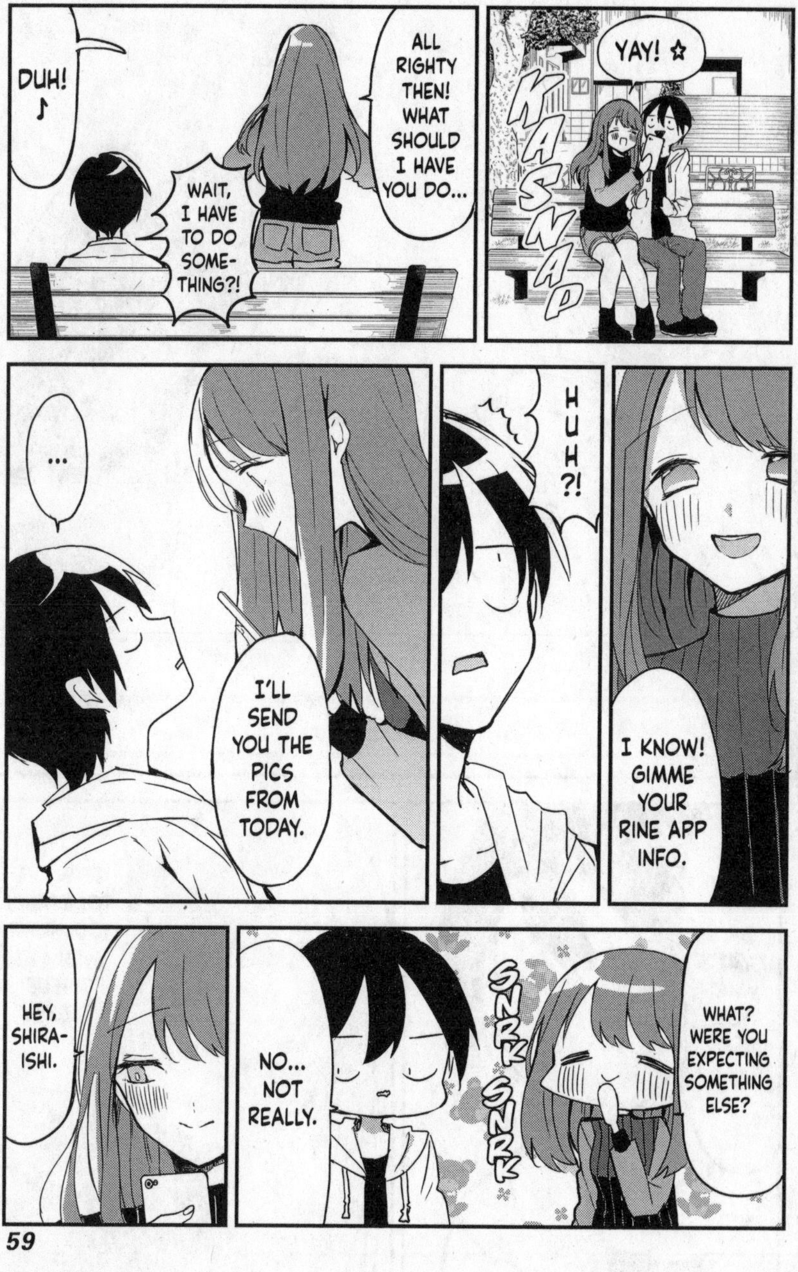
YAY! ✩
KASNAP
ALL RIGHTY THEN! WHAT SHOULD I HAVE YOU DO...
WAIT, I HAVE TO DO SOME-THING?!
DUH! ♪
I KNOW! GIMME YOUR RINE APP INFO.
HUH?!
I'LL SEND YOU THE PICS FROM TODAY.
...
WHAT? WERE YOU EXPECTING SOMETHING ELSE?
SNRK SNRK
NO... NOT REALLY.
HEY, SHIRA-ISHI.

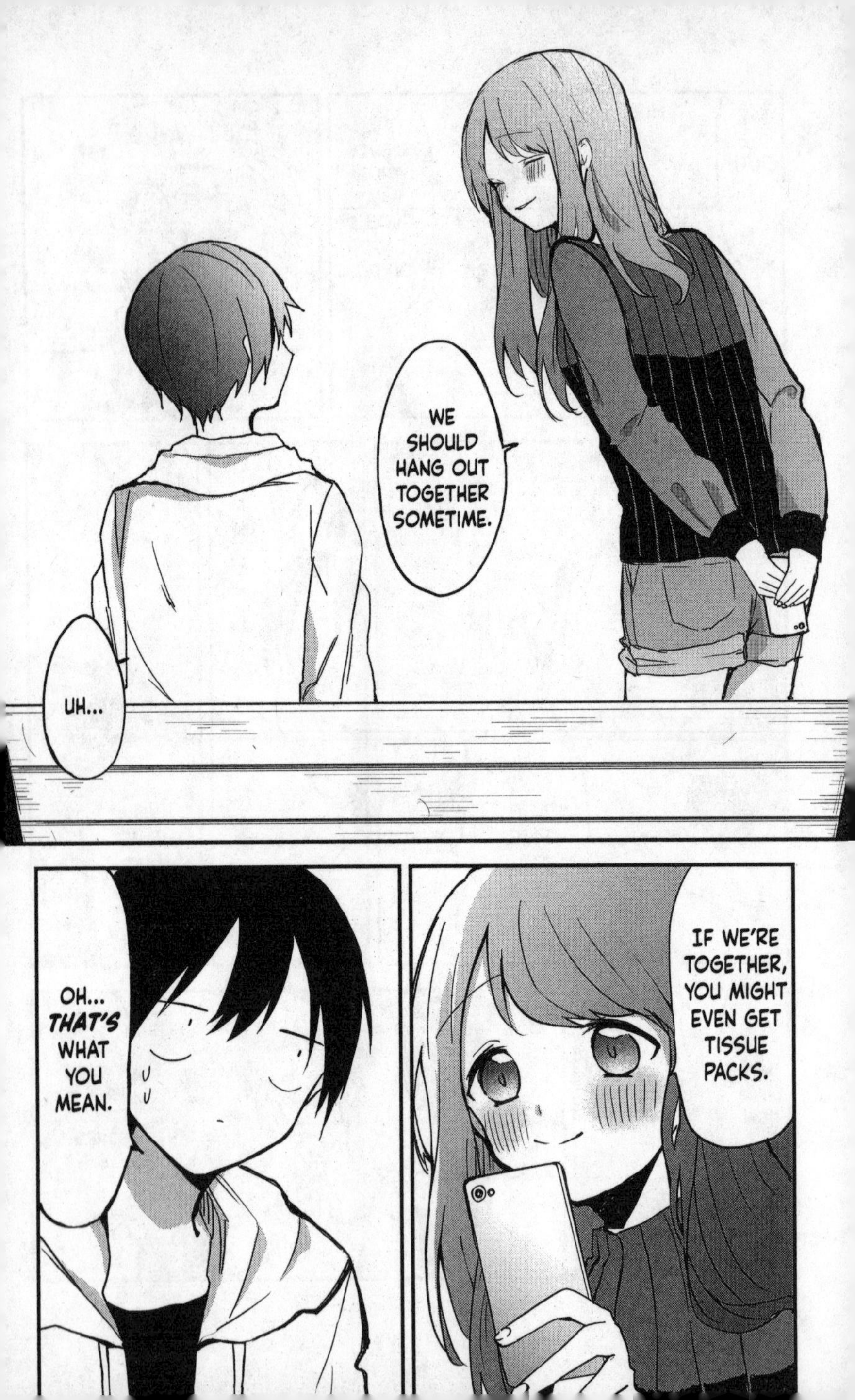
WE SHOULD HANG OUT TOGETHER SOMETIME.
UH...
IF WE'RE TOGETHER, YOU MIGHT EVEN GET TISSUE PACKS.
OH... *THAT'S* WHAT YOU MEAN.

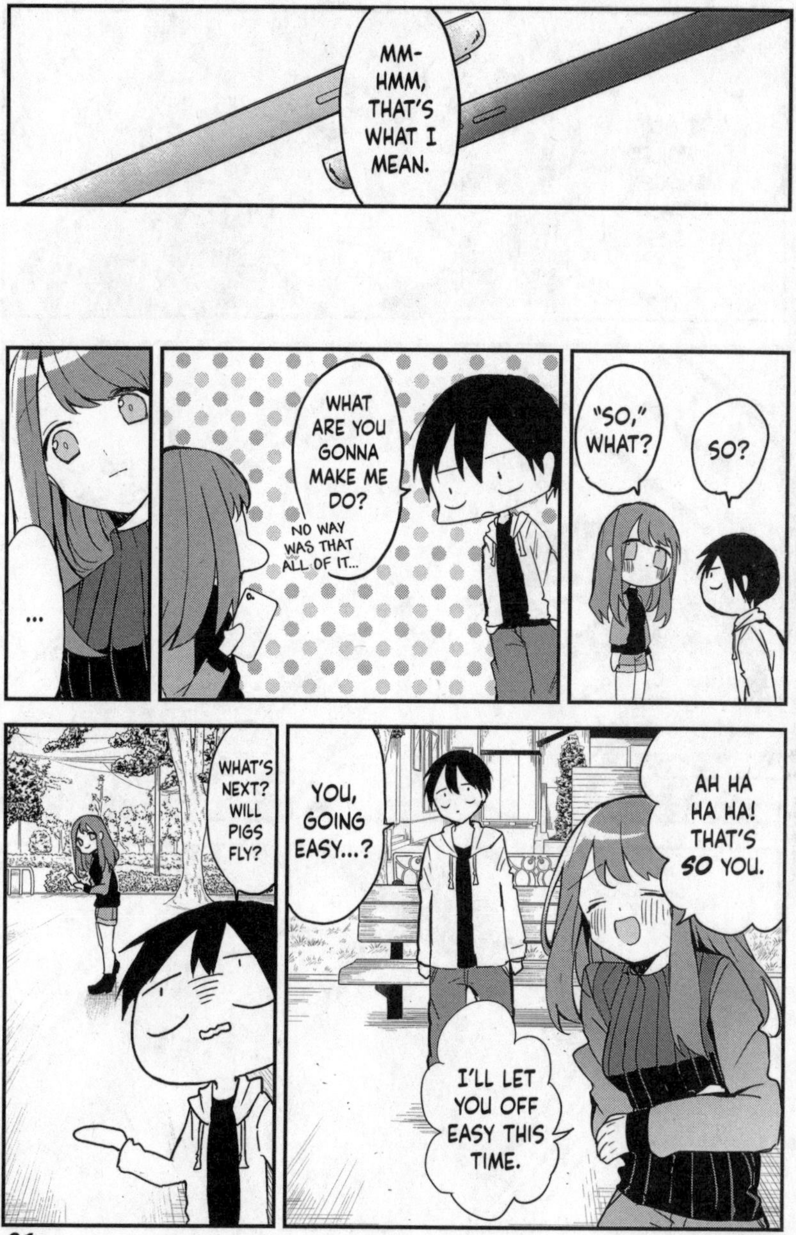
MM-HMM, THAT'S WHAT I MEAN.
SO?
"SO," WHAT?
WHAT ARE YOU GONNA MAKE ME DO?
NO WAY WAS THAT ALL OF IT...
...
AH HA HA HA! THAT'S *SO* YOU.
YOU, GOING EASY...?
I'LL LET YOU OFF EASY THIS TIME.
WHAT'S NEXT? WILL PIGS FLY?

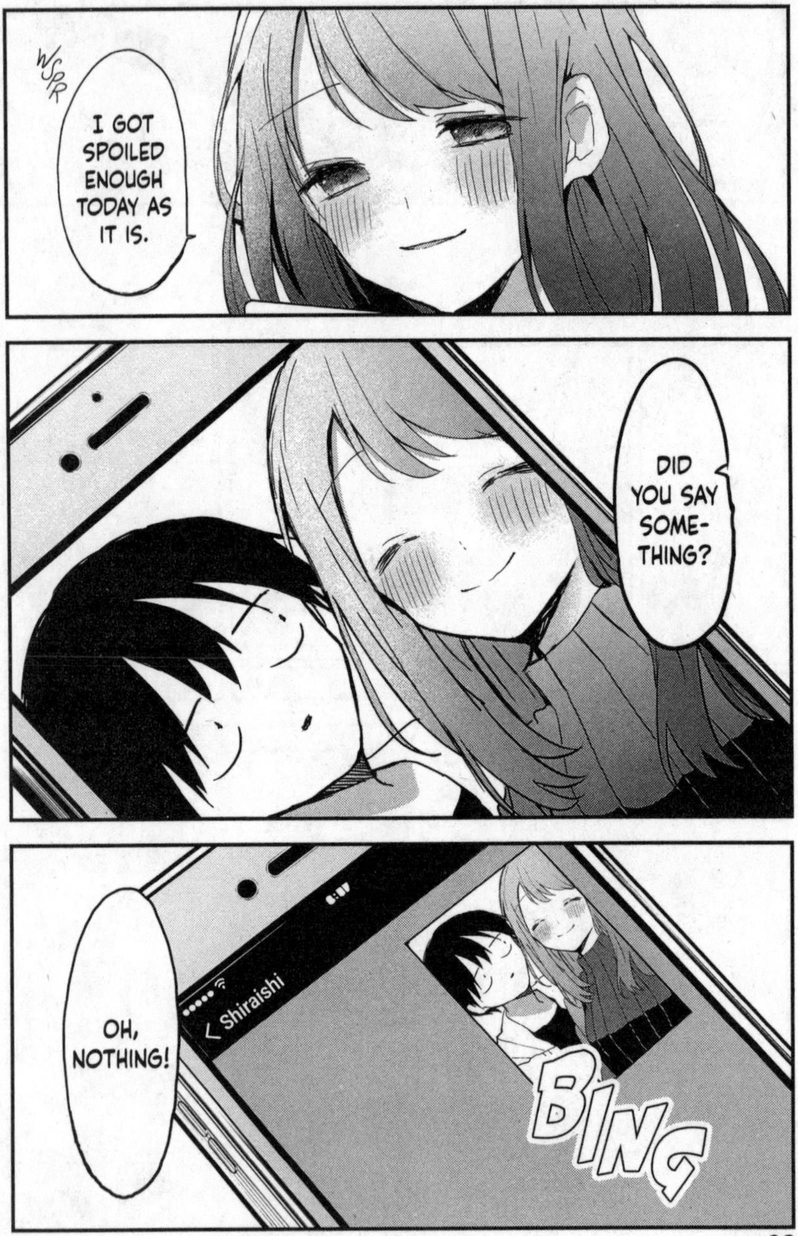
WSPR
I GOT SPOILED ENOUGH TODAY AS IT IS.
DID YOU SAY SOME-THING?
Shiraishi
OH, NOTHING!
BING

episode 005

PONYTAIL AND BODY WIPES

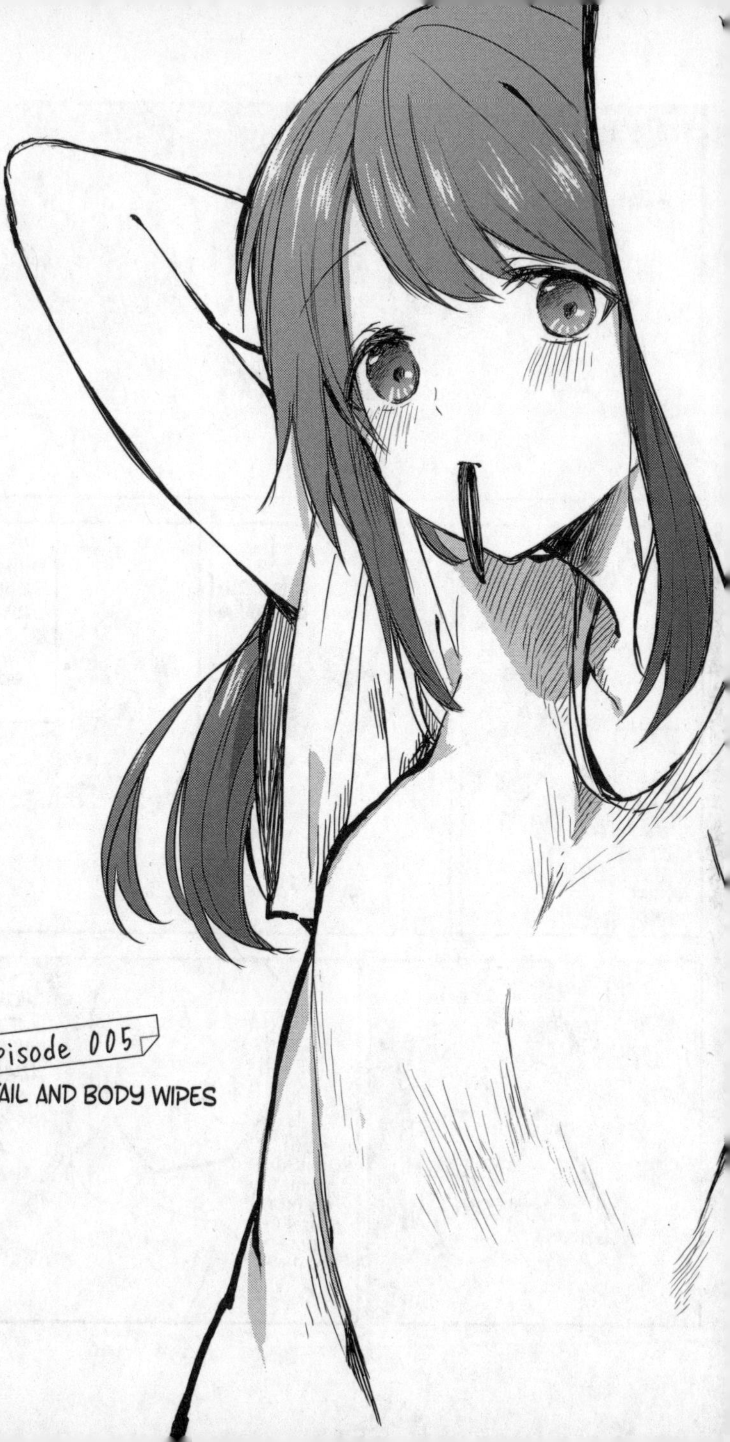

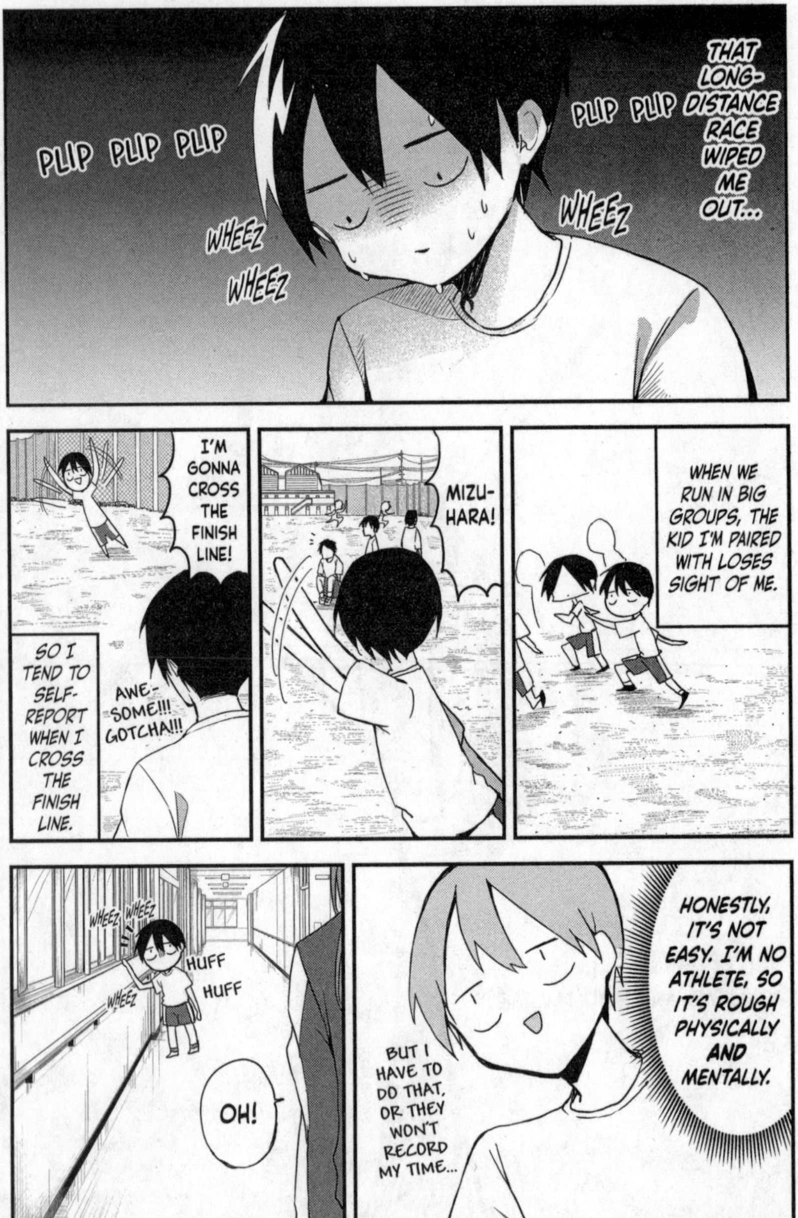
THAT LONG-DISTANCE RACE WIPED ME OUT...
PLIP PLIP
WHEEZ
PLIP PLIP PLIP
WHEEZ
WHEEZ
WHEN WE RUN IN BIG GROUPS, THE KID I'M PAIRED WITH LOSES SIGHT OF ME.
MIZU-HARA!
I'M GONNA CROSS THE FINISH LINE!
AWE-SOME!!! GOTCHA!!!
SO I TEND TO SELF-REPORT WHEN I CROSS THE FINISH LINE.
HONESTLY, IT'S NOT EASY. I'M NO ATHLETE, SO IT'S ROUGH PHYSICALLY AND MENTALLY.
BUT I HAVE TO DO THAT, OR THEY WON'T RECORD MY TIME...
WHEEZ WHEEZ
HUFF
HUFF
WHEEZ
OH!

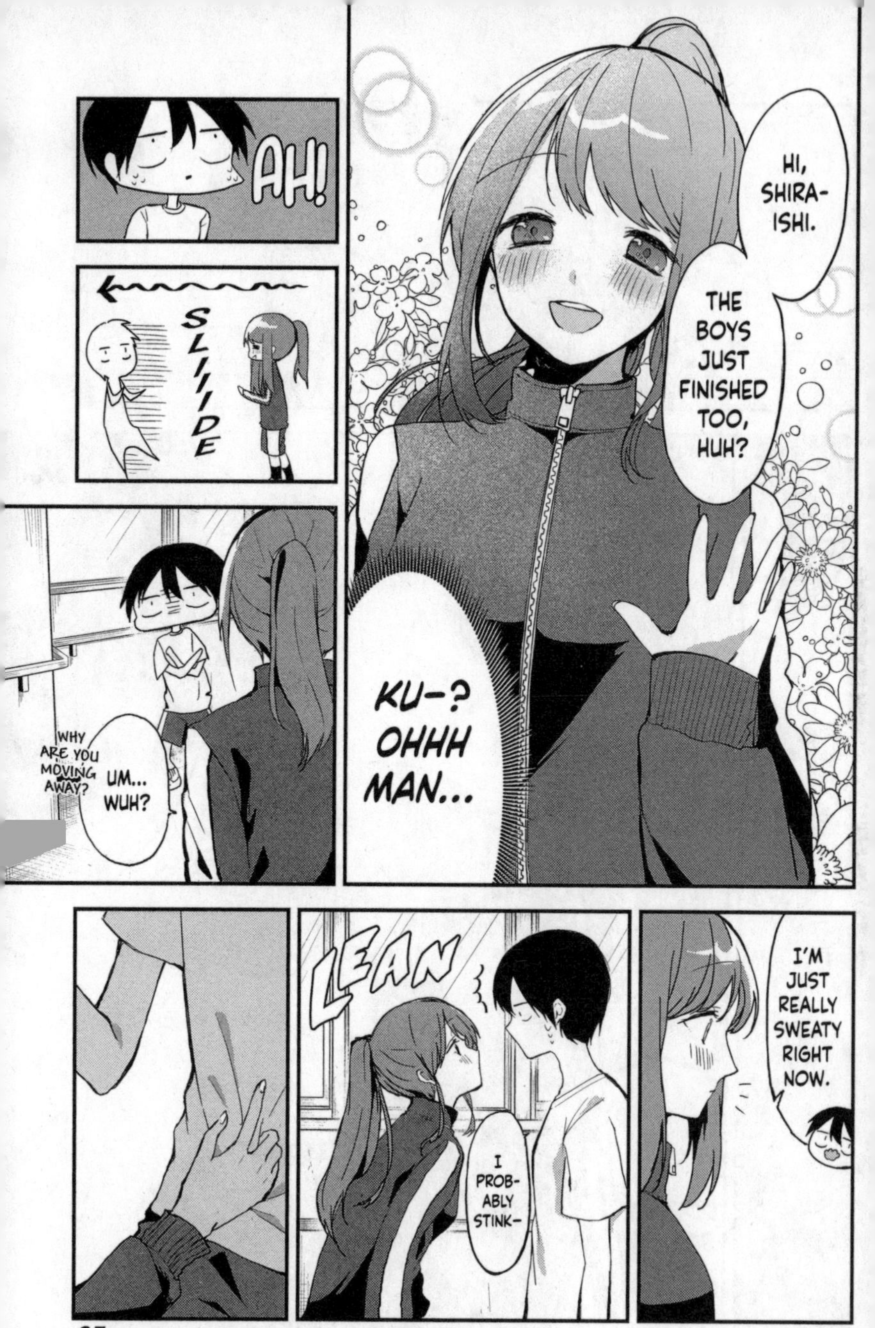
HI, SHIRA-ISHI.
THE BOYS JUST FINISHED TOO, HUH?
KU-? OHHH MAN...
AH!
SLIIIDE
UM... WUH?
WHY ARE YOU MOVING AWAY?
I'M JUST REALLY SWEATY RIGHT NOW.
LEAN
I PROB-ABLY STINK-

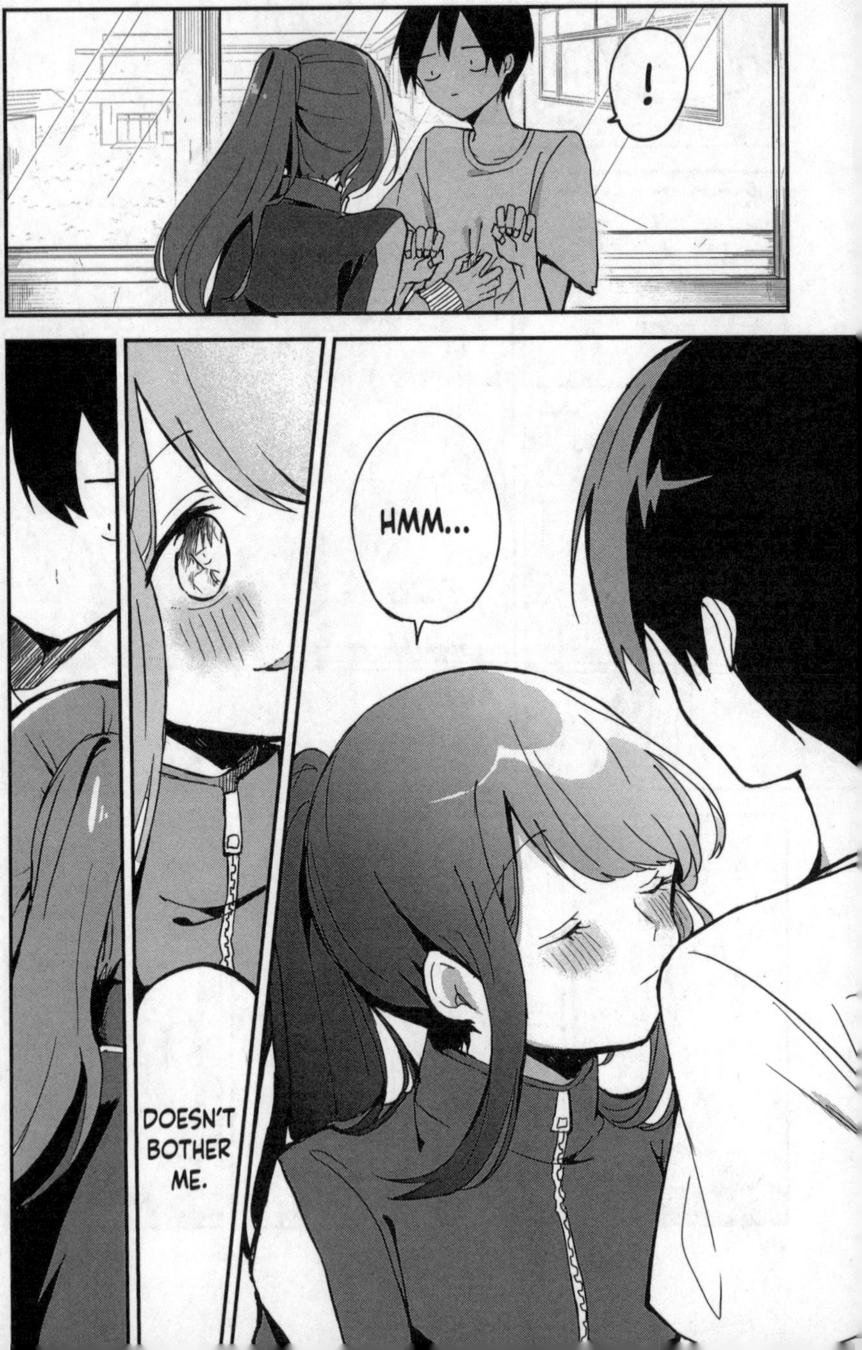
!
HMM...
DOESN'T BOTHER ME.

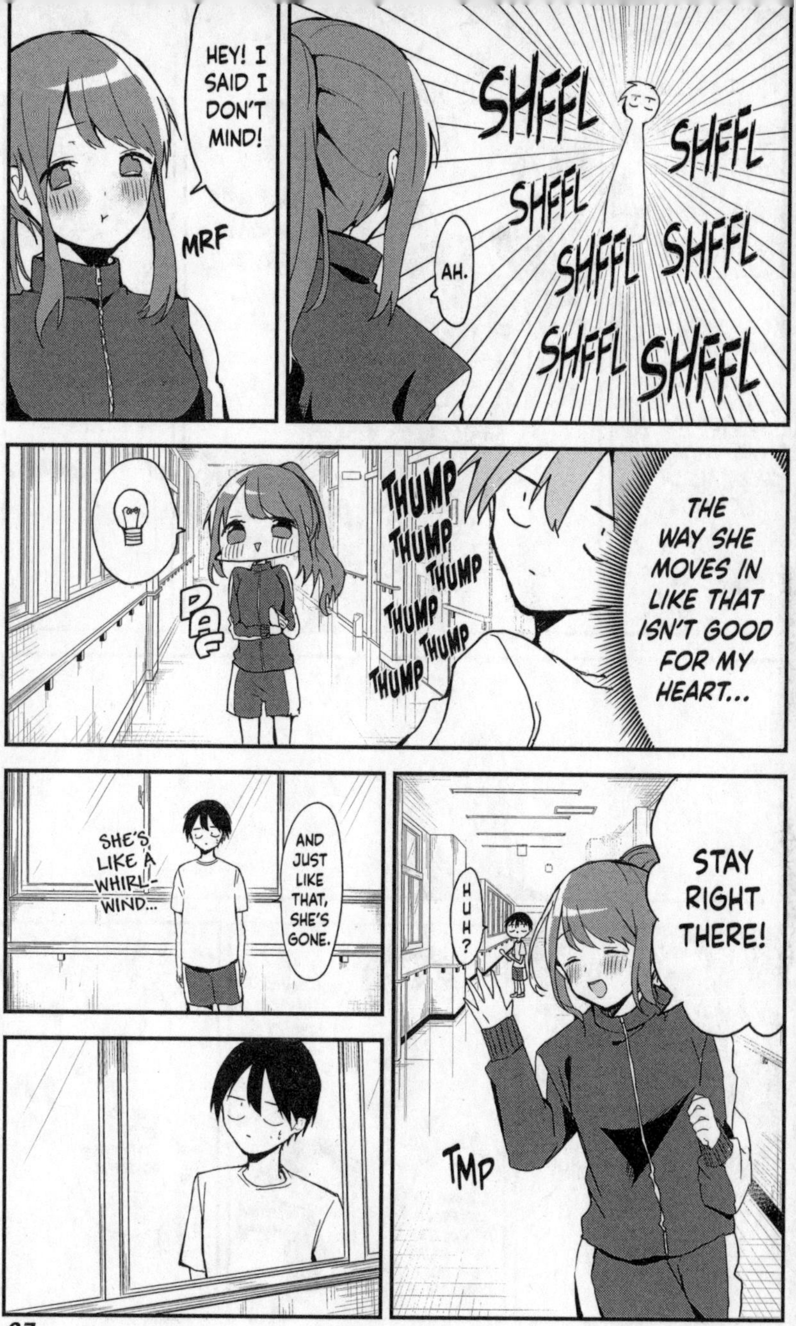
SHFFL SHFFL SHFFL SHFFL SHFFL SHFFL SHFFL
AH.
HEY! I SAID I DON'T MIND!
MRF
THE WAY SHE MOVES IN LIKE THAT ISN'T GOOD FOR MY HEART...
THUMP THUMP THUMP THUMP THUMP THUMP
PAF
STAY RIGHT THERE!
HUH?
TMP
AND JUST LIKE THAT, SHE'S GONE.
SHE'S LIKE A WHIRL-WIND...

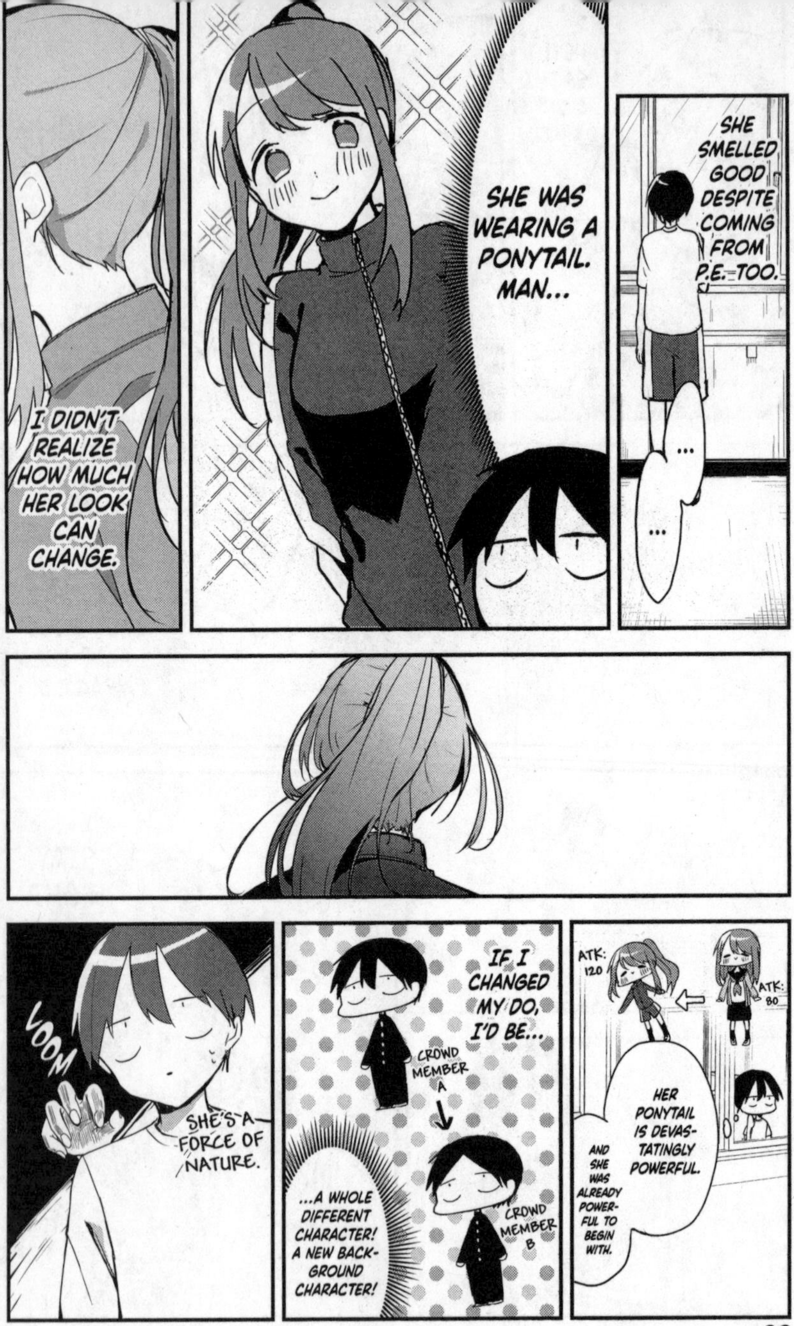
SHE SMELLED GOOD DESPITE COMING FROM P.E. TOO.
...
...
SHE WAS WEARING A PONYTAIL. MAN...
I DIDN'T REALIZE HOW MUCH HER LOOK CAN CHANGE.
ATK: 120
ATK: 80
HER PONYTAIL IS DEVAS-TATINGLY POWERFUL.
AND SHE WAS ALREADY POWER-FUL TO BEGIN WITH.
IF I CHANGED MY DO, I'D BE...
CROWD MEMBER A
CROWD MEMBER B
...A WHOLE DIFFERENT CHARACTER! A NEW BACK-GROUND CHARACTER!
VOOM
SHE'S A FORCE OF NATURE.

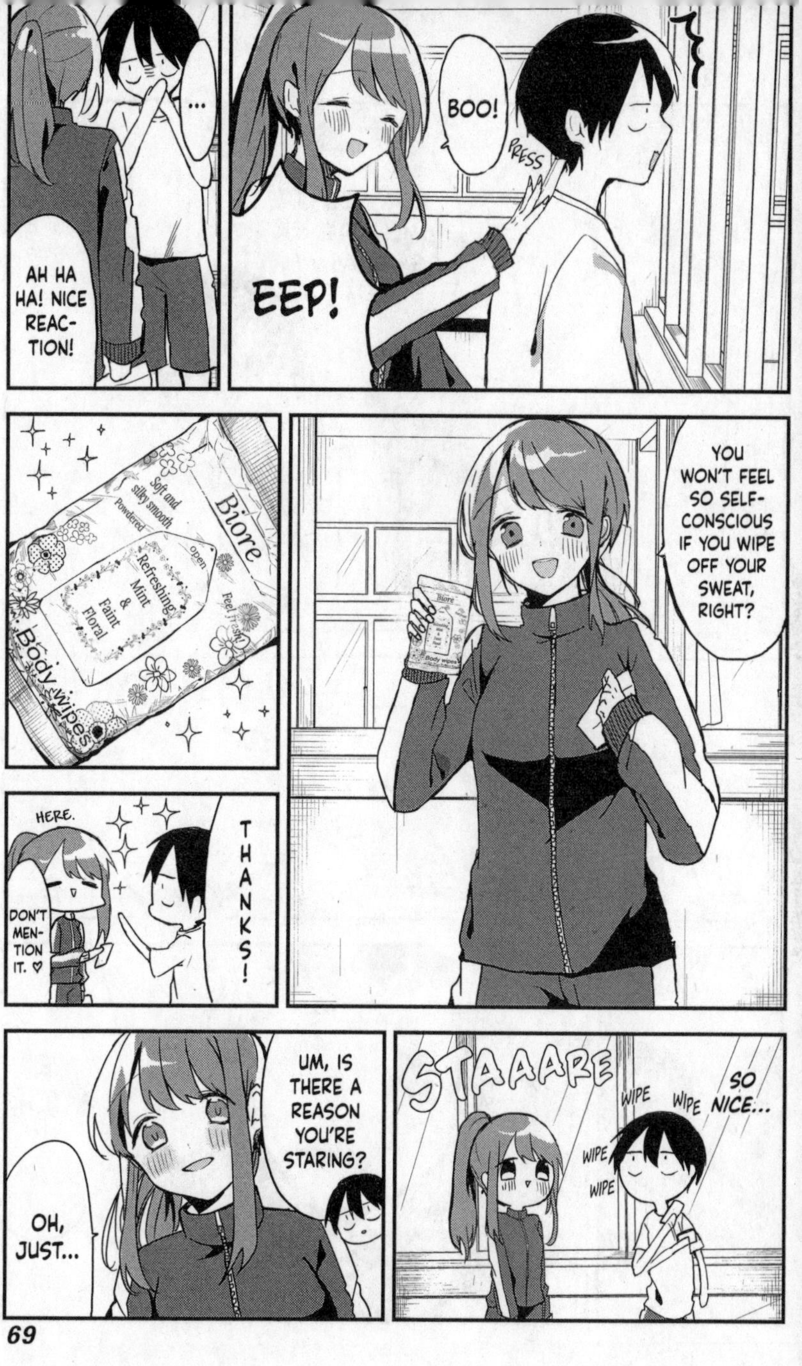
BOO!
PRESS
EEP!
...
AH HA HA! NICE REACTION!
YOU WON'T FEEL SO SELF-CONSCIOUS IF YOU WIPE OFF YOUR SWEAT, RIGHT?
Biore
Soft and silky smooth
Powdered
Refreshing Mint & Faint Floral
open
Feel fresh!
Body wipes
HERE.
THANKS!
DON'T MENTION IT. ♡
STAAARE
WIPE
WIPE
SO NICE...
WIPE
WIPE
UM, IS THERE A REASON YOU'RE STARING?
OH, JUST...

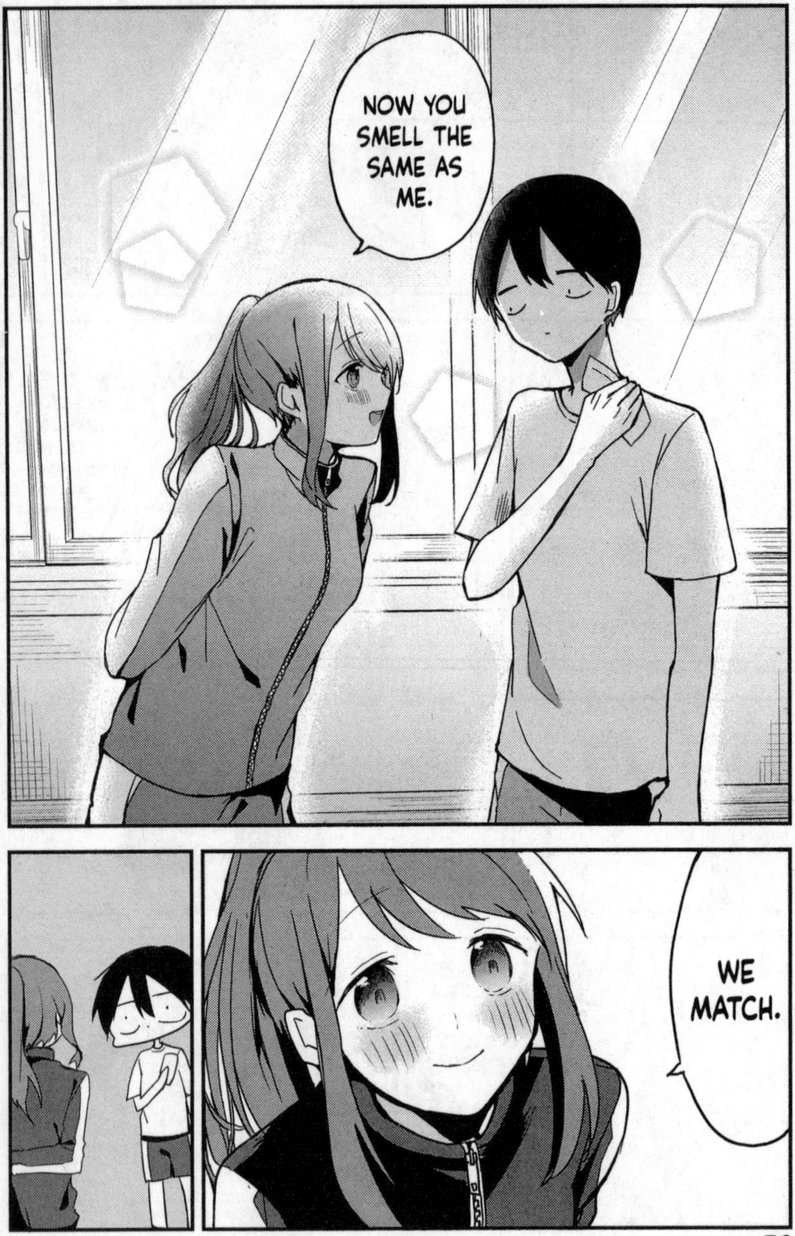
NOW YOU SMELL THE SAME AS ME.
WE MATCH.

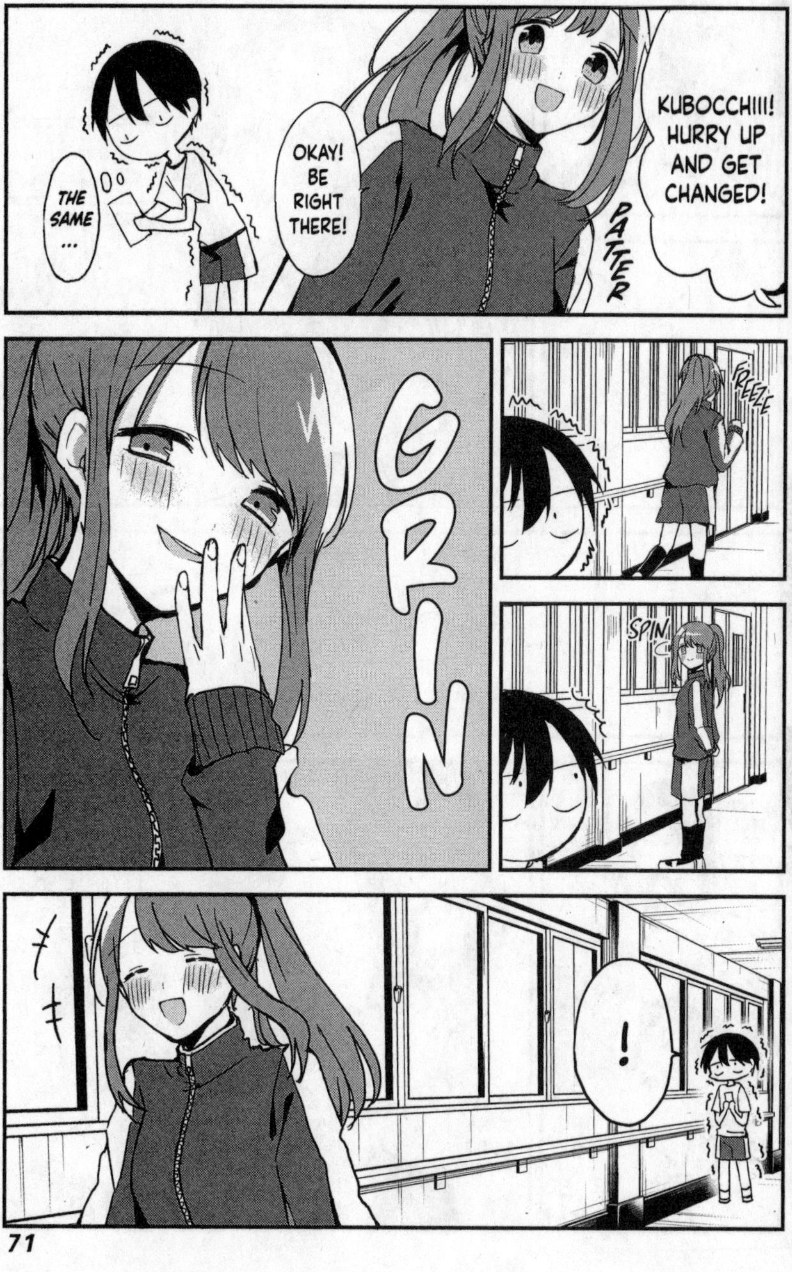
KUBOCCHIIII! HURRY UP AND GET CHANGED!
PATTER
OKAY! BE RIGHT THERE!
THE SAME ...
FREEZE
SPIN
GRIN
!

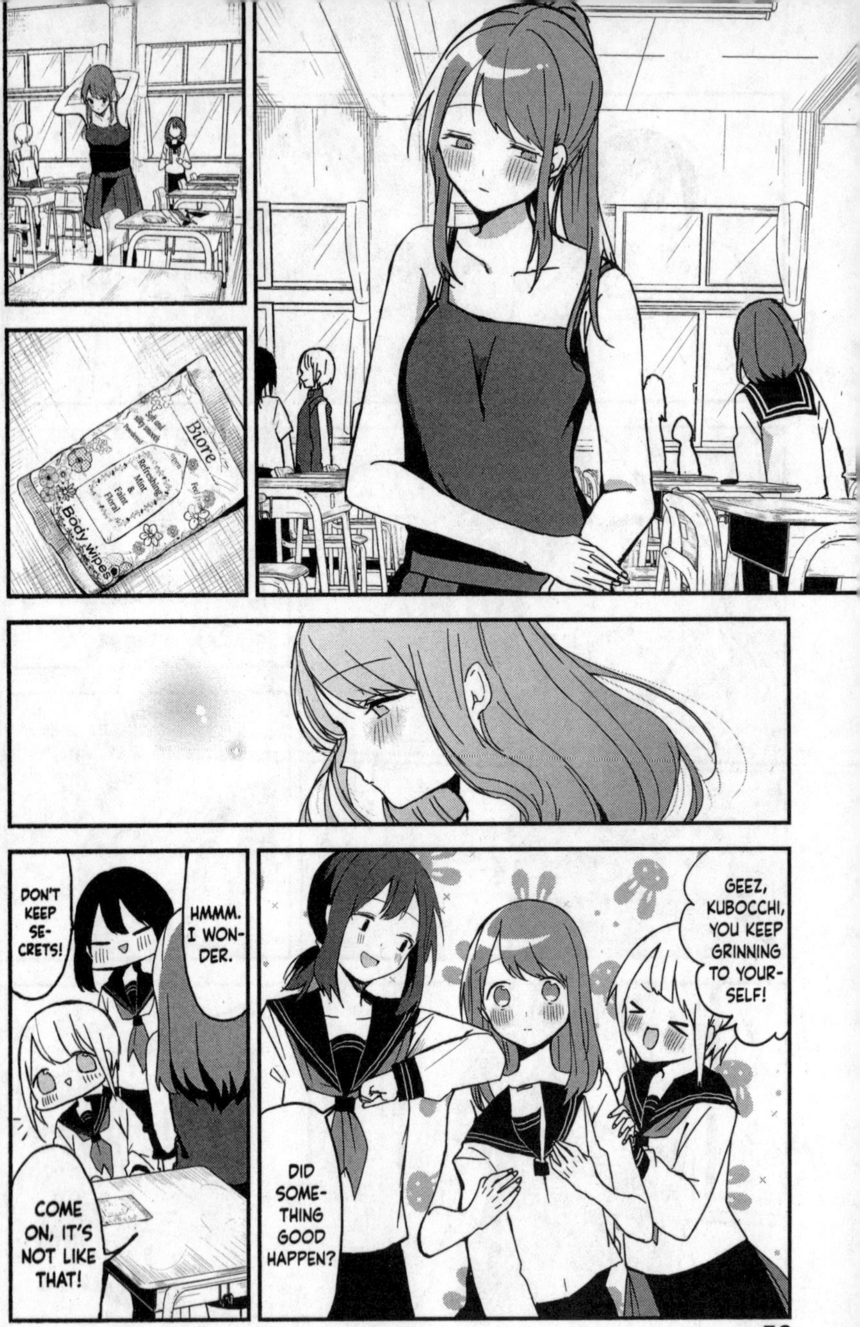
Biore
Refreshing Mint & Faint Floral
Body wipes
GEEZ, KUBOCCHI, YOU KEEP GRINNING TO YOURSELF!
DID SOMETHING GOOD HAPPEN?
HMMM. I WONDER.
DON'T KEEP SECRETS!
COME ON, IT'S NOT LIKE THAT!

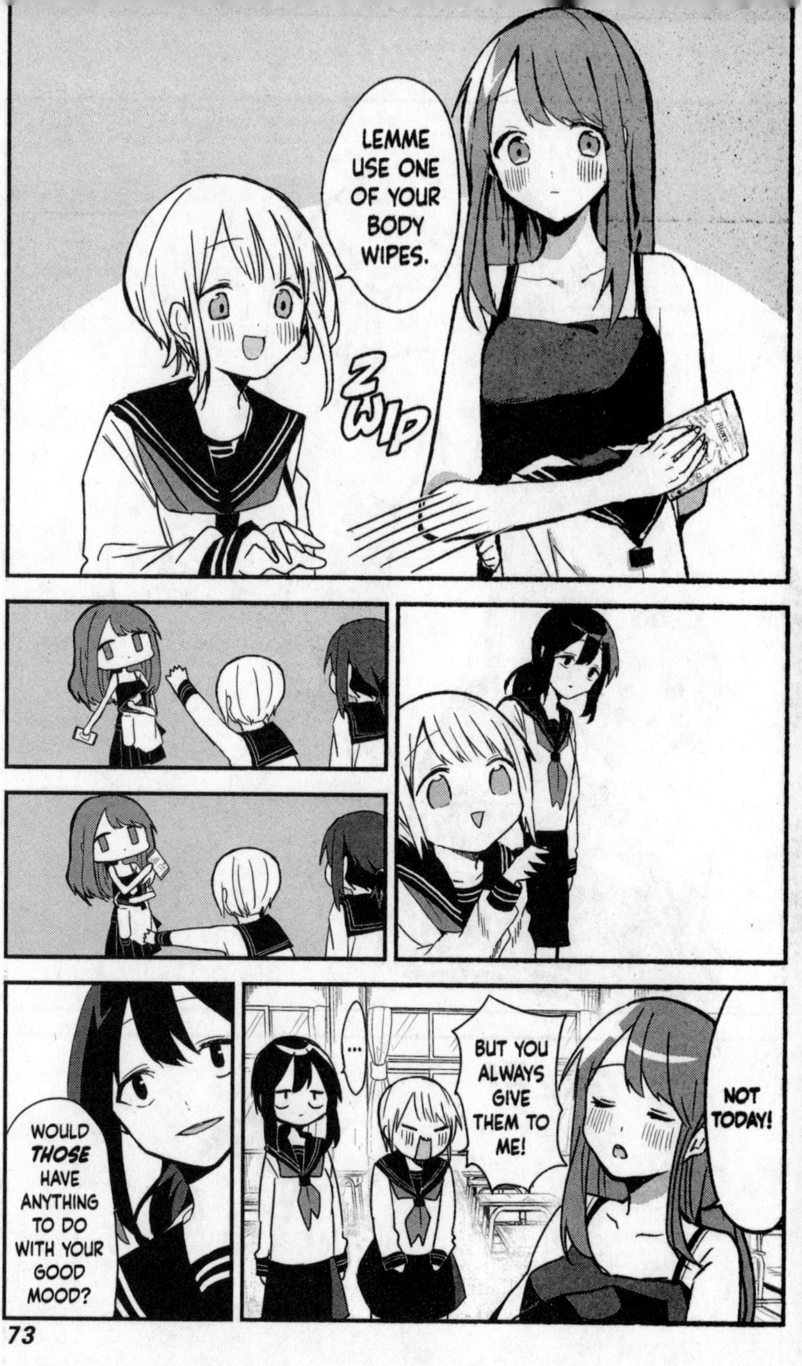
LEMME USE ONE OF YOUR BODY WIPES.
ZWIP
NOT TODAY!
BUT YOU ALWAYS GIVE THEM TO ME!
...
WOULD *THOSE* HAVE ANYTHING TO DO WITH YOUR GOOD MOOD?

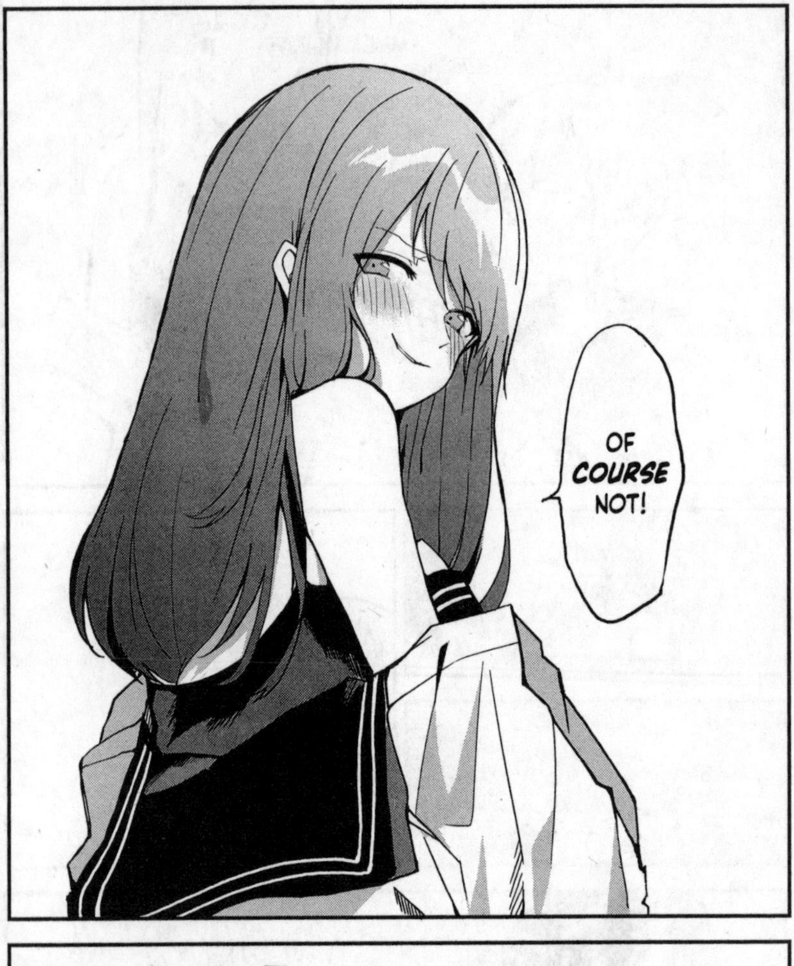
OF COURSE NOT!
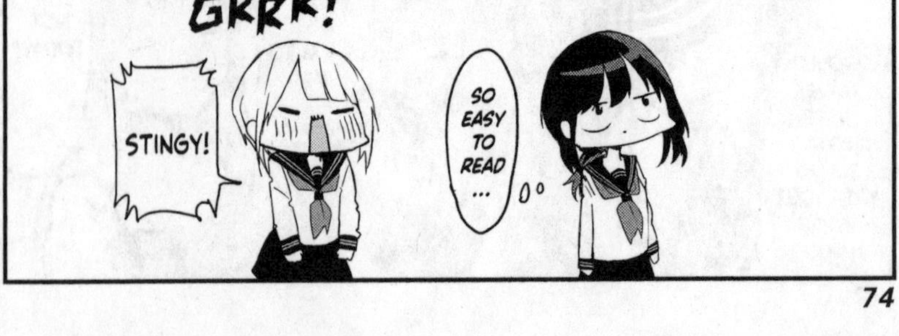
SO EASY TO READ...
GRRR!
STINGY!

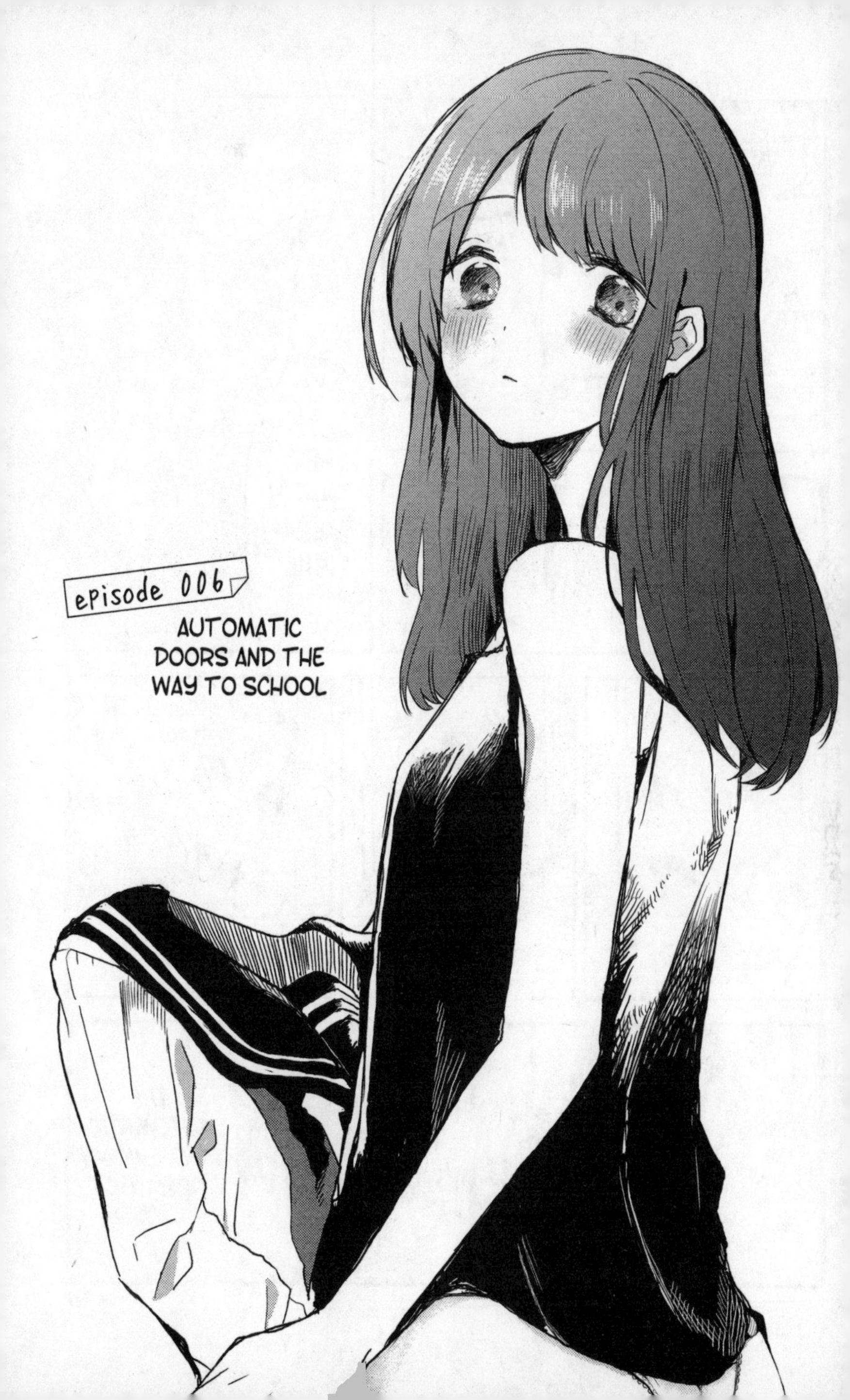
episode 006
AUTOMATIC DOORS AND THE WAY TO SCHOOL

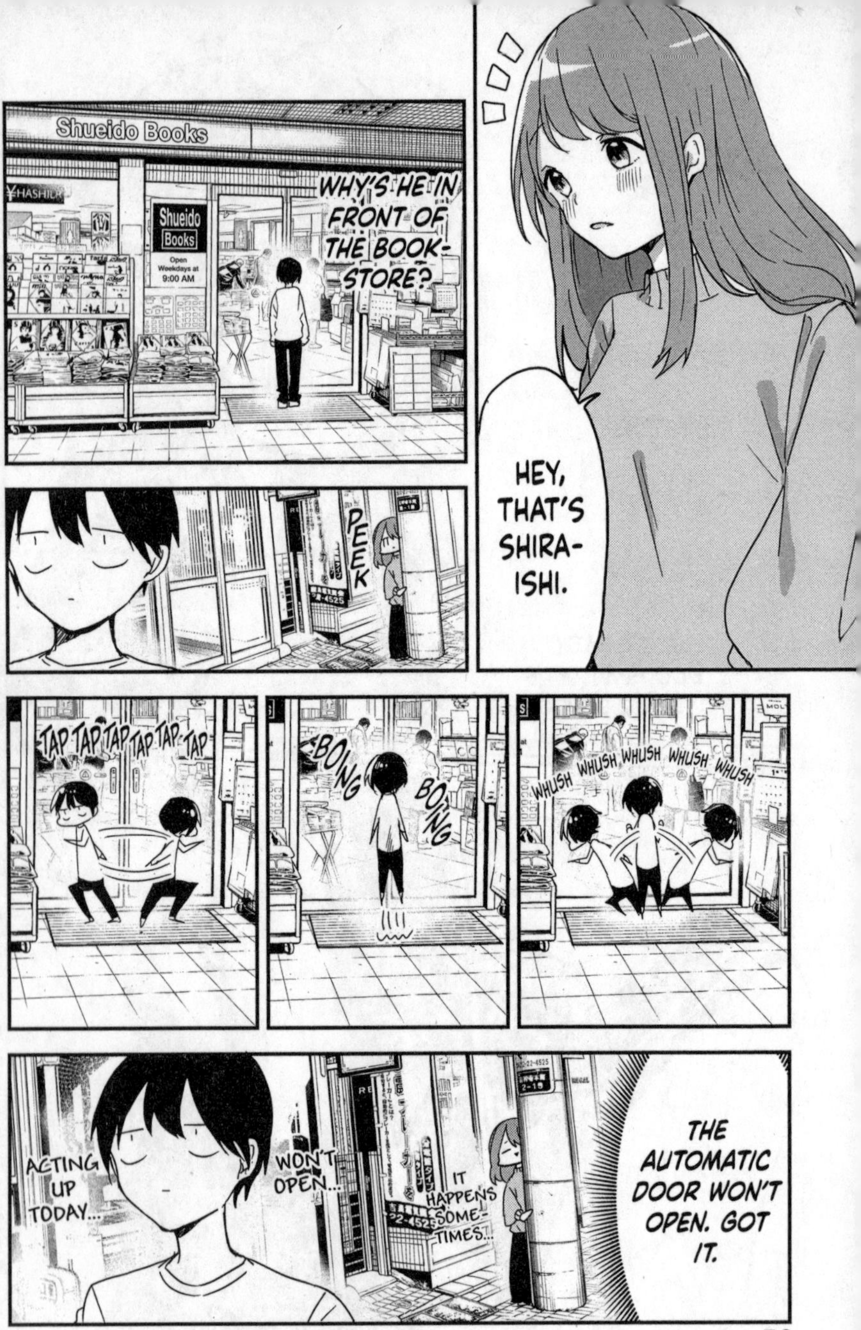
HEY, THAT'S SHIRA-ISHI.
Shueido Books
WHY'S HE IN FRONT OF THE BOOK-STORE?
Shueido Books
Open Weekdays at 9:00 AM
PEEK
WHUSH WHUSH WHUSH WHUSH WHUSH
BOING BOING
TAP TAP TAP TAP TAP TAP
THE AUTOMATIC DOOR WON'T OPEN. GOT IT.
IT HAPPENS SOMETIMES...
WON'T OPEN...
ACTING UP TODAY...

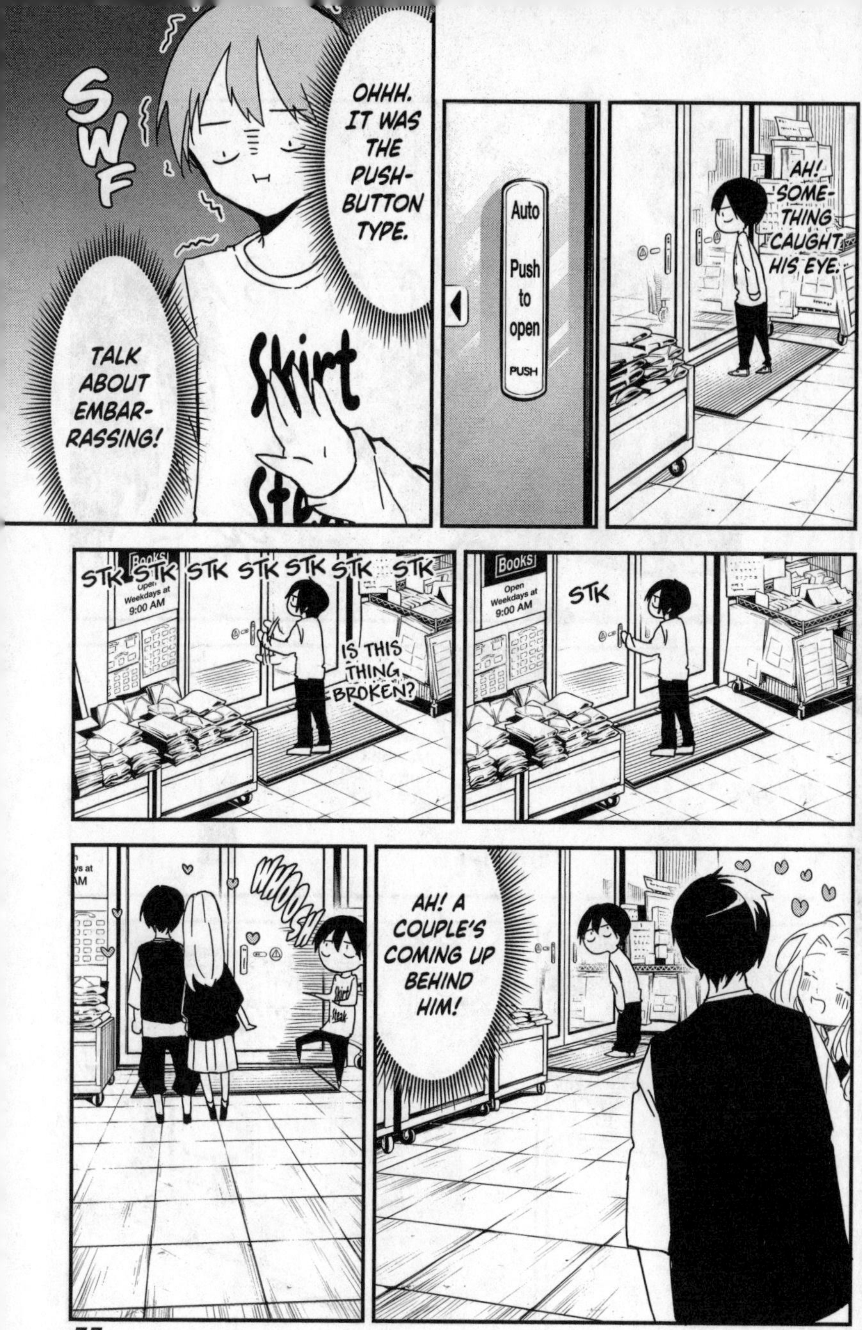
AH! SOMETHING CAUGHT HIS EYE.
Auto
Push to open
PUSH
SWF
OHHH. IT WAS THE PUSH-BUTTON TYPE.
TALK ABOUT EMBARRASSING!
Skirt
Books
Open Weekdays at 9:00 AM
STK
STK STK STK STK STK STK STK
Books
Open Weekdays at 9:00 AM
IS THIS THING BROKEN?
AH! A COUPLE'S COMING UP BEHIND HIM!
WHOOOSH
Skirt
Steak

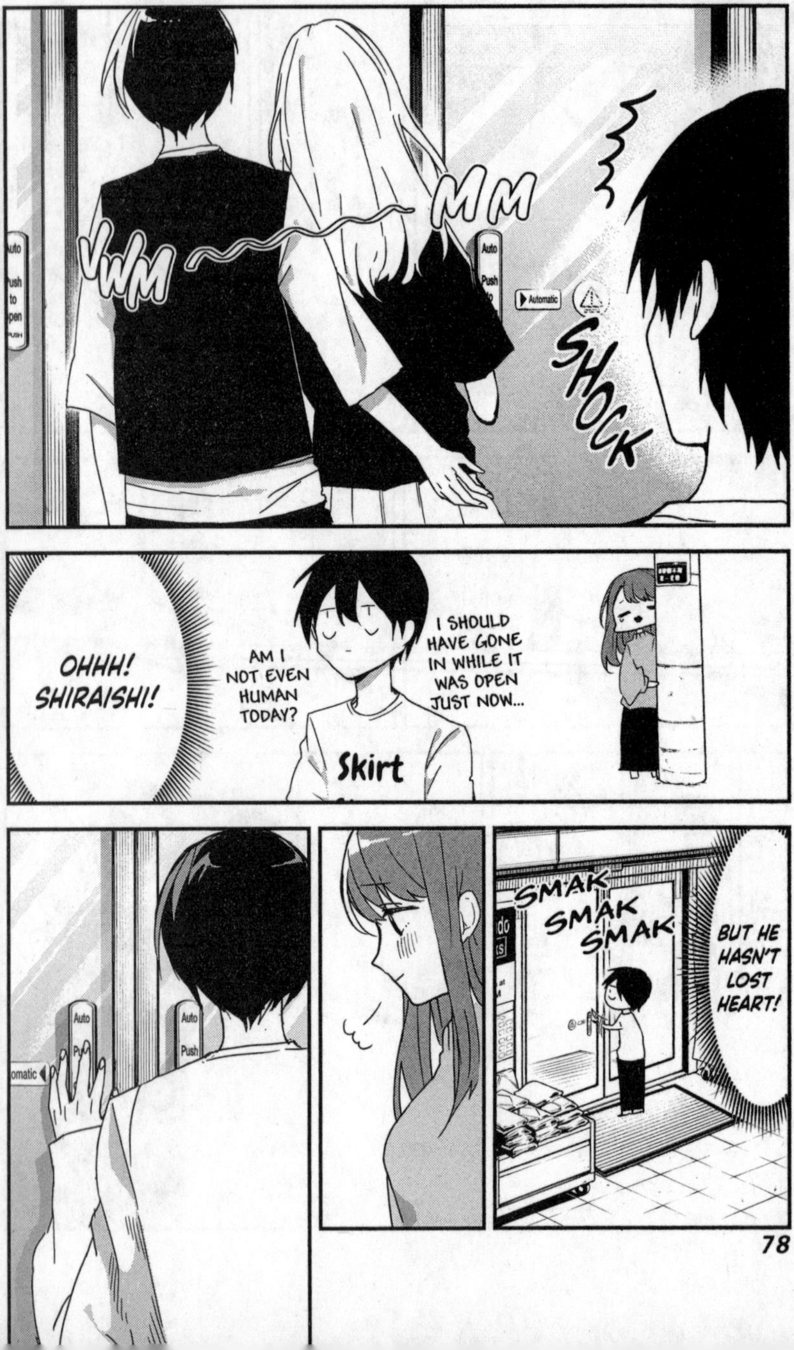
MM
VWM
Auto
Push to open
PUSH
Auto
Push
Automatic
SHOCK
I SHOULD HAVE GONE IN WHILE IT WAS OPEN JUST NOW...
AM I NOT EVEN HUMAN TODAY?
Skirt
OHHH! SHIRAISHI!
BUT HE HASN'T LOST HEART!
SMAK SMAK SMAK
Auto
Push
Auto
omatic

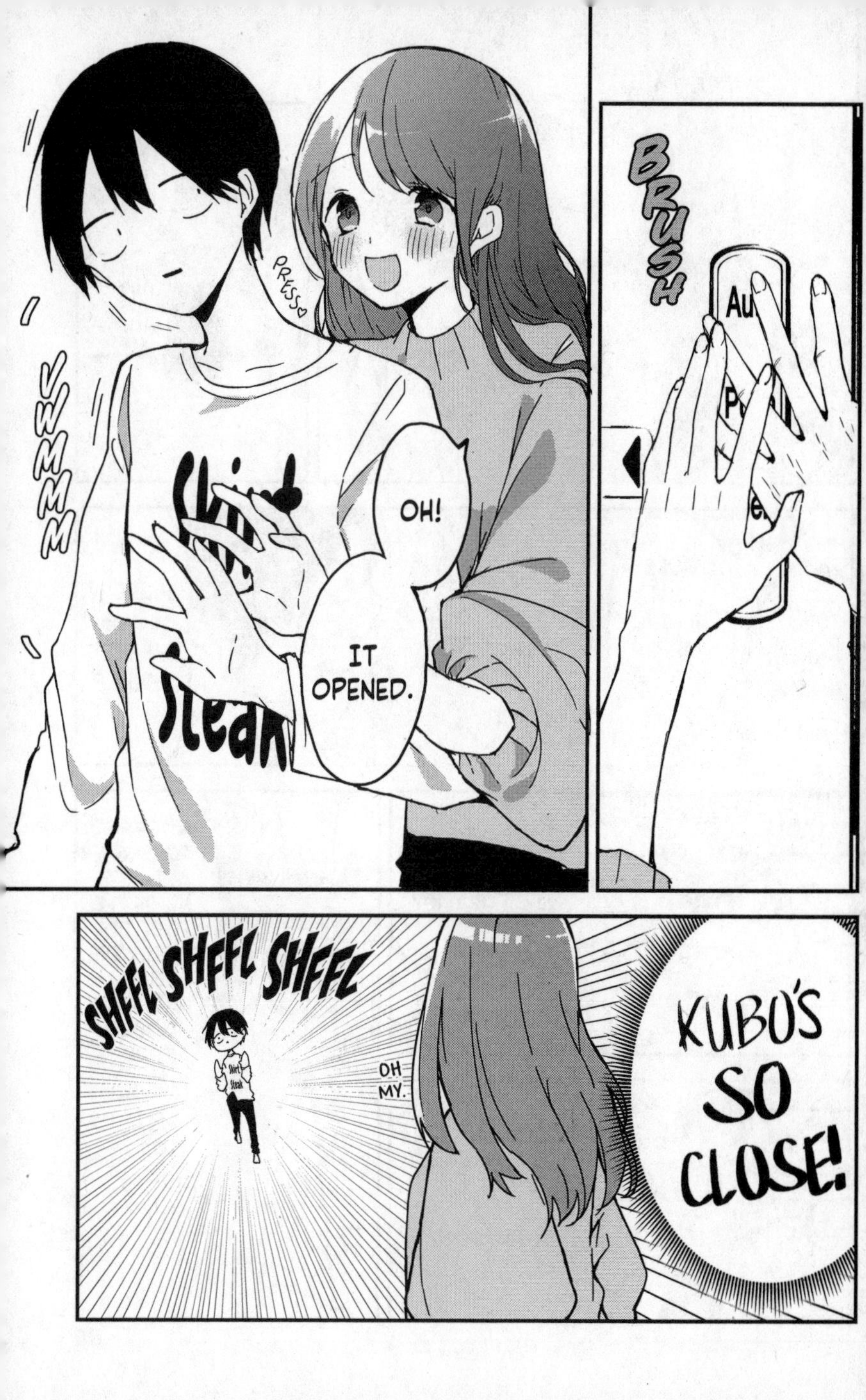
BRUSH
PRESS♡
OH!
IT OPENED.
VWMMM
KUBO'S SO CLOSE!
OH MY.
Skirt Steak
SHFFL SHFFL SHFFL

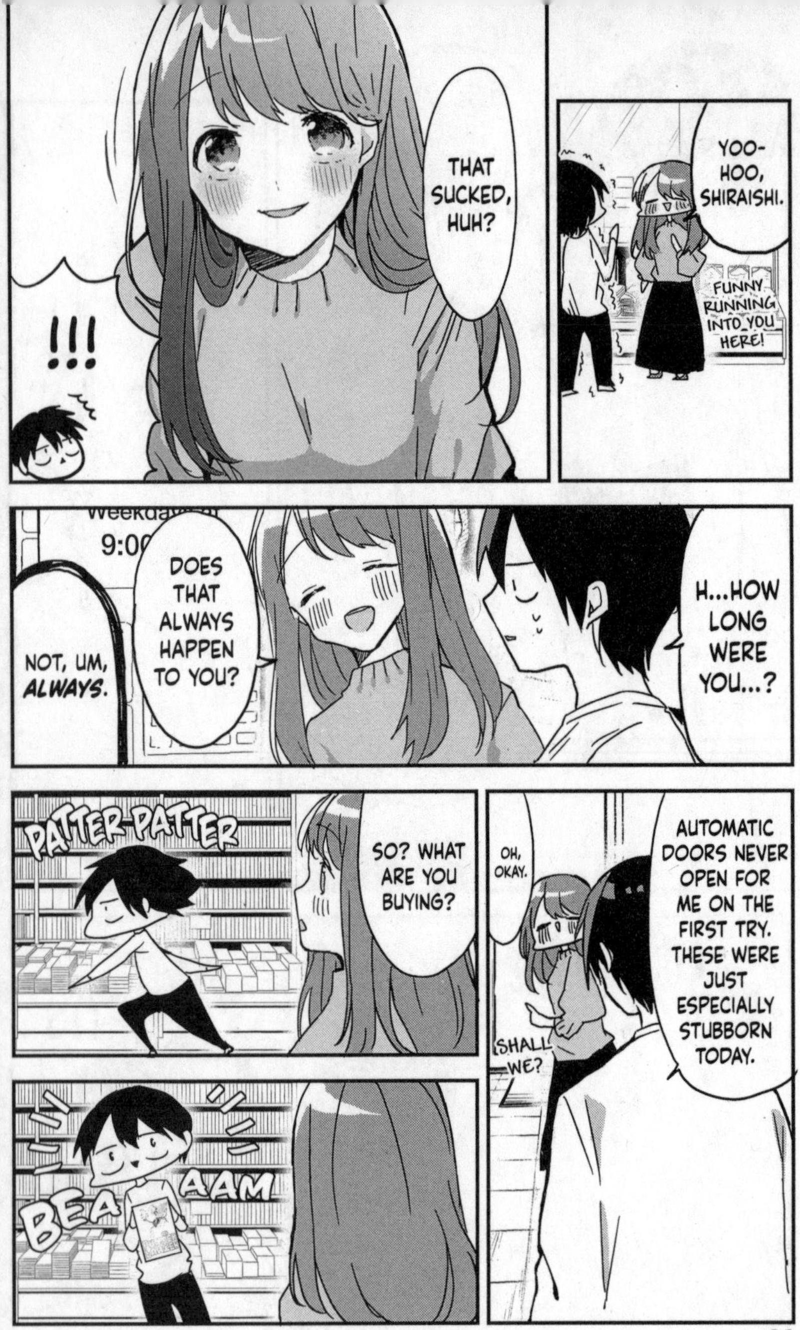
YOO-HOO, SHIRAISHI.
FUNNY RUNNING INTO YOU HERE!
THAT SUCKED, HUH?
!!!
H...HOW LONG WERE YOU...?
DOES THAT ALWAYS HAPPEN TO YOU?
NOT, UM, ALWAYS.
AUTOMATIC DOORS NEVER OPEN FOR ME ON THE FIRST TRY. THESE WERE JUST ESPECIALLY STUBBORN TODAY.
OH, OKAY.
SHALL WE?
SO? WHAT ARE YOU BUYING?
PATTER PATTER
BEAAAM

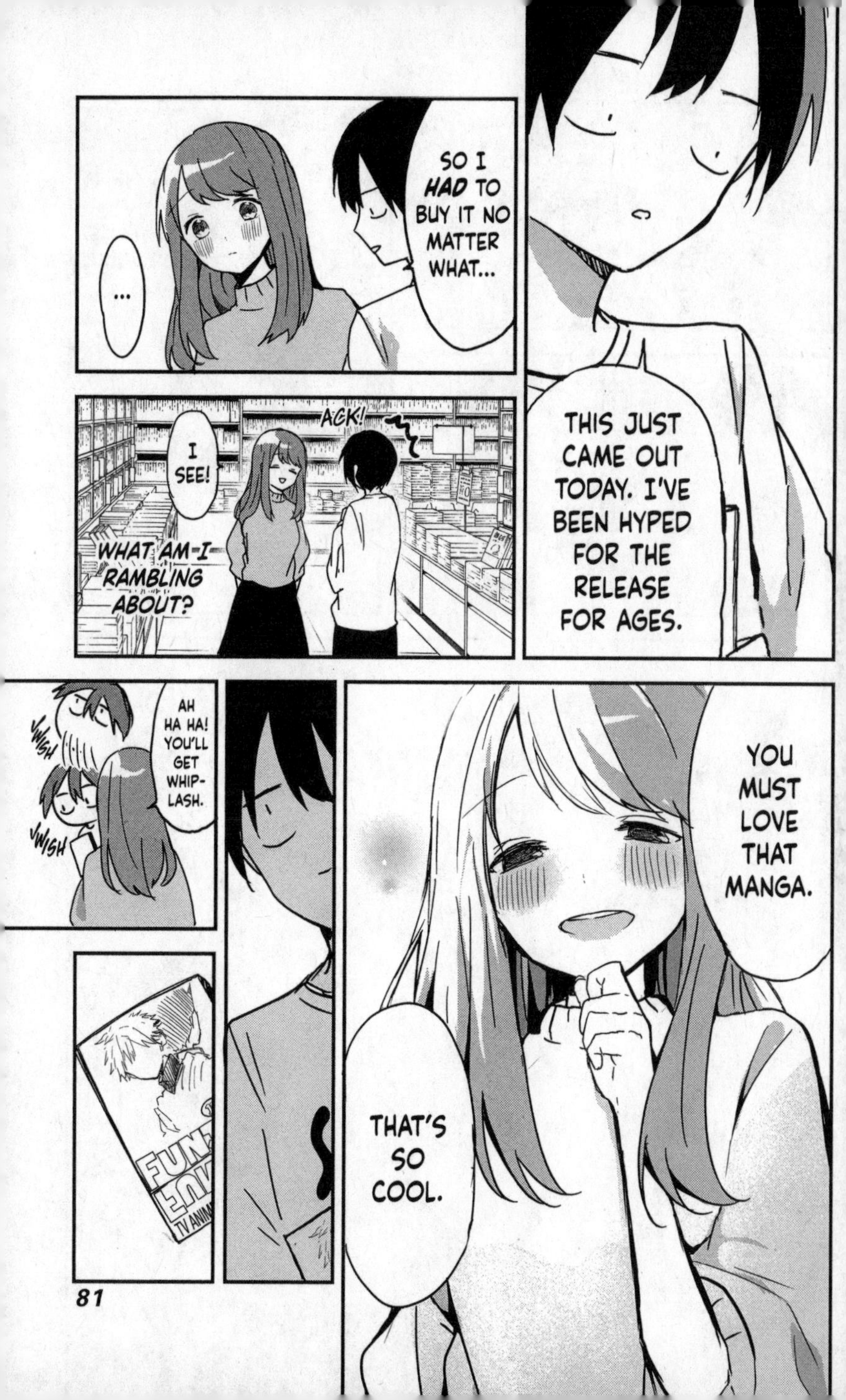
THIS JUST CAME OUT TODAY. I'VE BEEN HYPED FOR THE RELEASE FOR AGES.
SO I ***HAD*** TO BUY IT NO MATTER WHAT...
...
ACK!
I SEE!
WHAT AM I RAMBLING ABOUT?
YOU MUST LOVE THAT MANGA.
THAT'S SO COOL.
AH HA HA! YOU'LL GET WHIP-LASH.
JWISH
JWISH

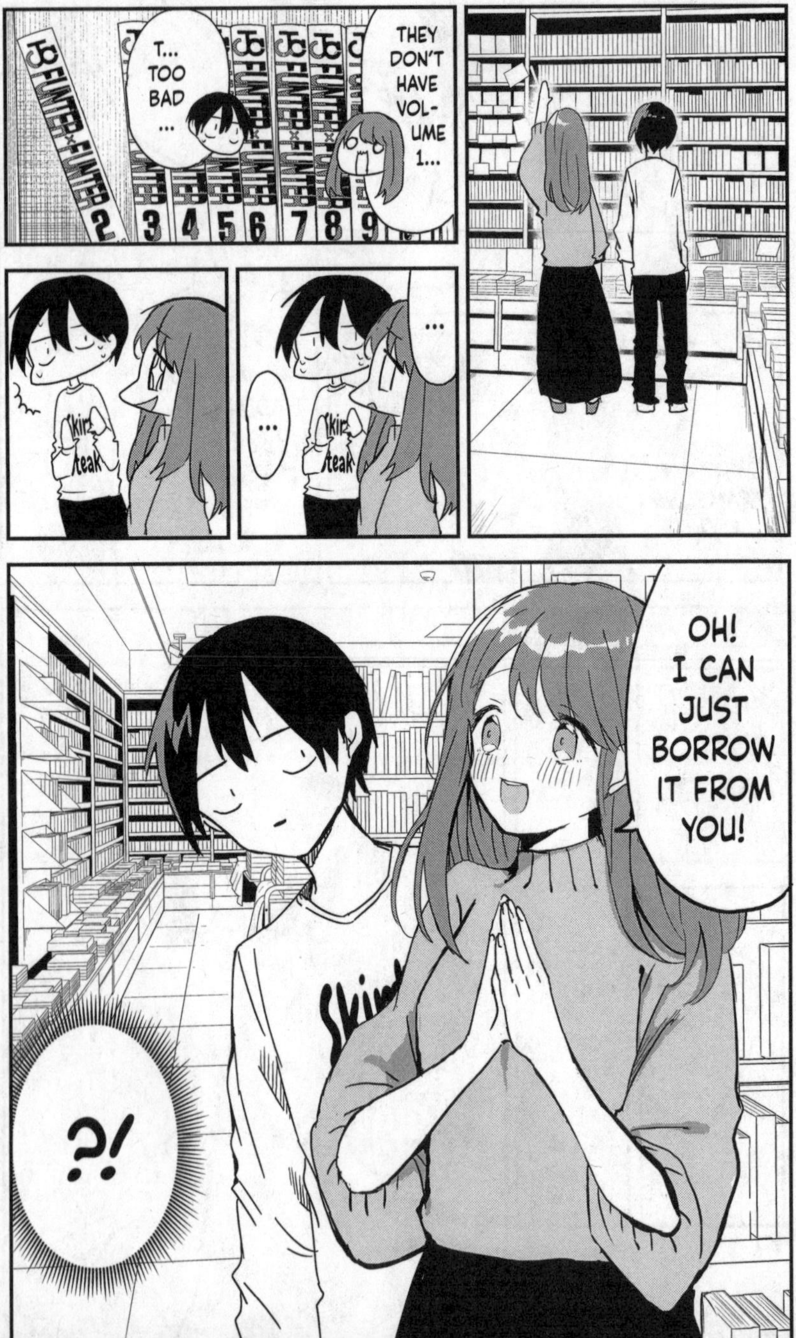
THEY DON'T HAVE VOL-UME 1...
T... TOO BAD ...
...
...
OH! I CAN JUST BORROW IT FROM YOU!
?!

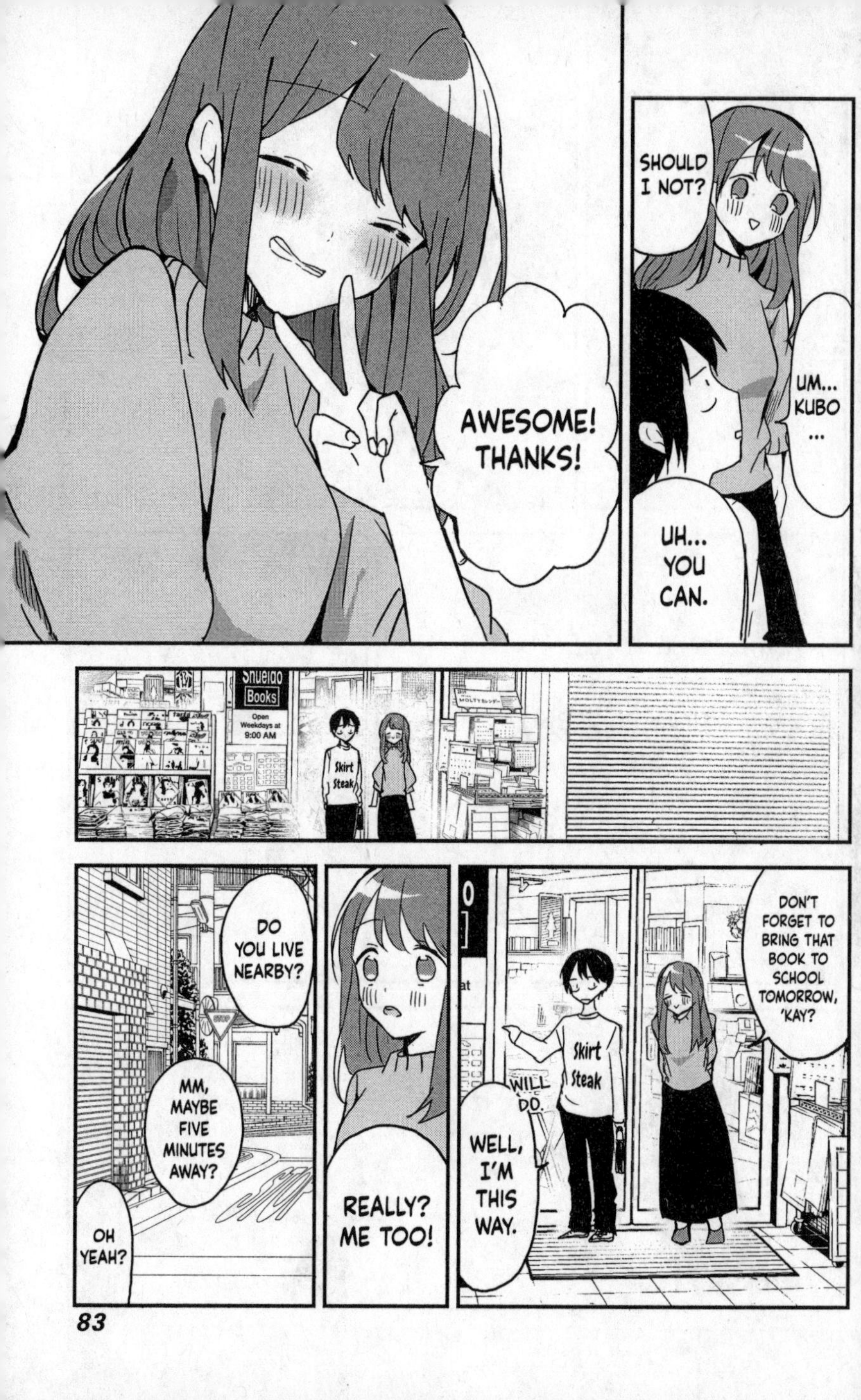
SHOULD I NOT?
UM... KUBO ...
UH... YOU CAN.
AWESOME! THANKS!
Shueido
Books
Open Weekdays at 9:00 AM
Skirt Steak
DON'T FORGET TO BRING THAT BOOK TO SCHOOL TOMORROW, 'KAY?
WILL DO.
WELL, I'M THIS WAY.
Skirt Steak
REALLY? ME TOO!
DO YOU LIVE NEARBY?
MM, MAYBE FIVE MINUTES AWAY?
OH YEAH?

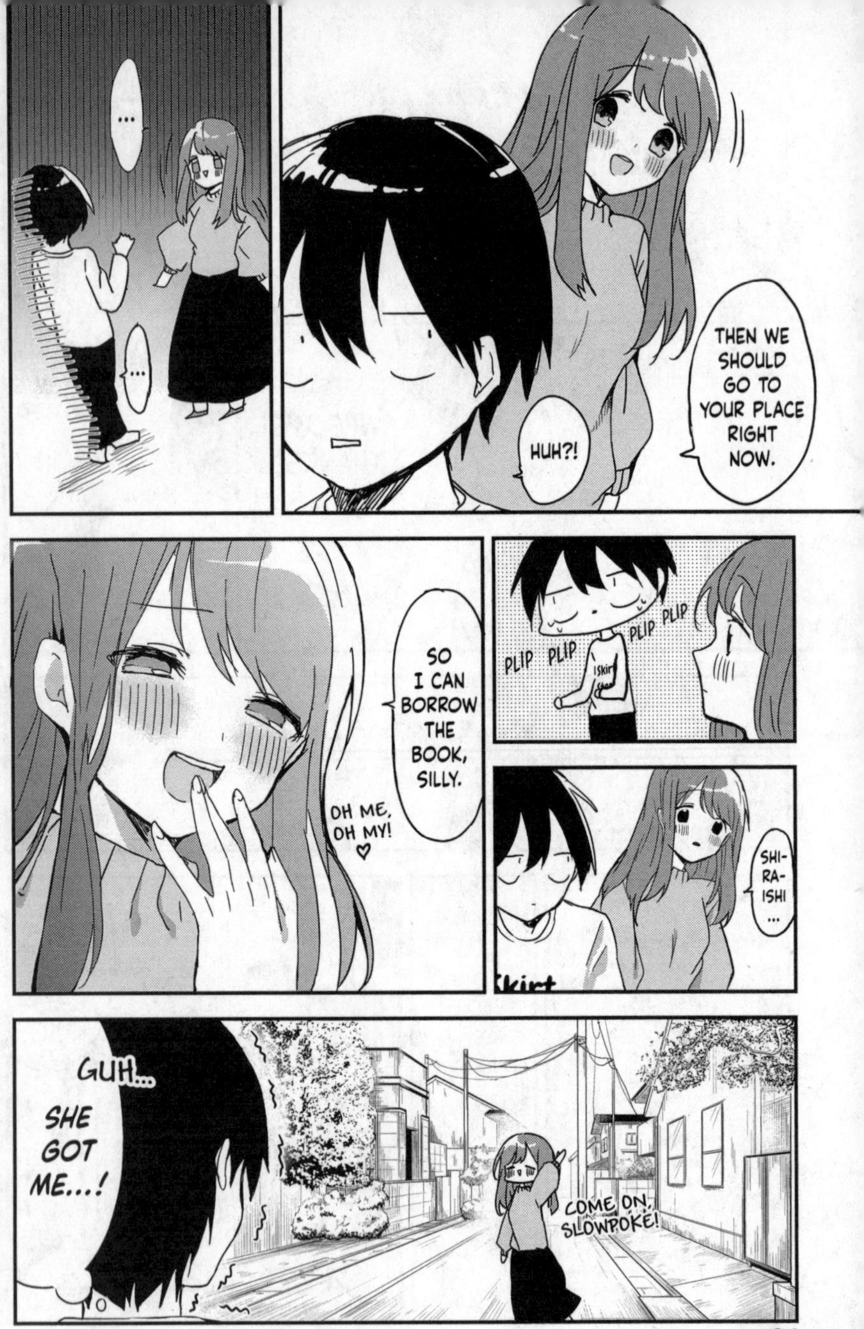
THEN WE SHOULD GO TO YOUR PLACE RIGHT NOW.
HUH?!
...
...
PLIP PLIP PLIP PLIP
SHI-RA-ISHI...
SO I CAN BORROW THE BOOK, SILLY.
OH ME, OH MY! ♡
COME ON, SLOWPOKE!
GUH...
SHE GOT ME...!

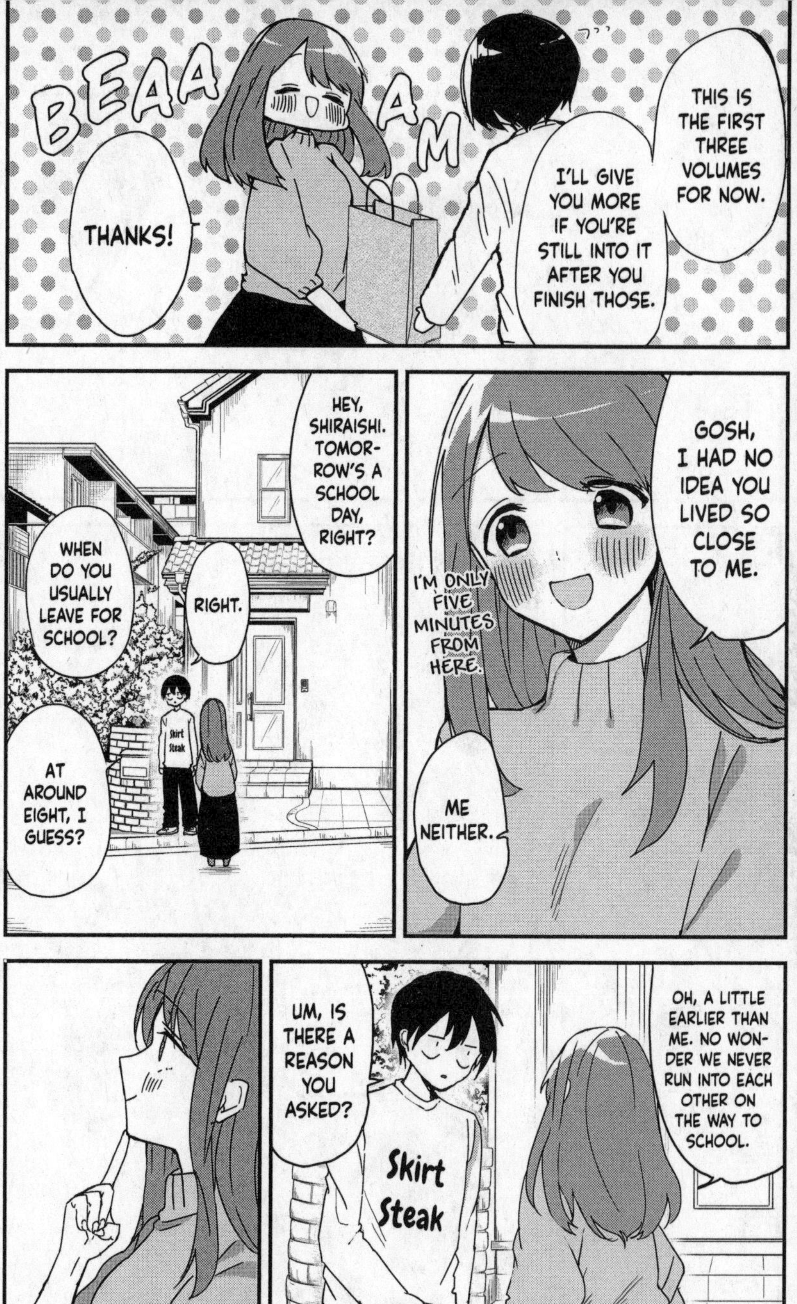
THIS IS THE FIRST THREE VOLUMES FOR NOW.
I'LL GIVE YOU MORE IF YOU'RE STILL INTO IT AFTER YOU FINISH THOSE.
BEAAAM
THANKS!
GOSH, I HAD NO IDEA YOU LIVED SO CLOSE TO ME.
I'M ONLY FIVE MINUTES FROM HERE.
ME NEITHER.
HEY, SHIRAISHI. TOMORROW'S A SCHOOL DAY, RIGHT?
RIGHT.
WHEN DO YOU USUALLY LEAVE FOR SCHOOL?
Skirt Steak
AT AROUND EIGHT, I GUESS?
OH, A LITTLE EARLIER THAN ME. NO WONDER WE NEVER RUN INTO EACH OTHER ON THE WAY TO SCHOOL.
UM, IS THERE A REASON YOU ASKED?
Skirt Steak

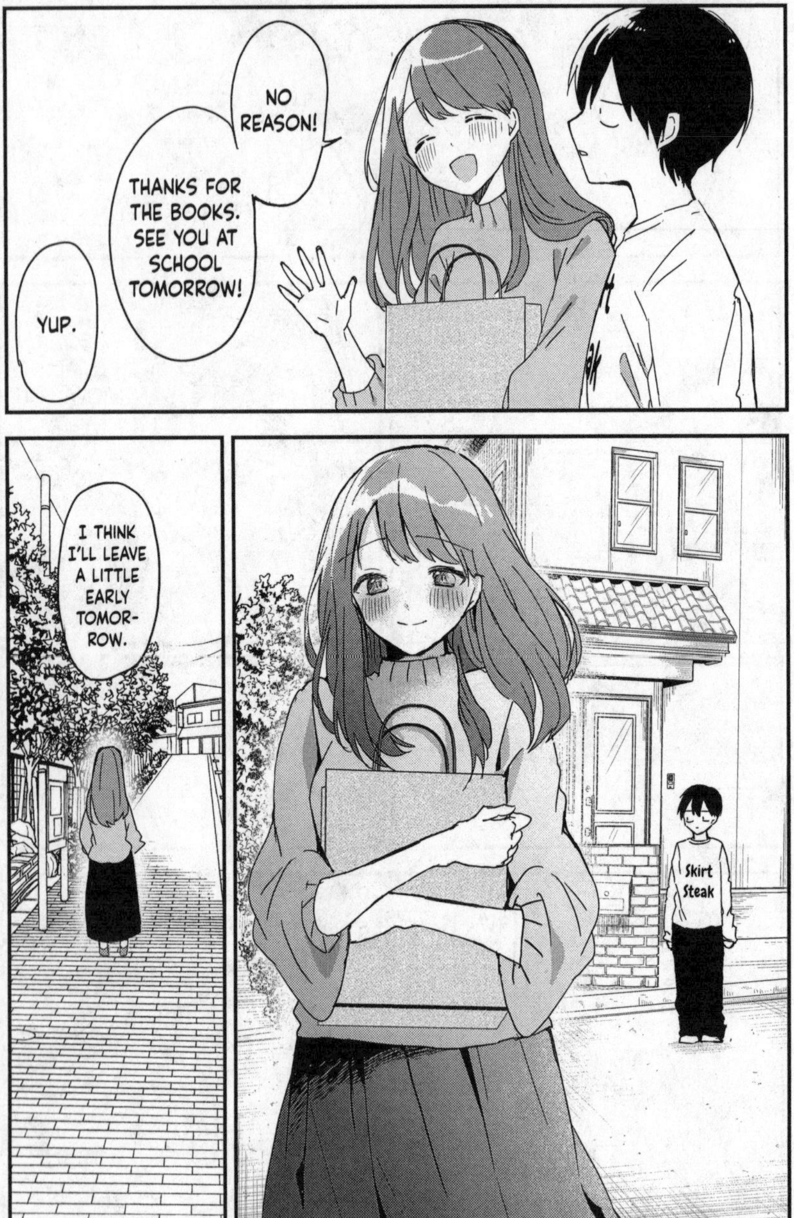
NO REASON!
THANKS FOR THE BOOKS. SEE YOU AT SCHOOL TOMORROW!
YUP.
Skirt Steak
I THINK I'LL LEAVE A LITTLE EARLY TOMOR-ROW.

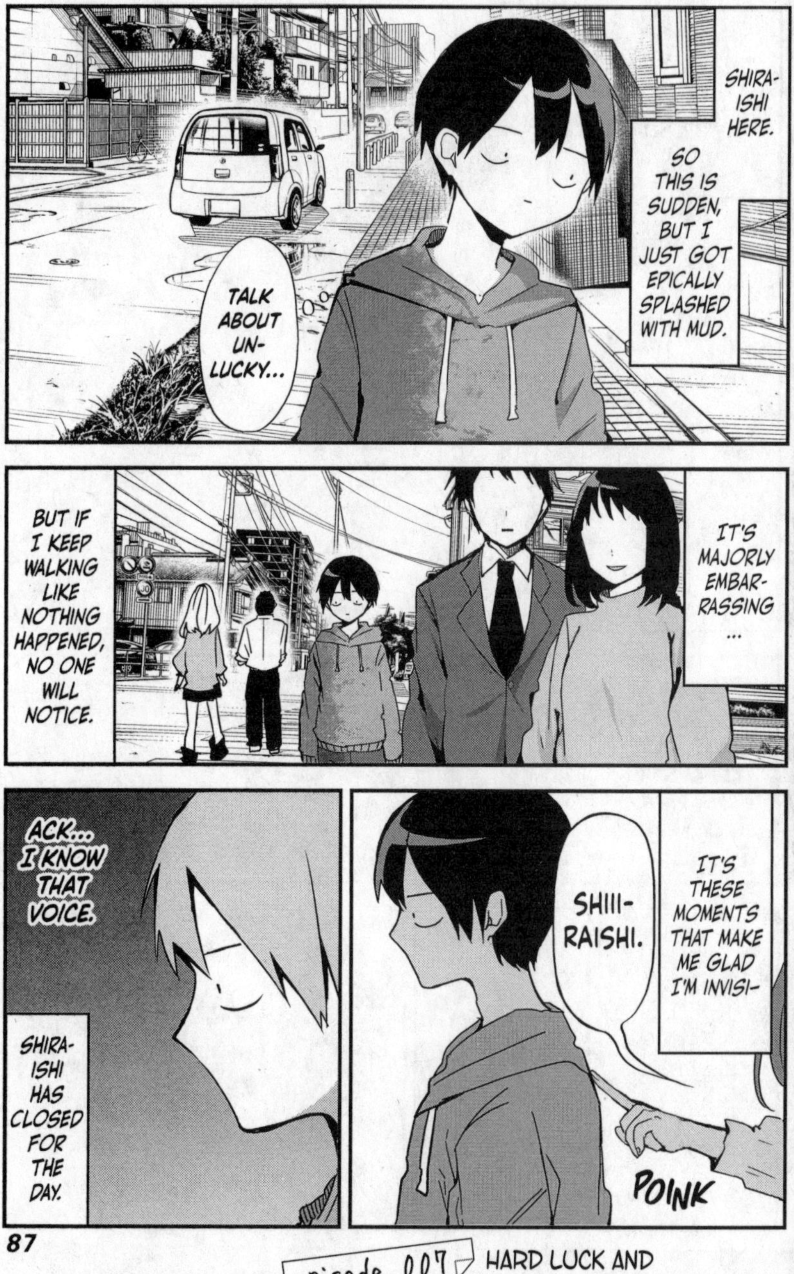
SHIRA-ISHI HERE.
SO THIS IS SUDDEN, BUT I JUST GOT EPICALLY SPLASHED WITH MUD.
TALK ABOUT UN-LUCKY...
IT'S MAJORLY EMBAR-RASSING ...
BUT IF I KEEP WALKING LIKE NOTHING HAPPENED, NO ONE WILL NOTICE.
IT'S THESE MOMENTS THAT MAKE ME GLAD I'M INVISI-
SHIII-RAISHI.
POINK
ACK... I KNOW THAT VOICE.
SHIRA-ISHI HAS CLOSED FOR THE DAY.

episode 007 HARD LUCK AND A HOME VISIT

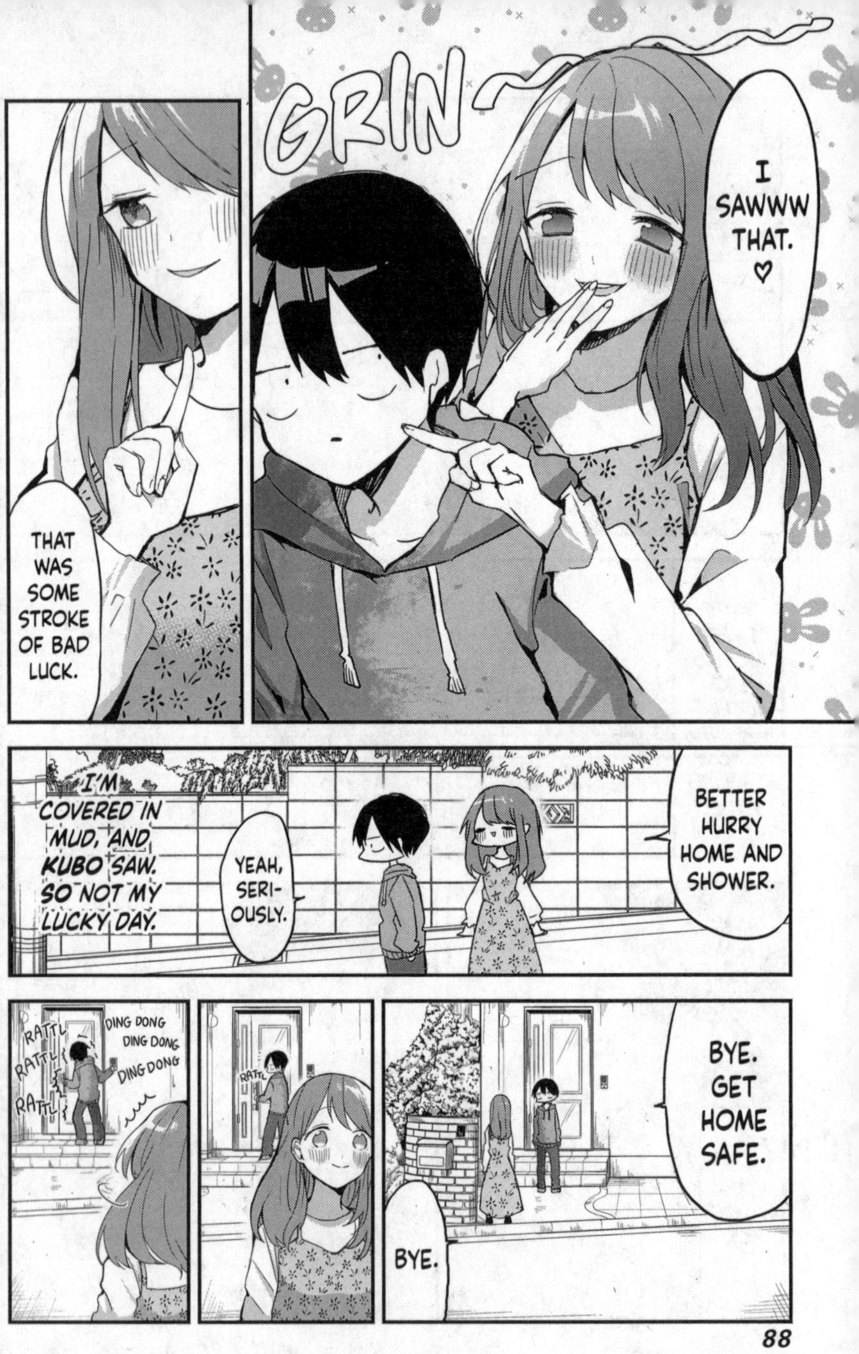
GRIN~
I SAWWW THAT. ♡
THAT WAS SOME STROKE OF BAD LUCK.
BETTER HURRY HOME AND SHOWER.
YEAH, SERI-OUSLY.
I'M COVERED IN MUD, AND KUBO SAW. SO NOT MY LUCKY DAY.
BYE. GET HOME SAFE.
BYE.
RATTL
RATTL
RATTL
RATTL
DING DONG
DING DONG
DING DONG

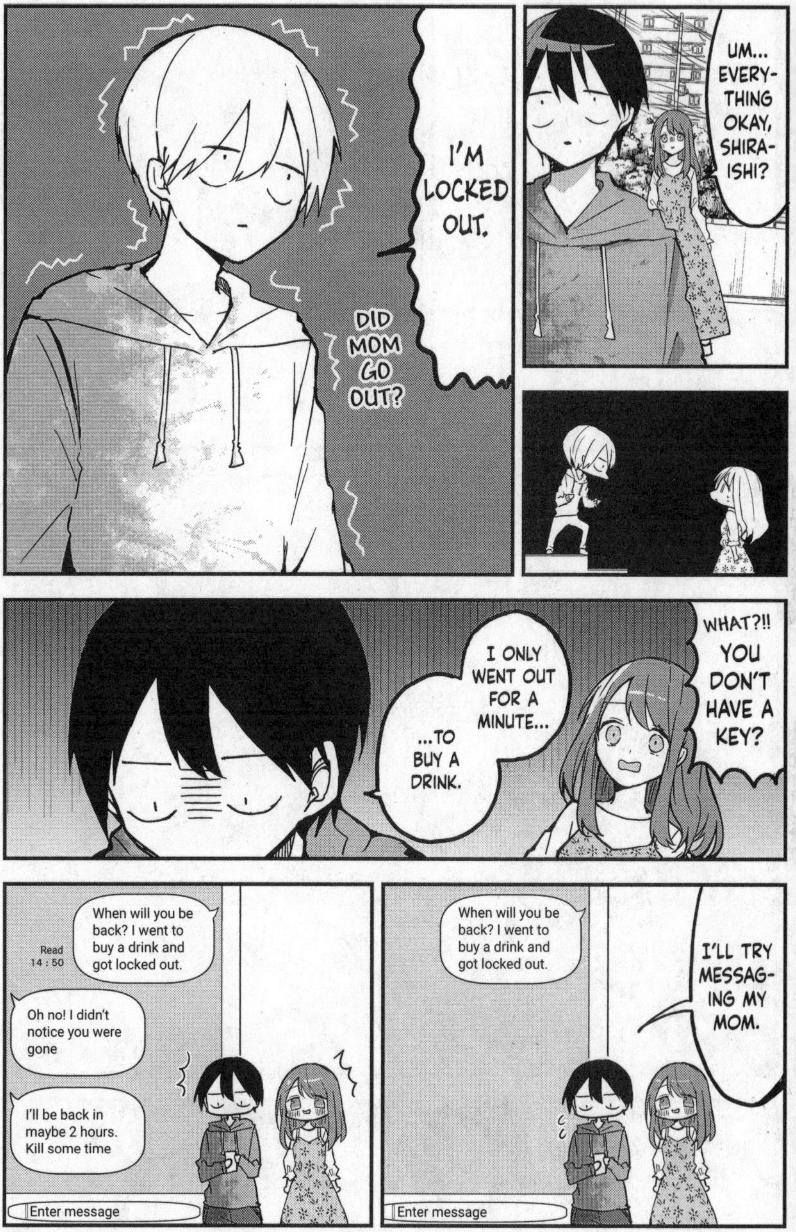
UM... EVERY-THING OKAY, SHIRA-ISHI?
I'M LOCKED OUT.
DID MOM GO OUT?
WHAT?!! YOU DON'T HAVE A KEY?
I ONLY WENT OUT FOR A MINUTE...
...TO BUY A DRINK.
I'LL TRY MESSAG-ING MY MOM.
When will you be back? I went to buy a drink and got locked out.
Enter message
Read 14 : 50
When will you be back? I went to buy a drink and got locked out.
Oh no! I didn't notice you were gone
I'll be back in maybe 2 hours. Kill some time
Enter message

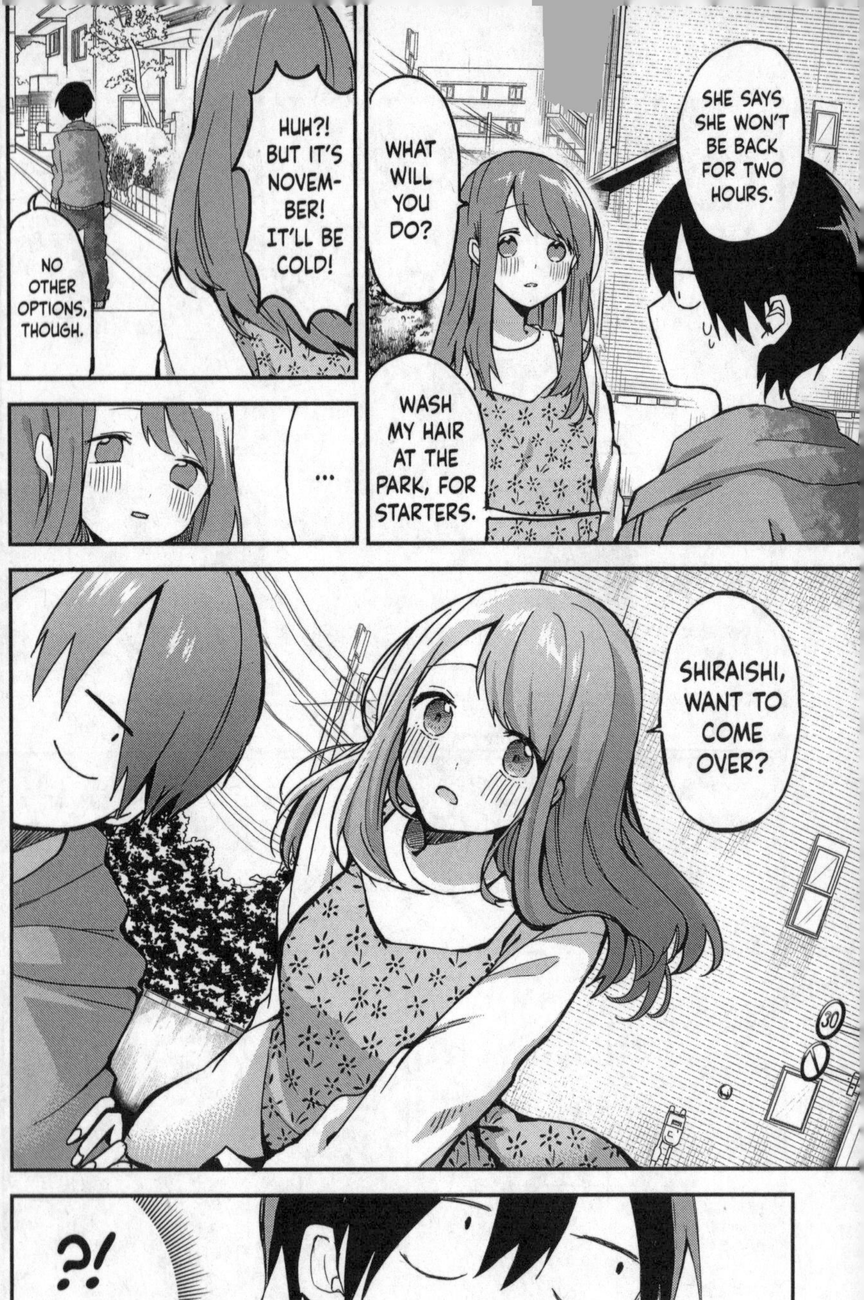
SHE SAYS SHE WON'T BE BACK FOR TWO HOURS.
WHAT WILL YOU DO?
WASH MY HAIR AT THE PARK, FOR STARTERS.
HUH?! BUT IT'S NOVEM-BER! IT'LL BE COLD!
NO OTHER OPTIONS, THOUGH.
...
SHIRAISHI, WANT TO COME OVER?
?!

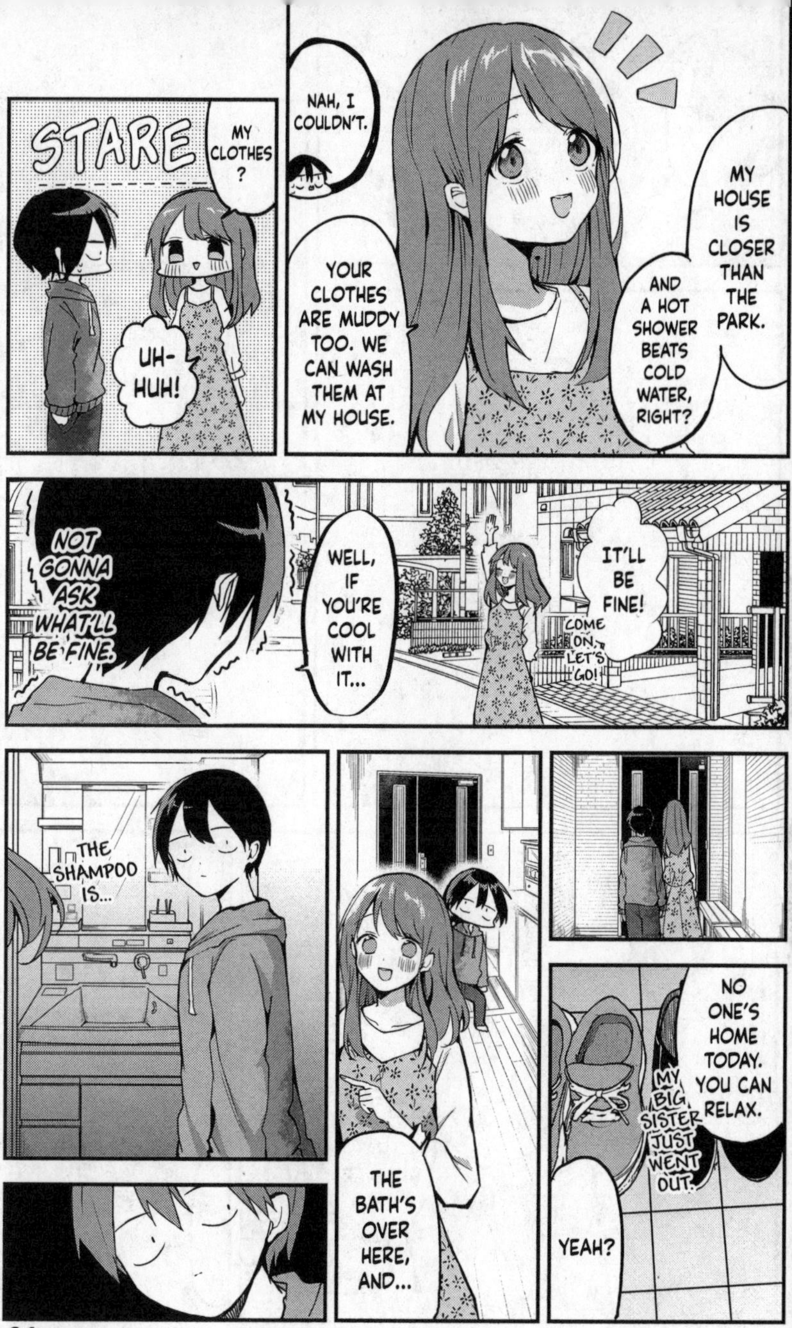
MY HOUSE IS CLOSER THAN THE PARK.
AND A HOT SHOWER BEATS COLD WATER, RIGHT?
NAH, I COULDN'T.
YOUR CLOTHES ARE MUDDY TOO. WE CAN WASH THEM AT MY HOUSE.
MY CLOTHES?
STARE
UH-HUH!
IT'LL BE FINE!
COME ON, LET'S GO!
WELL, IF YOU'RE COOL WITH IT...
NOT GONNA ASK WHAT'LL BE FINE.
NO ONE'S HOME TODAY. YOU CAN RELAX.
MY BIG SISTER JUST WENT OUT.
YEAH?
THE BATH'S OVER HERE, AND...
THE SHAMPOO IS...

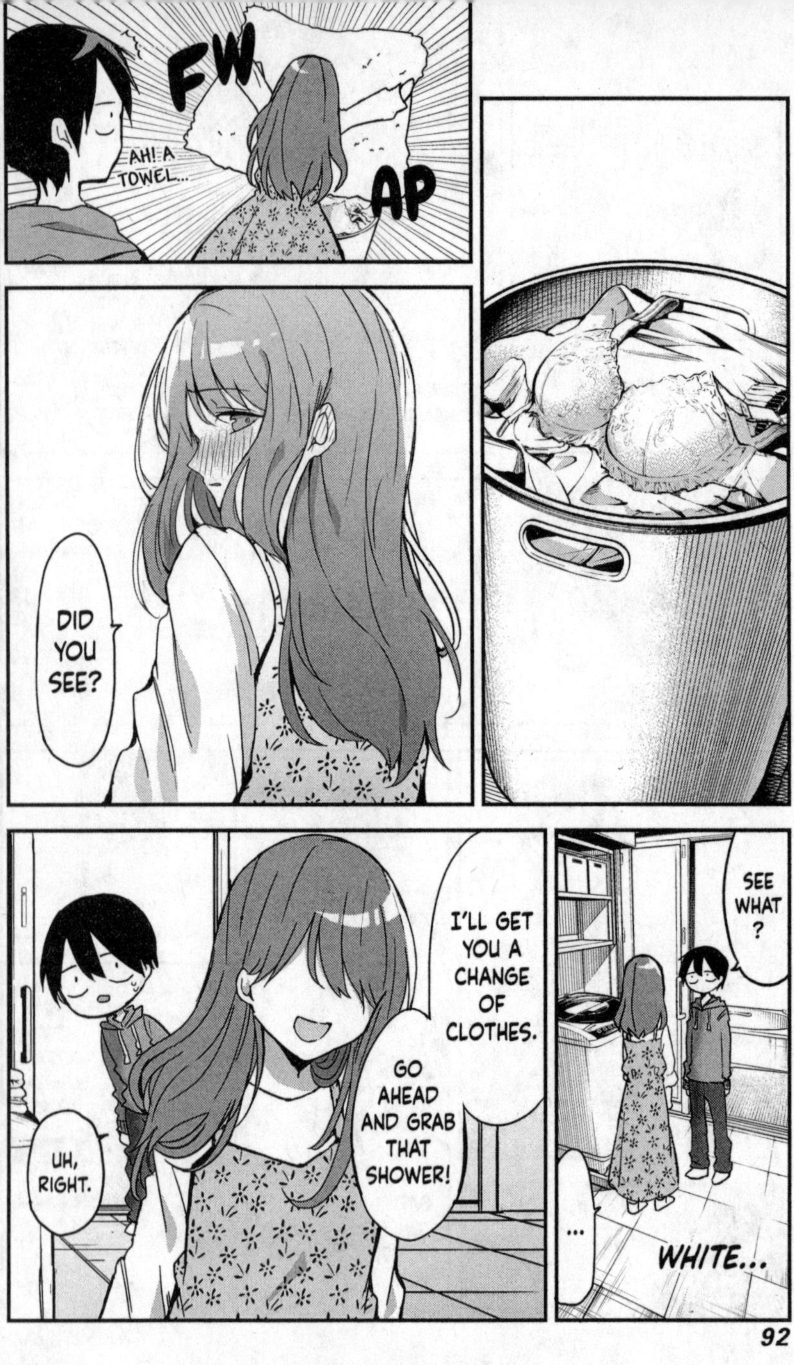
FW
AP
AH! A TOWEL...
DID YOU SEE?
SEE WHAT?
...
WHITE...
I'LL GET YOU A CHANGE OF CLOTHES.
GO AHEAD AND GRAB THAT SHOWER!
UH, RIGHT.

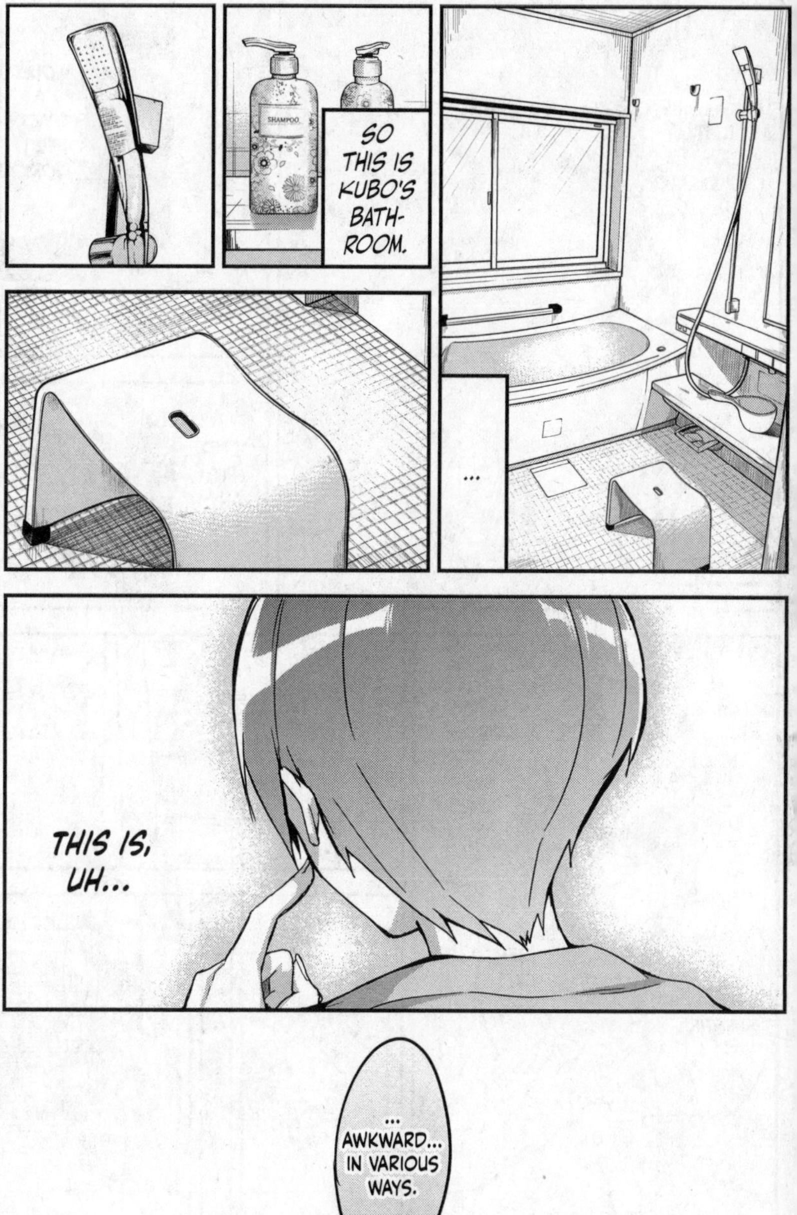
...
SO THIS IS KUBO'S BATH-ROOM.
SHAMPOO
THIS IS, UH...
...AWKWARD... IN VARIOUS WAYS.

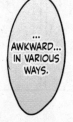

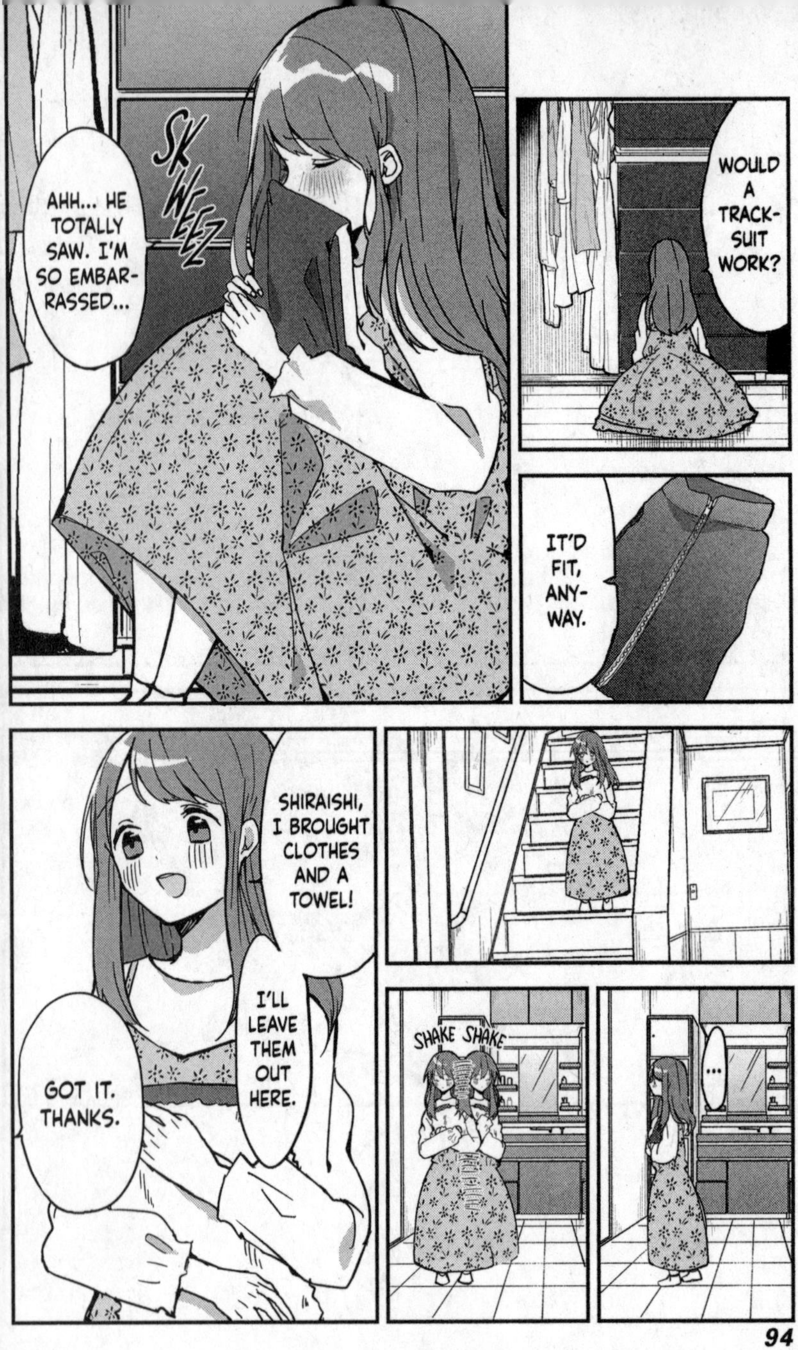
WOULD A TRACK-SUIT WORK?
IT'D FIT, ANY-WAY.
SKWEEZ
AHH... HE TOTALLY SAW. I'M SO EMBAR-RASSED...
...
SHAKE SHAKE
SHIRAISHI, I BROUGHT CLOTHES AND A TOWEL!
I'LL LEAVE THEM OUT HERE.
GOT IT. THANKS.

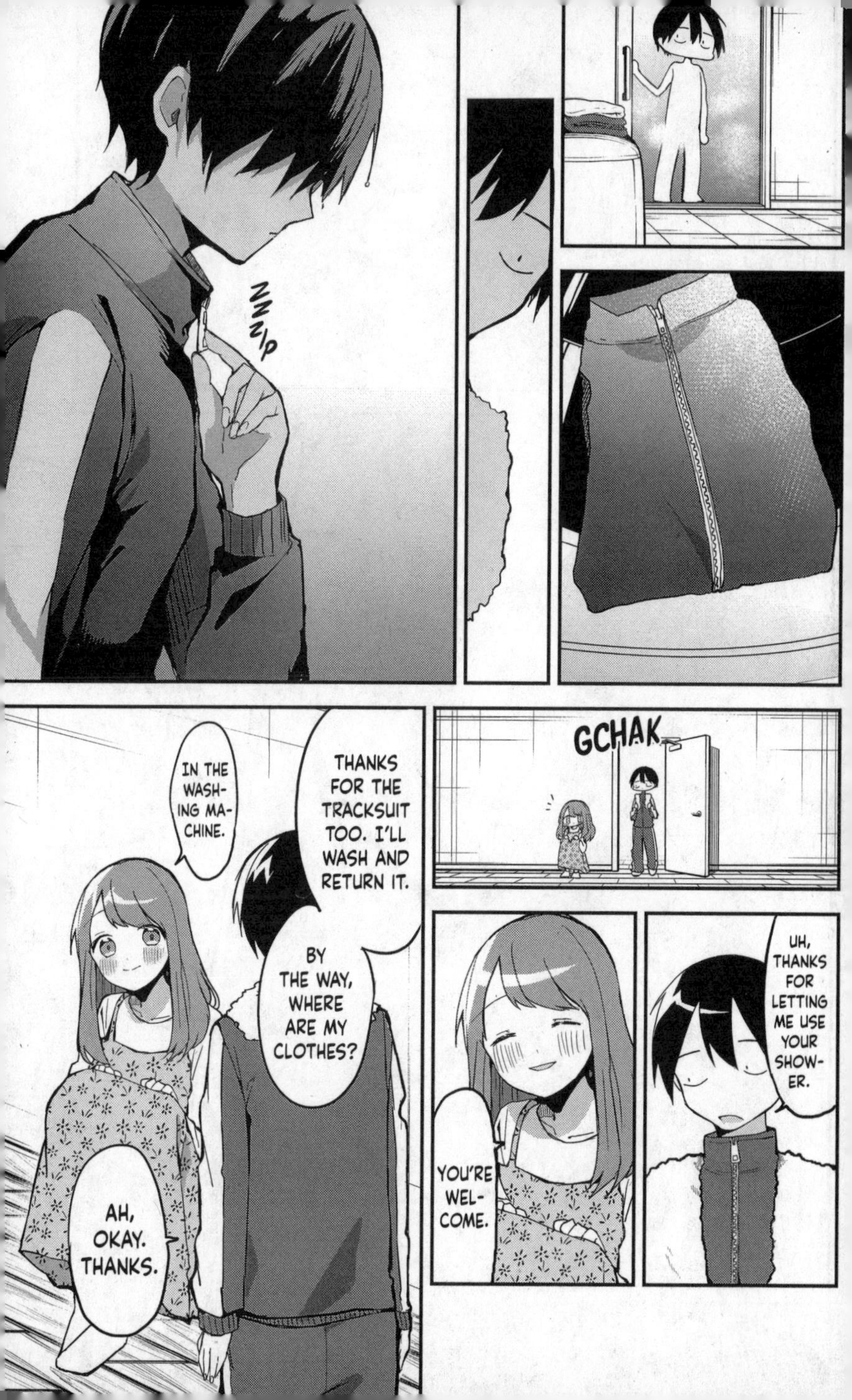
ZZZIP
GCHAK
UH, THANKS FOR LETTING ME USE YOUR SHOWER.
YOU'RE WELCOME.
THANKS FOR THE TRACKSUIT TOO. I'LL WASH AND RETURN IT.
BY THE WAY, WHERE ARE MY CLOTHES?
IN THE WASHING MACHINE.
AH, OKAY. THANKS.

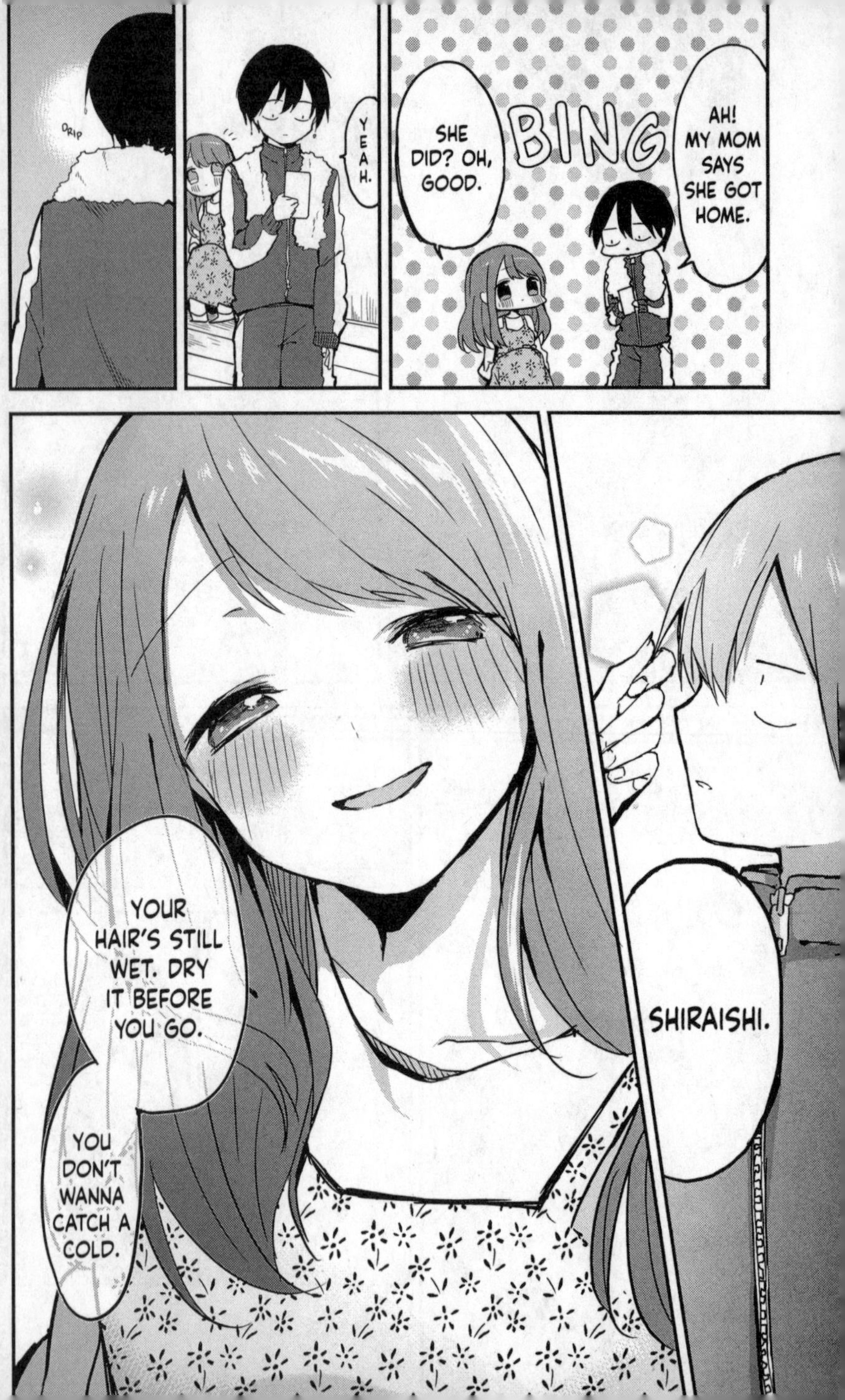
AH! MY MOM SAYS SHE GOT HOME.
BING
SHE DID? OH, GOOD.
YEAH.
DRIP
SHIRAISHI.
YOUR HAIR'S STILL WET. DRY IT BEFORE YOU GO.
YOU DON'T WANNA CATCH A COLD.

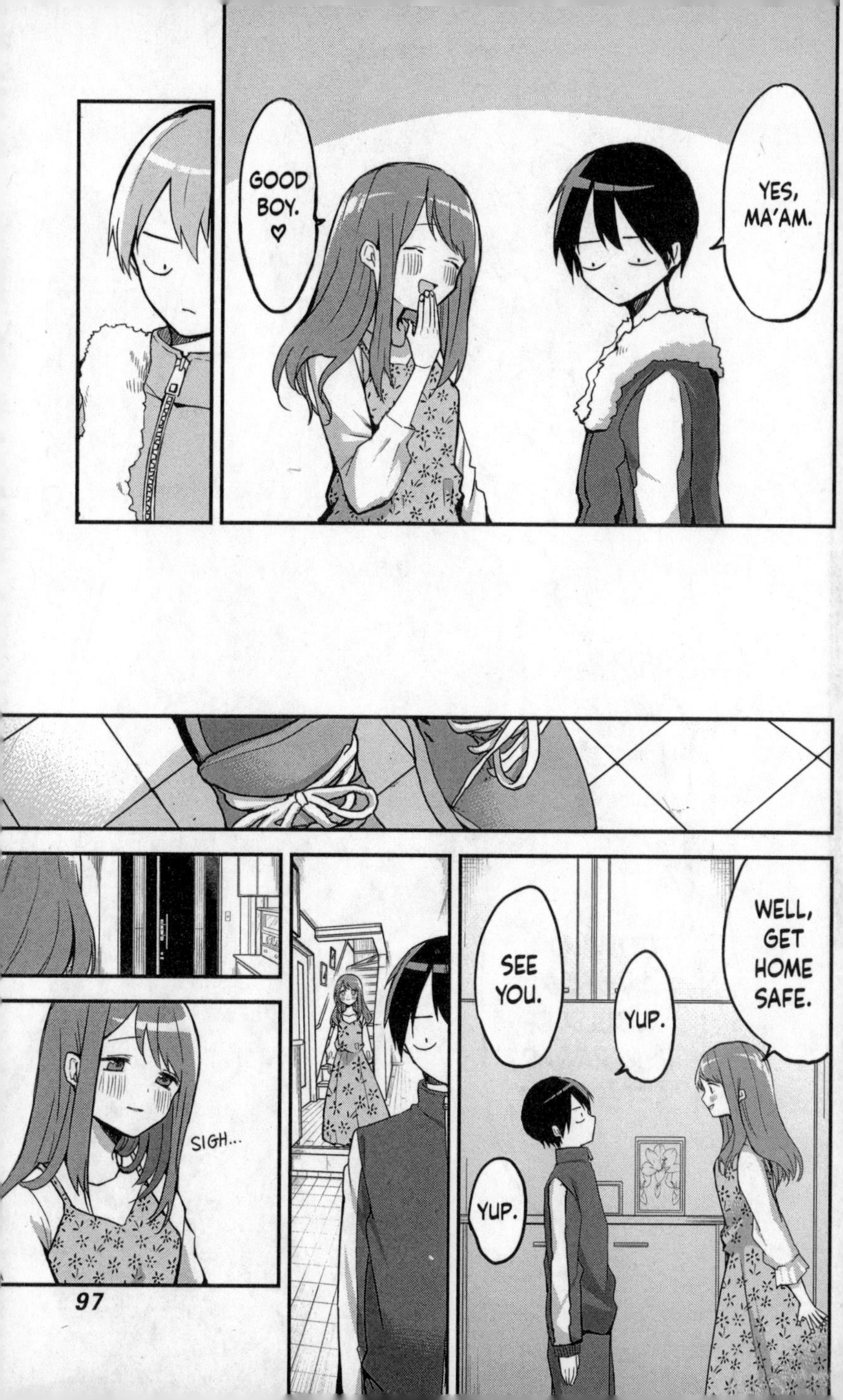
YES, MA'AM.
GOOD BOY. ♥
WELL, GET HOME SAFE.
YUP.
SEE YOU.
YUP.
SIGH...

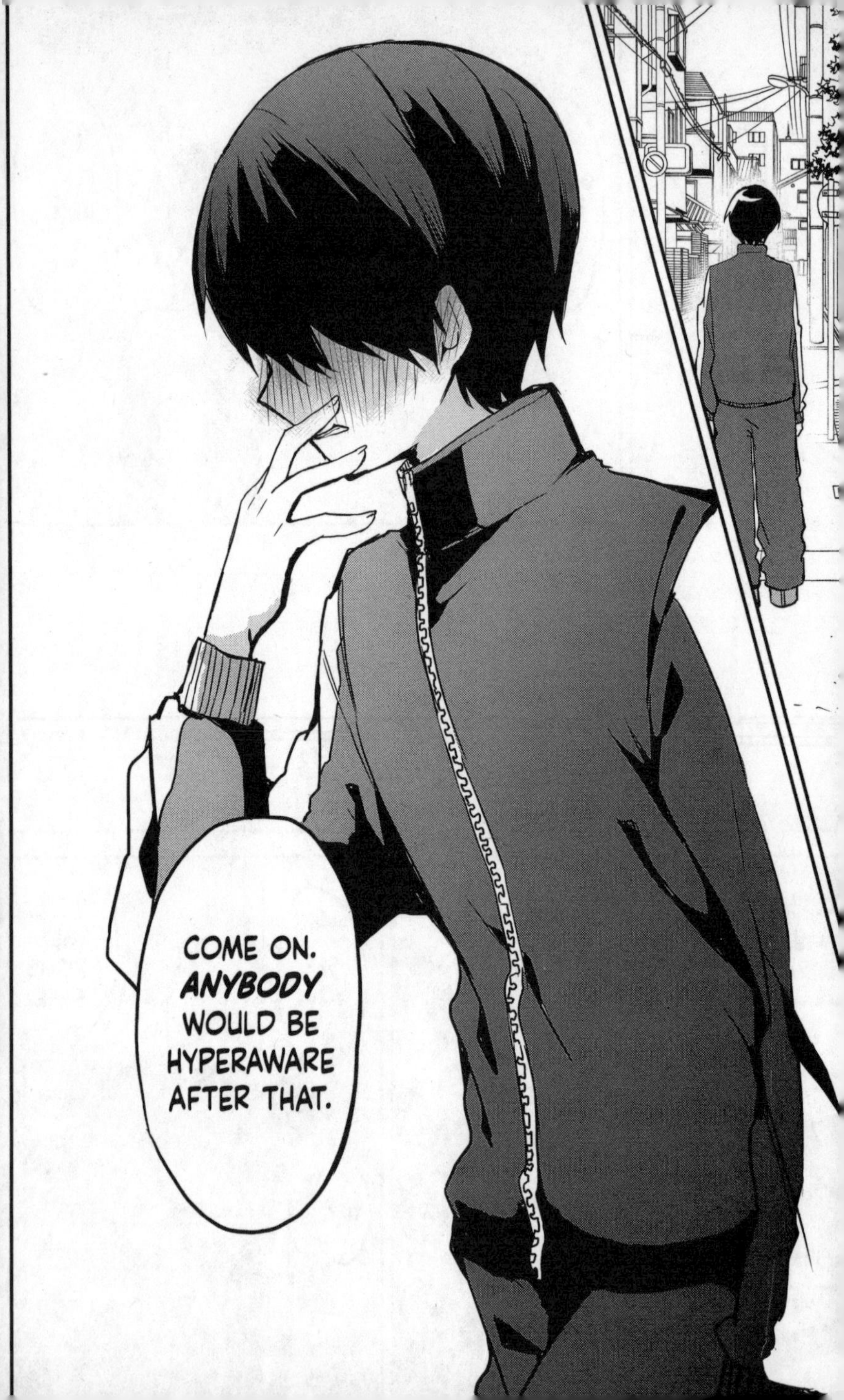
COME ON. ***ANYBODY*** WOULD BE HYPERAWARE AFTER THAT.

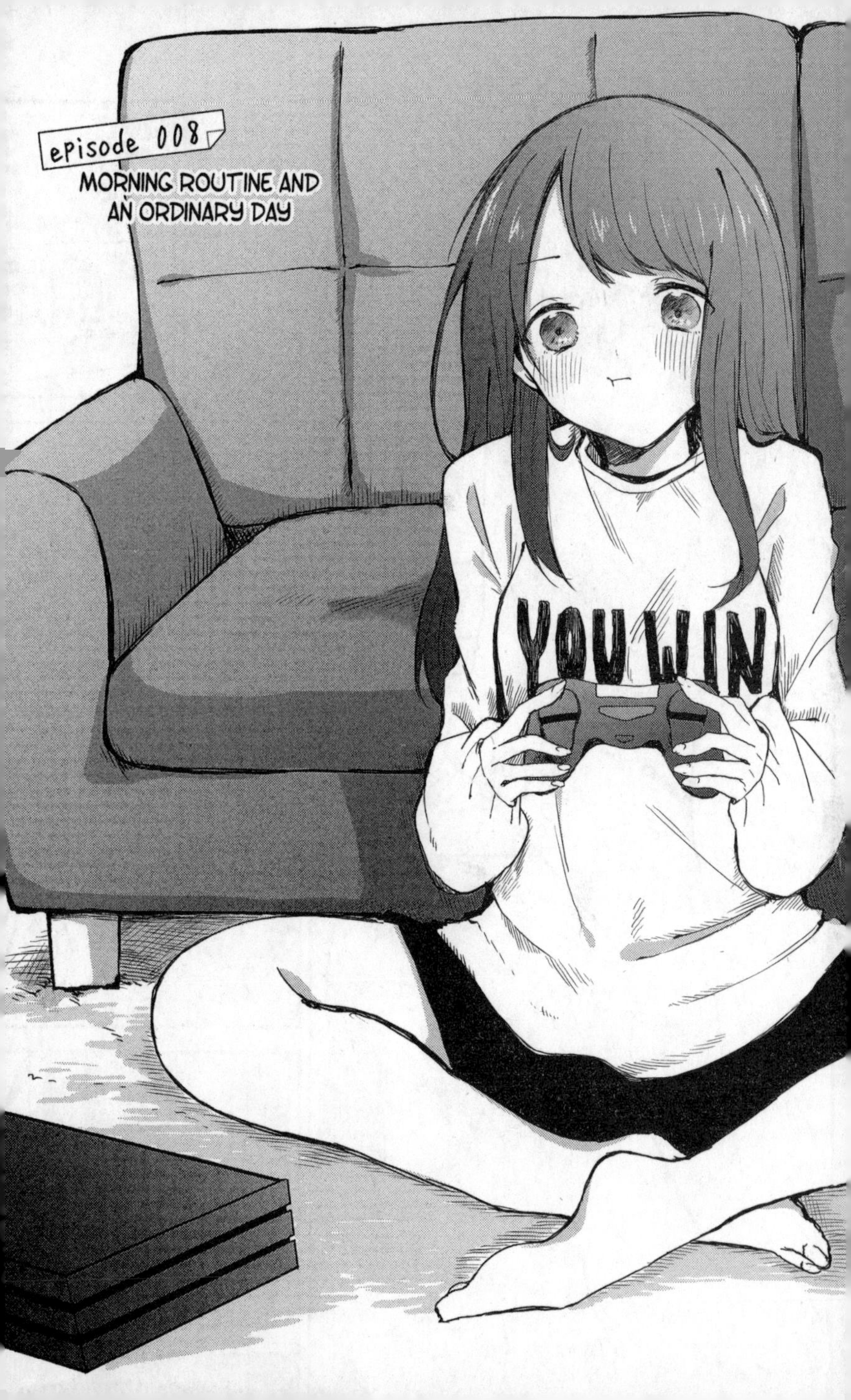
episode 008
MORNING ROUTINE AND AN ORDINARY DAY
YOU WIN

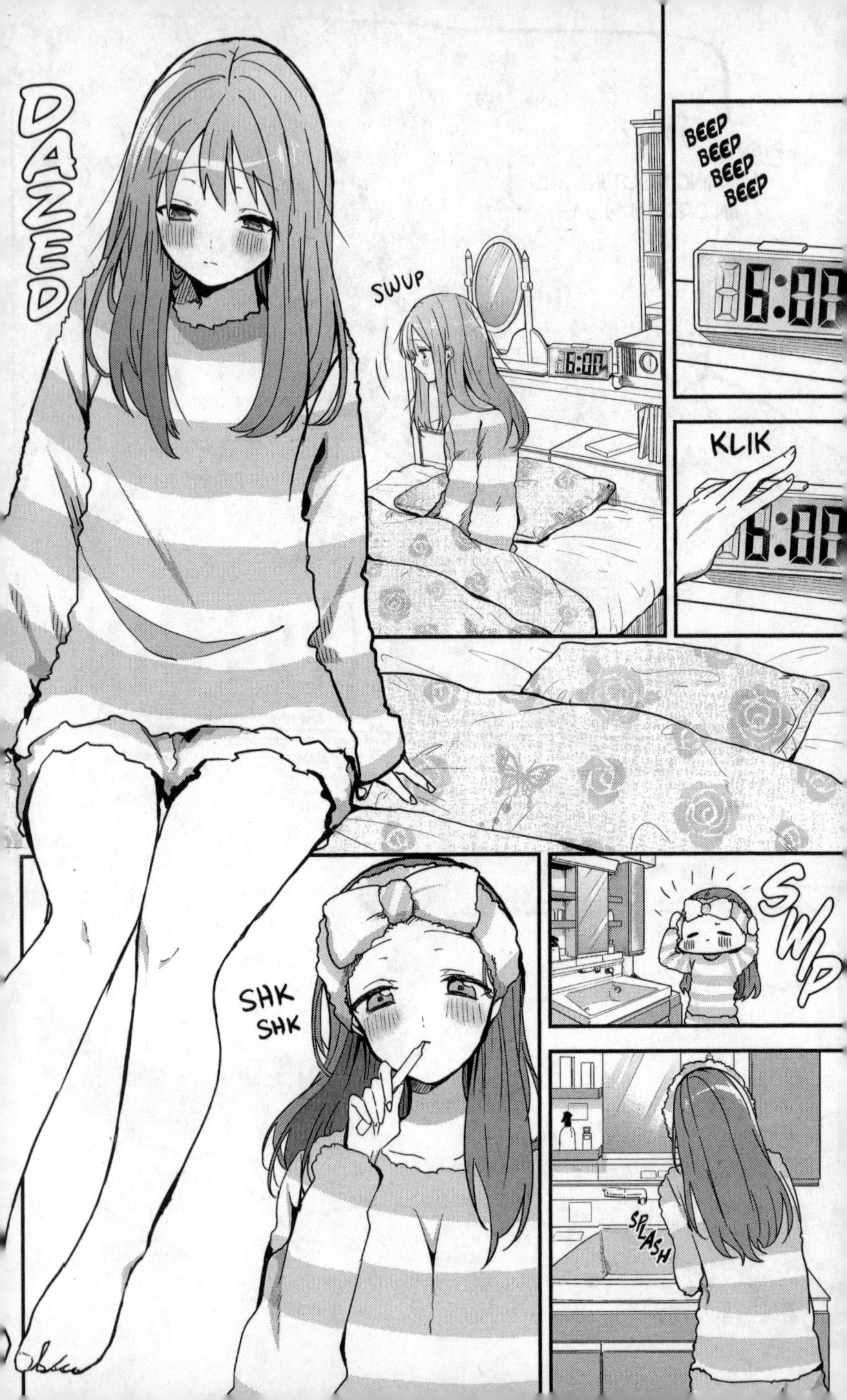
BEEP
BEEP
BEEP
BEEP
KLIK
SWUP
DAZED
SWIP
SPLASH
SHK
SHK

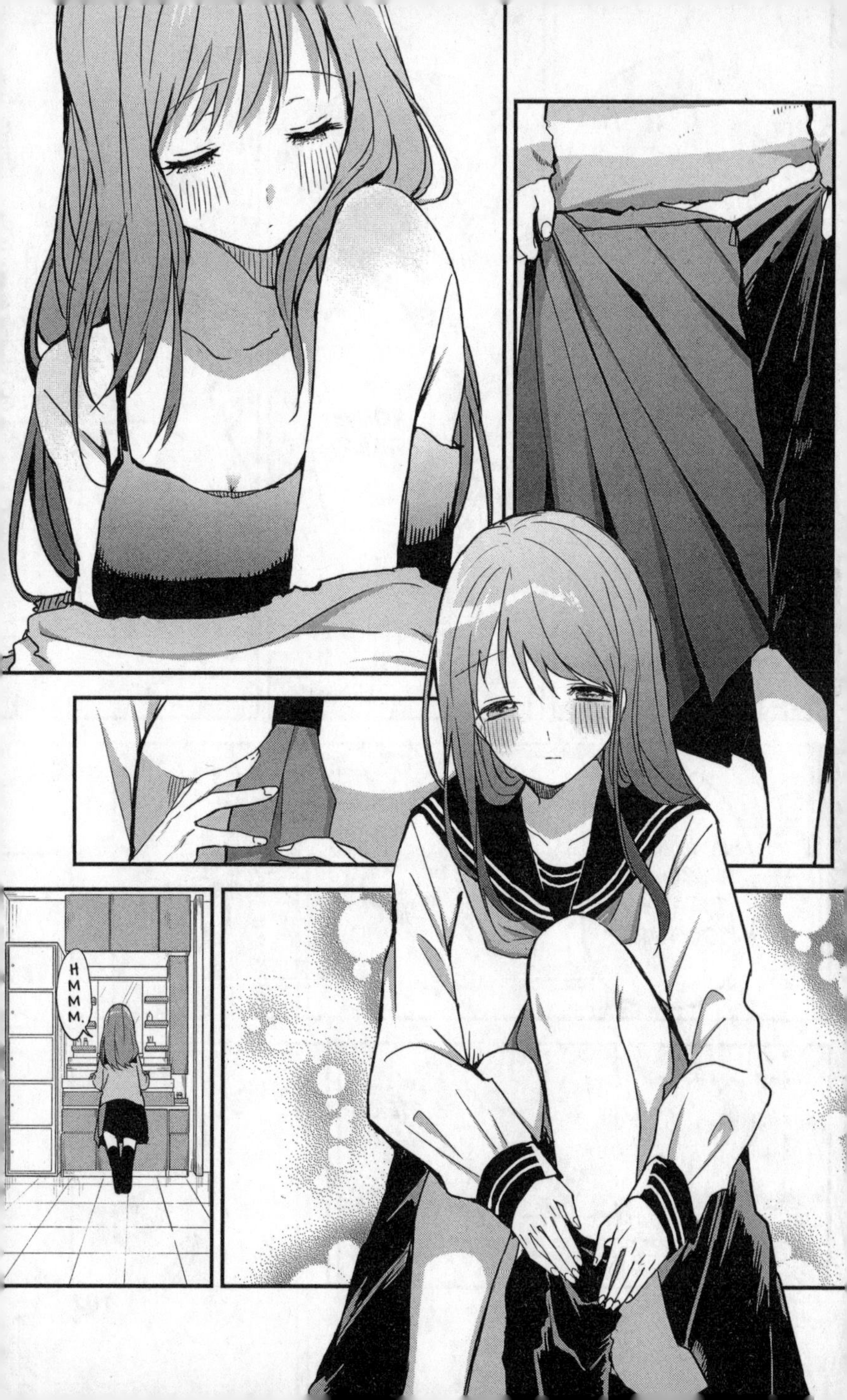
HMMM.

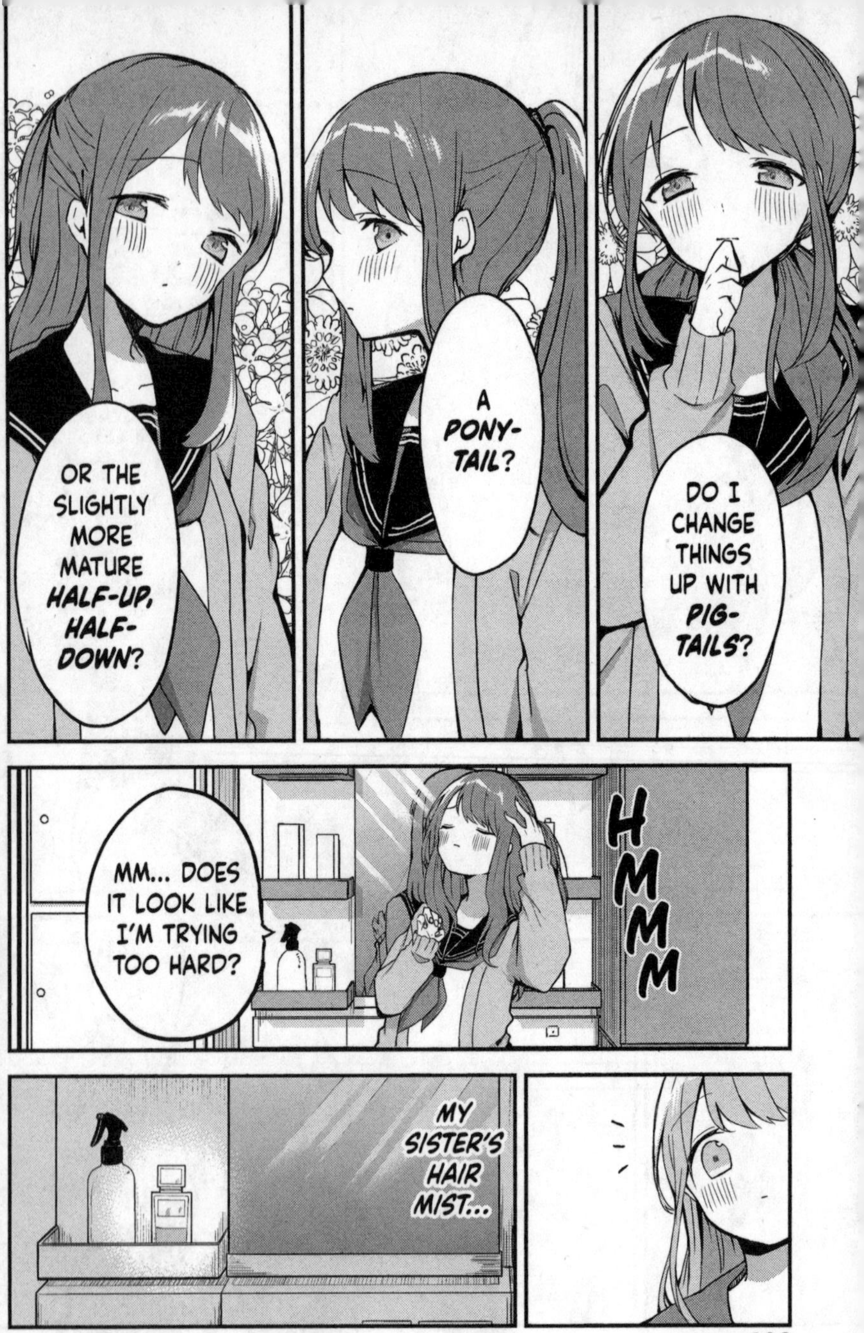
DO I CHANGE THINGS UP WITH PIG-TAILS?
A PONY-TAIL?
OR THE SLIGHTLY MORE MATURE HALF-UP, HALF-DOWN?
HMMM
MM... DOES IT LOOK LIKE I'M TRYING TOO HARD?
MY SISTER'S HAIR MIST...

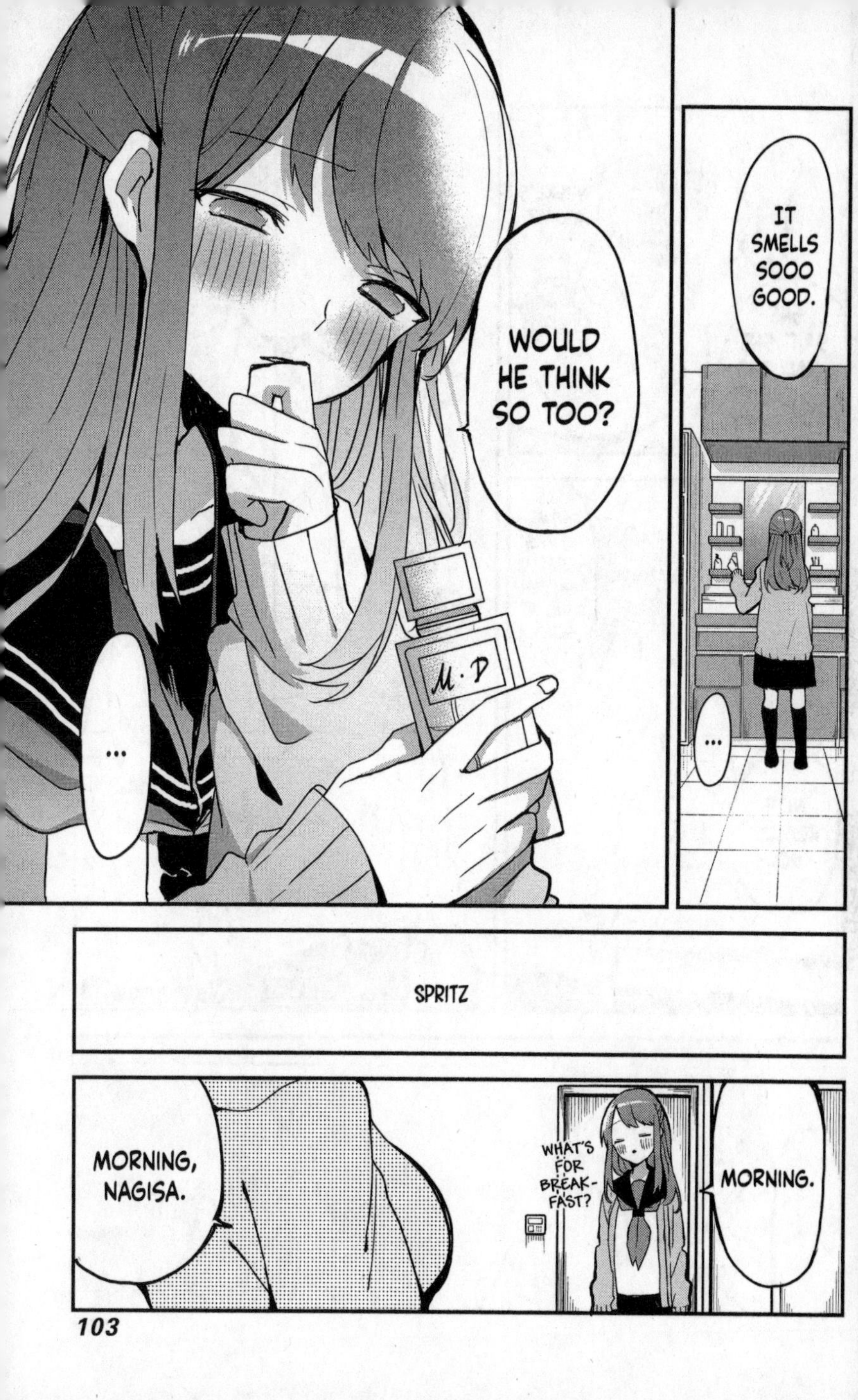
IT SMELLS SOOO GOOD.
...
WOULD HE THINK SO TOO?
M·D
...
SPRITZ
MORNING.
WHAT'S FOR BREAK-FAST?
MORNING, NAGISA.

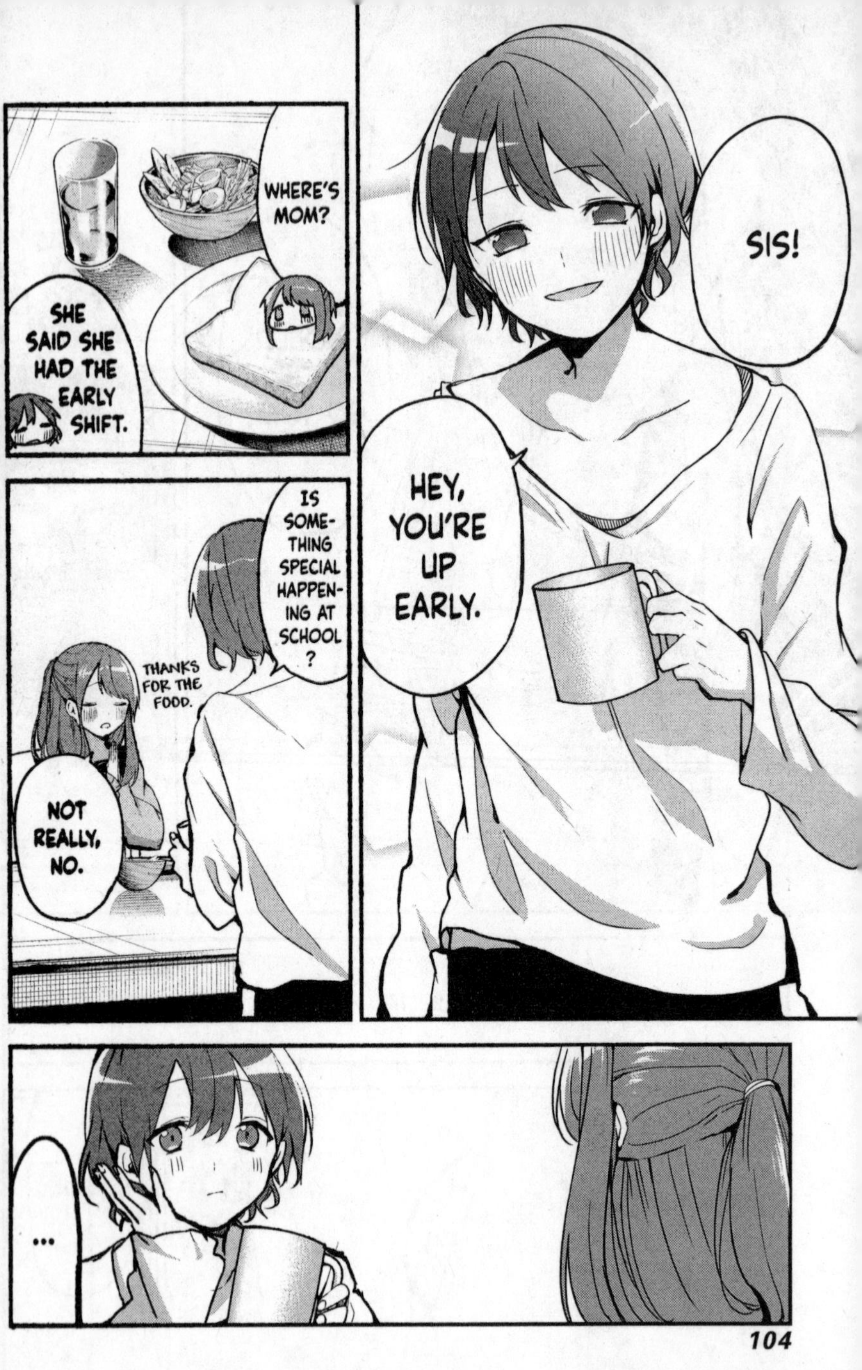
SIS!
HEY, YOU'RE UP EARLY.
WHERE'S MOM?
SHE SAID SHE HAD THE EARLY SHIFT.
IS SOME-THING SPECIAL HAPPEN-ING AT SCHOOL?
THANKS FOR THE FOOD.
NOT REALLY, NO.
...

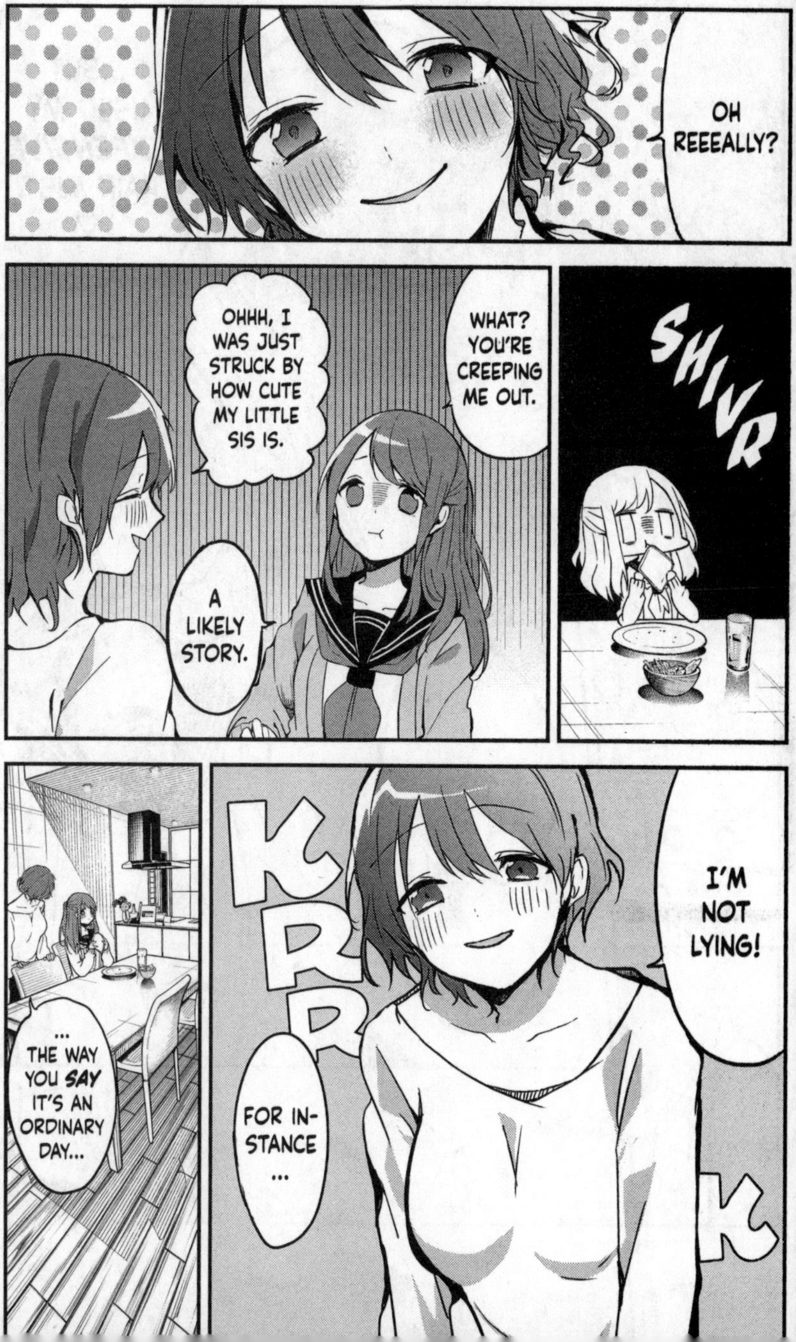
OH REEEALLY?
SHIVR
WHAT? YOU'RE CREEPING ME OUT.
OHHH, I WAS JUST STRUCK BY HOW CUTE MY LITTLE SIS IS.
A LIKELY STORY.
I'M NOT LYING!
KRRK
FOR IN-STANCE ...
... THE WAY YOU *SAY* IT'S AN ORDINARY DAY...

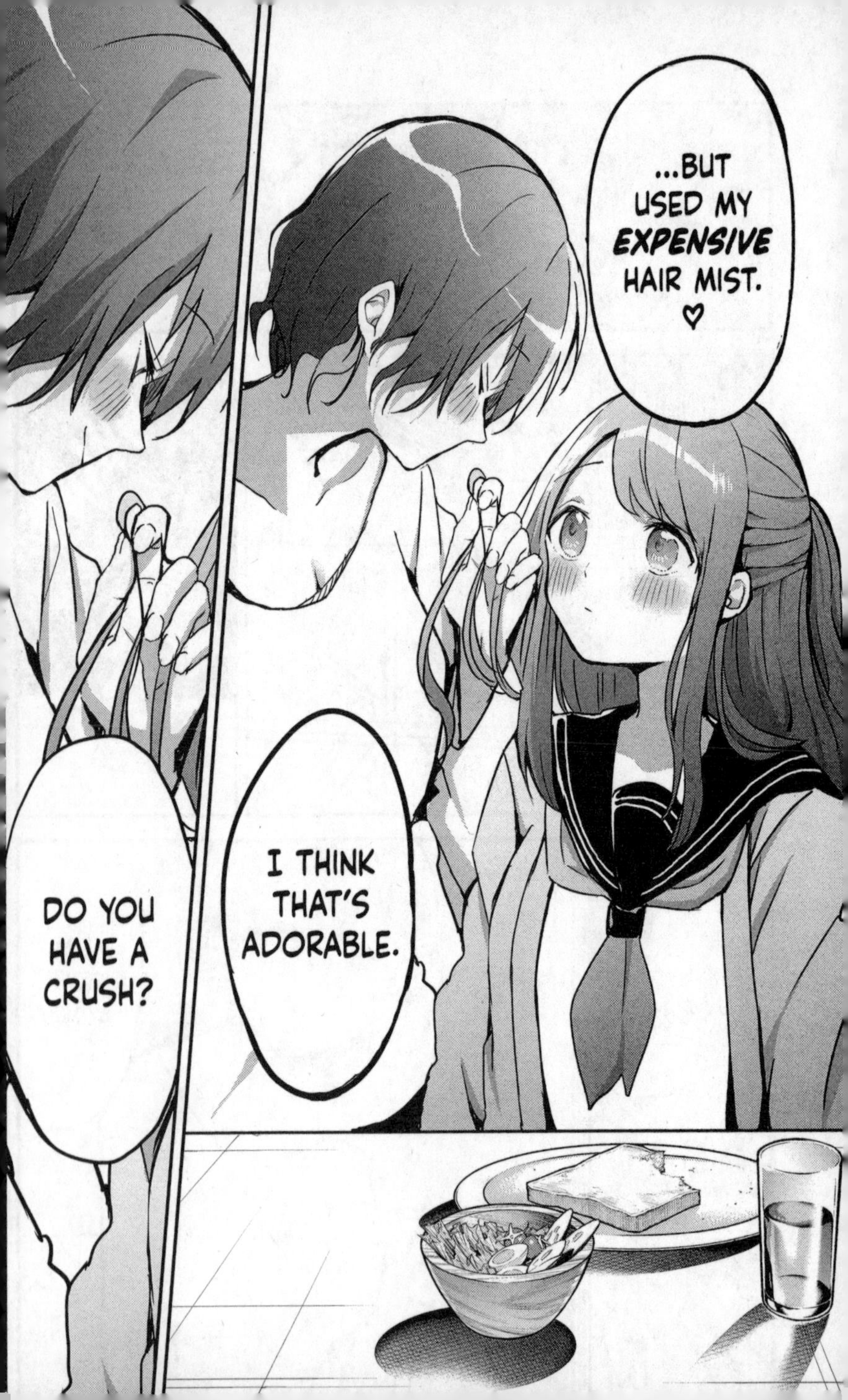
...BUT USED MY ***EXPENSIVE*** HAIR MIST. ♡
I THINK THAT'S ADORABLE.
DO YOU HAVE A CRUSH?

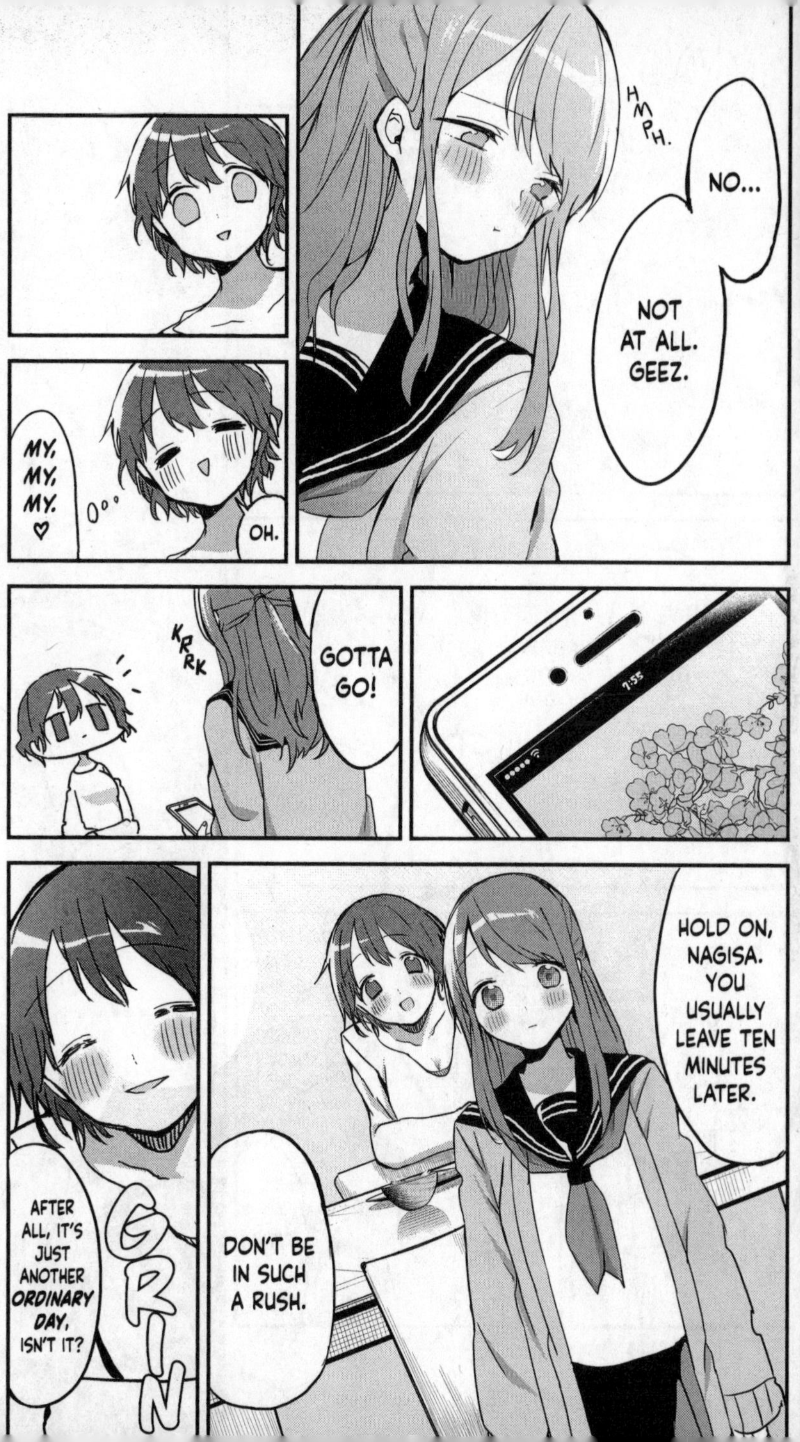
NO...
NOT AT ALL. GEEZ.
HMPH.
OH.
MY, MY, MY. ♡
7:55
GOTTA GO!
KRRK
HOLD ON, NAGISA. YOU USUALLY LEAVE TEN MINUTES LATER.
DON'T BE IN SUCH A RUSH.
GRIN
AFTER ALL, IT'S JUST ANOTHER ORDINARY DAY, ISN'T IT?

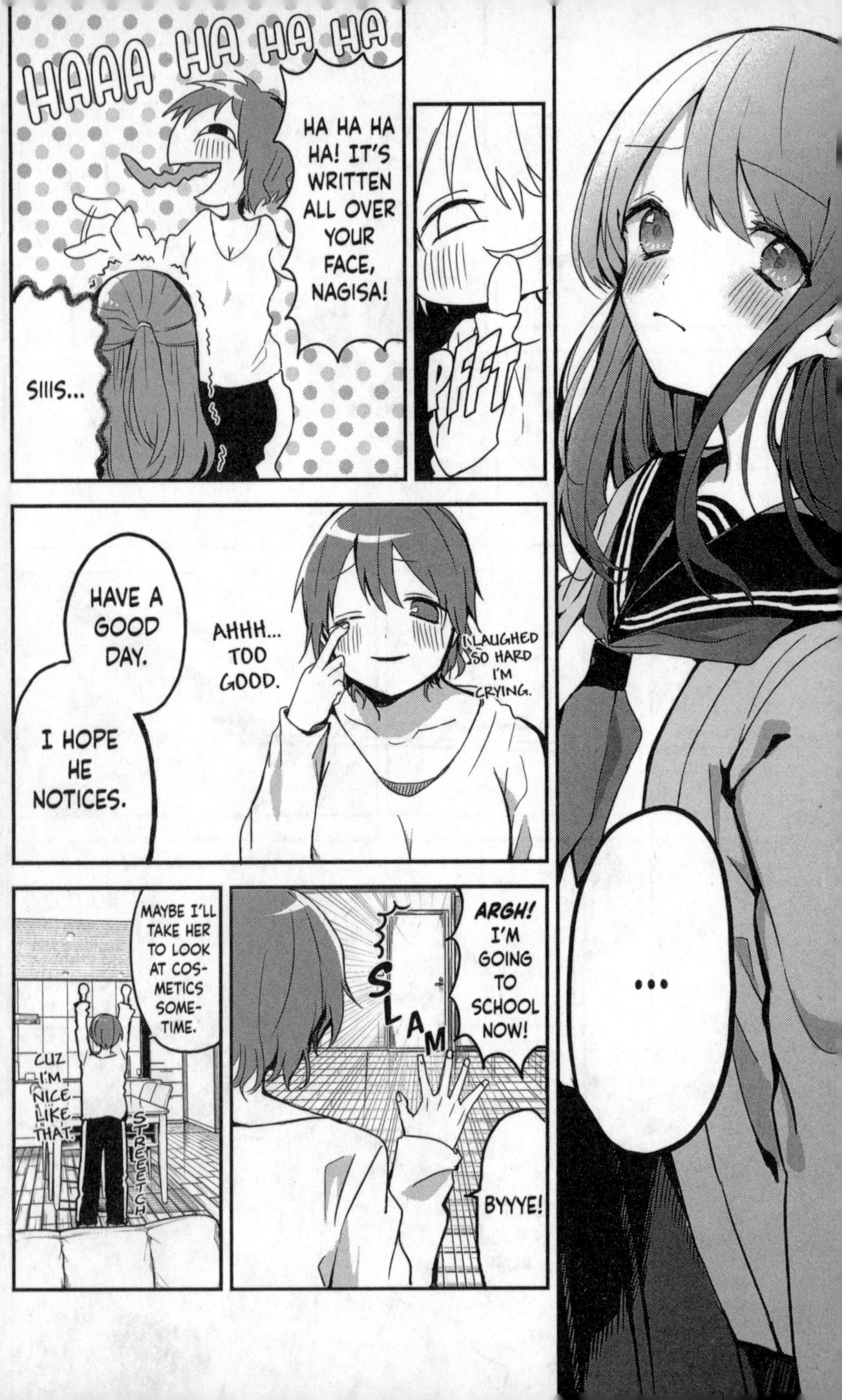
...
PFFT
HAAA HA HA HA
HA HA HA HA! IT'S WRITTEN ALL OVER YOUR FACE, NAGISA!
SIIIS...
I LAUGHED SO HARD I'M CRYING.
AHHH... TOO GOOD.
HAVE A GOOD DAY.
I HOPE HE NOTICES.
ARGH! I'M GOING TO SCHOOL NOW!
SLAM
BYYYE!
MAYBE I'LL TAKE HER TO LOOK AT COS-METICS SOME-TIME.
CUZ I'M NICE LIKE THAT.
STREEETCH

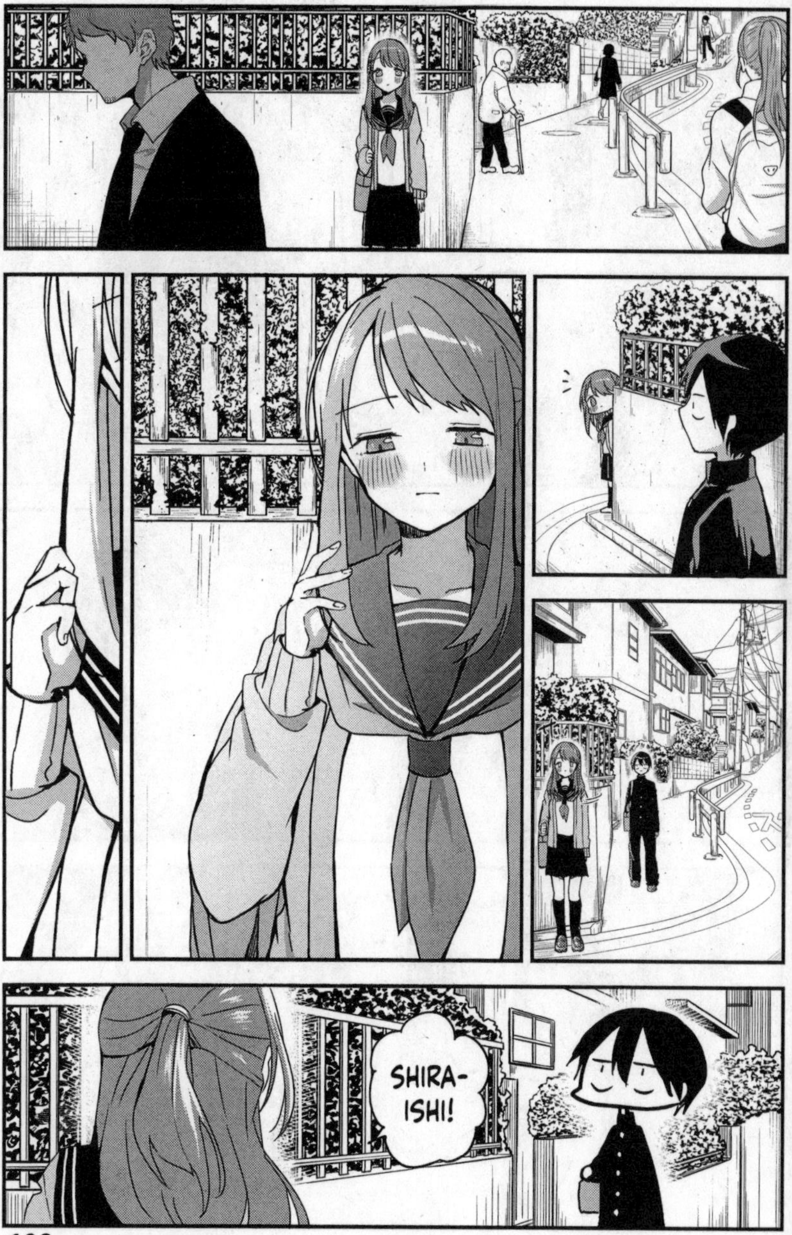
SHIRA-ISHI!

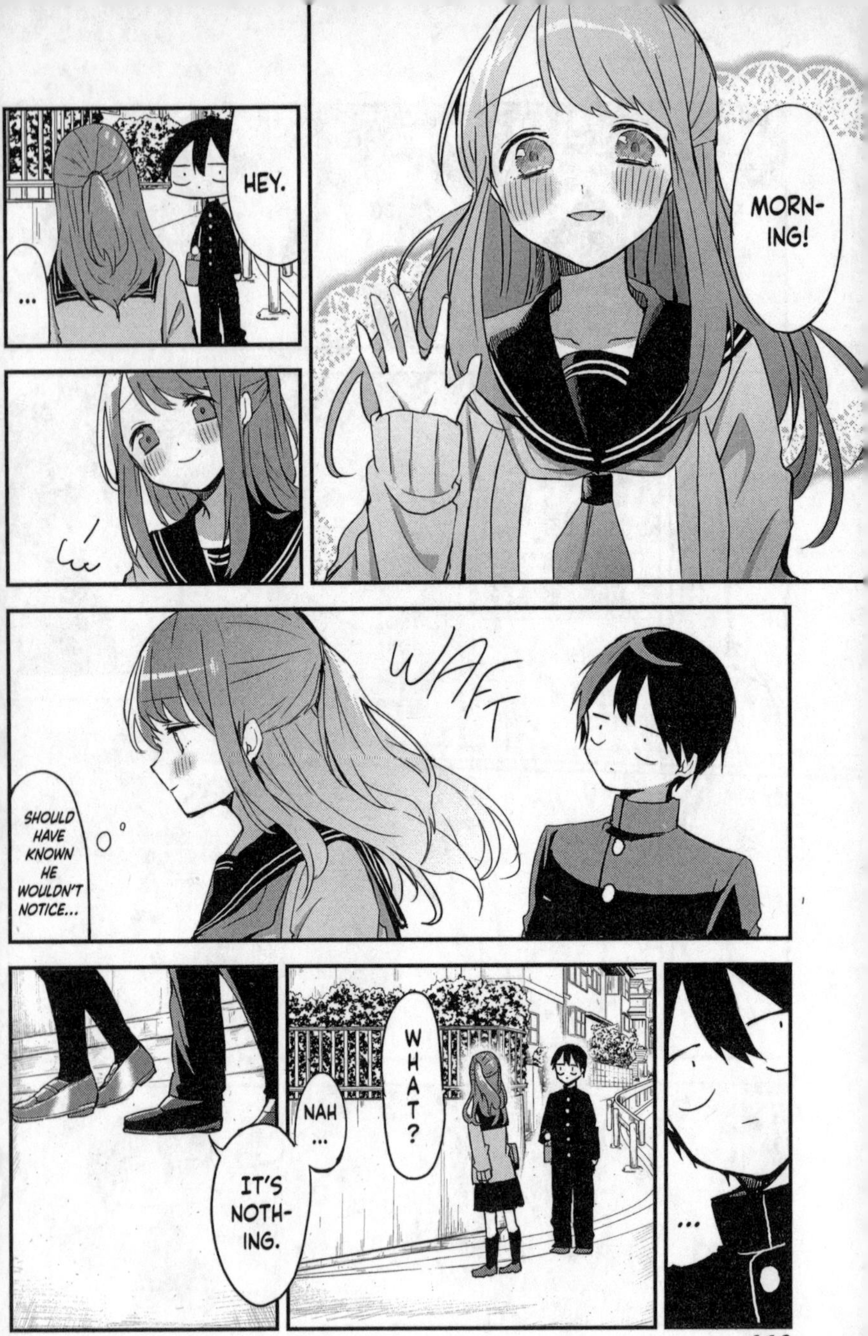
MORN-ING!
HEY.
...
WAFT
SHOULD HAVE KNOWN HE WOULDN'T NOTICE...
...
WHAT?
NAH...
IT'S NOTH-ING.

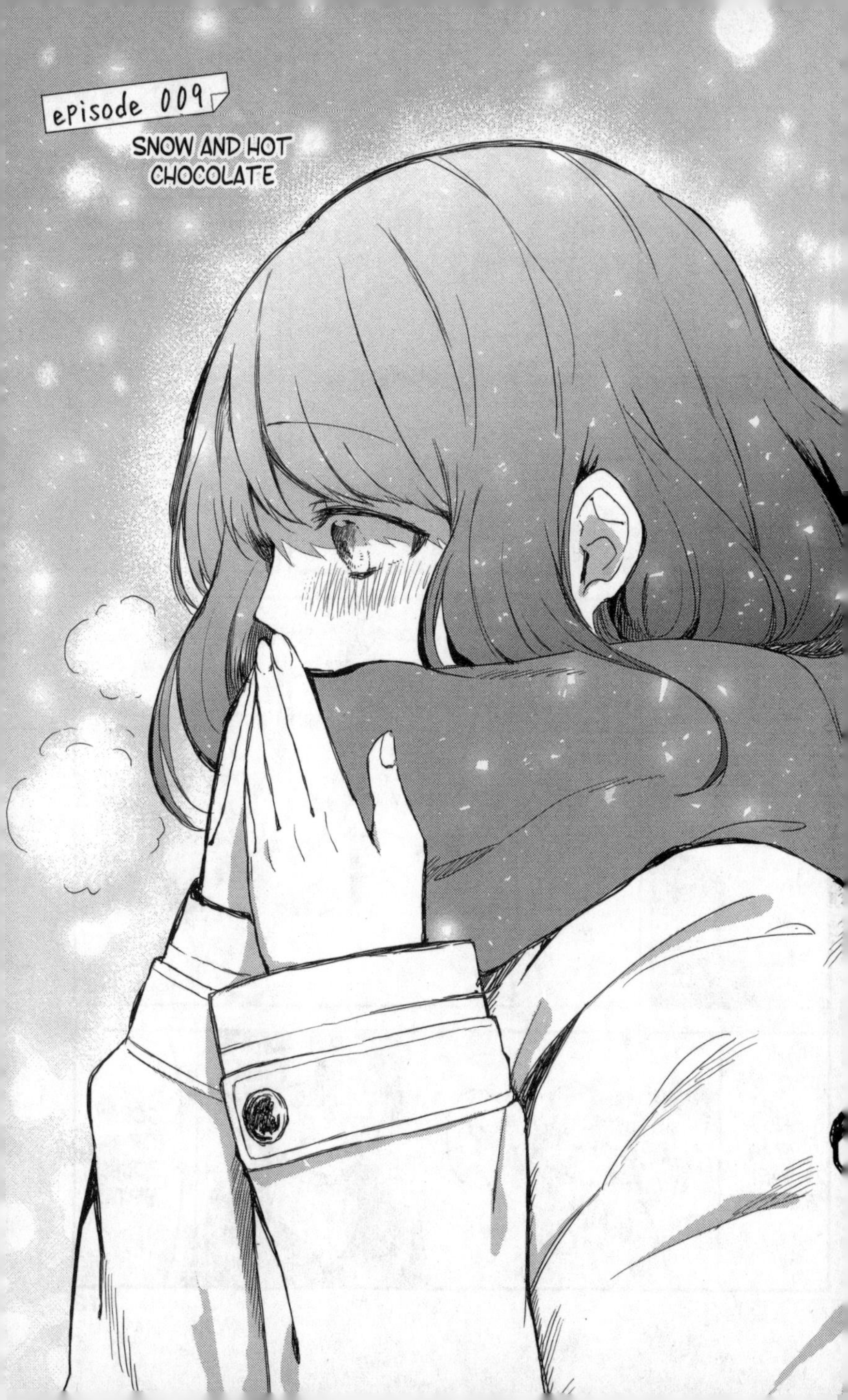
episode 009
SNOW AND HOT CHOCOLATE

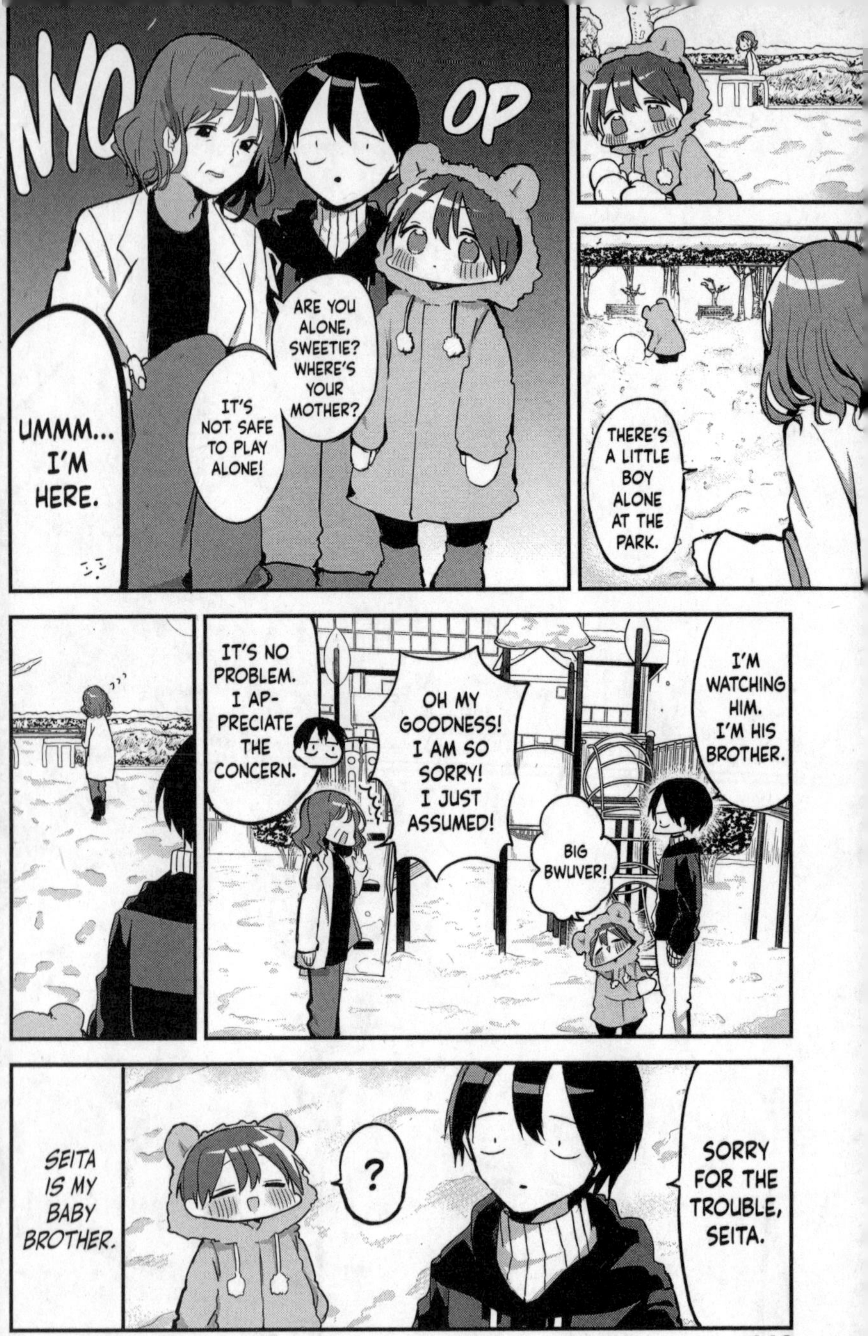
THERE'S A LITTLE BOY ALONE AT THE PARK.
NYO OP
ARE YOU ALONE, SWEETIE? WHERE'S YOUR MOTHER?
IT'S NOT SAFE TO PLAY ALONE!
UMMM... I'M HERE.
I'M WATCHING HIM. I'M HIS BROTHER.
BIG BWUVER!
OH MY GOODNESS! I AM SO SORRY! I JUST ASSUMED!
IT'S NO PROBLEM. I APPRECIATE THE CONCERN.
SORRY FOR THE TROUBLE, SEITA.
?
SEITA IS MY BABY BROTHER.

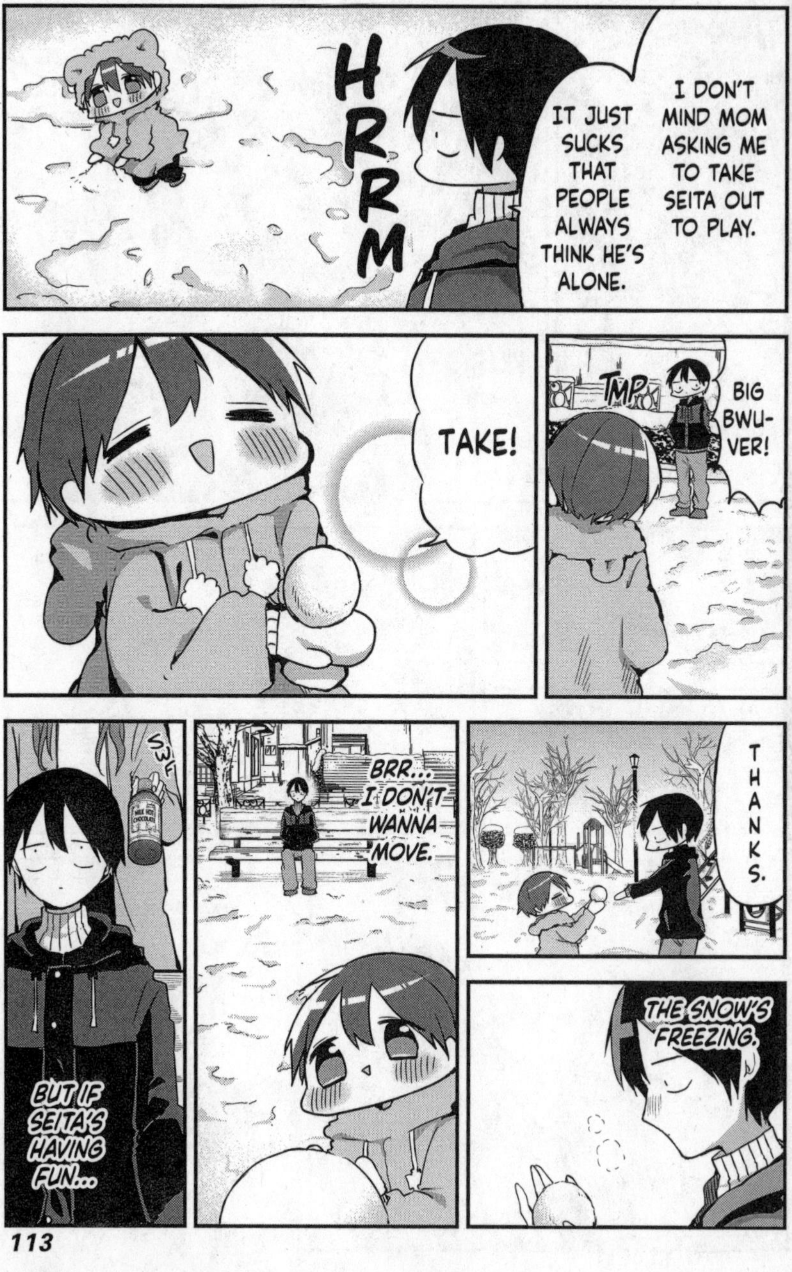
I DON'T MIND MOM ASKING ME TO TAKE SEITA OUT TO PLAY.
IT JUST SUCKS THAT PEOPLE ALWAYS THINK HE'S ALONE.
HRRM
BIG BWU-VER!
TMP
TAKE!
THANKS.
THE SNOW'S FREEZING.
BRR... I DON'T WANNA MOVE.
SWF
MILK HOT CHOCOLATE
BUT IF SEITA'S HAVING FUN...

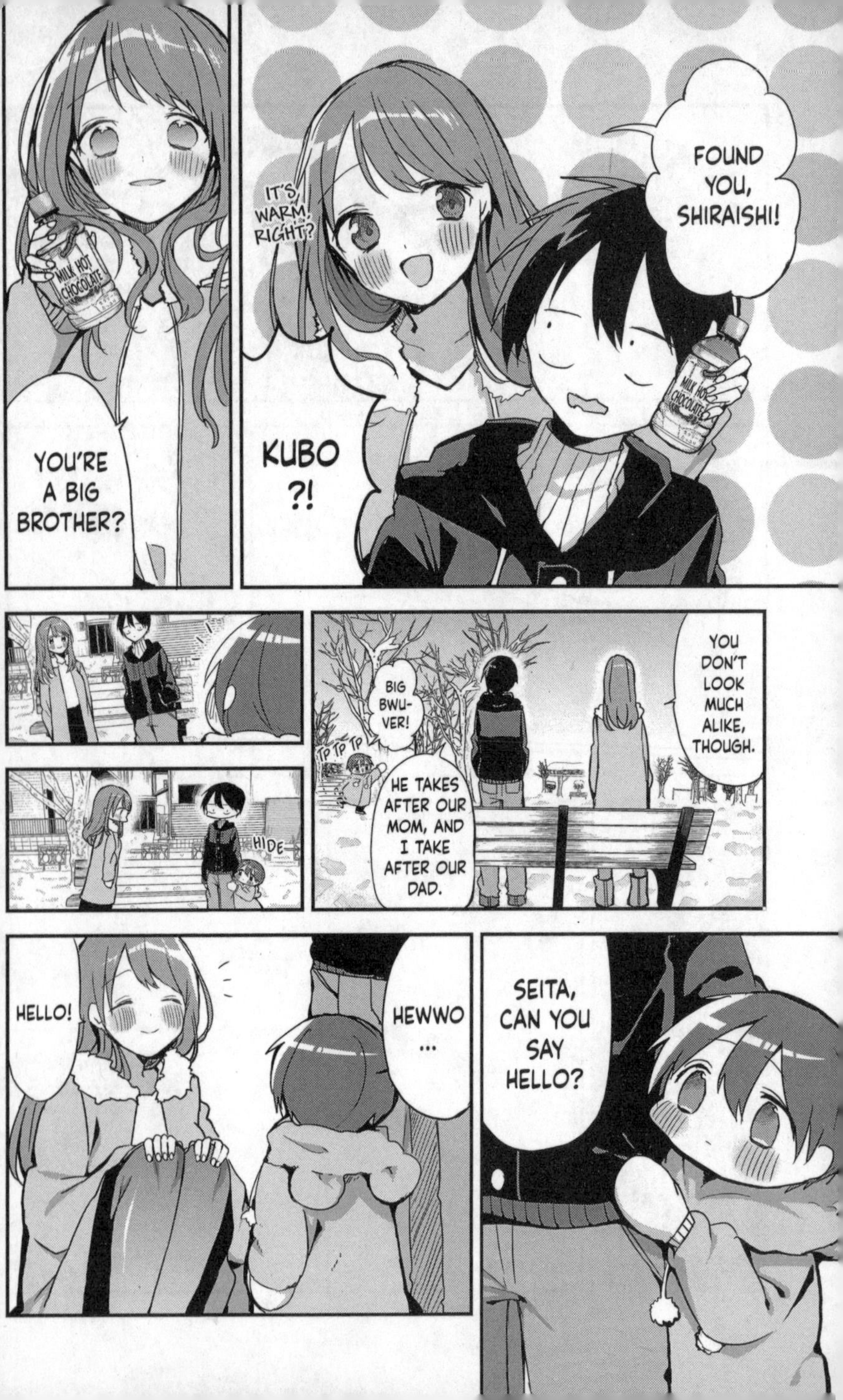
FOUND YOU, SHIRAISHI!
IT'S WARM, RIGHT?
MILK HOT CHOCOLATE
KUBO ?!
MILK HOT CHOCOLATE
YOU'RE A BIG BROTHER?
YOU DON'T LOOK MUCH ALIKE, THOUGH.
BIG BWU-VER!
TP TP TP
HE TAKES AFTER OUR MOM, AND I TAKE AFTER OUR DAD.
HIDE
SEITA, CAN YOU SAY HELLO?
HEWWO ...
HELLO!

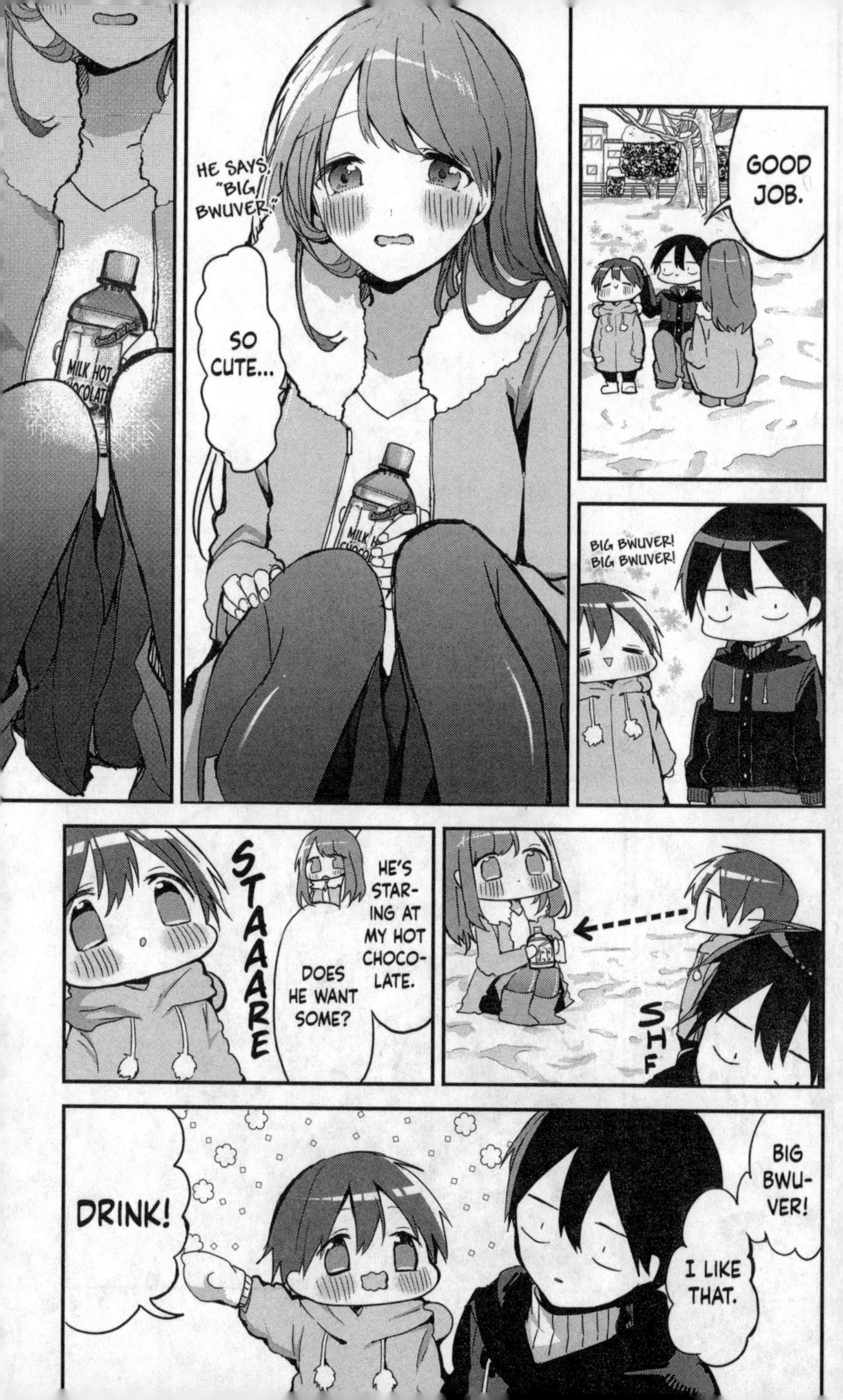
GOOD JOB.
BIG BWUVER! BIG BWUVER!
HE SAYS, "BIG BWUVER."
SO CUTE...
MILK HOT CHOCOLATE
MILK HOT CHOCO
SHF
STAAARE
HE'S STARING AT MY HOT CHOCOLATE.
DOES HE WANT SOME?
BIG BWUVER!
I LIKE THAT.
DRINK!

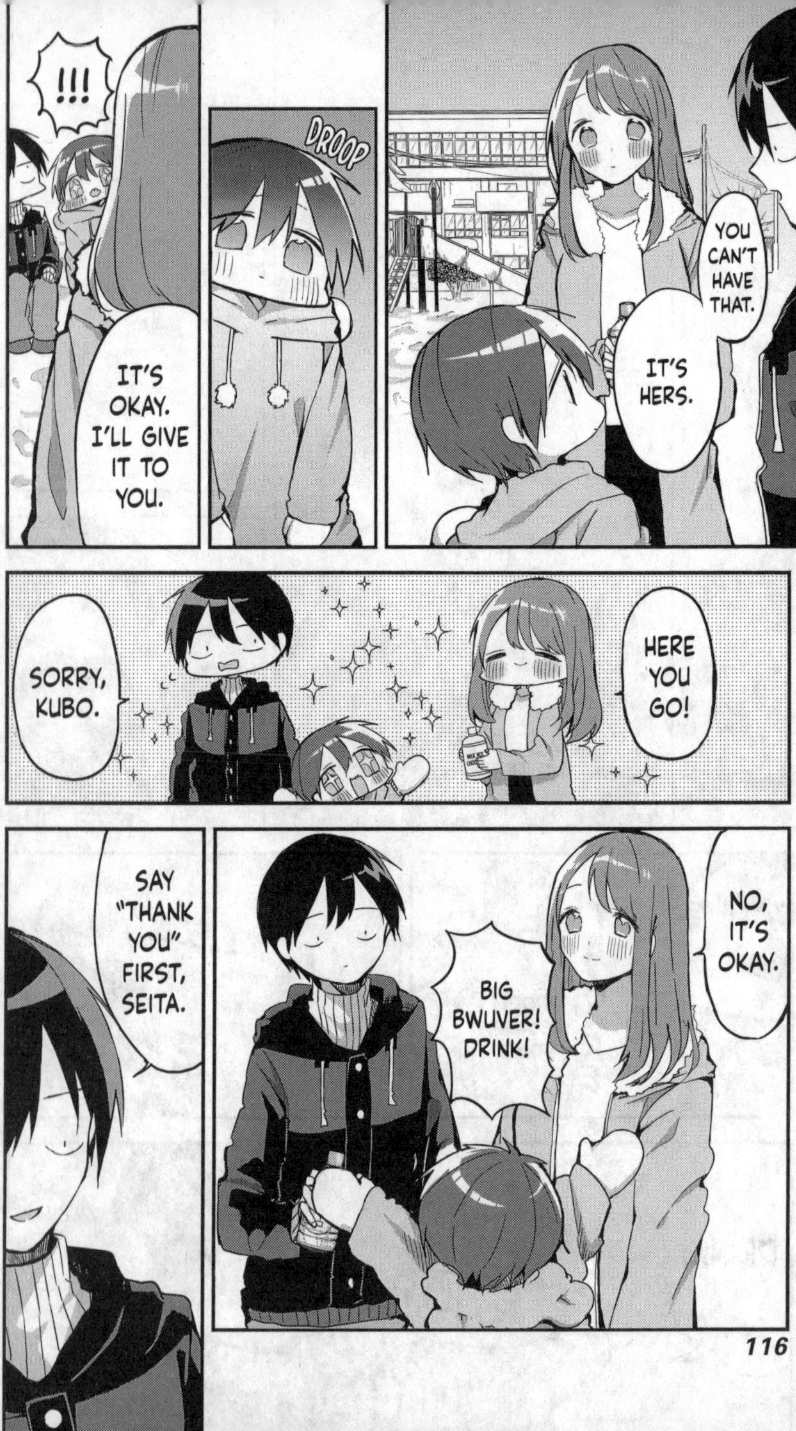
YOU CAN'T HAVE THAT.
IT'S HERS.
DROOP
IT'S OKAY. I'LL GIVE IT TO YOU.
!!!
HERE YOU GO!
SORRY, KUBO.
NO, IT'S OKAY.
BIG BWUVER! DRINK!
SAY "THANK YOU" FIRST, SEITA.

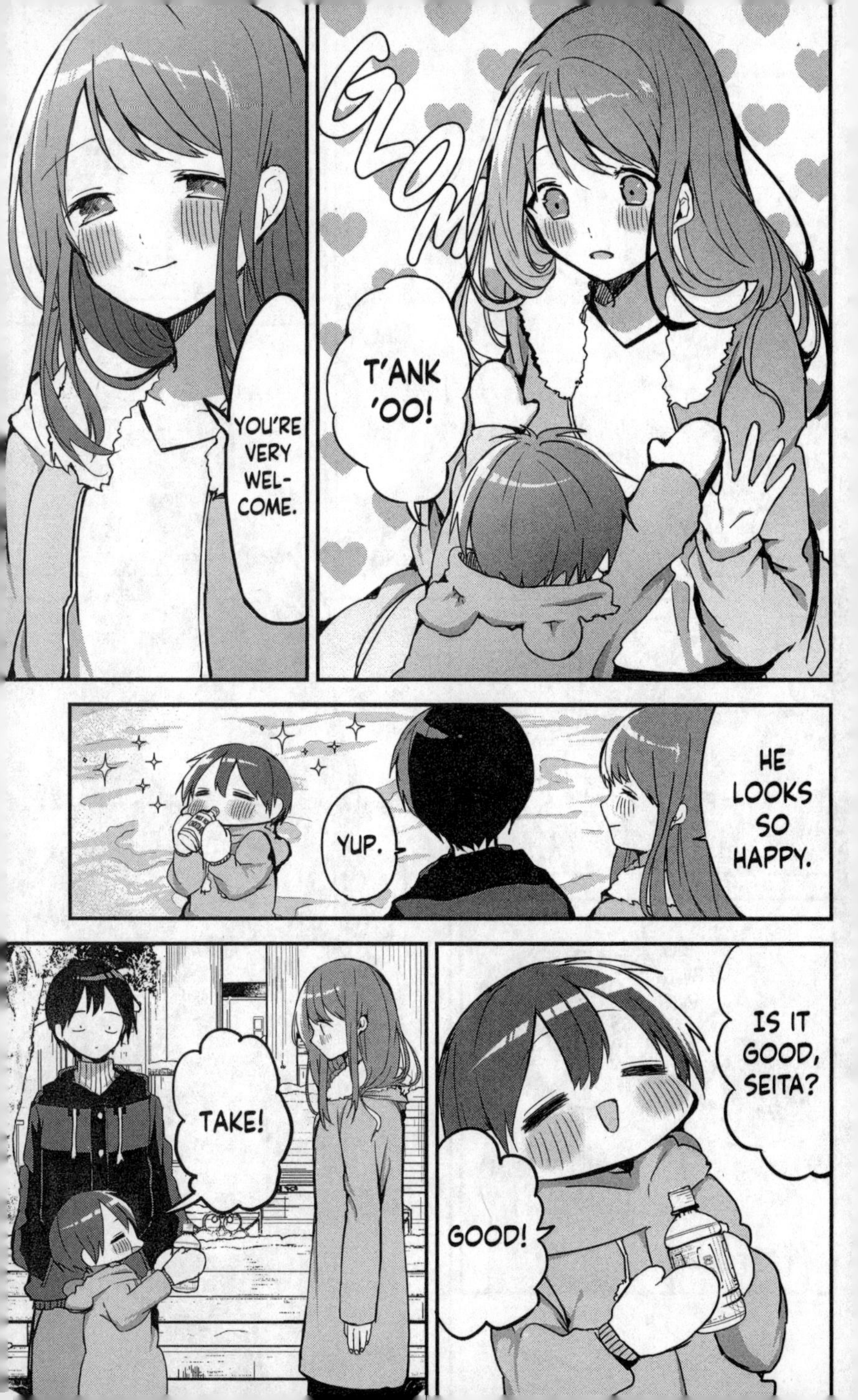
GLOMP
T'ANK 'OO!
YOU'RE VERY WEL-COME.
HE LOOKS SO HAPPY.
YUP.
IS IT GOOD, SEITA?
GOOD!
TAKE!

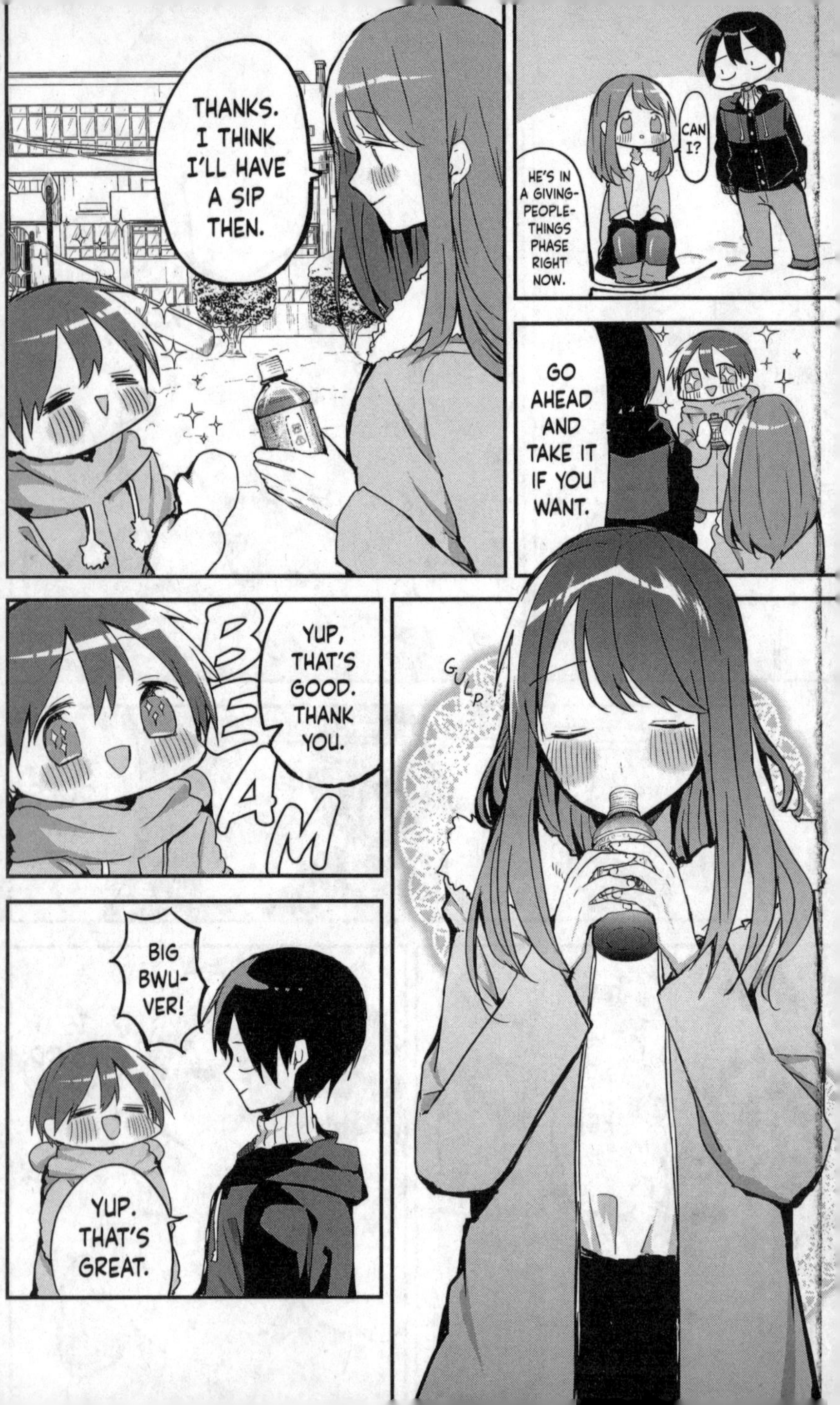
CAN I?
HE'S IN A GIVING-PEOPLE-THINGS PHASE RIGHT NOW.
GO AHEAD AND TAKE IT IF YOU WANT.
THANKS. I THINK I'LL HAVE A SIP THEN.
GULP
BEAM
YUP, THAT'S GOOD. THANK YOU.
BIG BWU-VER!
YUP. THAT'S GREAT.

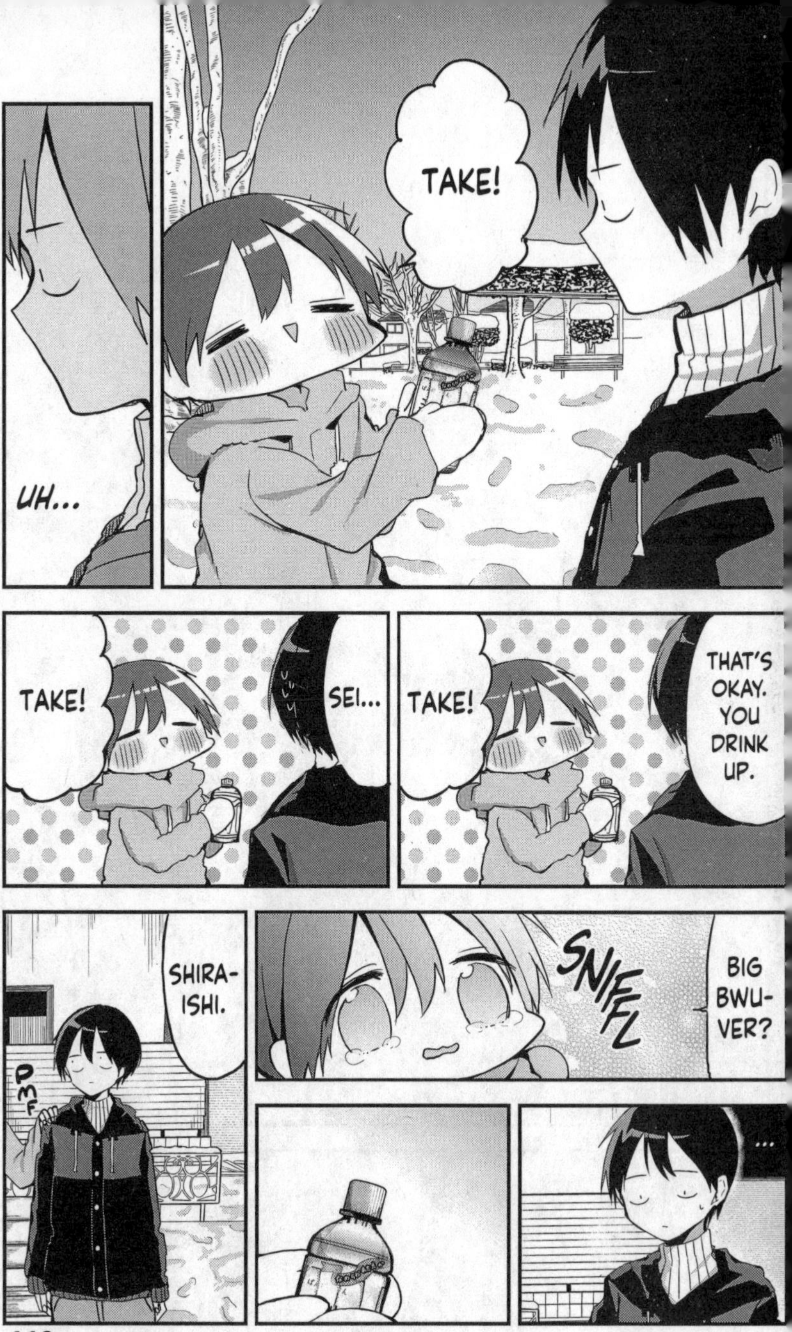
TAKE!
UH...
THAT'S OKAY. YOU DRINK UP.
TAKE!
SEI...
TAKE!
BIG BWU-VER?
SNIFFL
...
SHIRA-ISHI.
PMF

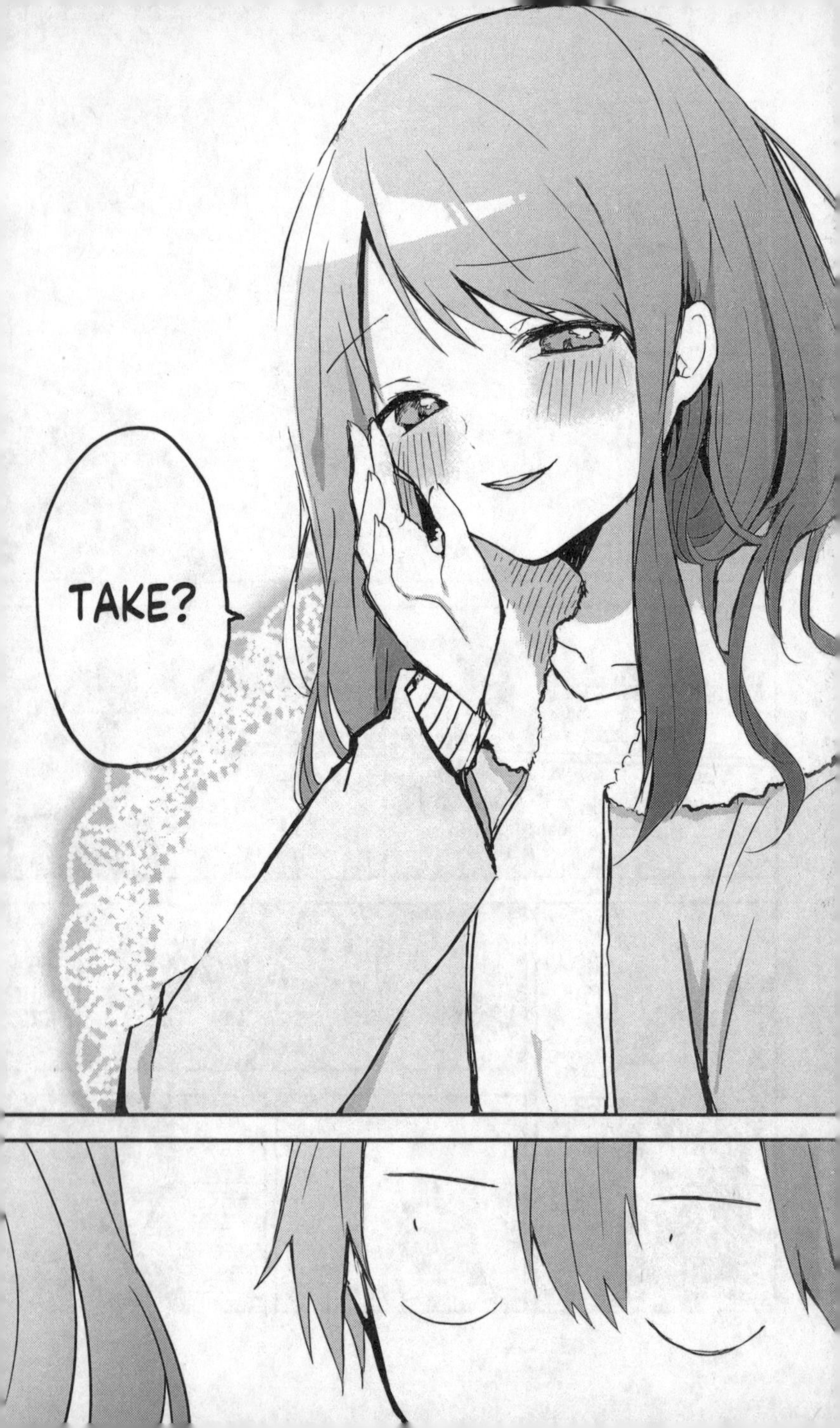
TAKE?

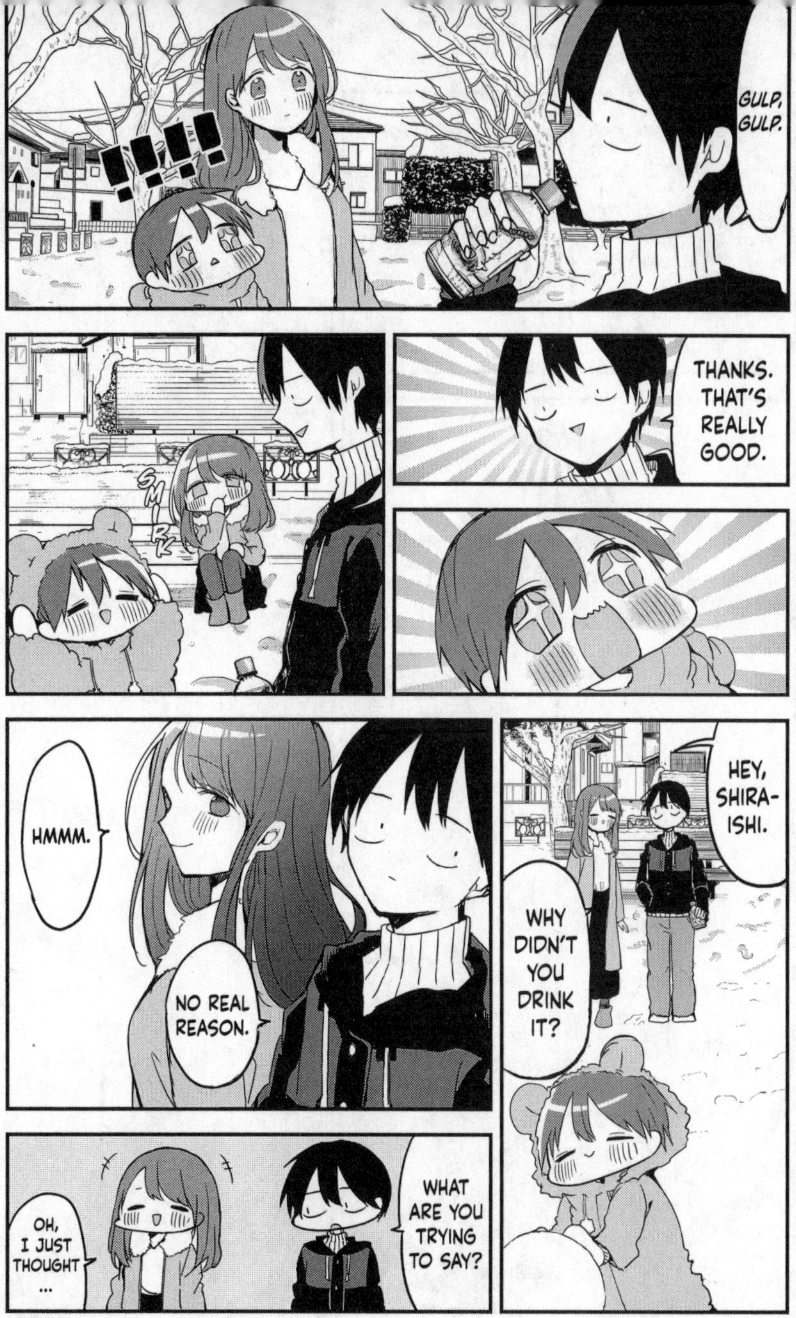
GULP, GULP.
THANKS. THAT'S REALLY GOOD.
SMIRK
HEY, SHIRA-ISHI.
WHY DIDN'T YOU DRINK IT?
NO REAL REASON.
HMMM.
WHAT ARE YOU TRYING TO SAY?
OH, I JUST THOUGHT...

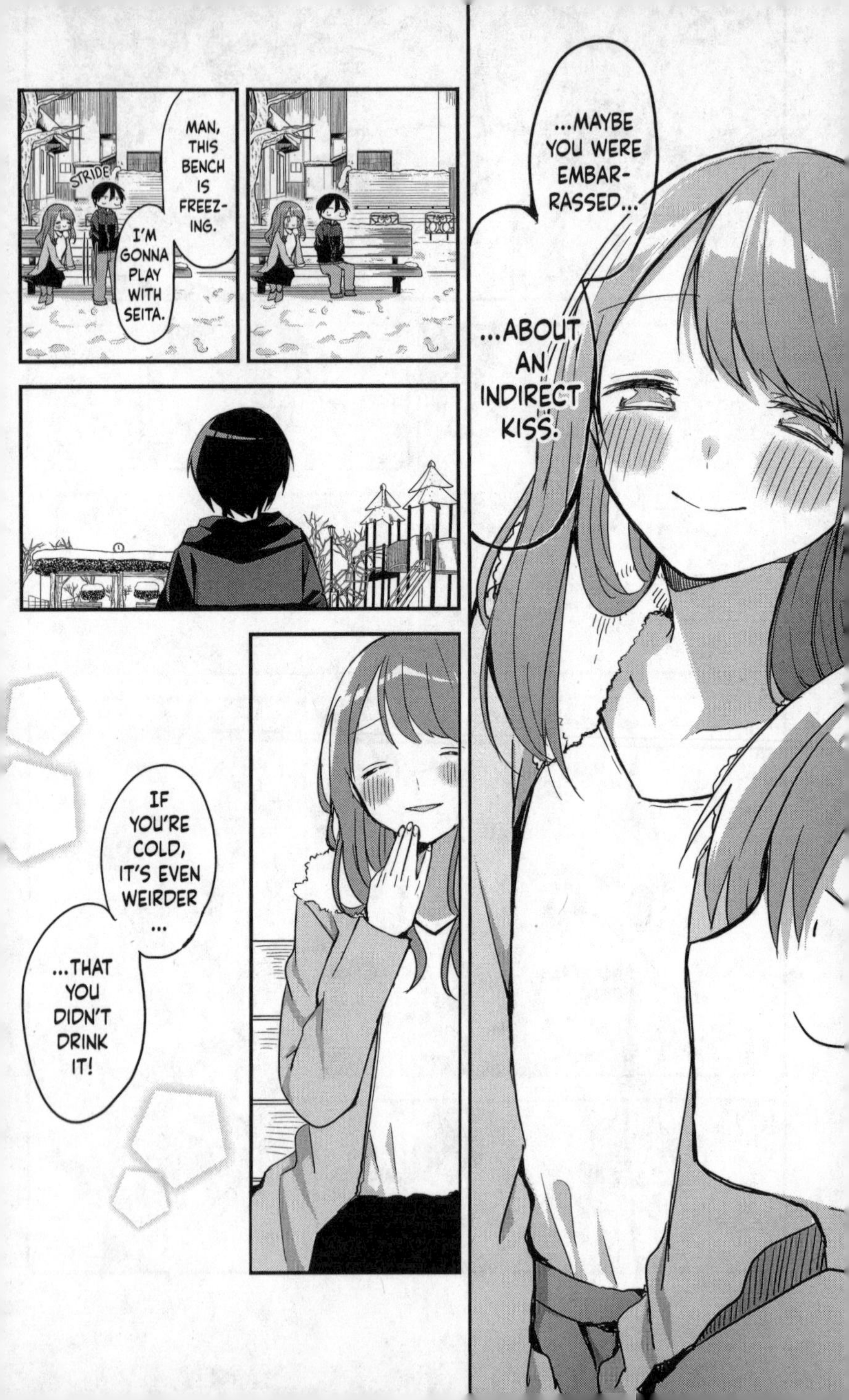
MAN, THIS BENCH IS FREEZ-ING.
STRIDE
I'M GONNA PLAY WITH SEITA.
IF YOU'RE COLD, IT'S EVEN WEIRDER ...
...THAT YOU DIDN'T DRINK IT!
...MAYBE YOU WERE EMBAR-RASSED...
...ABOUT AN INDIRECT KISS.

episode 010

BOOKSTORE AND COMPLEX

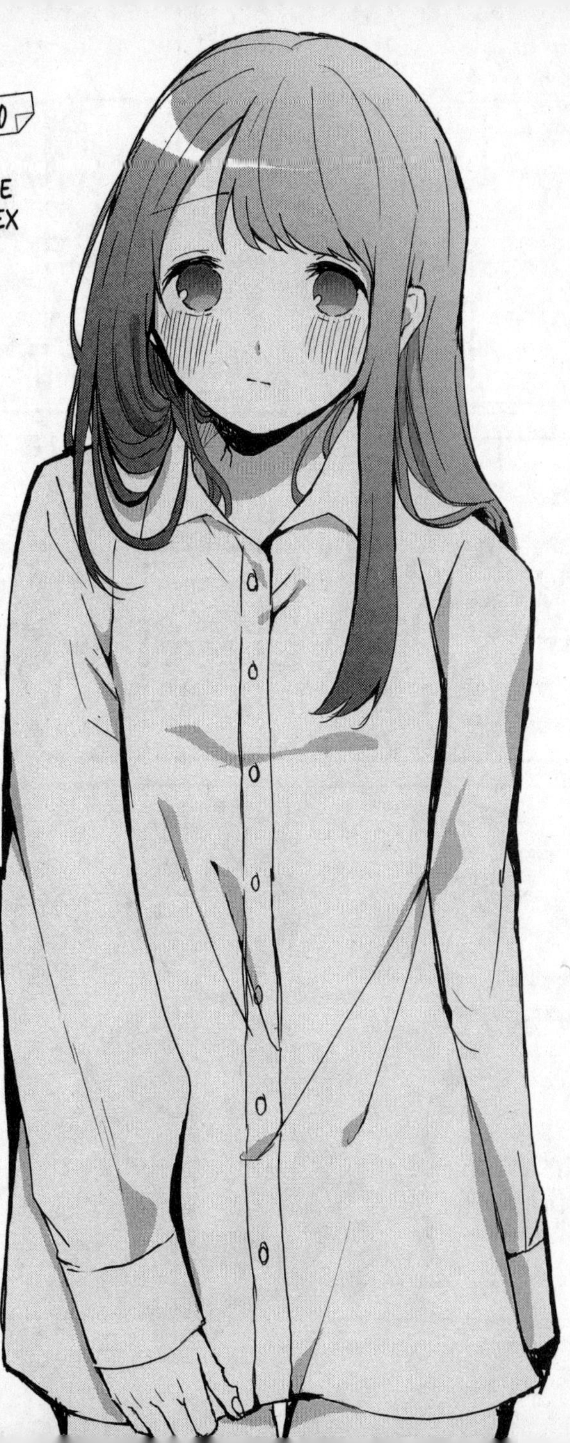

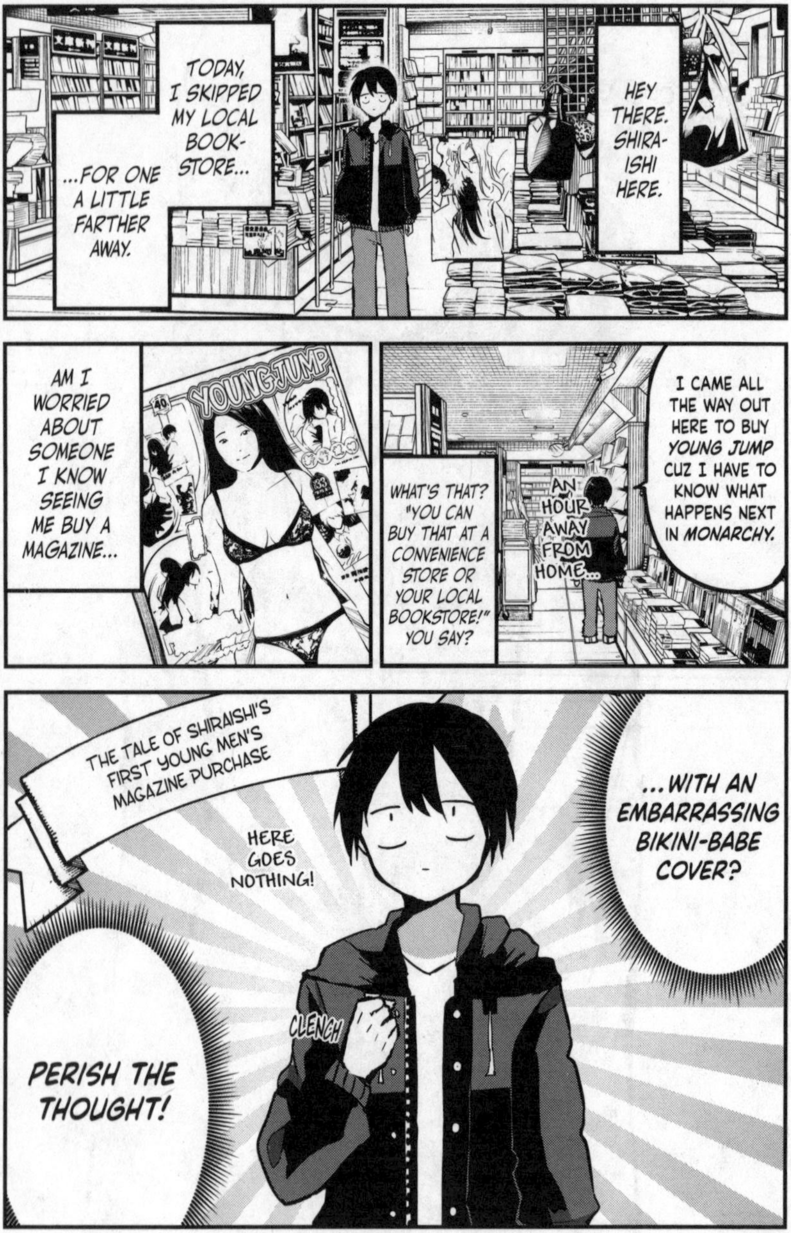
HEY THERE. SHIRAISHI HERE.
TODAY, I SKIPPED MY LOCAL BOOKSTORE...
...FOR ONE A LITTLE FARTHER AWAY.
I CAME ALL THE WAY OUT HERE TO BUY YOUNG JUMP CUZ I HAVE TO KNOW WHAT HAPPENS NEXT IN MONARCHY.
AN HOUR AWAY FROM HOME...
WHAT'S THAT? "YOU CAN BUY THAT AT A CONVENIENCE STORE OR YOUR LOCAL BOOKSTORE!" YOU SAY?
YOUNG JUMP
AM I WORRIED ABOUT SOMEONE I KNOW SEEING ME BUY A MAGAZINE...
...WITH AN EMBARRASSING BIKINI-BABE COVER?
THE TALE OF SHIRAISHI'S FIRST YOUNG MEN'S MAGAZINE PURCHASE
HERE GOES NOTHING!
CLENCH
PERISH THE THOUGHT!

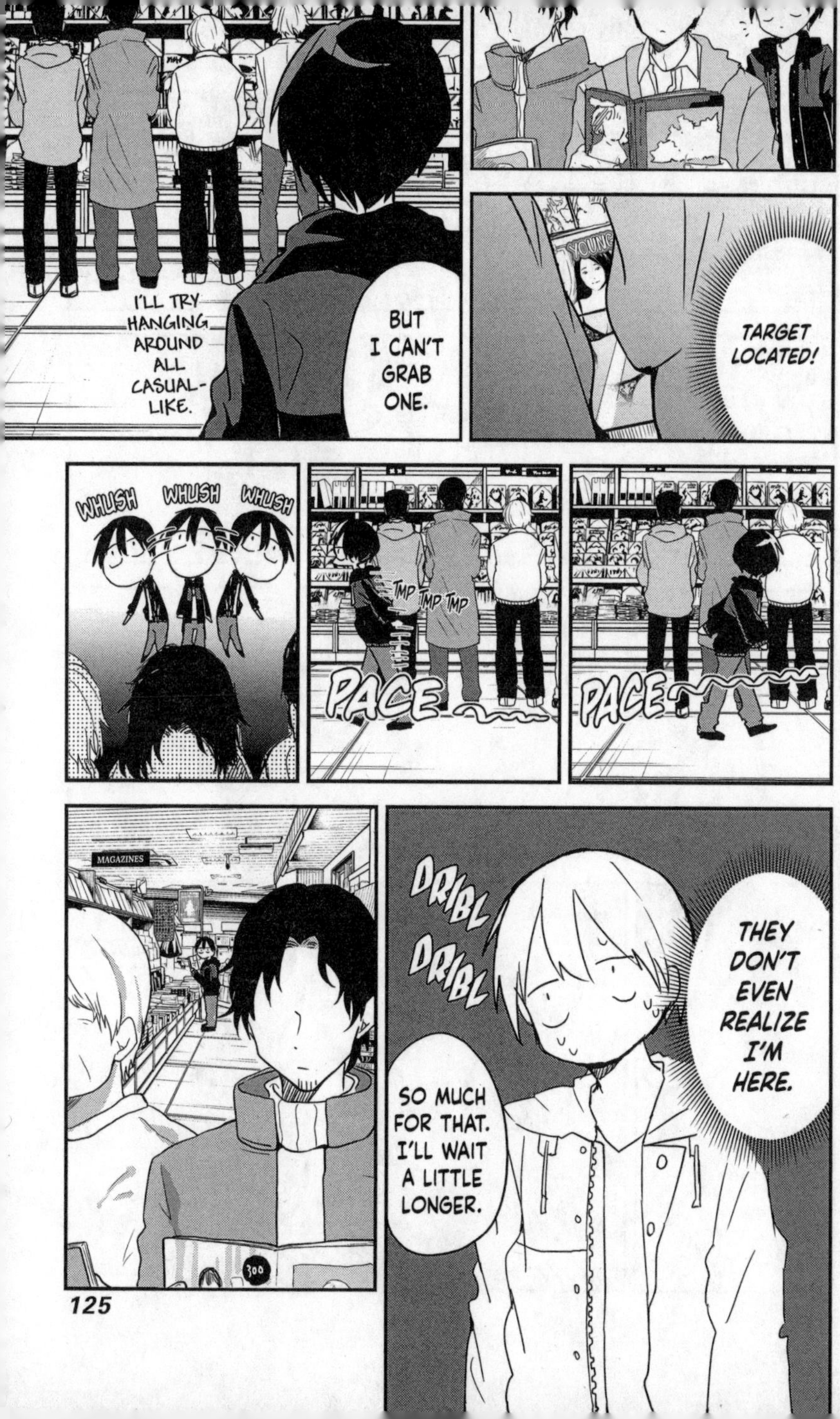
YOUNG
TARGET LOCATED!
BUT I CAN'T GRAB ONE.
I'LL TRY HANGING AROUND ALL CASUAL-LIKE.
PACE
TMP TMP TMP
PACE
WHUSH
WHUSH
WHUSH
DRIBL
DRIBL
THEY DON'T EVEN REALIZE I'M HERE.
SO MUCH FOR THAT. I'LL WAIT A LITTLE LONGER.
MAGAZINES
300

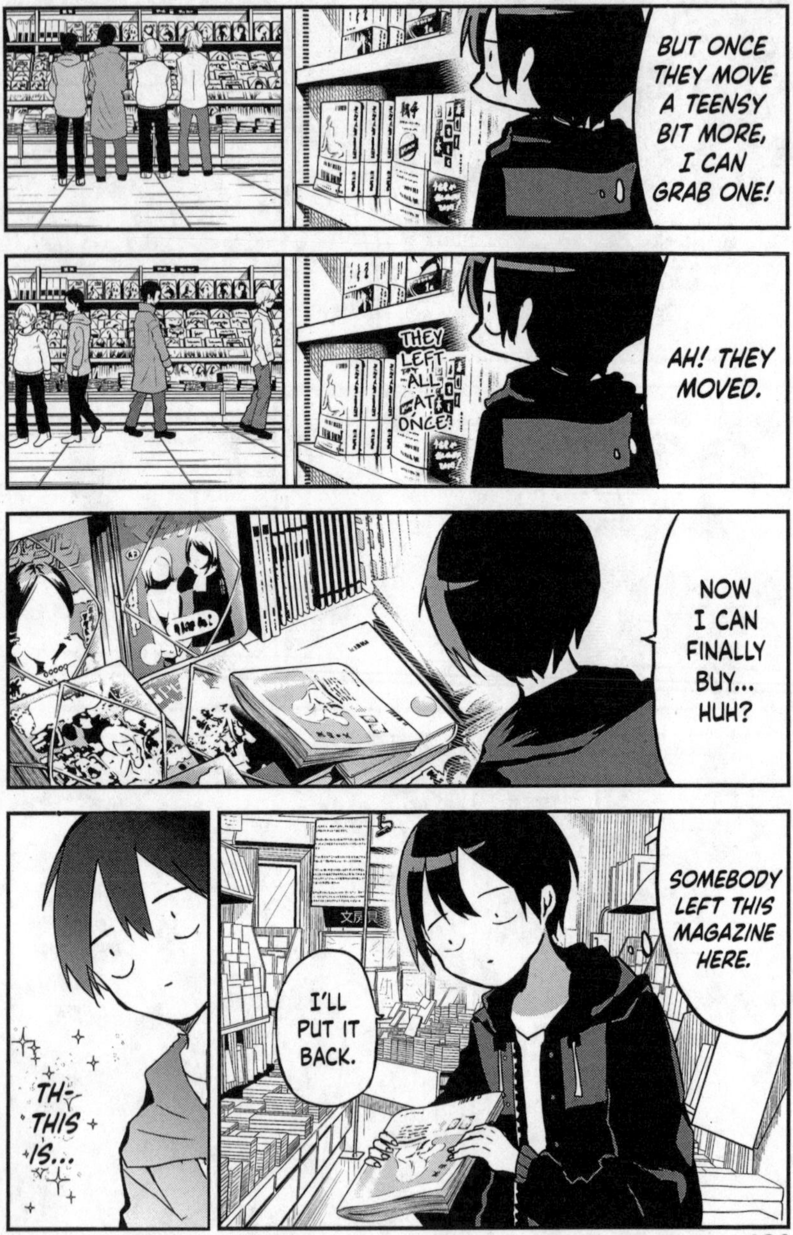
BUT ONCE THEY MOVE A TEENSY BIT MORE, I CAN GRAB ONE!
AH! THEY MOVED.
THEY LEFT ALL AT ONCE!
NOW I CAN FINALLY BUY... HUH?
SOMEBODY LEFT THIS MAGAZINE HERE.
I'LL PUT IT BACK.
TH-THIS IS...

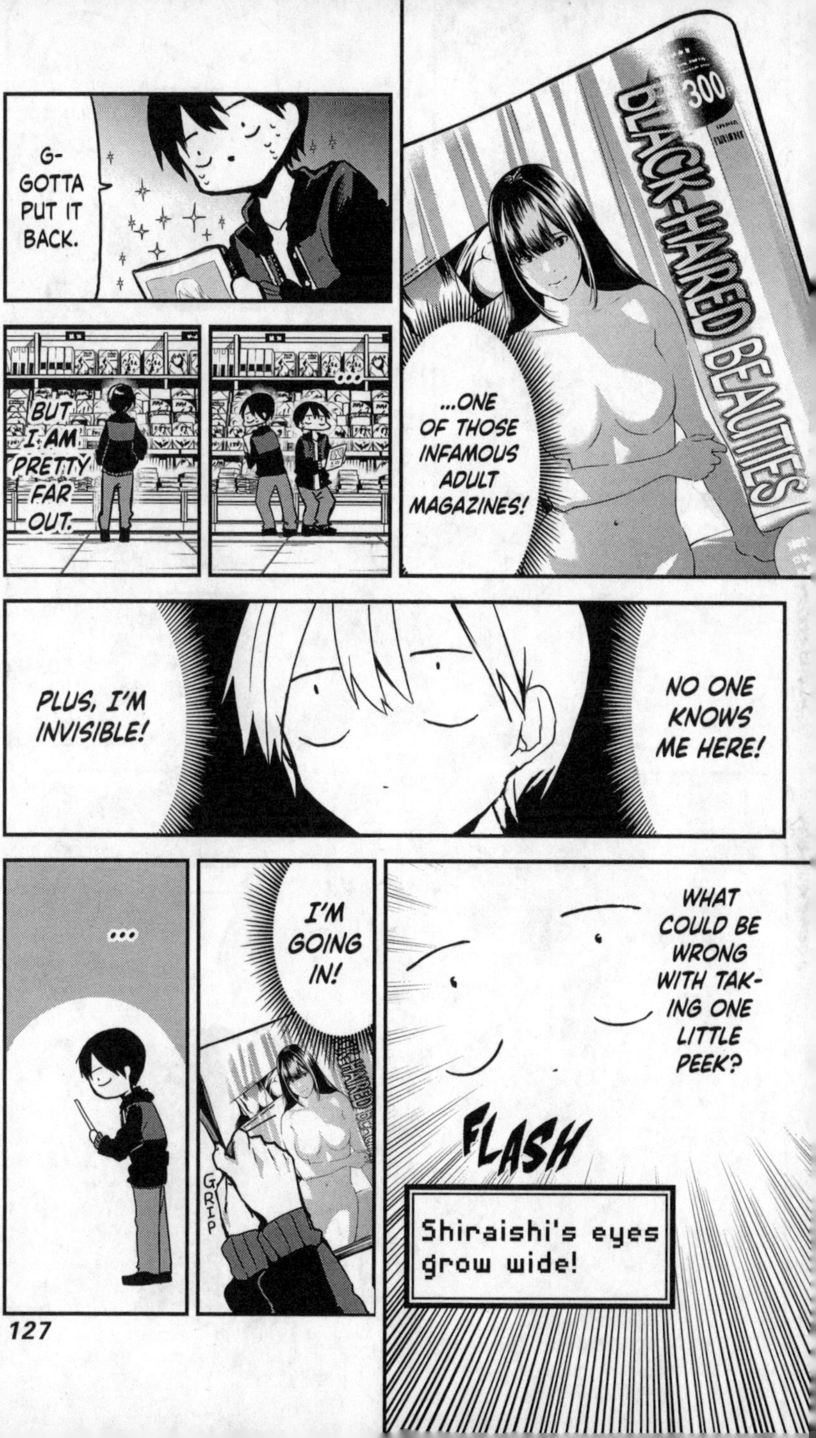
300
BLACK-HAIRED BEAUTIES
...ONE OF THOSE INFAMOUS ADULT MAGAZINES!
G-GOTTA PUT IT BACK.
...
BUT I AM PRETTY FAR OUT.
NO ONE KNOWS ME HERE!
PLUS, I'M INVISIBLE!
WHAT COULD BE WRONG WITH TAK-ING ONE LITTLE PEEK?
FLASH
Shiraishi's eyes grow wide!
I'M GOING IN!
GRIP
...

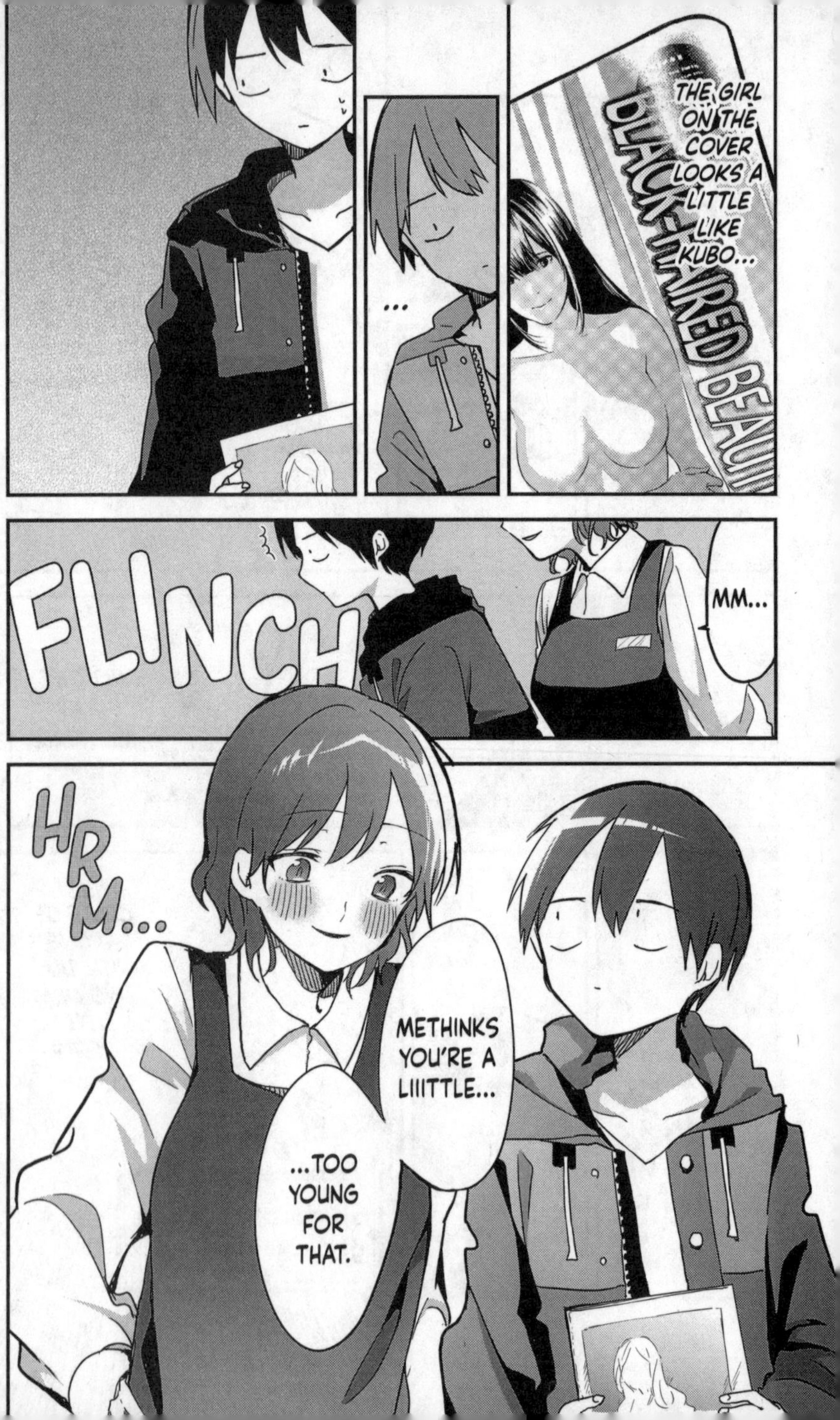
THE GIRL ON THE COVER LOOKS A LITTLE LIKE KUBO...
BLACK-HAIRED BEAUT
...
MM...
FLINCH
HRM...
METHINKS YOU'RE A LIIITTLE...
...TOO YOUNG FOR THAT.

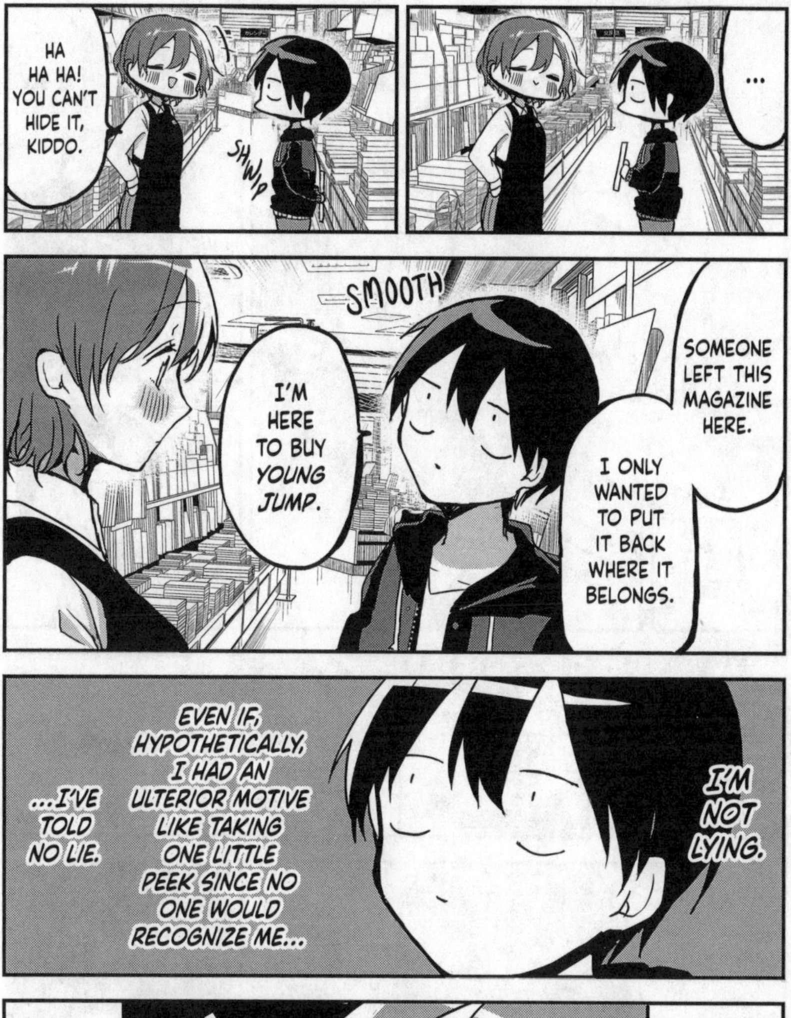
...
HA HA HA! YOU CAN'T HIDE IT, KIDDO.
SHWIP
SOMEONE LEFT THIS MAGAZINE HERE.
I ONLY WANTED TO PUT IT BACK WHERE IT BELONGS.
SMOOTH
I'M HERE TO BUY YOUNG JUMP.
I'M NOT LYING.
EVEN IF, HYPOTHETICALLY, I HAD AN ULTERIOR MOTIVE LIKE TAKING ONE LITTLE PEEK SINCE NO ONE WOULD RECOGNIZE ME...
...I'VE TOLD NO LIE.
BY THE WAY, BENEATH THE POKER FACE...
B-BMP B-BMP B-BMP B-BMP B-BMP
...MY HEART'S RACING A MILE A MINUTE.

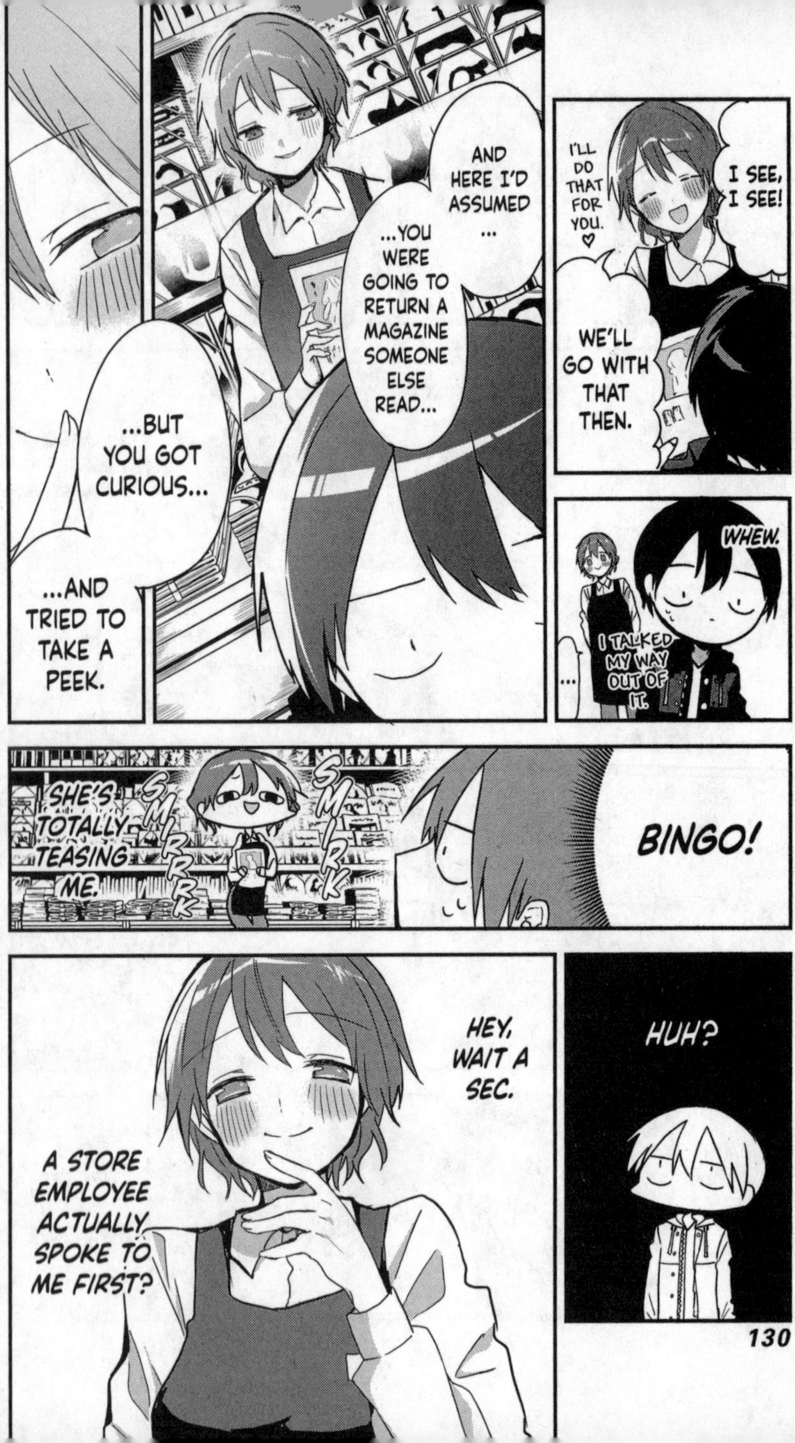
I SEE, I SEE!
I'LL DO THAT FOR YOU. ♡
WE'LL GO WITH THAT THEN.
WHEW.
I TALKED MY WAY OUT OF IT.
...
AND HERE I'D ASSUMED...
...YOU WERE GOING TO RETURN A MAGAZINE SOMEONE ELSE READ...
...BUT YOU GOT CURIOUS...
...AND TRIED TO TAKE A PEEK.
BINGO!
SMIRK
SMIRRRK
SHE'S TOTALLY TEASING ME.
HUH?
HEY, WAIT A SEC.
A STORE EMPLOYEE ACTUALLY SPOKE TO ME FIRST?

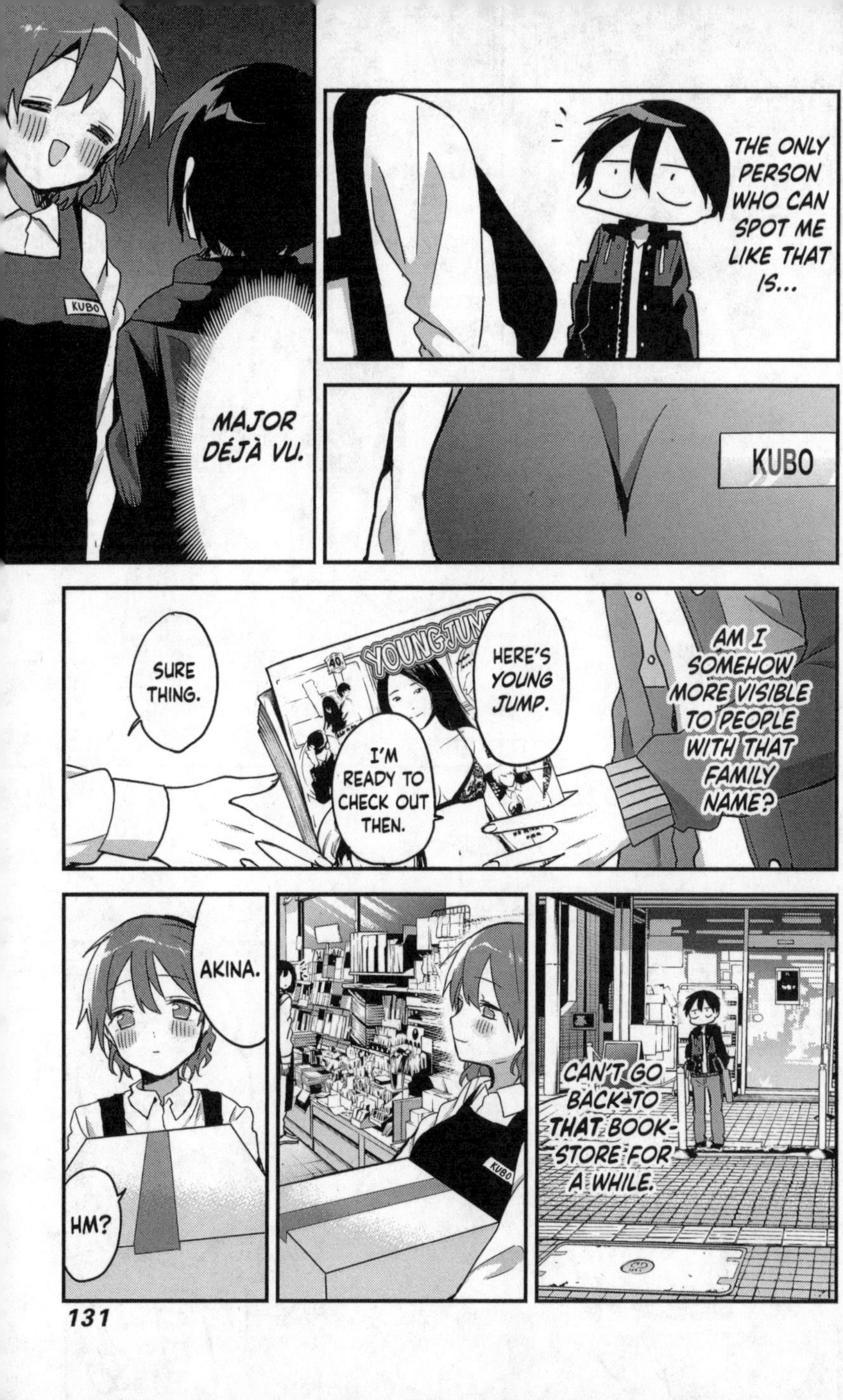

THE ONLY PERSON WHO CAN SPOT ME LIKE THAT IS...
KUBO
MAJOR DÉJÀ VU.
KUBO
AM I SOMEHOW MORE VISIBLE TO PEOPLE WITH THAT FAMILY NAME?
HERE'S YOUNG JUMP.
I'M READY TO CHECK OUT THEN.
SURE THING.
CAN'T GO BACK TO THAT BOOK-STORE FOR A WHILE.
KUBO
AKINA.
HM?

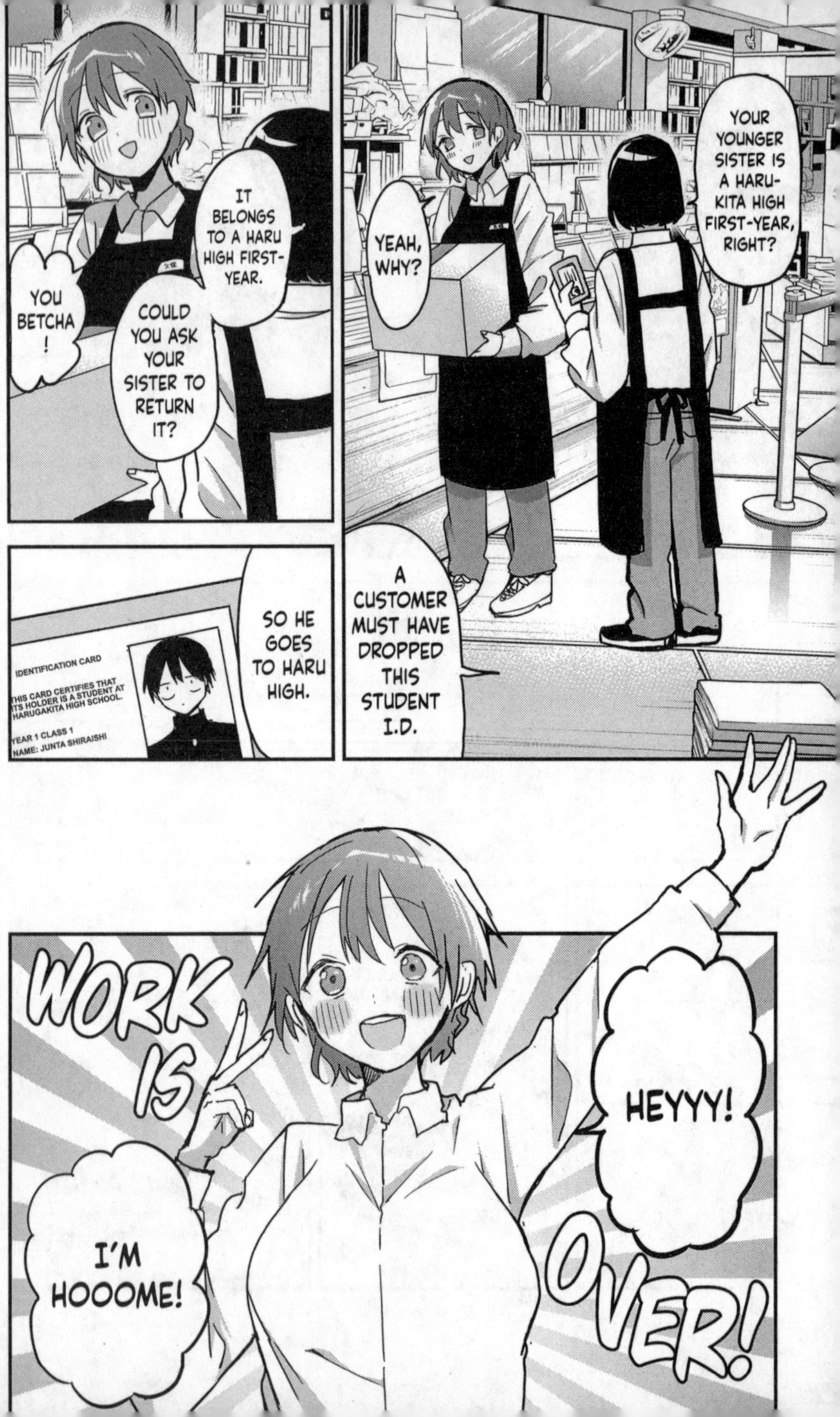
YOUR YOUNGER SISTER IS A HARU-KITA HIGH FIRST-YEAR, RIGHT?
YEAH, WHY?
A CUSTOMER MUST HAVE DROPPED THIS STUDENT I.D.
IT BELONGS TO A HARU HIGH FIRST-YEAR.
COULD YOU ASK YOUR SISTER TO RETURN IT?
YOU BETCHA!
SO HE GOES TO HARU HIGH.
IDENTIFICATION CARD
THIS CARD CERTIFIES THAT ITS HOLDER IS A STUDENT AT HARUGAKITA HIGH SCHOOL.
YEAR 1 CLASS 1
NAME: JUNTA SHIRAISHI
HEYYY!
WORK IS OVER!
I'M HOOOME!

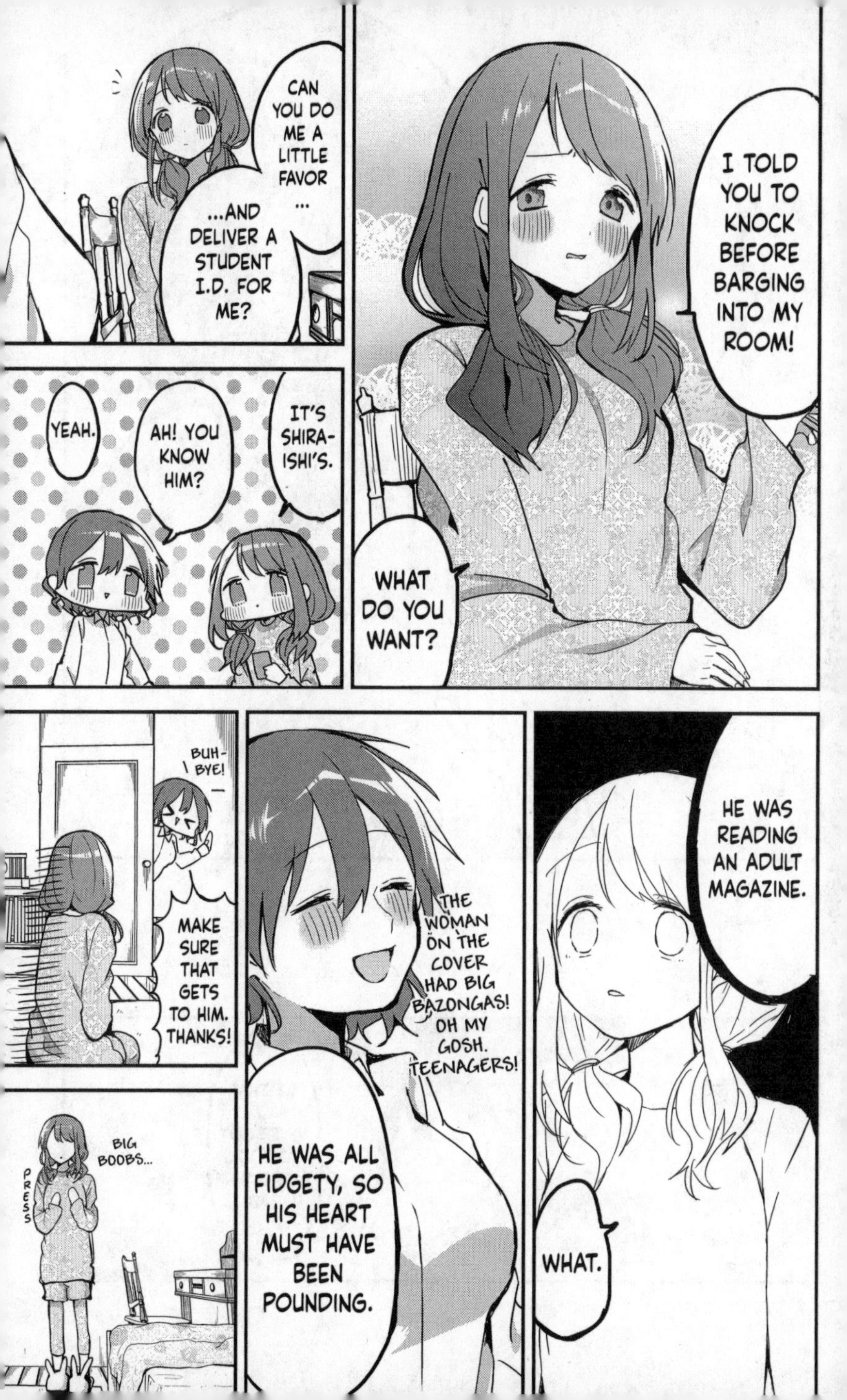

I TOLD YOU TO KNOCK BEFORE BARGING INTO MY ROOM!
WHAT DO YOU WANT?
CAN YOU DO ME A LITTLE FAVOR ...
...AND DELIVER A STUDENT I.D. FOR ME?
IT'S SHIRA-ISHI'S.
AH! YOU KNOW HIM?
YEAH.
HE WAS READING AN ADULT MAGAZINE.
WHAT.
THE WOMAN ON THE COVER HAD BIG BAZONGAS! OH MY GOSH. TEENAGERS!
HE WAS ALL FIDGETY, SO HIS HEART MUST HAVE BEEN POUNDING.
BUH-BYE!
MAKE SURE THAT GETS TO HIM. THANKS!
BIG BOOBS...
PRESS

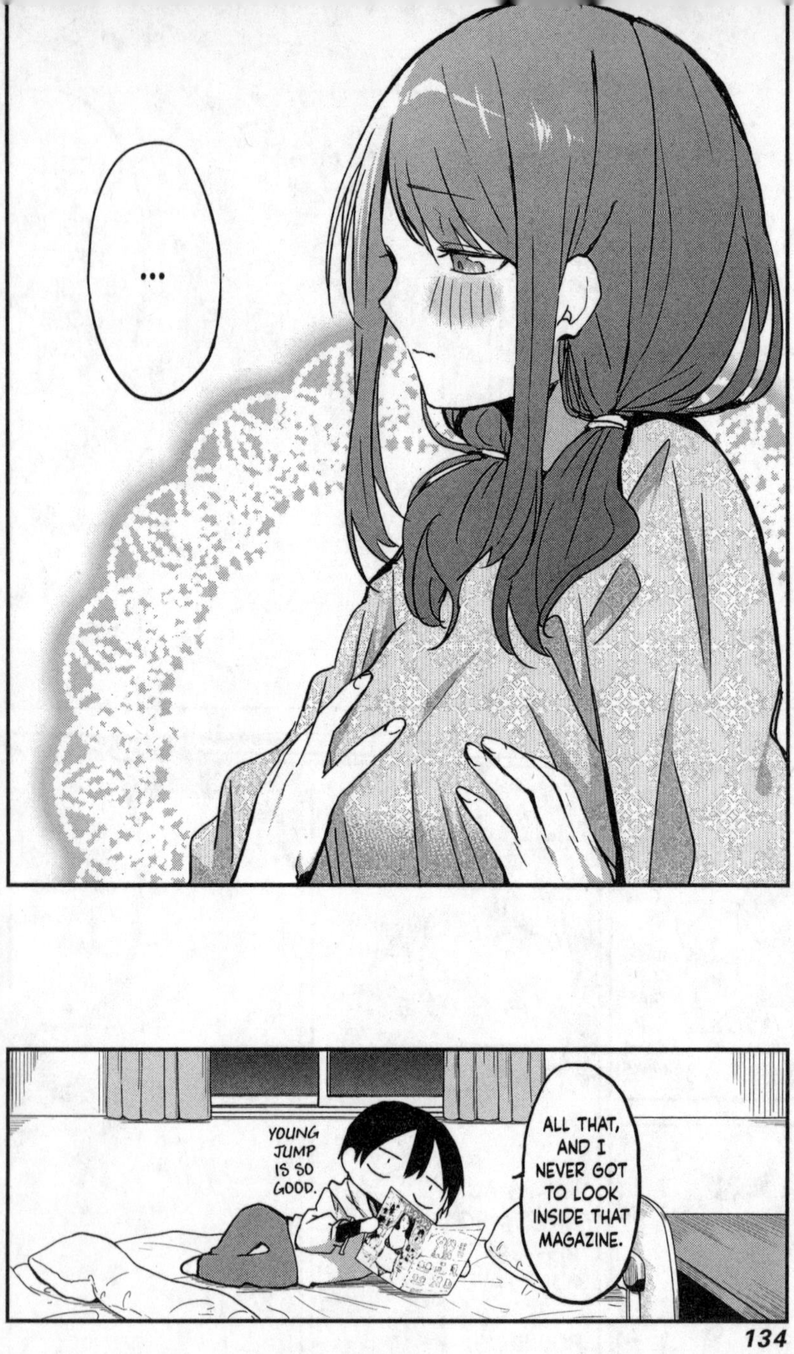
...
ALL THAT, AND I NEVER GOT TO LOOK INSIDE THAT MAGAZINE.
YOUNG JUMP IS SO GOOD.

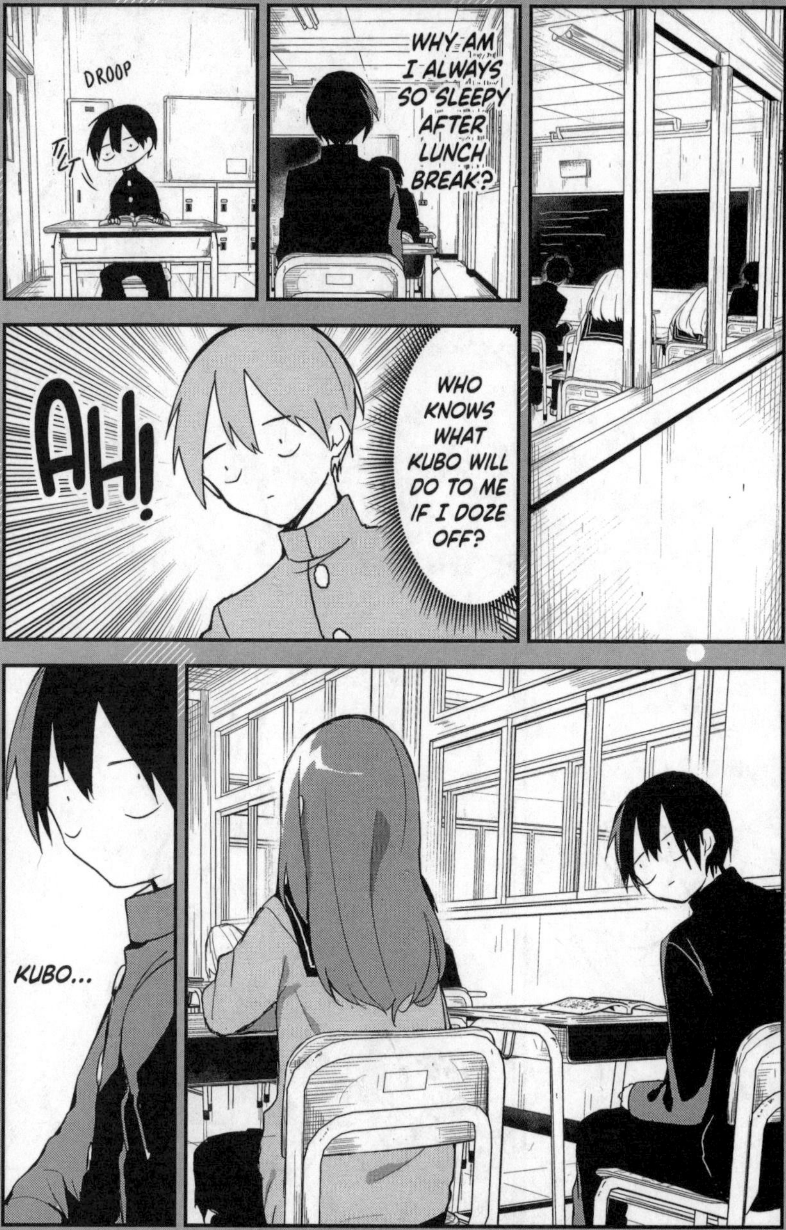
WHY AM I ALWAYS SO SLEEPY AFTER LUNCH BREAK?
DROOP
TILT
WHO KNOWS WHAT KUBO WILL DO TO ME IF I DOZE OFF?
AH!
KUBO...

extra episode DOZING OFF

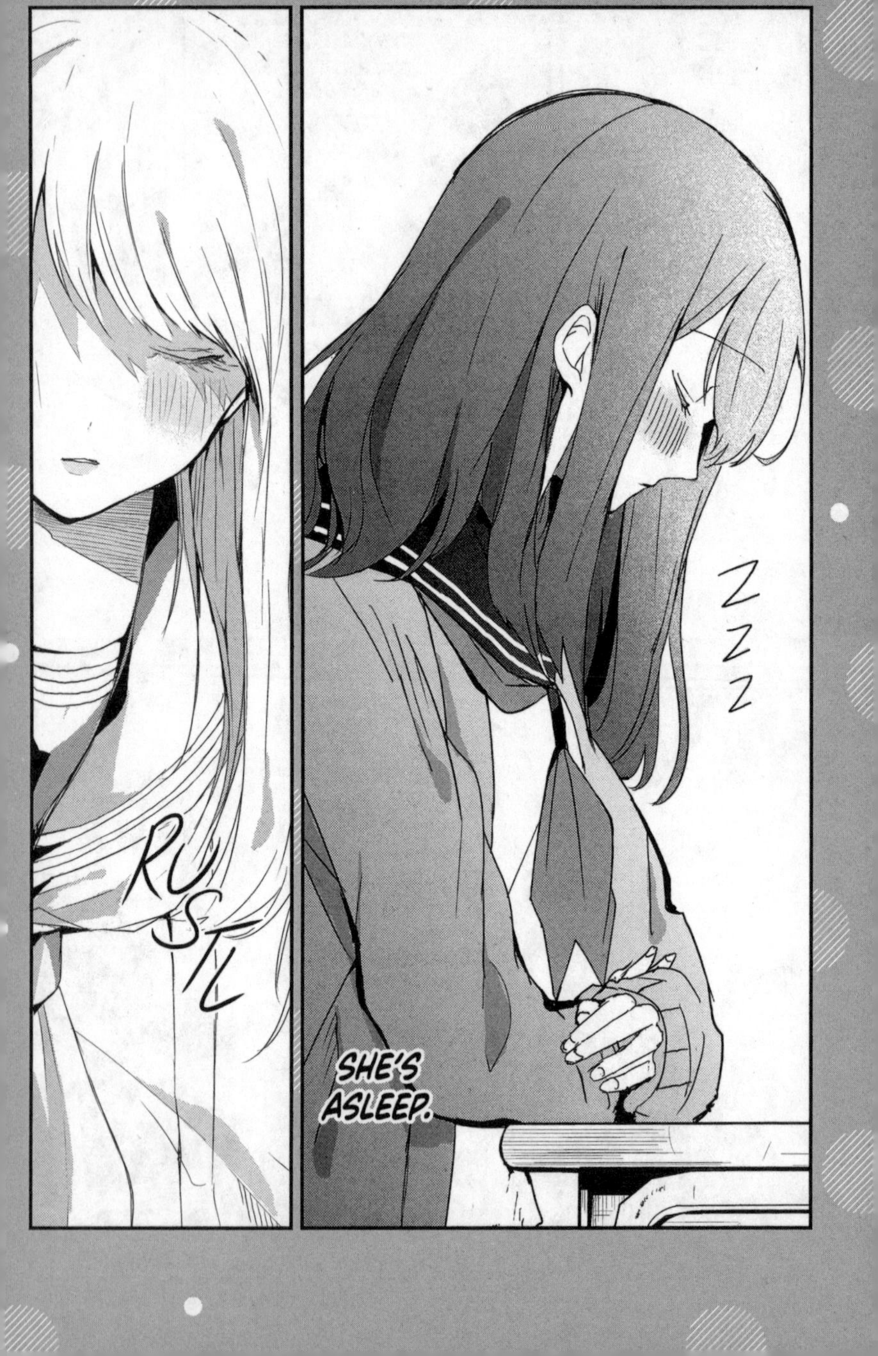
ZZZ
SHE'S ASLEEP.
RUSTL

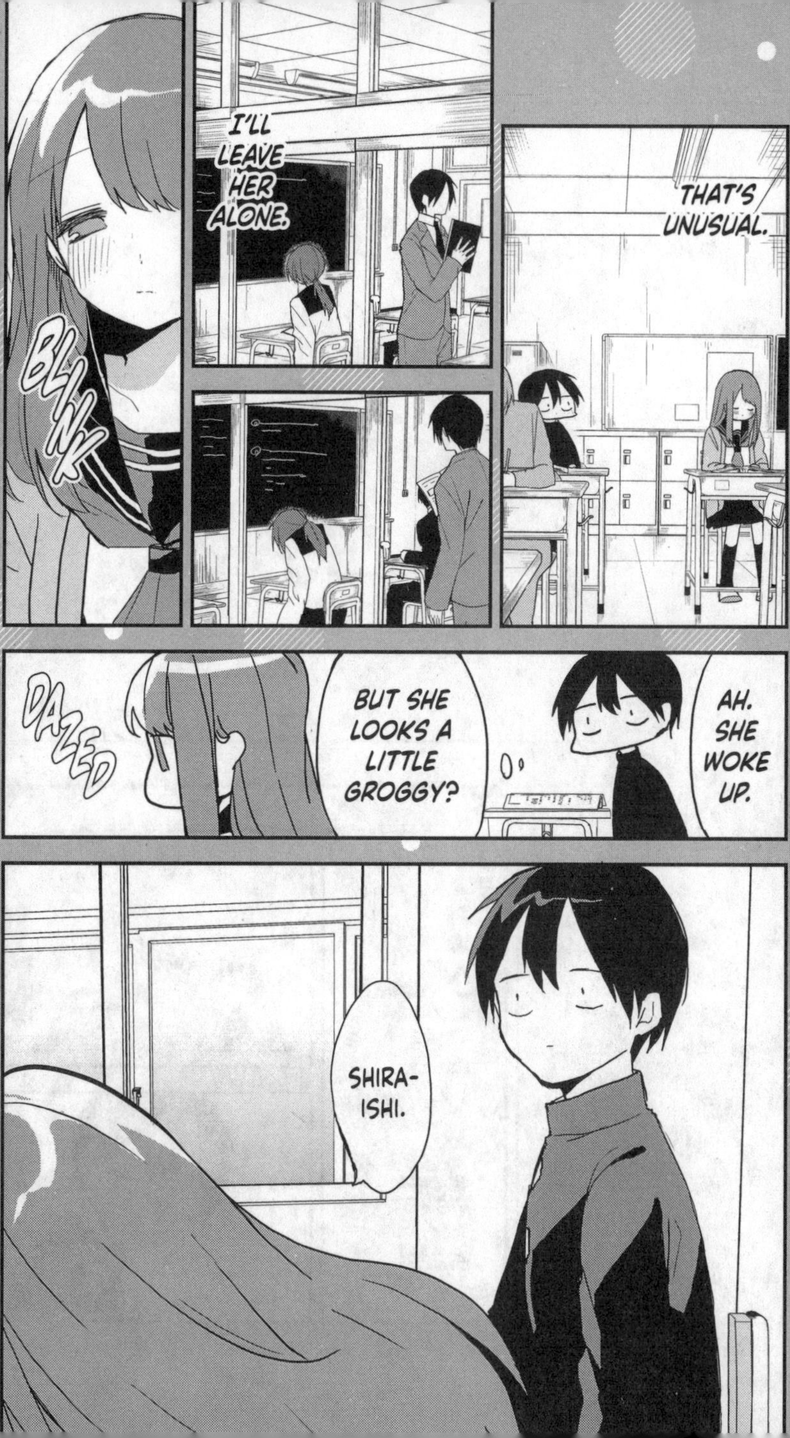
THAT'S UNUSUAL.
I'LL LEAVE HER ALONE.
BLINK
AH. SHE WOKE UP.
BUT SHE LOOKS A LITTLE GROGGY?
DAZED
SHIRA-ISHI.

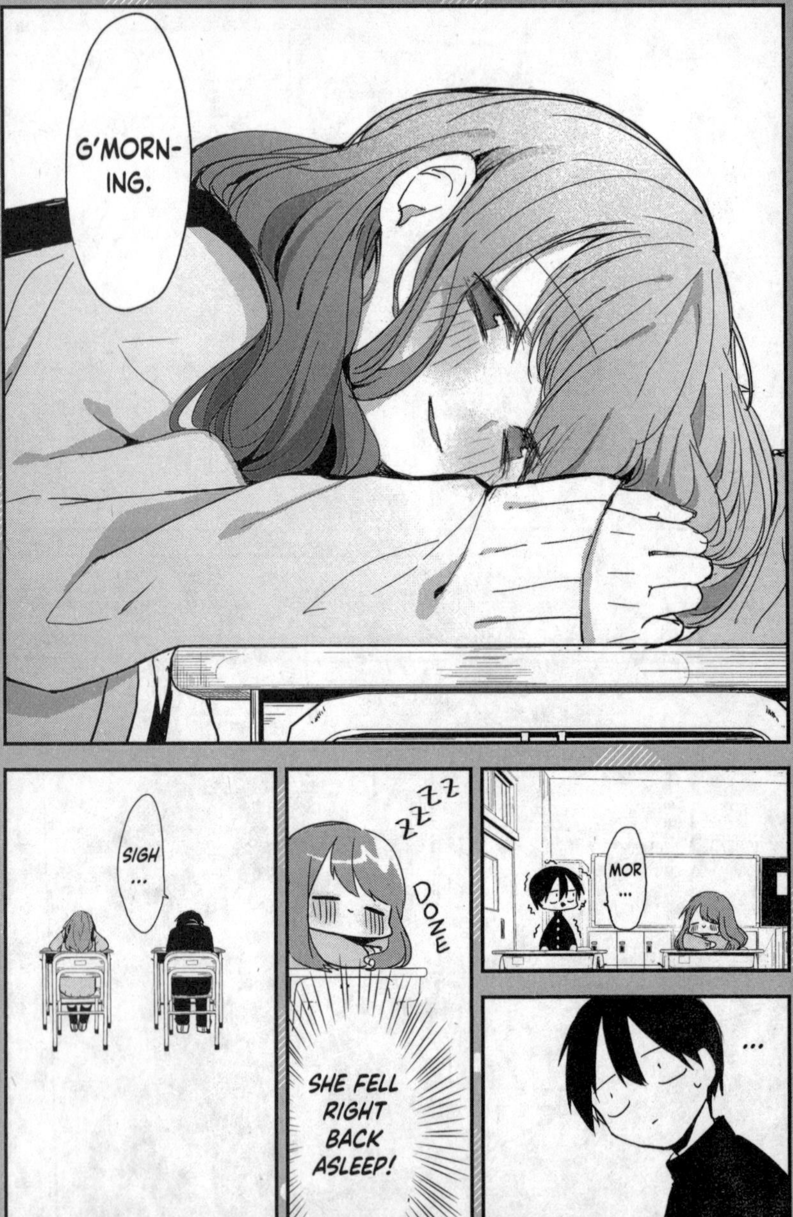
G'MORNING.
MOR...
...
ZZZZ
DOZE
SHE FELL RIGHT BACK ASLEEP!
SIGH...

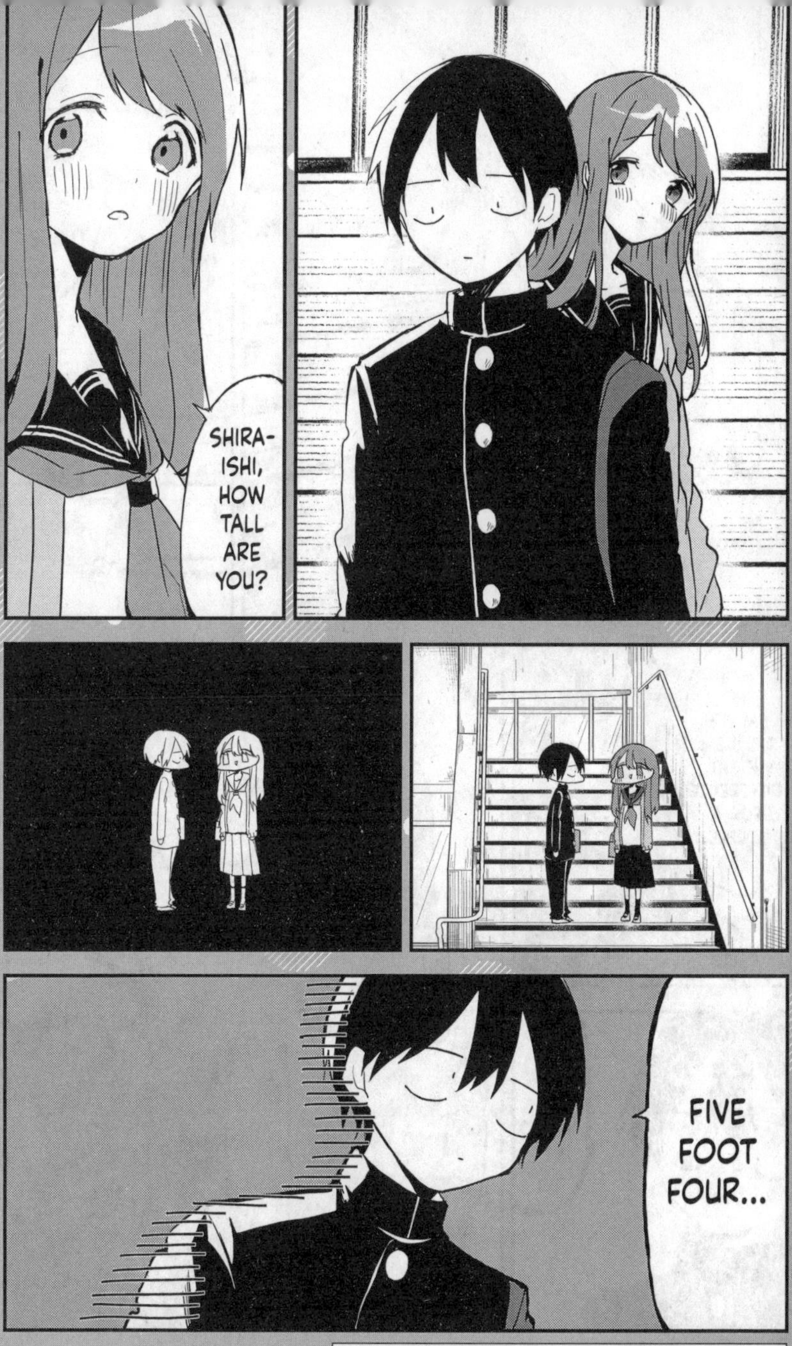
SHIRA-ISHI, HOW TALL ARE YOU?
FIVE FOOT FOUR...

extra episode HEIGHT DIFFERENCE

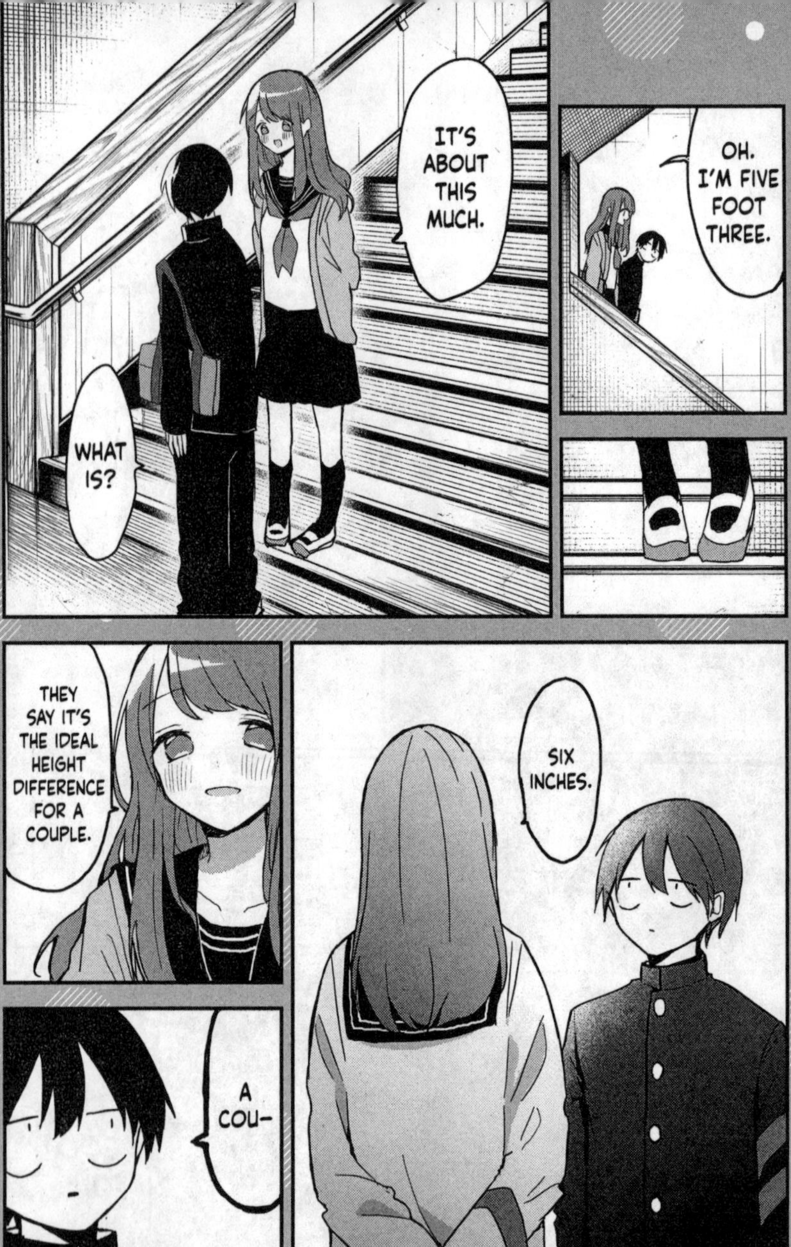
OH. I'M FIVE FOOT THREE.
IT'S ABOUT THIS MUCH.
WHAT IS?
SIX INCHES.
THEY SAY IT'S THE IDEAL HEIGHT DIFFERENCE FOR A COUPLE.
A COU-

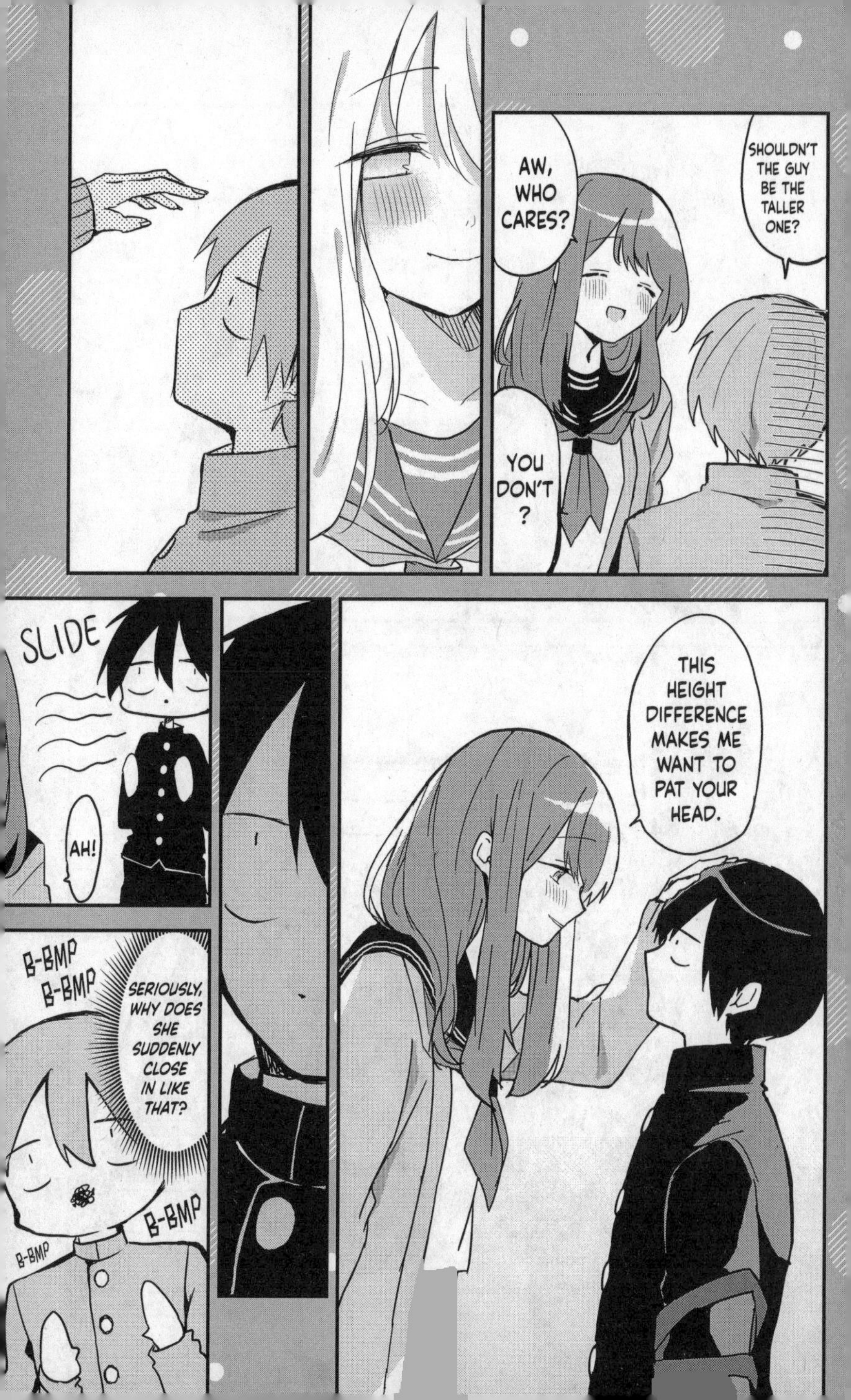
SHOULDN'T THE GUY BE THE TALLER ONE?
AW, WHO CARES?
YOU DON'T ?
THIS HEIGHT DIFFERENCE MAKES ME WANT TO PAT YOUR HEAD.
SLIDE
AH!
B-BMP
B-BMP
SERIOUSLY, WHY DOES SHE SUDDENLY CLOSE IN LIKE THAT?
B-BMP
B-BMP

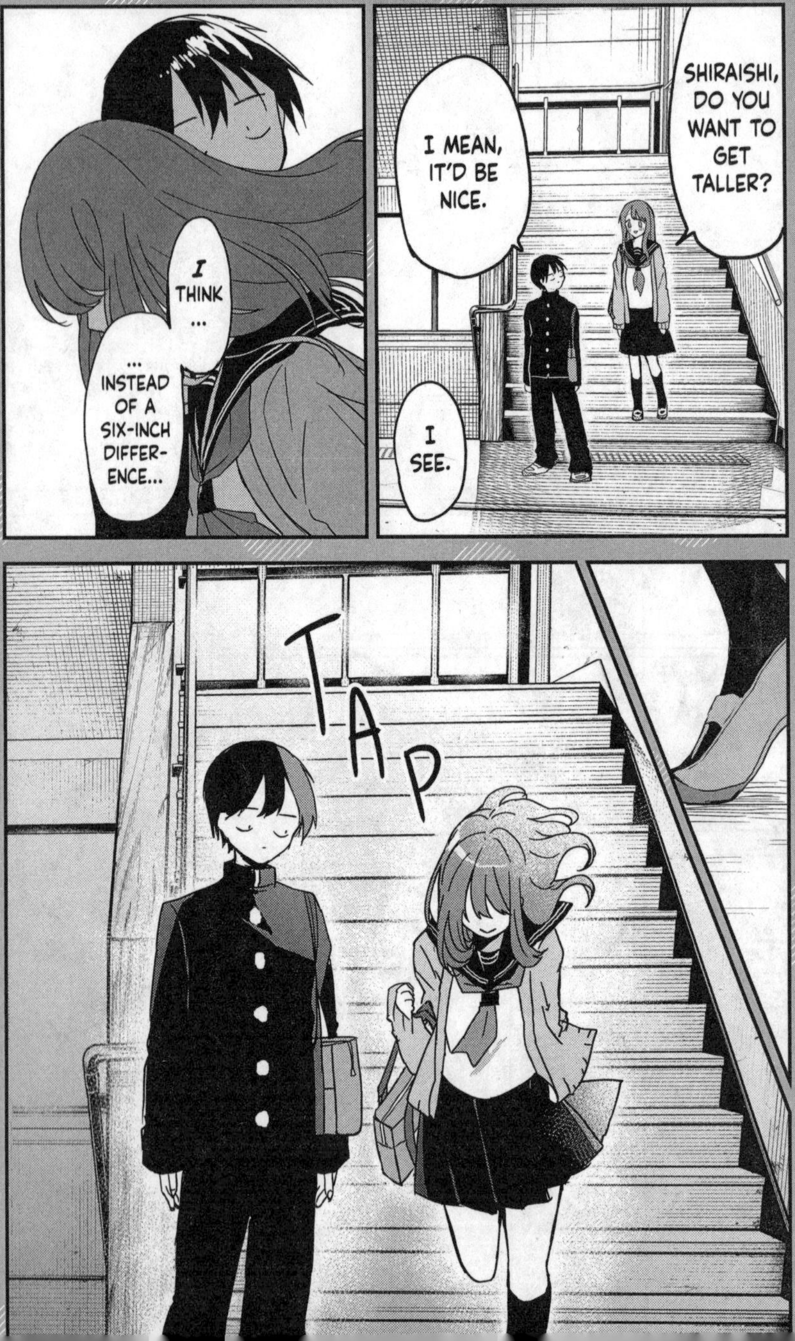
SHIRAISHI, DO YOU WANT TO GET TALLER?
I MEAN, IT'D BE NICE.
I SEE.
I THINK ...
... INSTEAD OF A SIX-INCH DIFFER-ENCE...
TAP

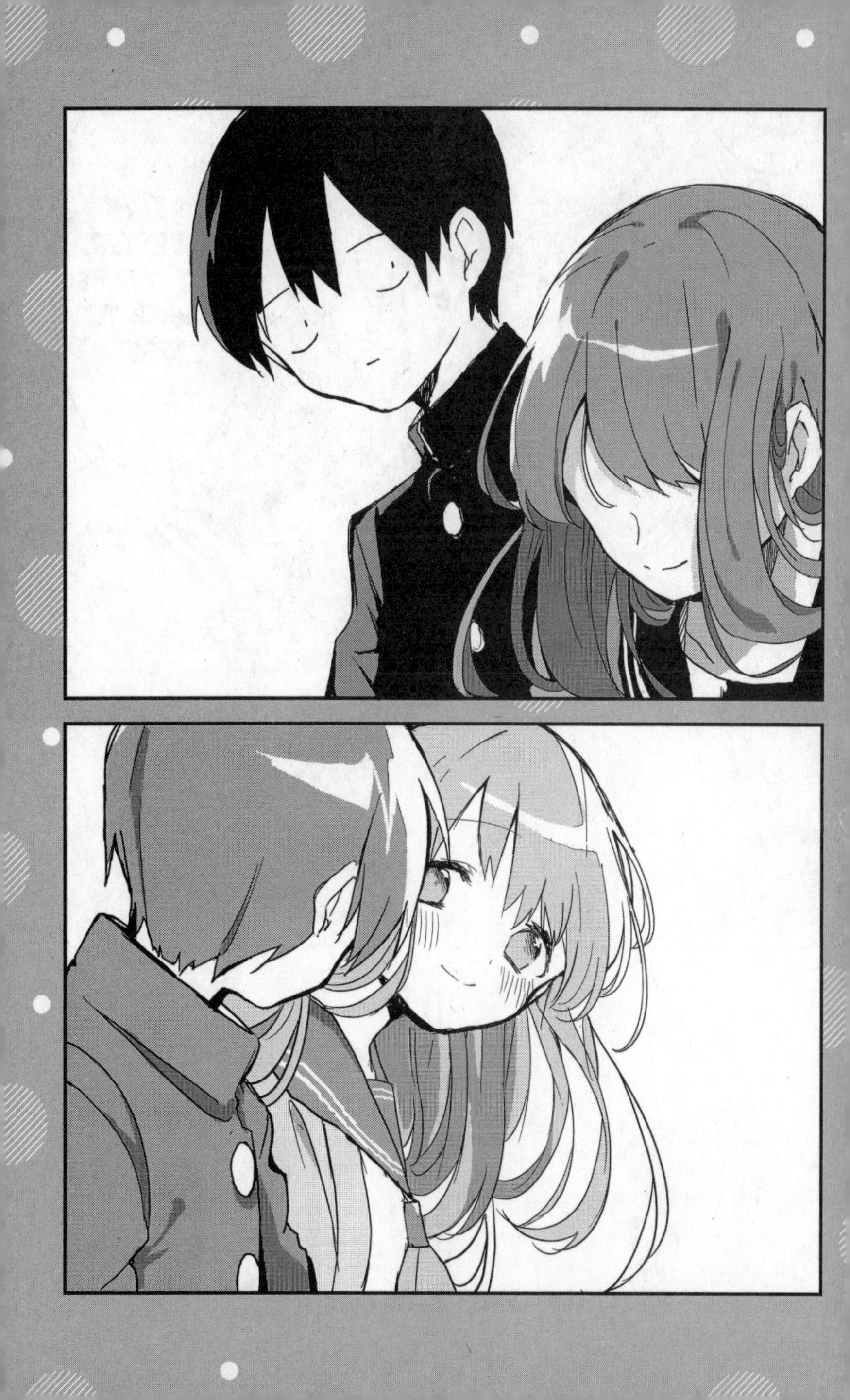

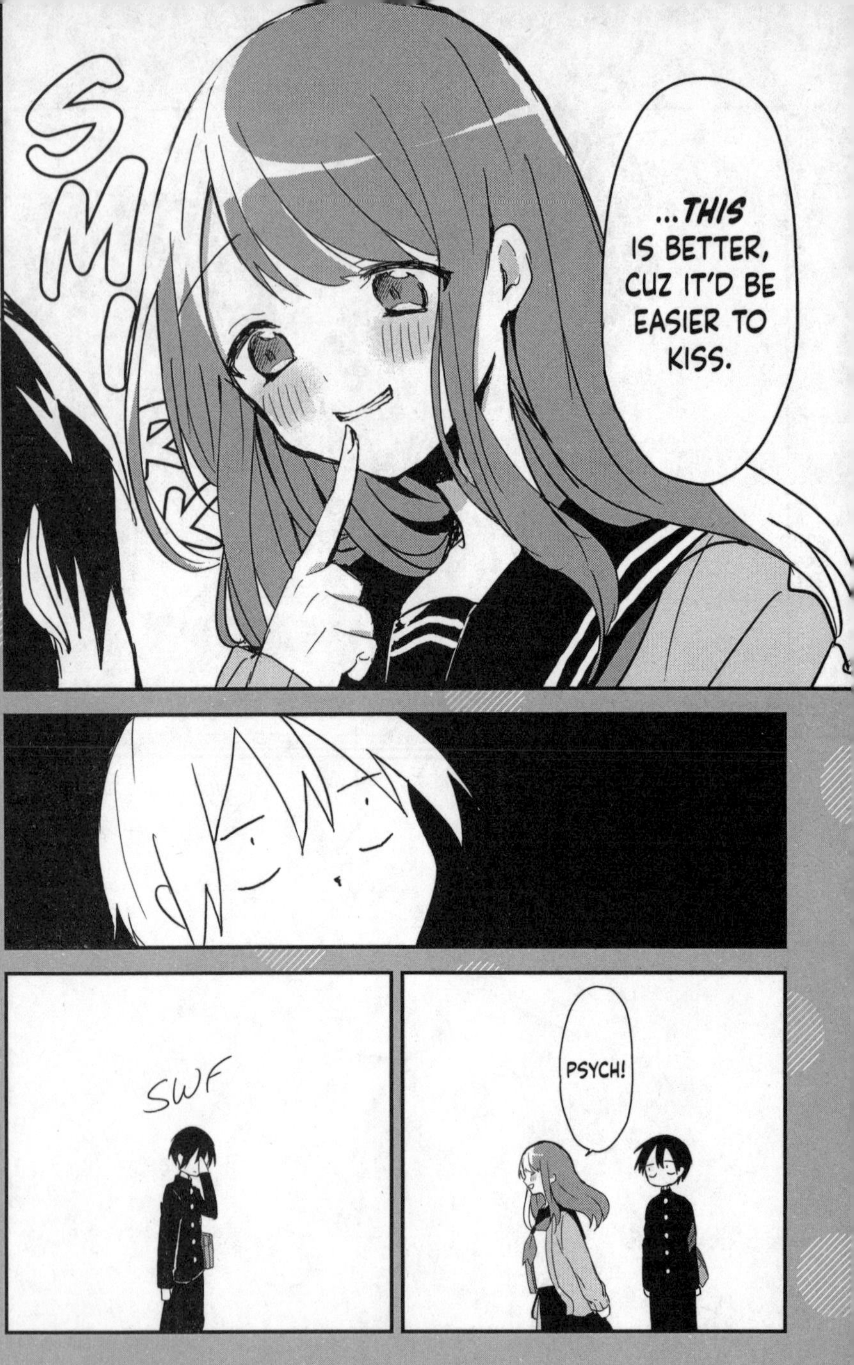
...THIS IS BETTER, CUZ IT'D BE EASIER TO KISS.
SMIRK
PSYCH!
SWF

special episode

THE NOBODY'S GIFT

This story was published in the December 2019 special issue of *Young Jump Love.*

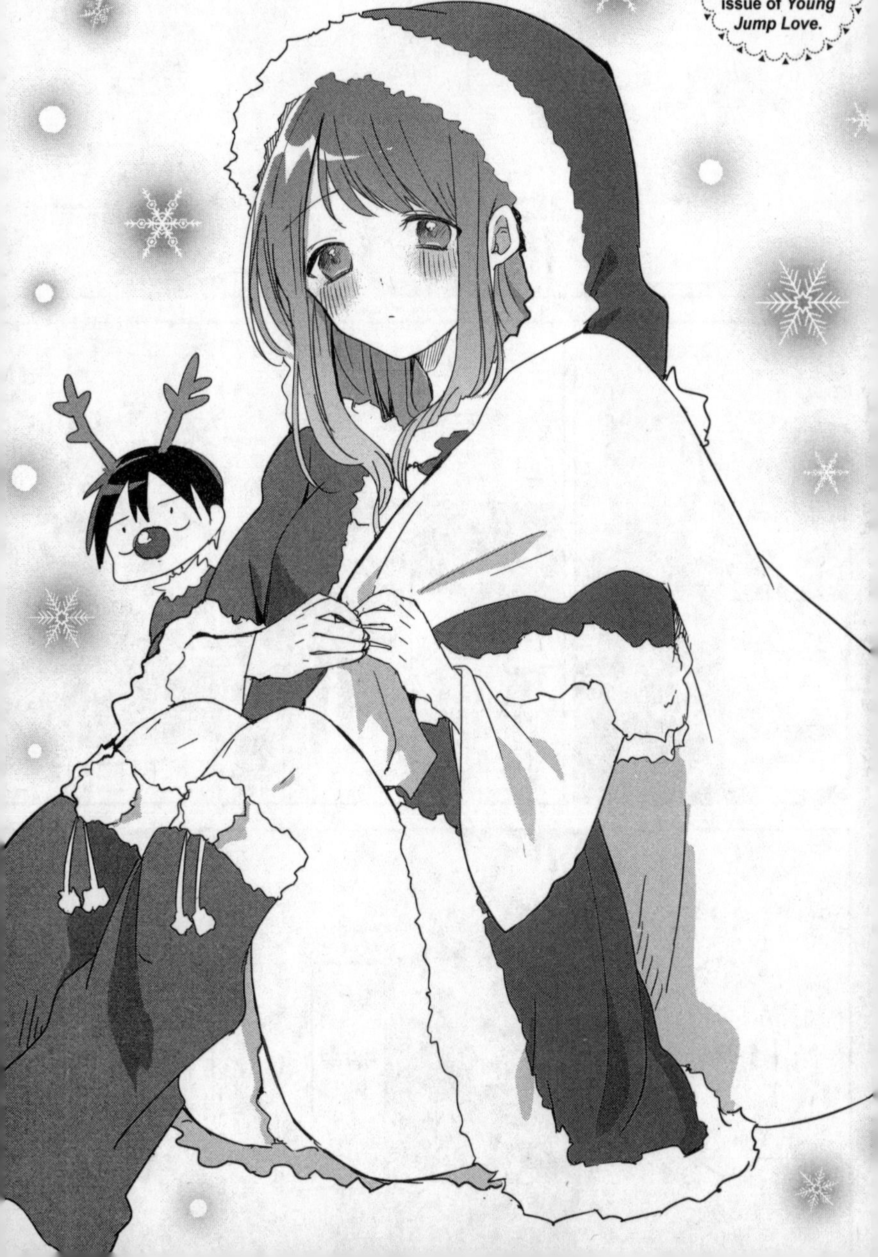

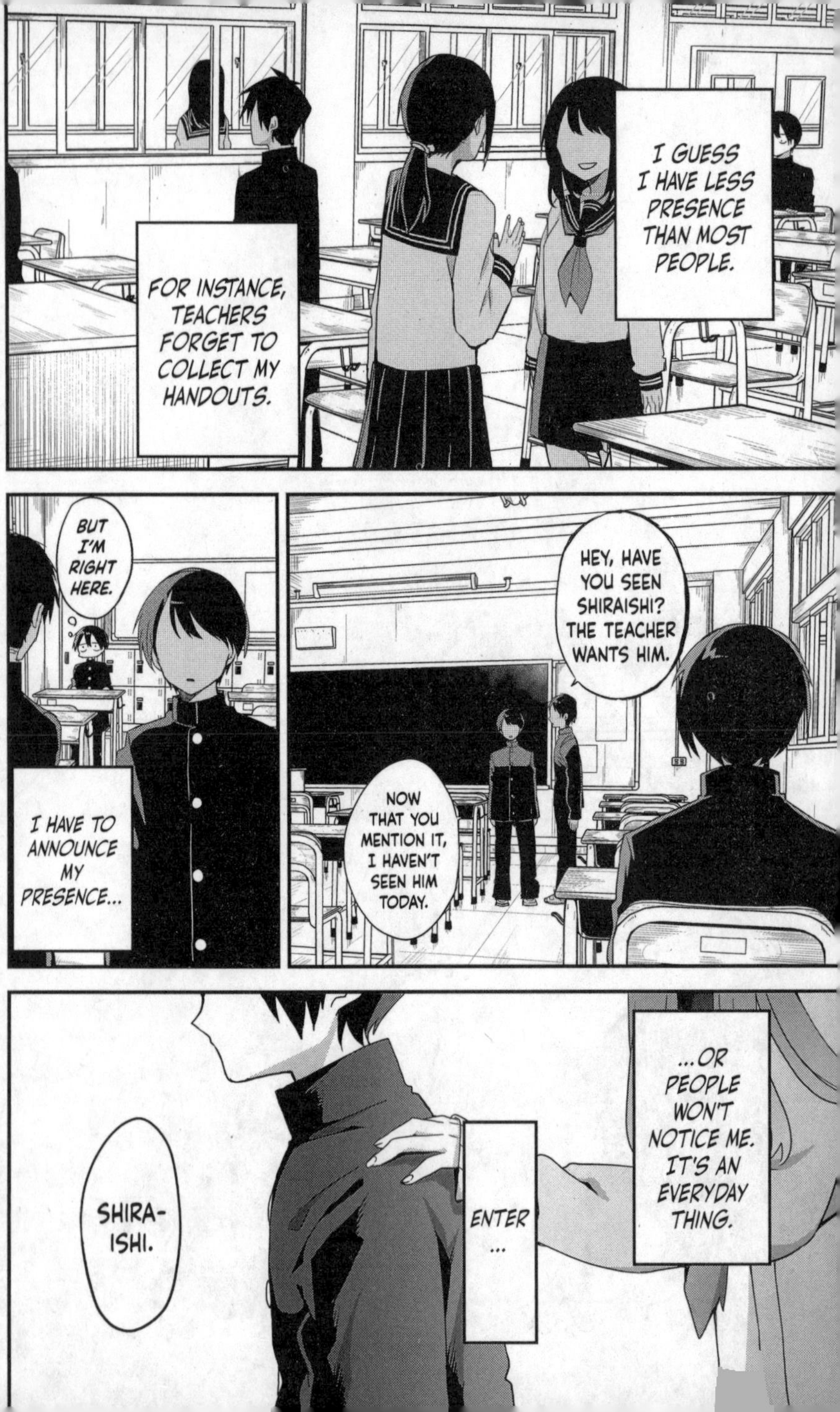
I GUESS I HAVE LESS PRESENCE THAN MOST PEOPLE.
FOR INSTANCE, TEACHERS FORGET TO COLLECT MY HANDOUTS.
HEY, HAVE YOU SEEN SHIRAISHI? THE TEACHER WANTS HIM.
NOW THAT YOU MENTION IT, I HAVEN'T SEEN HIM TODAY.
BUT I'M RIGHT HERE.
I HAVE TO ANNOUNCE MY PRESENCE...
...OR PEOPLE WON'T NOTICE ME. IT'S AN EVERYDAY THING.
ENTER...
SHIRA-ISHI.

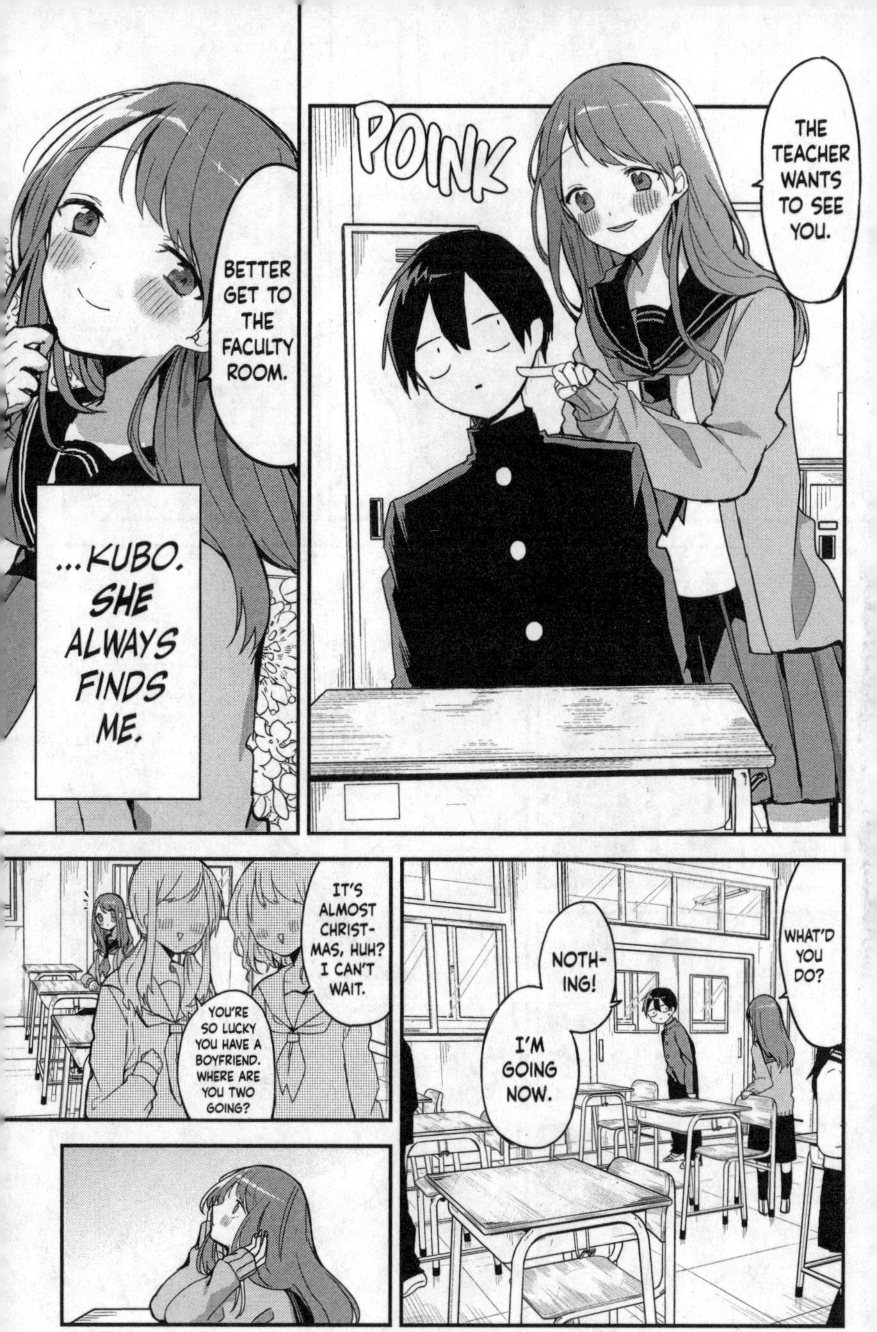
POINK
THE TEACHER WANTS TO SEE YOU.
BETTER GET TO THE FACULTY ROOM.
...KUBO. SHE ALWAYS FINDS ME.
WHAT'D YOU DO?
NOTHING!
I'M GOING NOW.
IT'S ALMOST CHRISTMAS, HUH? I CAN'T WAIT.
YOU'RE SO LUCKY YOU HAVE A BOYFRIEND. WHERE ARE YOU TWO GOING?

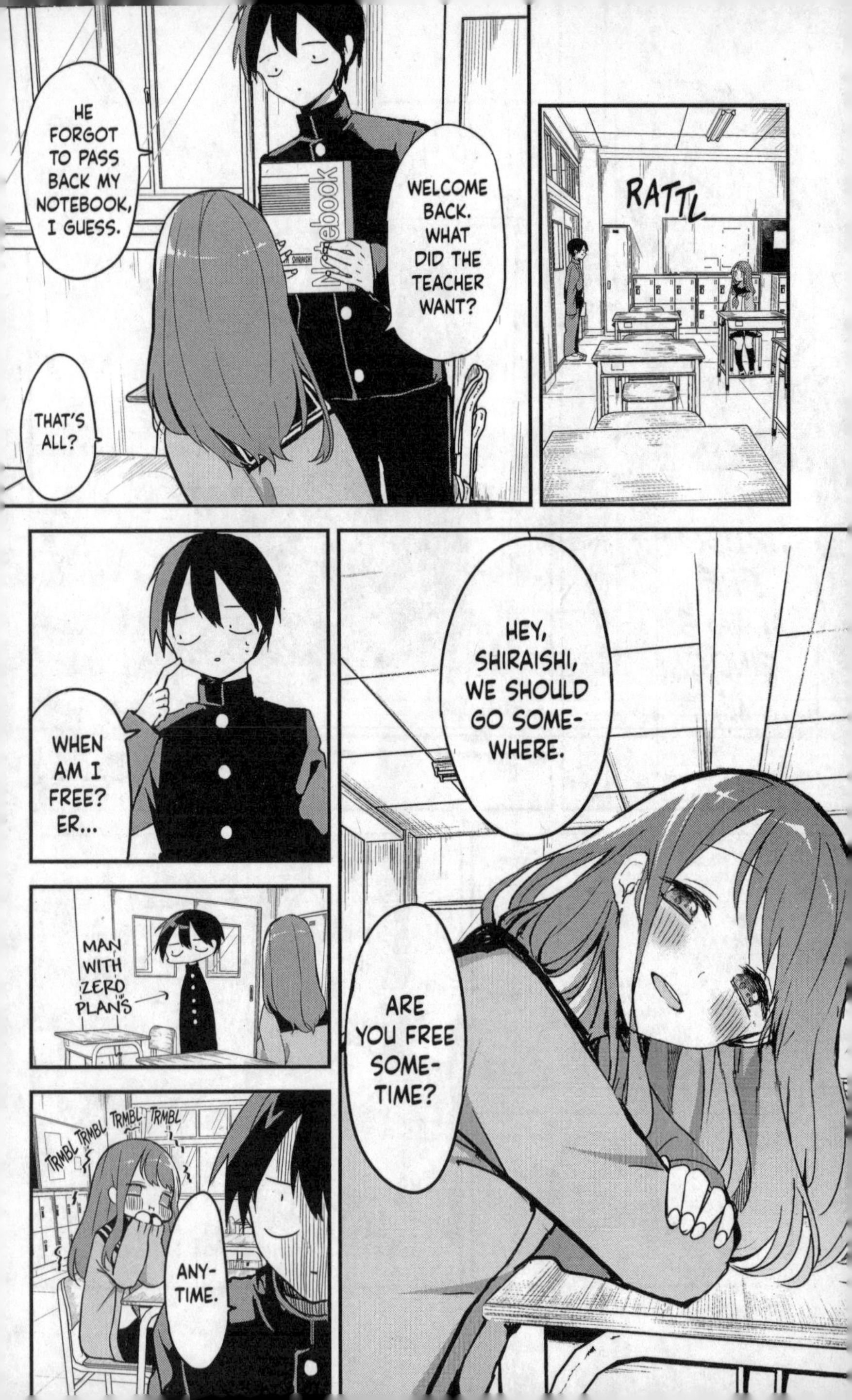
RATTL
WELCOME BACK. WHAT DID THE TEACHER WANT?
Notebook
HE FORGOT TO PASS BACK MY NOTEBOOK, I GUESS.
THAT'S ALL?
HEY, SHIRAISHI, WE SHOULD GO SOME-WHERE.
ARE YOU FREE SOME-TIME?
WHEN AM I FREE? ER...
MAN WITH ZERO PLANS
TRMBL TRMBL TRMBL TRMBL
ANY-TIME.

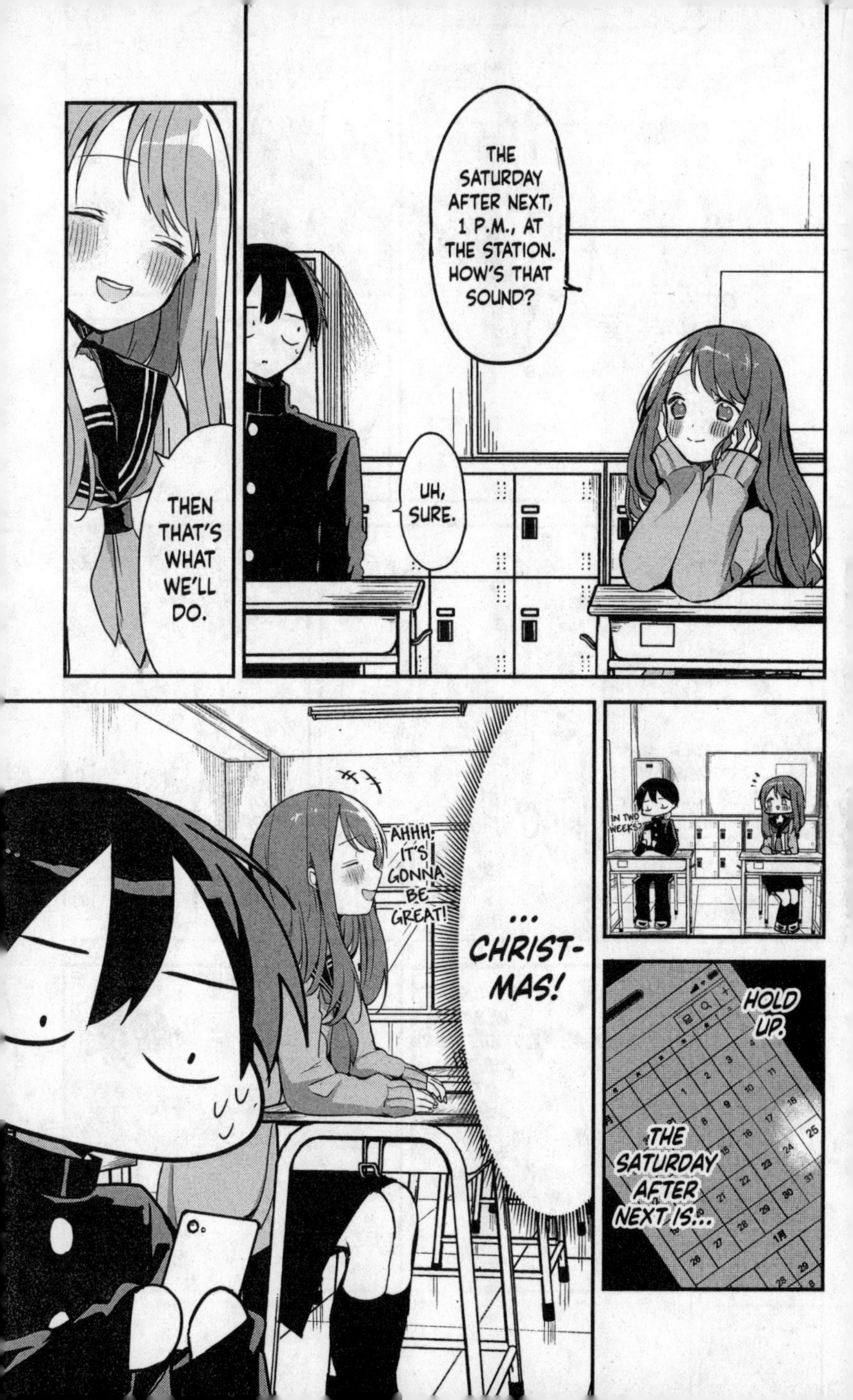
THE SATURDAY AFTER NEXT, 1 P.M., AT THE STATION. HOW'S THAT SOUND?
UH, SURE.
THEN THAT'S WHAT WE'LL DO.
IN TWO WEEKS?
HOLD UP.
THE SATURDAY AFTER NEXT IS...
AHHH, IT'S GONNA BE GREAT!
...CHRISTMAS!

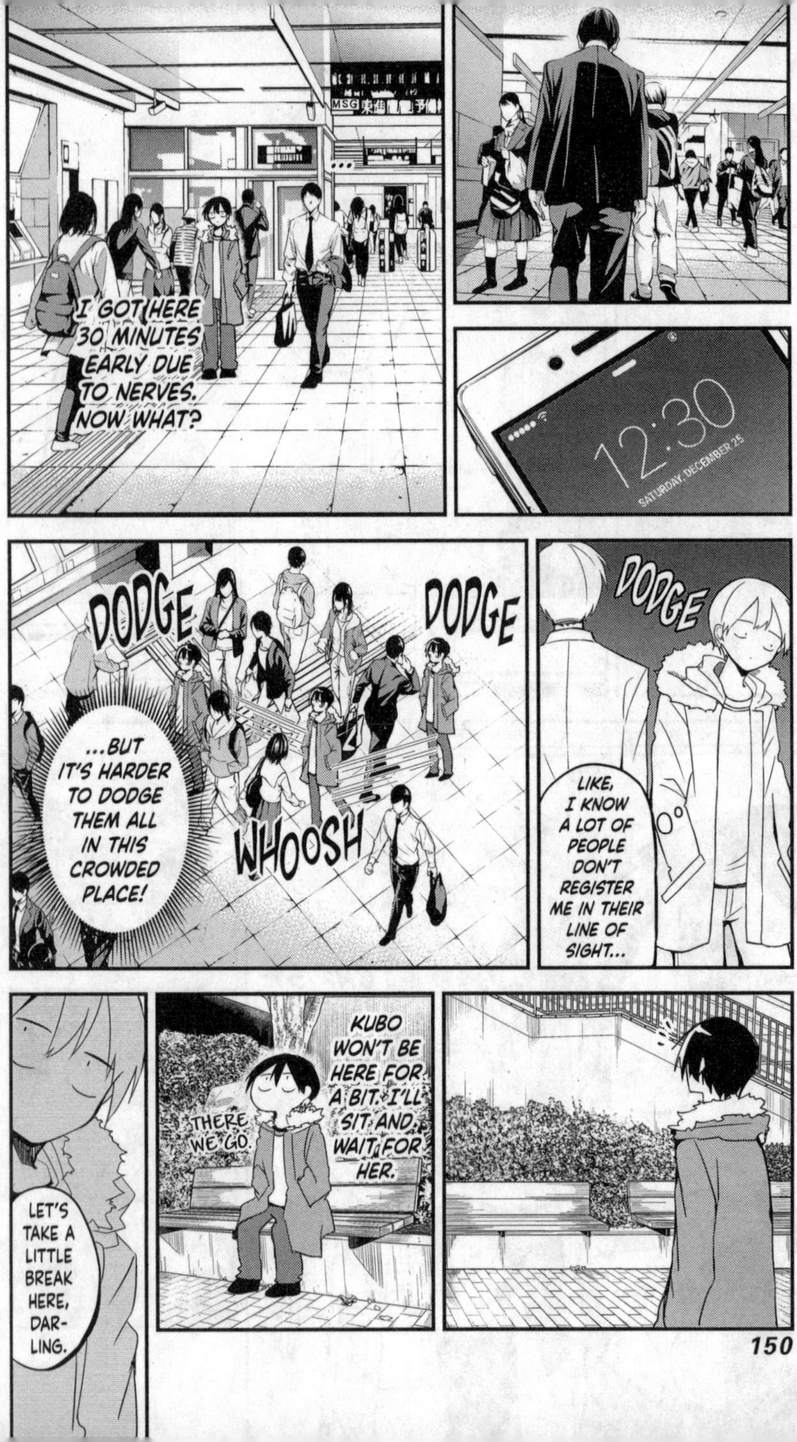
12:30
SATURDAY, DECEMBER 25
...
I GOT HERE 30 MINUTES EARLY DUE TO NERVES. NOW WHAT?
DODGE
LIKE, I KNOW A LOT OF PEOPLE DON'T REGISTER ME IN THEIR LINE OF SIGHT...
DODGE
DODGE
...BUT IT'S HARDER TO DODGE THEM ALL IN THIS CROWDED PLACE!
WHOOSH
KUBO WON'T BE HERE FOR A BIT. I'LL SIT AND WAIT FOR HER.
THERE WE GO.
LET'S TAKE A LITTLE BREAK HERE, DARLING.

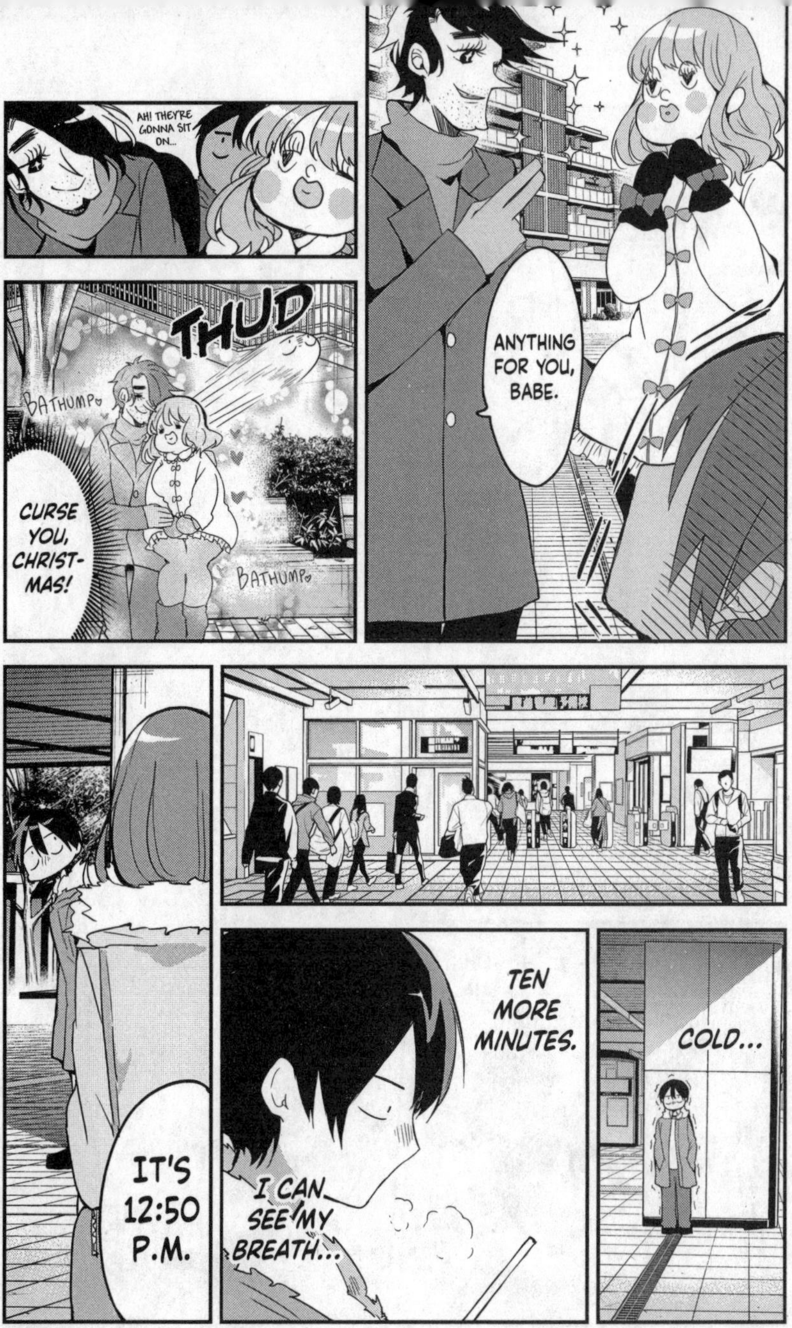
ANYTHING FOR YOU, BABE.
AH! THEY'RE GONNA SIT ON...
THUD
BATHUMP
BATHUMP
CURSE YOU, CHRIST-MAS!
COLD...
TEN MORE MINUTES.
I CAN SEE MY BREATH...
IT'S 12:50 P.M.

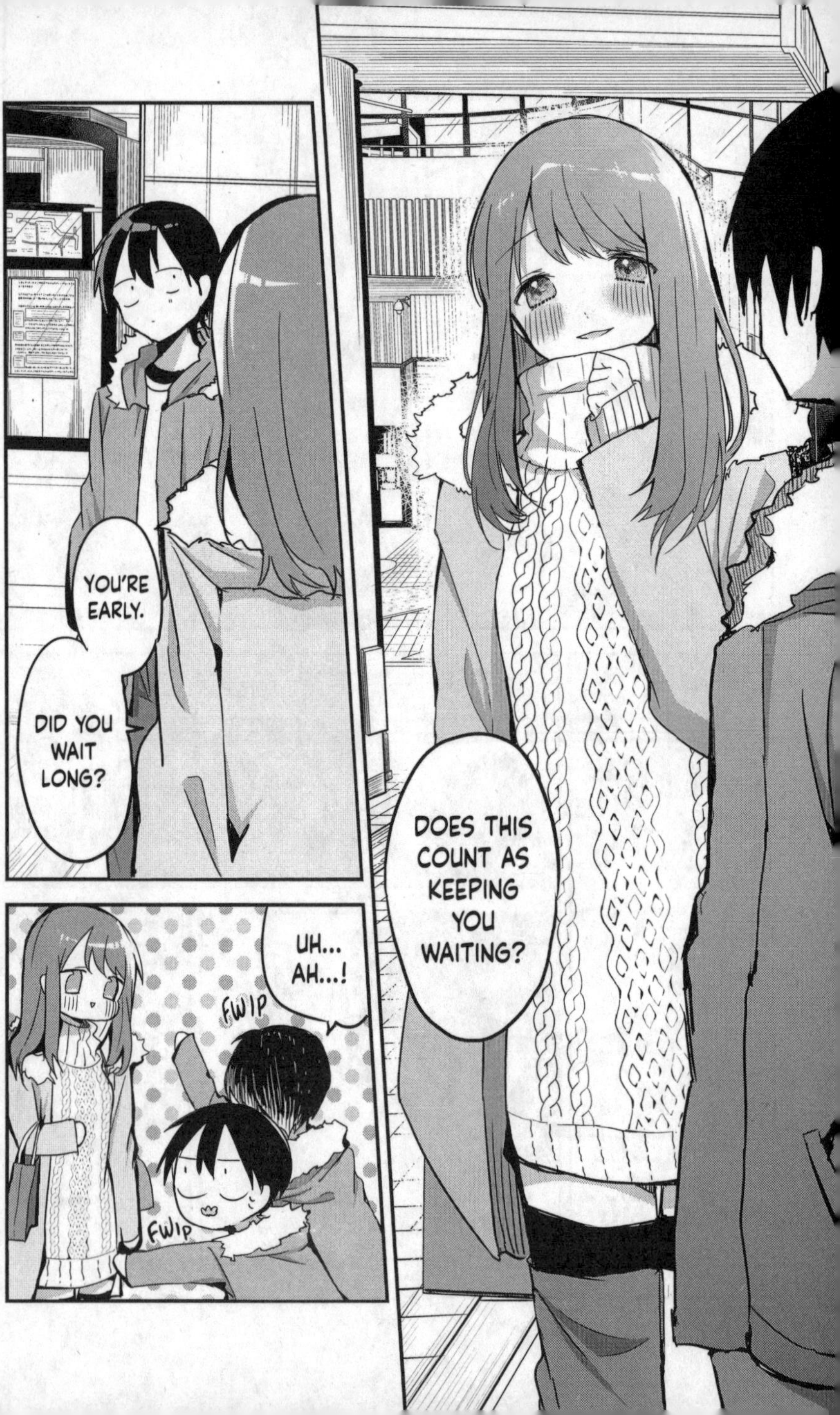
DOES THIS COUNT AS KEEPING YOU WAITING?
YOU'RE EARLY.
DID YOU WAIT LONG?
UH... AH...!
FWIP
FWIP

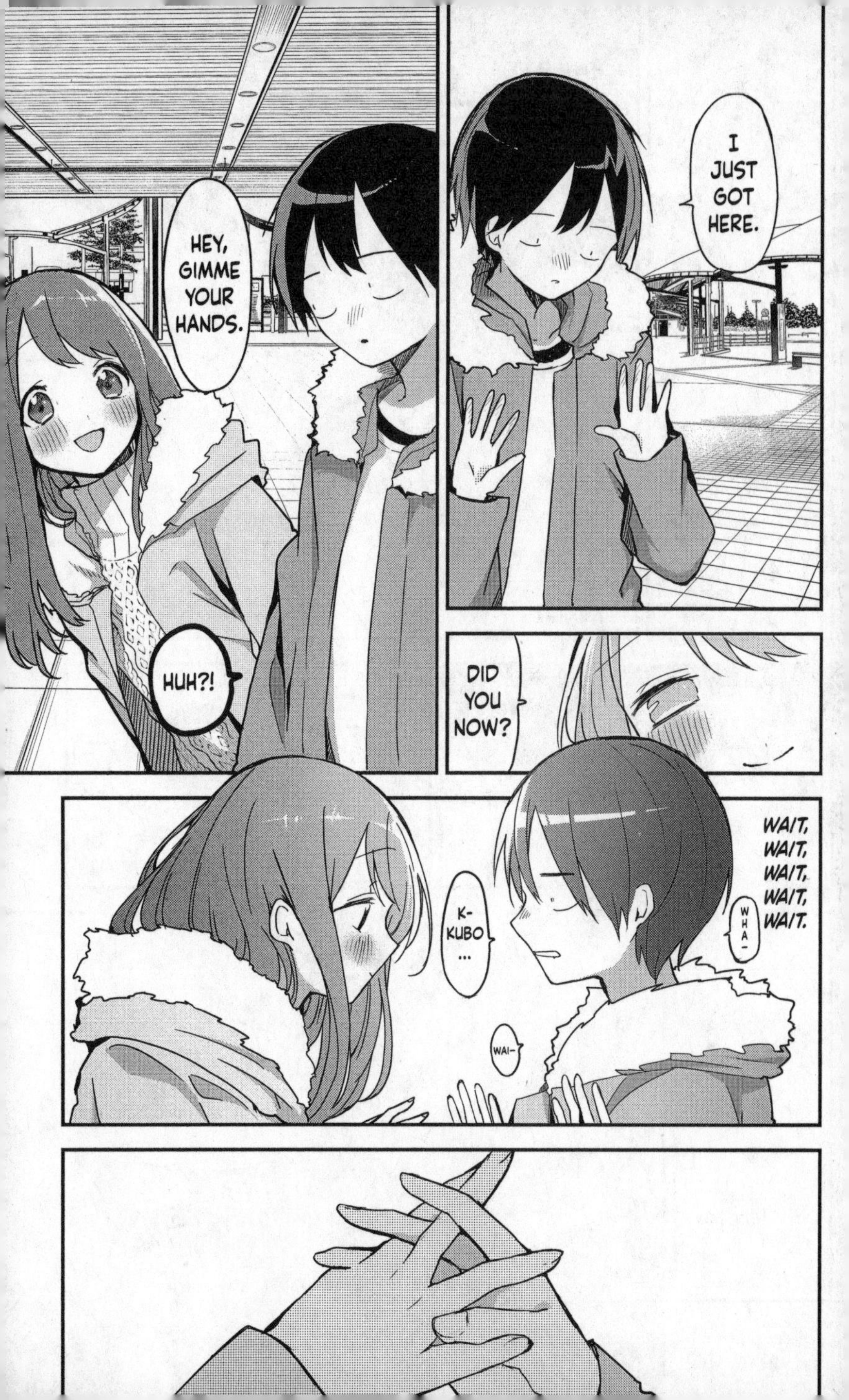
I JUST GOT HERE.
DID YOU NOW?
HEY, GIMME YOUR HANDS.
HUH?!
WAIT, WAIT, WAIT, WAIT, WAIT.
WHA—
K-KUBO...
WAI—

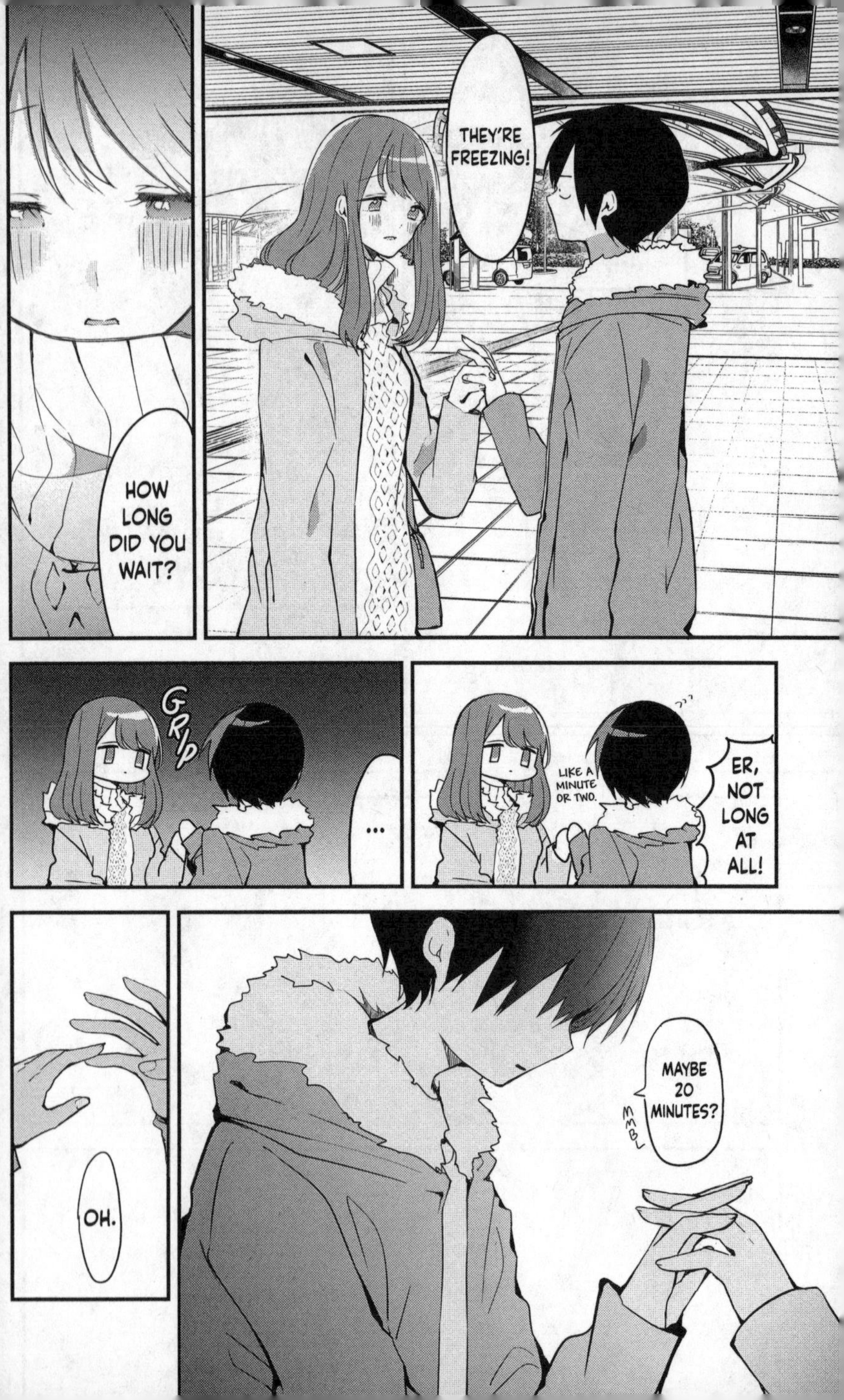
THEY'RE FREEZING!
HOW LONG DID YOU WAIT?
ER, NOT LONG AT ALL!
LIKE A MINUTE OR TWO.
GRIP
...
MAYBE 20 MINUTES?
MMBL
OH.

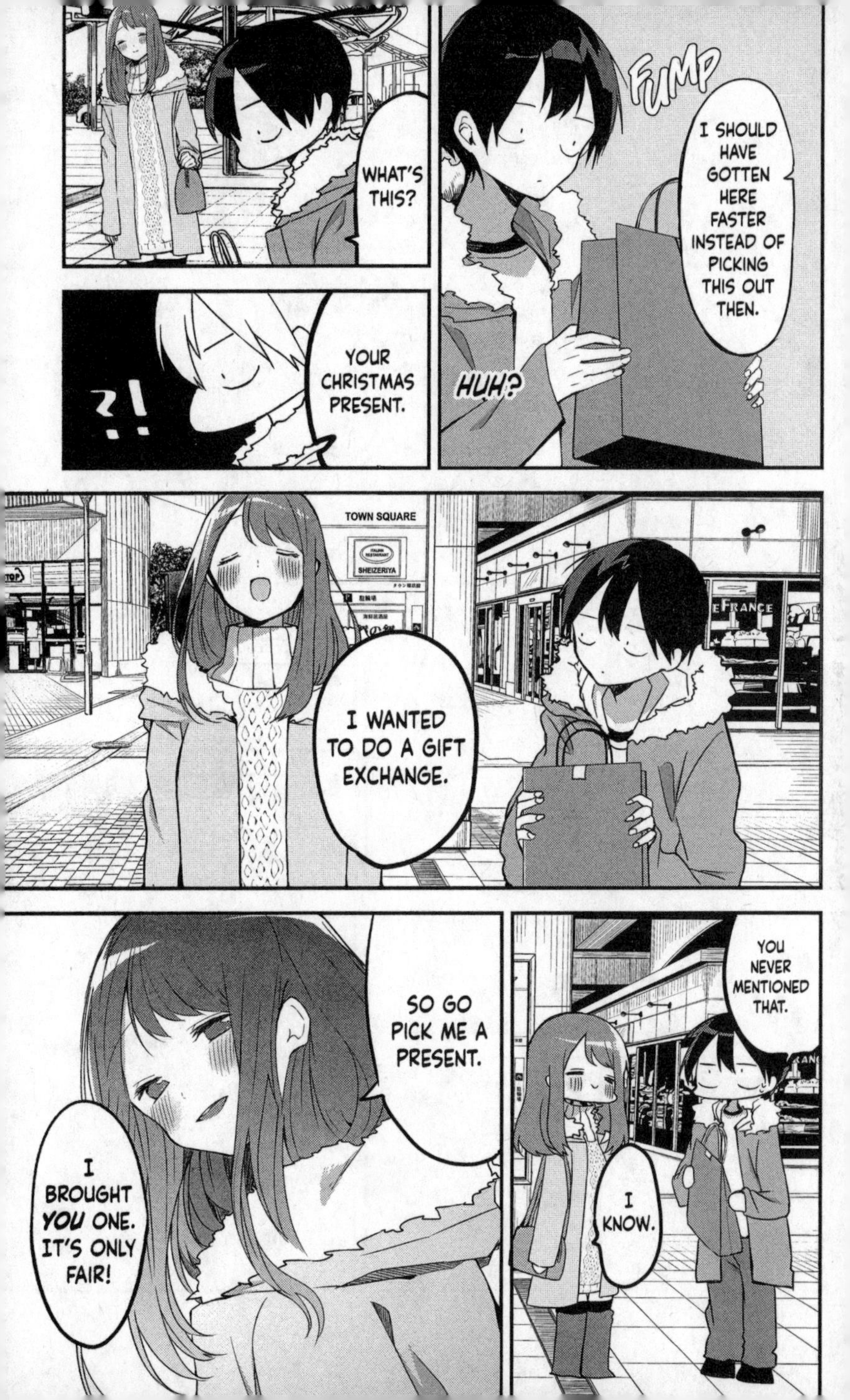
FUMP
I SHOULD HAVE GOTTEN HERE FASTER INSTEAD OF PICKING THIS OUT THEN.
HUH?
WHAT'S THIS?
YOUR CHRISTMAS PRESENT.
?!
TOWN SQUARE
SHEIZERIYA
I WANTED TO DO A GIFT EXCHANGE.
YOU NEVER MENTIONED THAT.
I KNOW.
SO GO PICK ME A PRESENT.
I BROUGHT YOU ONE. IT'S ONLY FAIR!

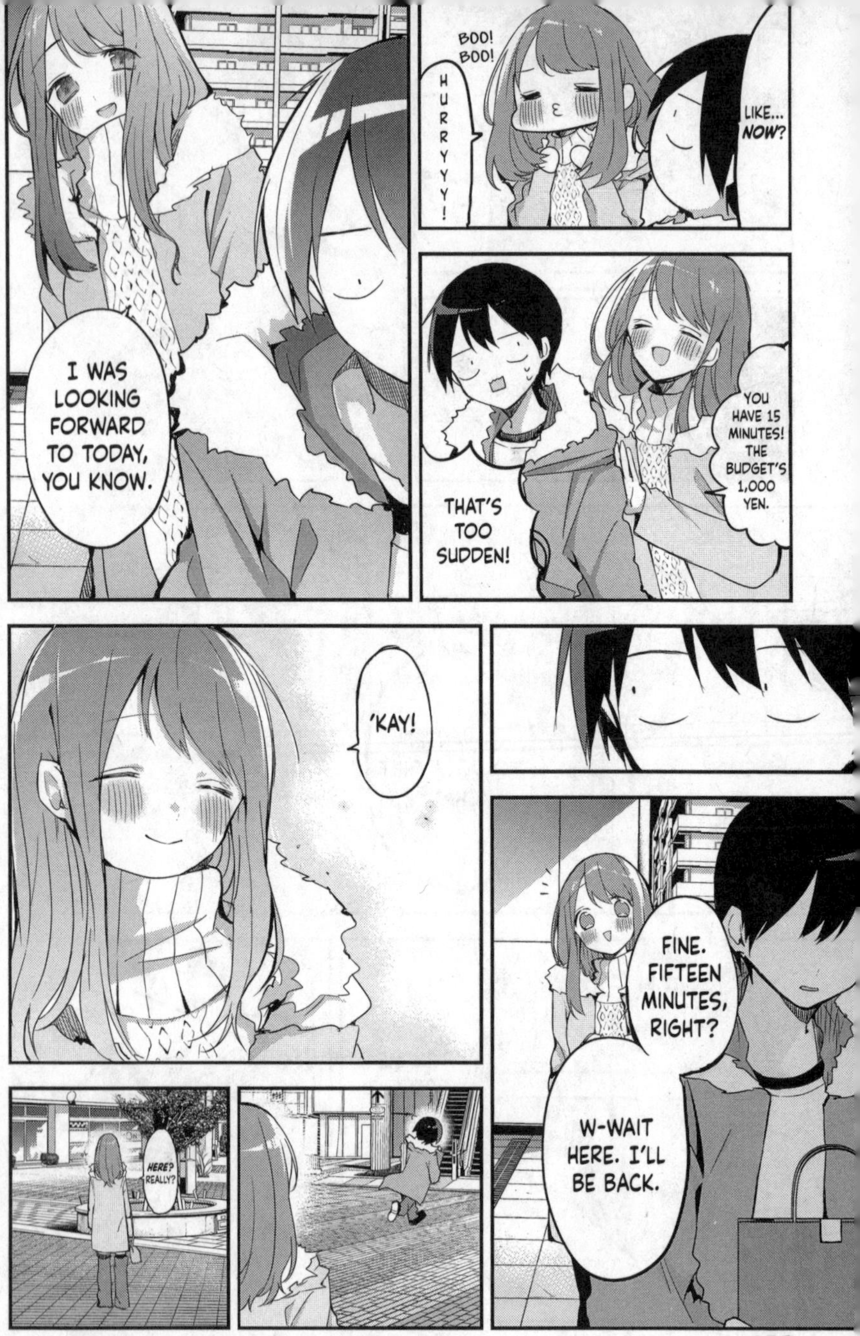
LIKE... NOW?
BOO! BOO!
HURRYYY!
YOU HAVE 15 MINUTES! THE BUDGET'S 1,000 YEN.
THAT'S TOO SUDDEN!
I WAS LOOKING FORWARD TO TODAY, YOU KNOW.
FINE. FIFTEEN MINUTES, RIGHT?
W-WAIT HERE. I'LL BE BACK.
'KAY!
HERE? REALLY?

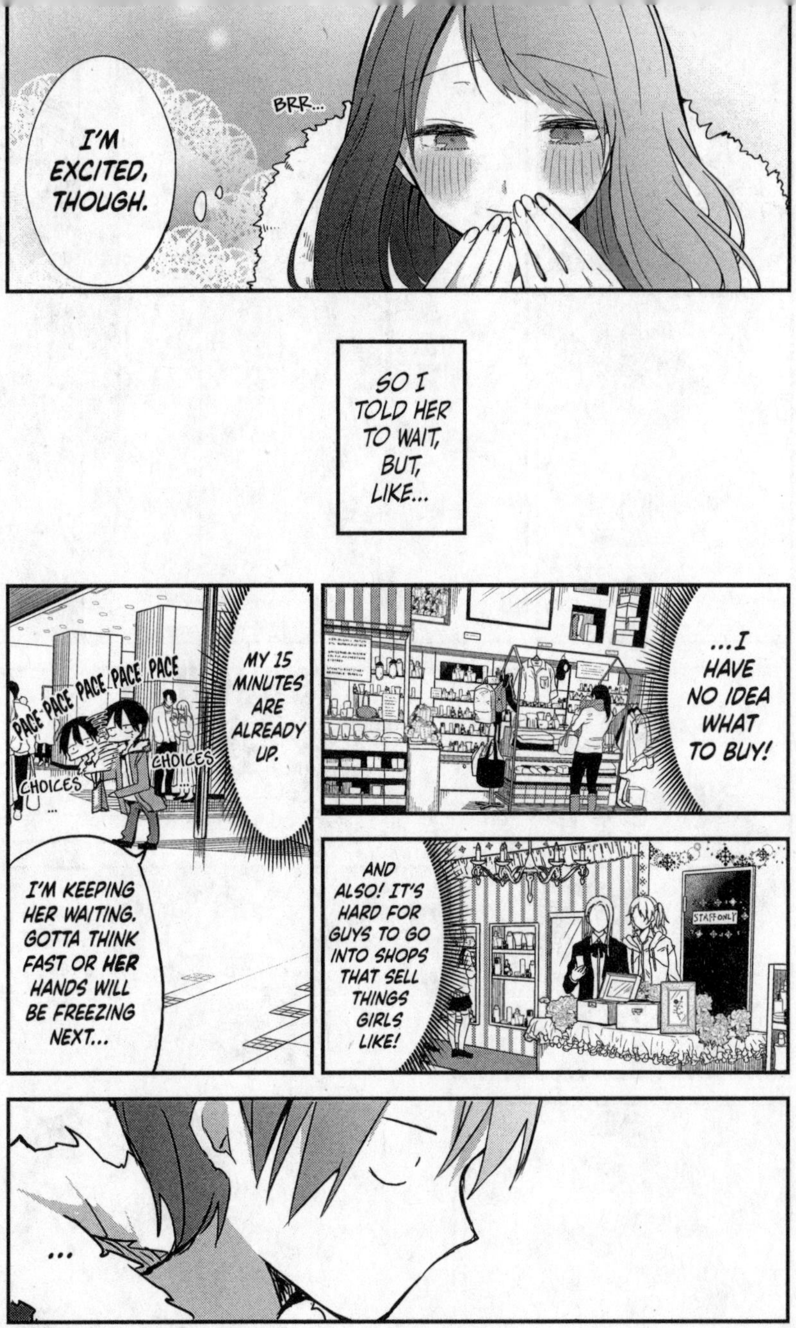
BRR...
I'M EXCITED, THOUGH.
SO I TOLD HER TO WAIT, BUT, LIKE...
...I HAVE NO IDEA WHAT TO BUY!
AND ALSO! IT'S HARD FOR GUYS TO GO INTO SHOPS THAT SELL THINGS GIRLS LIKE!
STAFF ONLY
MY 15 MINUTES ARE ALREADY UP.
PACE PACE PACE PACE PACE
CHOICES
CHOICES...
I'M KEEPING HER WAITING. GOTTA THINK FAST OR HER HANDS WILL BE FREEZING NEXT...
...

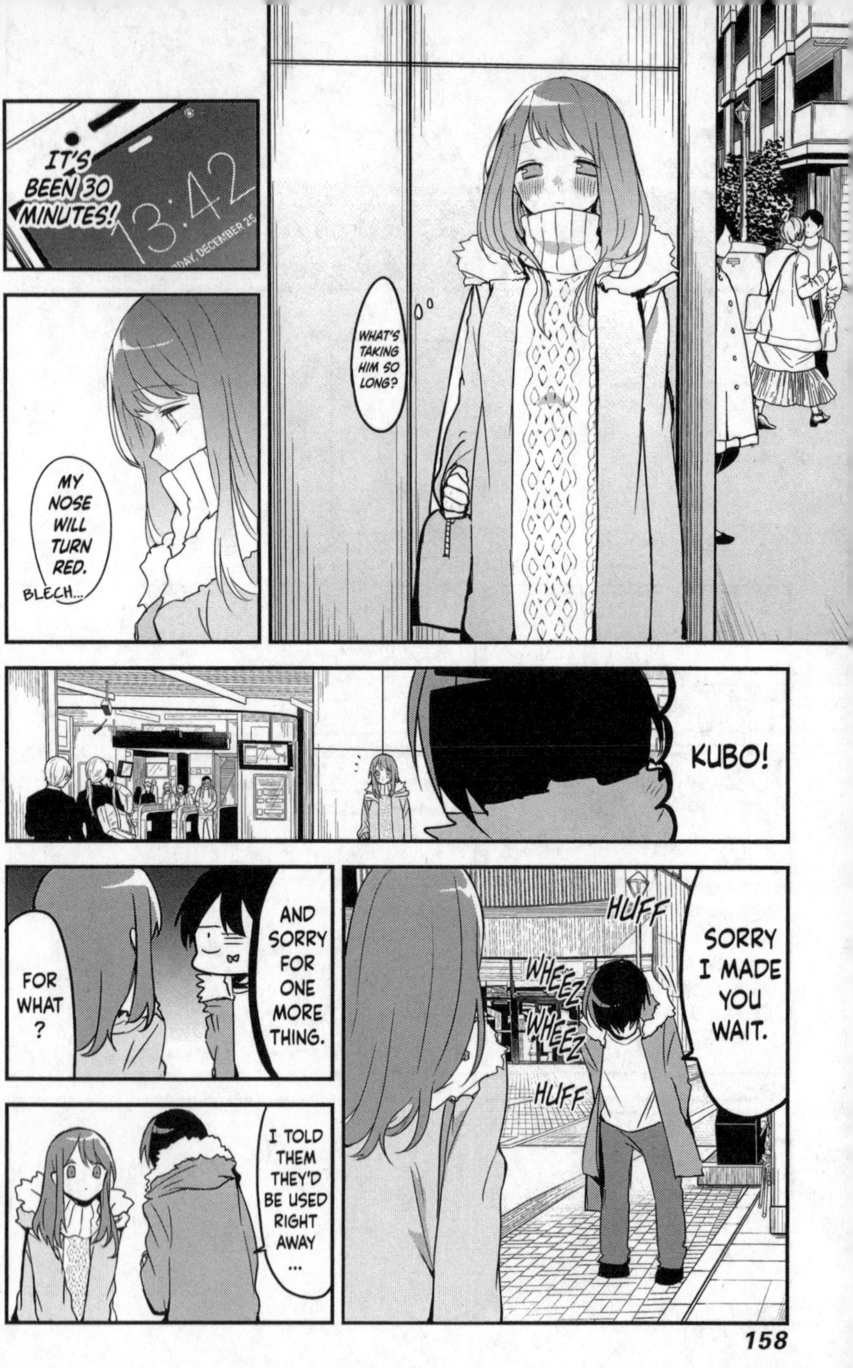
WHAT'S TAKING HIM SO LONG?
IT'S BEEN 30 MINUTES!
13:42
DECEMBER 25
MY NOSE WILL TURN RED.
BLECH...
KUBO!
SORRY I MADE YOU WAIT.
HUFF
WHEEZ
WHEEZ
HUFF
AND SORRY FOR ONE MORE THING.
FOR WHAT?
I TOLD THEM THEY'D BE USED RIGHT AWAY...

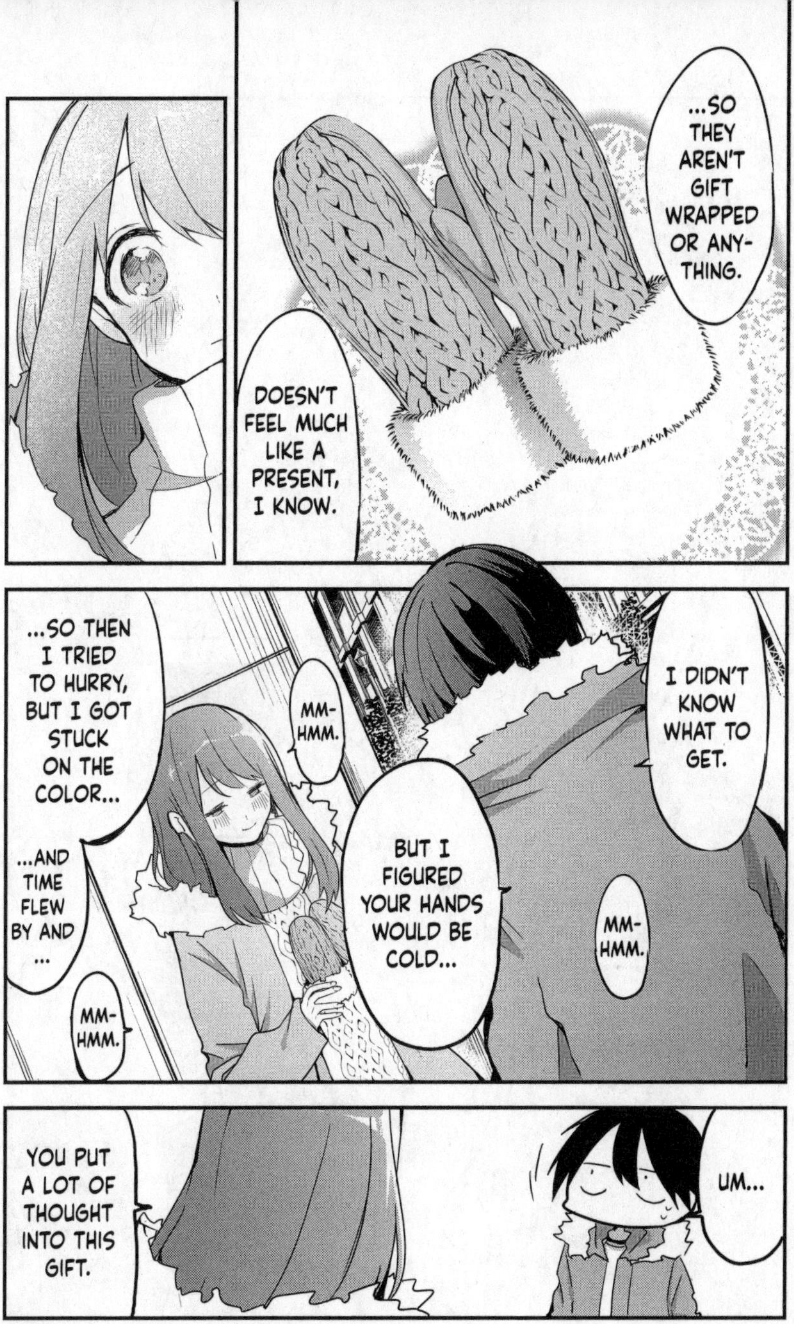
...SO THEY AREN'T GIFT WRAPPED OR ANY-THING.
DOESN'T FEEL MUCH LIKE A PRESENT, I KNOW.
I DIDN'T KNOW WHAT TO GET.
MM-HMM.
BUT I FIGURED YOUR HANDS WOULD BE COLD...
MM-HMM.
...SO THEN I TRIED TO HURRY, BUT I GOT STUCK ON THE COLOR...
...AND TIME FLEW BY AND ...
MM-HMM.
UM...
YOU PUT A LOT OF THOUGHT INTO THIS GIFT.

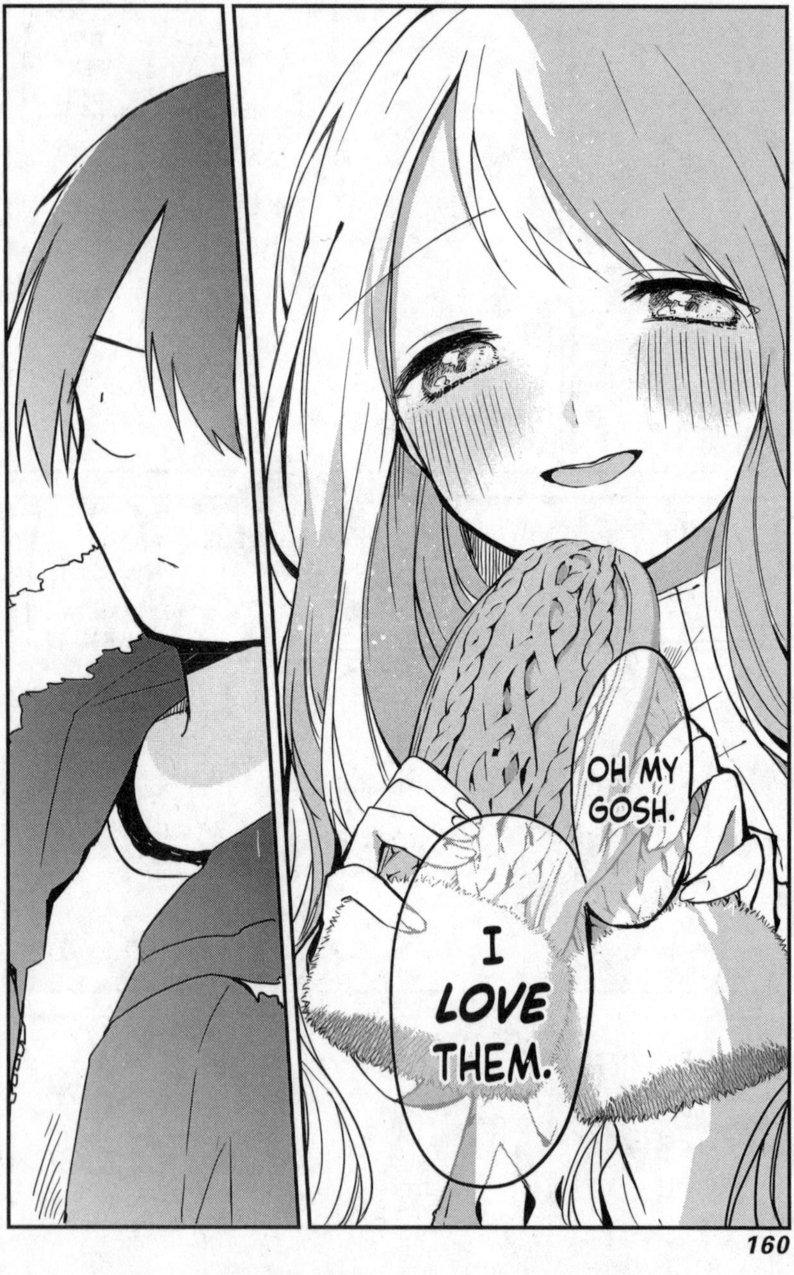
OH MY GOSH.
I *LOVE* THEM.

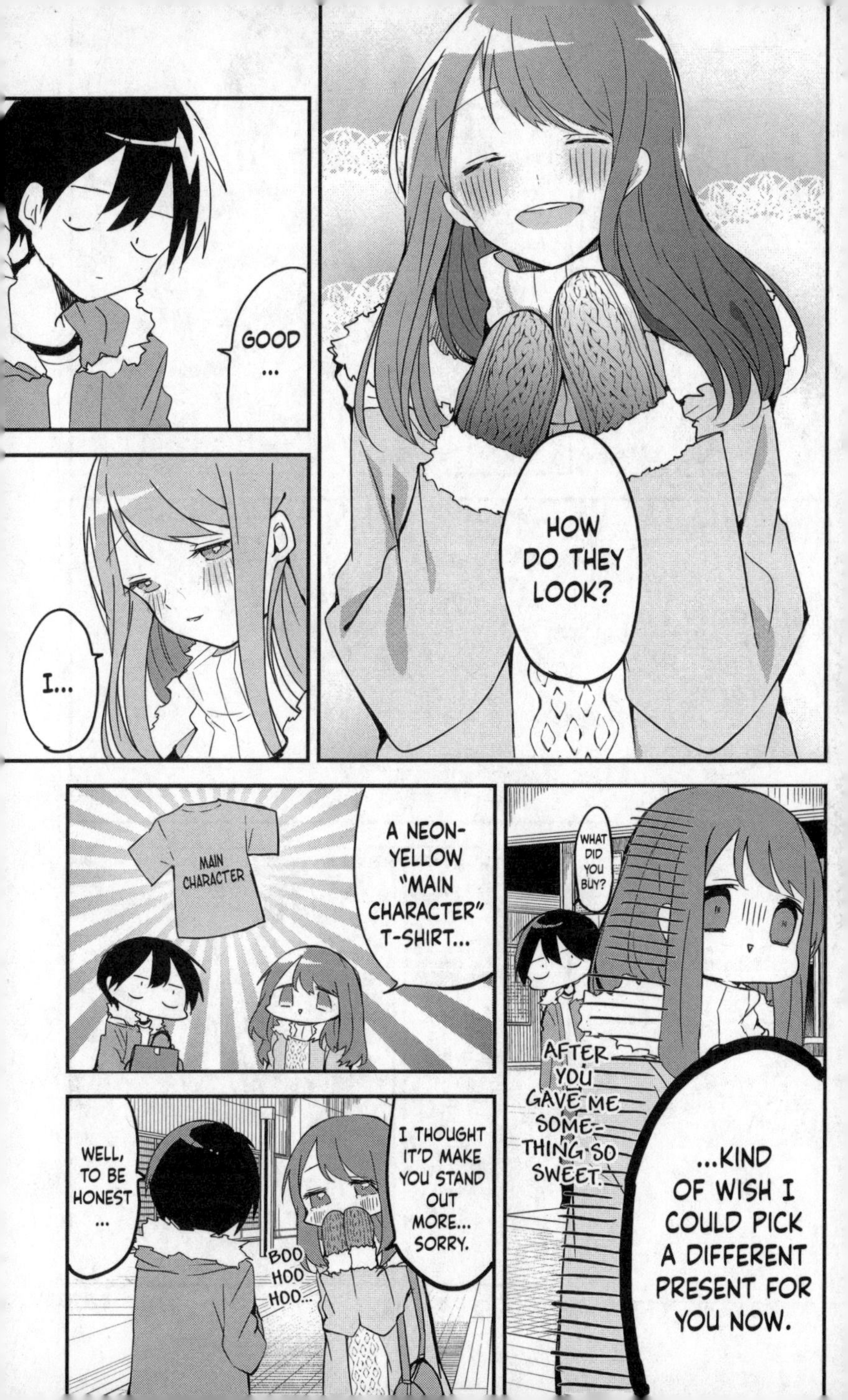
HOW DO THEY LOOK?
GOOD ...
I...
WHAT DID YOU BUY?
AFTER YOU GAVE ME SOME-THING SO SWEET.
...KIND OF WISH I COULD PICK A DIFFERENT PRESENT FOR YOU NOW.
A NEON-YELLOW "MAIN CHARACTER" T-SHIRT...
MAIN CHARACTER
I THOUGHT IT'D MAKE YOU STAND OUT MORE... SORRY.
BOO HOO HOO...
WELL, TO BE HONEST ...

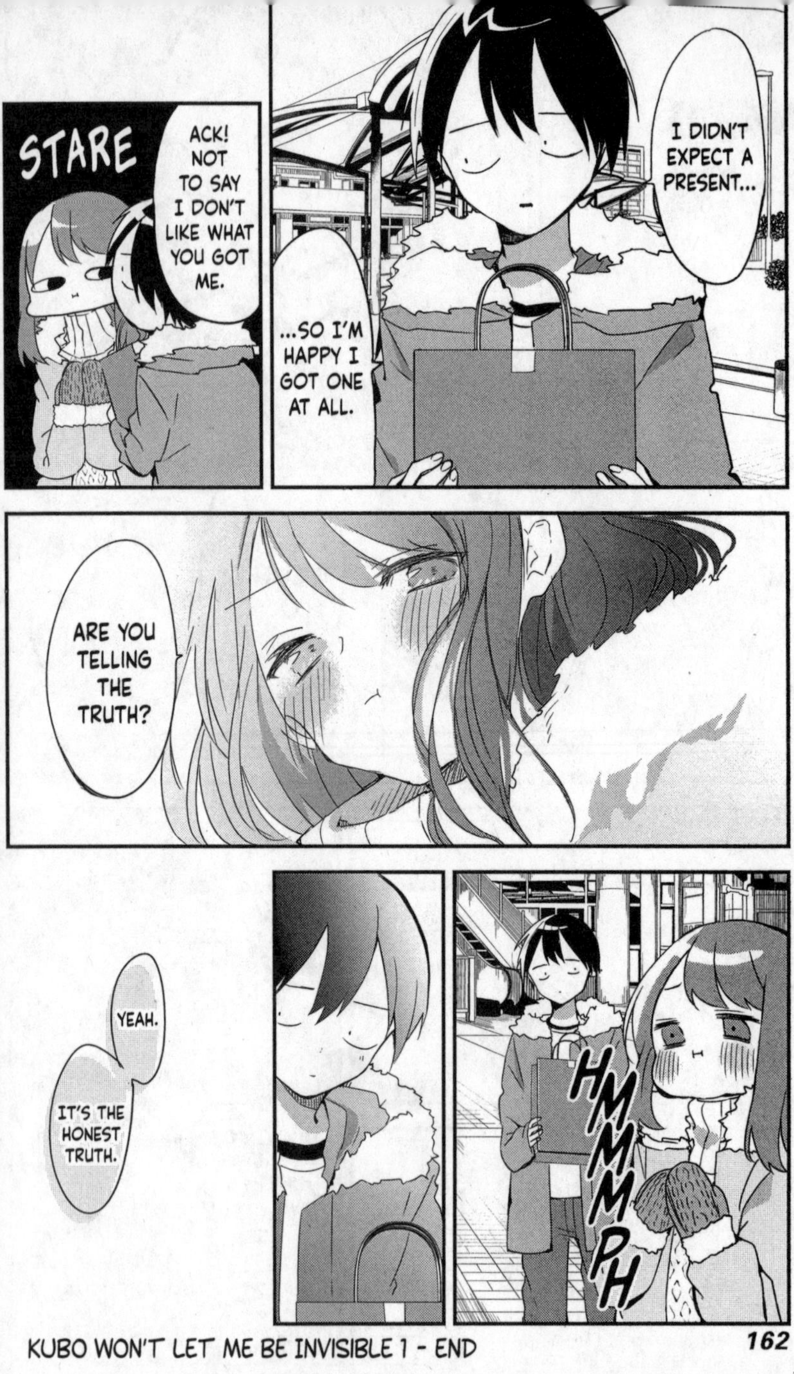
I DIDN'T EXPECT A PRESENT...
...SO I'M HAPPY I GOT ONE AT ALL.
ACK! NOT TO SAY I DON'T LIKE WHAT YOU GOT ME.
STARE
ARE YOU TELLING THE TRUTH?
HMMMMPH
YEAH.
IT'S THE HONEST TRUTH.

KUBO WON'T LET ME BE INVISIBLE 1 - END

MEET THE ASSISTANTS

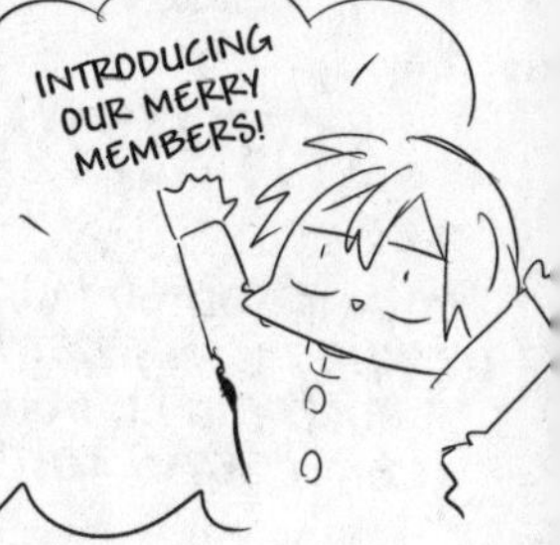
INTRODUCING OUR MERRY MEMBERS!

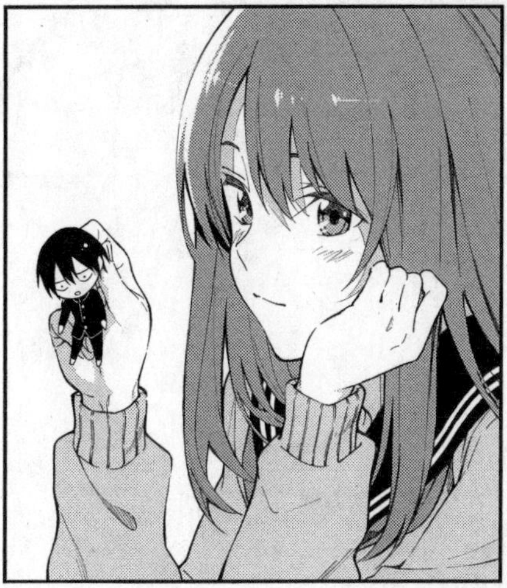

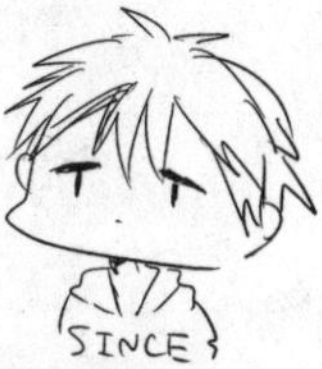
SINCE

Nakao

Can draw anything. Kind, polite, and randomly klutzy. Always worrying. Chatty when B'z comes up. Your *FGO* servants are too strong. I want your five-star servants.

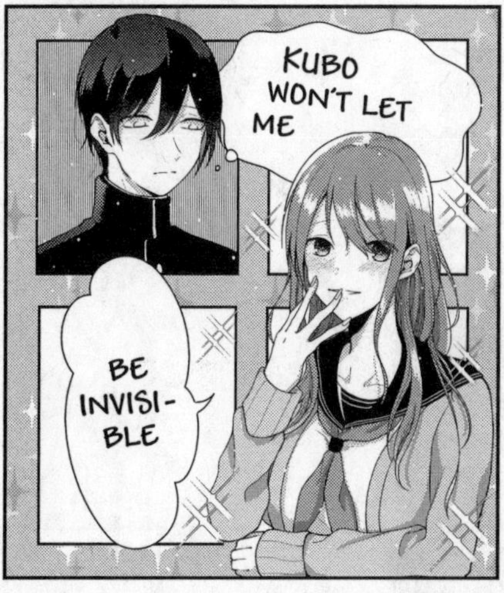
KUBO WON'T LET ME
BE INVISI-BLE

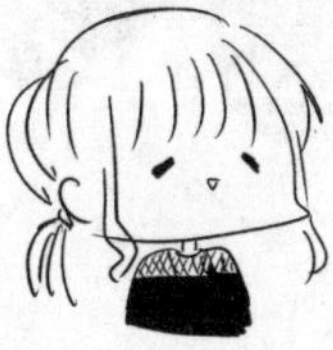

Egui

Fast worker. "Thank you" and "time-out." And to her own energy, "stay." Quick to tear up when talking about absolute faves. Overbearing love. Her love is 100 percent Gilles de Rais in *FGO* chapter 1. Has a unique way of rolling gacha.

AFTERWORD

THANK YOU SO MUCH FOR PICKING UP *KUBO WON'T LET ME BE INVISIBLE*! I HOPE YOU LIKED IT. IT'S MY FIRST WEEKLY SERIALIZATION, BUT THANKS TO THE SUPPORT OF MANY PEOPLE, I NOW HAVE A HANDLE ON IT AND CAN ENJOY THE PROCESS. I'M GOING TO WORK EVEN HARDER, SO PLEASE STICK AROUND.

NENE YUKIMORI

THANKS!

NAKAO, EGUI,
EDITOR R,
HACHIJO HIGH SCHOOL,
EVERYONE INVOLVED
IN THE MAKING OF
THIS MANGA,
AND YOU!

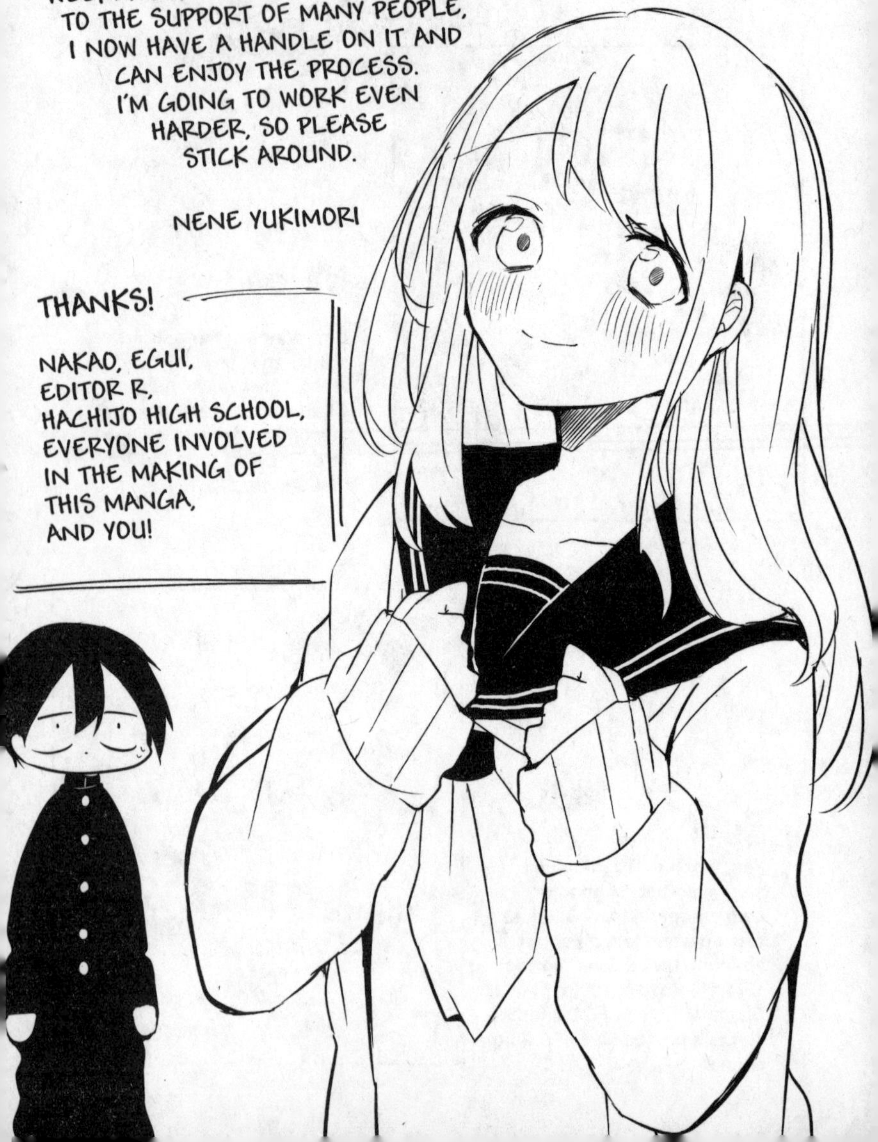

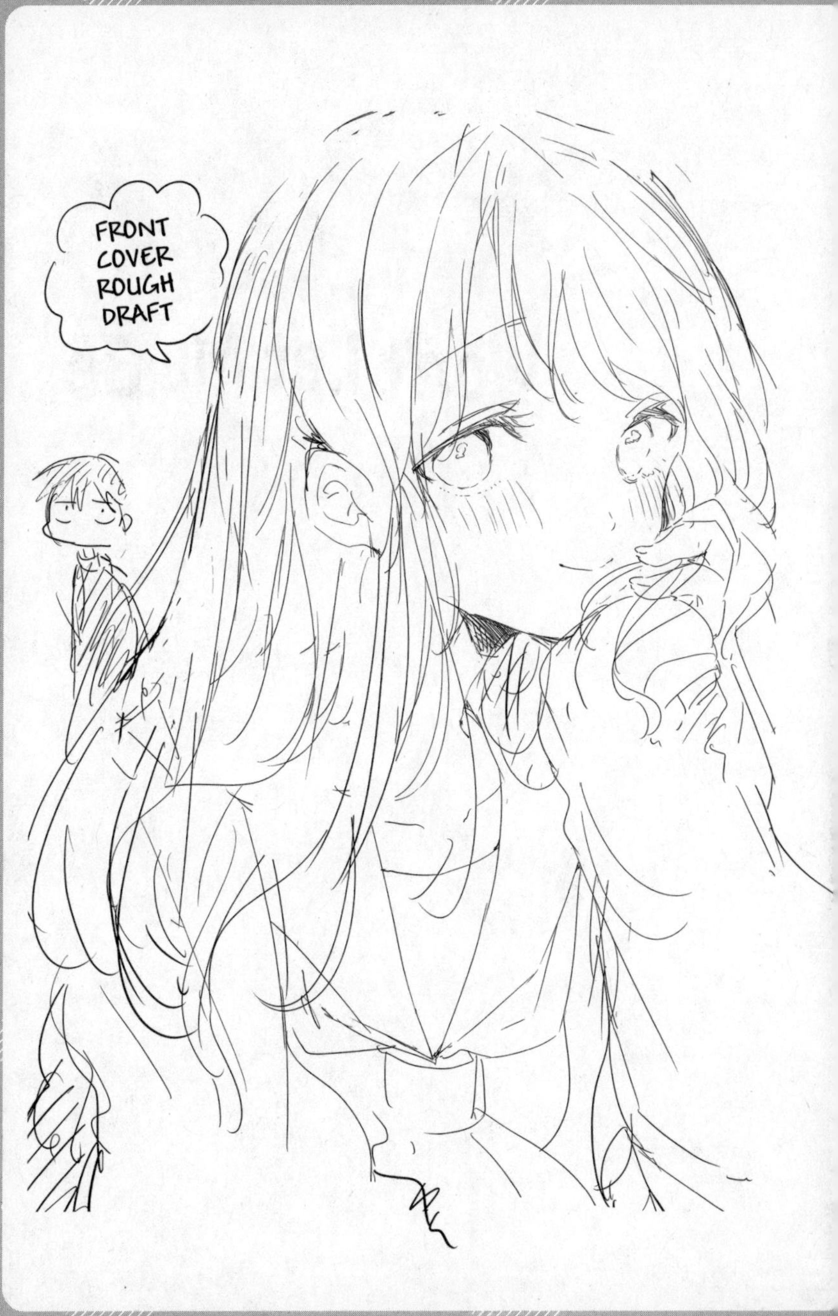
FRONT COVER ROUGH DRAFT

Kubo
Won't Let Me Be
Invisible

Even if everyone else misses you,
I'll always find you.
Because you, someone who "can't be special,"
are the most special to me.

Your name is
my theme song, the shortest in the world.

I left all the sad words in a love
in a previous life.

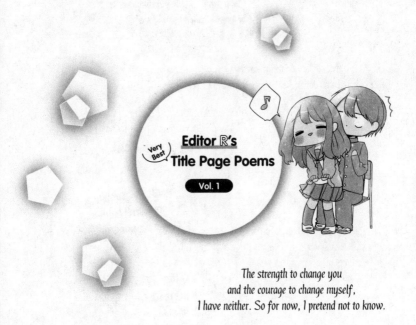

Editor R's Very Best Title Page Poems

Vol. 1

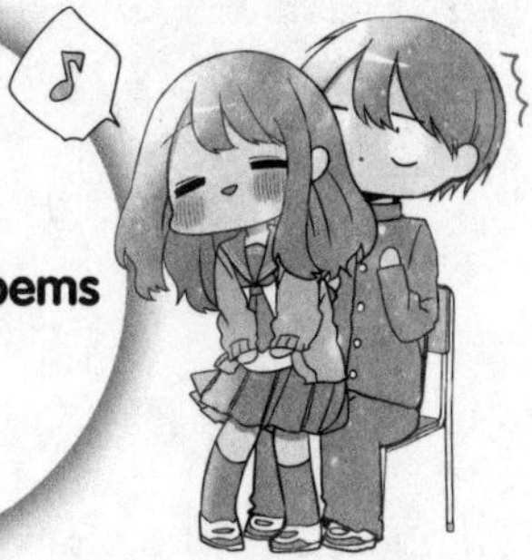

The strength to change you
and the courage to change myself,
I have neither. So for now, I pretend not to know.

The reason I like to be alone is
because there's someone I want to remember on anxious nights.

I tried standing just a little taller
so I could watch the sunset at the same speed as you hunched over.

We forget that glass is a liquid
and thoughtlessly swear an eternity of time together.

Intricate wrapping.
A thoughtful surprise.
Both requests to you, who neither suits.

Do you remember
the murmur of these feelings
before we called them "love"?

Magic limited to the season.
A message streams down: "Stay close because it's cold."

From the center of the world to its corners,
my feelings always ignore my coordinates
and dash off in a straight line.

Readers, do you sometimes feel like you don't quite understand Editor R's poems? I do.

Also, Editor R wants to turn these poems into a page-a-day calendar.

Whatever makes my editor happy.

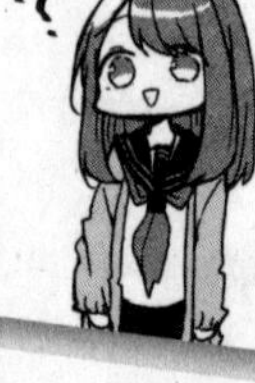

Nene Yukimori

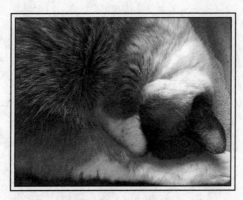

Nene Yukimori

I couldn't have made it this far on my own. I want to pay it forward by bringing others to places they couldn't see without me and never forget my gratitude for the people in my life.

Nene Yukimori earned the right to serialize *Kubo Won't Let Me Be Invisible* in *Young Jump* after the manga's one-shot version won the magazine's Shinman GP 2019 Season 5 contest. The manga then began serialization in October 2019. The work is Yukimori's first to receive an English release.

Kubo Won't Let Me Be Invisible

1

SHONEN JUMP EDITION

STORY AND ART BY
NENE YUKIMORI

TRANSLATION
AMANDA HALEY

TOUCH-UP ART & LETTERING
SNIR AHARON

DESIGN
ALICE LEWIS

EDITOR
JENNIFER SHERMAN

Printed in the U.S.A.

Published by VIZ Media, LLC
P.O. Box 77010
San Francisco, CA 94107

10 9 8 7 6 5 4 3 2 1
First printing, May 2022

ratings.viz.com
RATED T+ OLDER TEEN

PARENTAL ADVISORY
KUBO WON'T LET ME BE INVISIBLE is rated T+ for Older Teen and is recommended for ages 16 and up. This volume contains suggestive themes.

VIZ MEDIA
viz.com

SHONEN JUMP

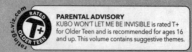

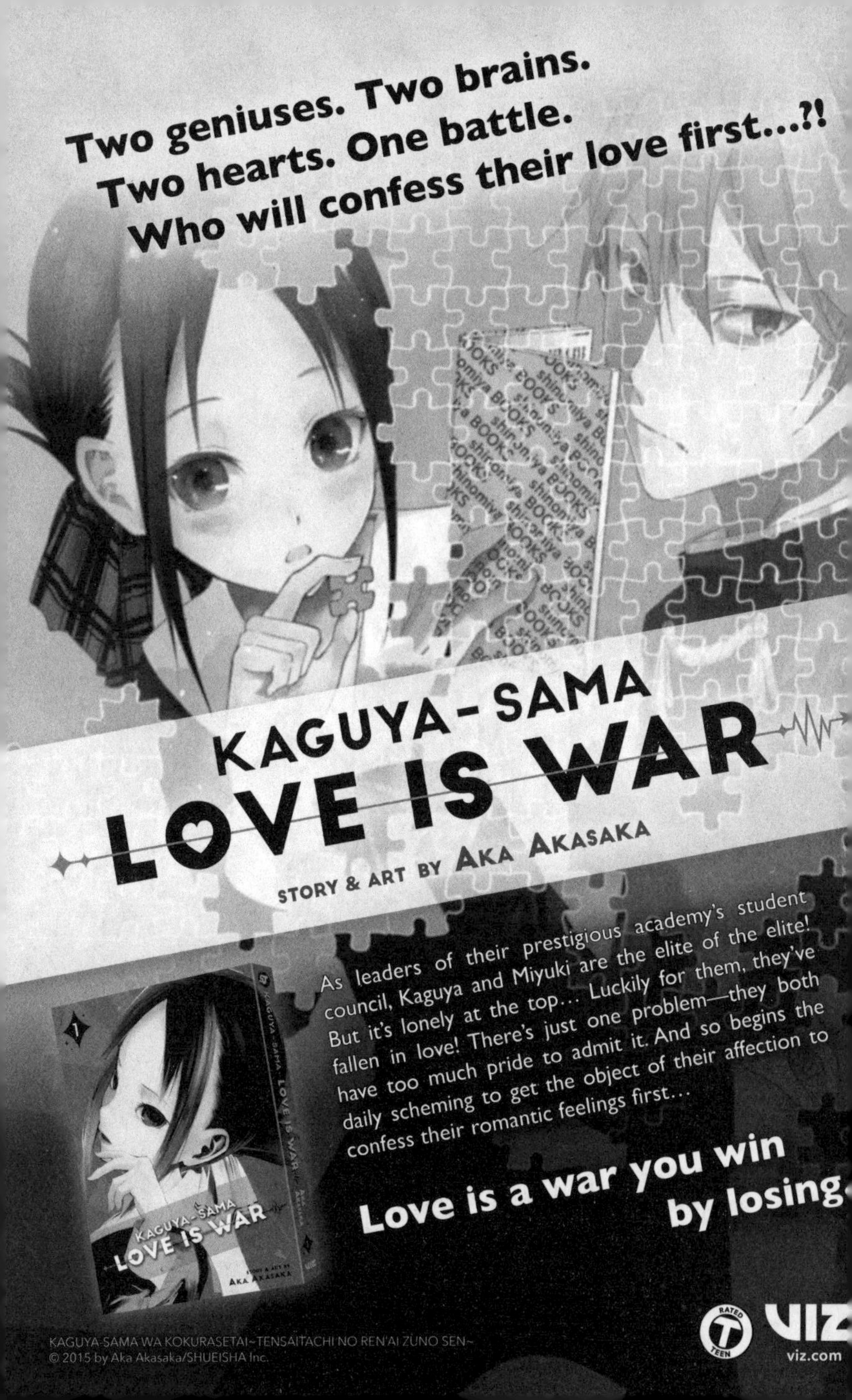
Two geniuses. Two brains.
Two hearts. One battle.
Who will confess their love first...?!
KAGUYA-SAMA
LOVE IS WAR
STORY & ART BY AKA AKASAKA
As leaders of their prestigious academy's student council, Kaguya and Miyuki are the elite of the elite! But it's lonely at the top... Luckily for them, they've fallen in love! There's just one problem—they both have too much pride to admit it. And so begins the daily scheming to get the object of their affection to confess their romantic feelings first...
Love is a war you win by losing.
KAGUYA-SAMA LOVE IS WAR
STORY & ART BY AKA AKASAKA
RATED T TEEN
VIZ
viz.com

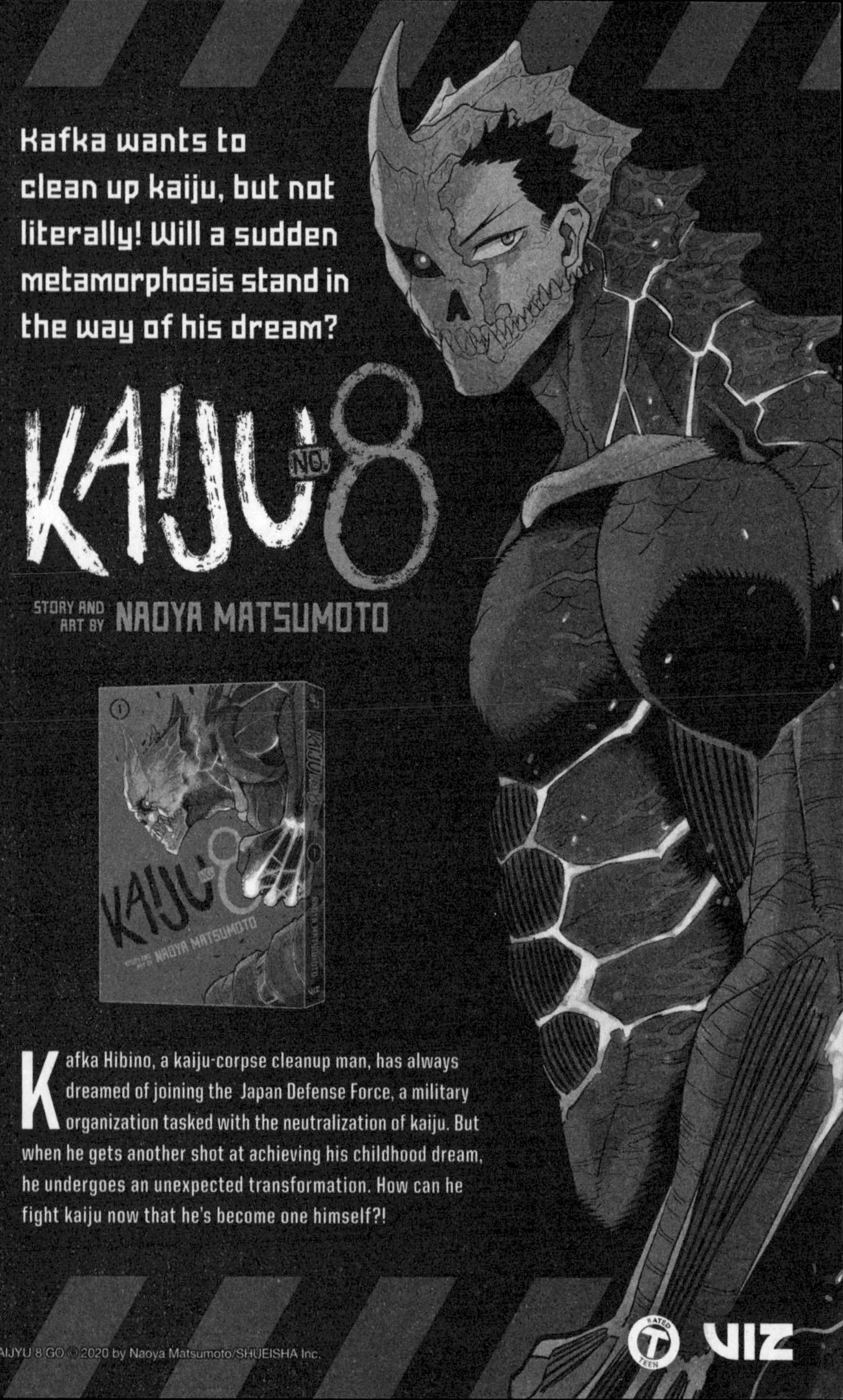
Kafka wants to clean up kaiju, but not literally! Will a sudden metamorphosis stand in the way of his dream?
KAIJU NO. 8
STORY AND ART BY NAOYA MATSUMOTO
Kafka Hibino, a kaiju-corpse cleanup man, has always dreamed of joining the Japan Defense Force, a military organization tasked with the neutralization of kaiju. But when he gets another shot at achieving his childhood dream, he undergoes an unexpected transformation. How can he fight kaiju now that he's become one himself?!
RATED T TEEN
VIZ
AIJYU 8 GO © 2020 by Naoya Matsumoto/SHUEISHA Inc.

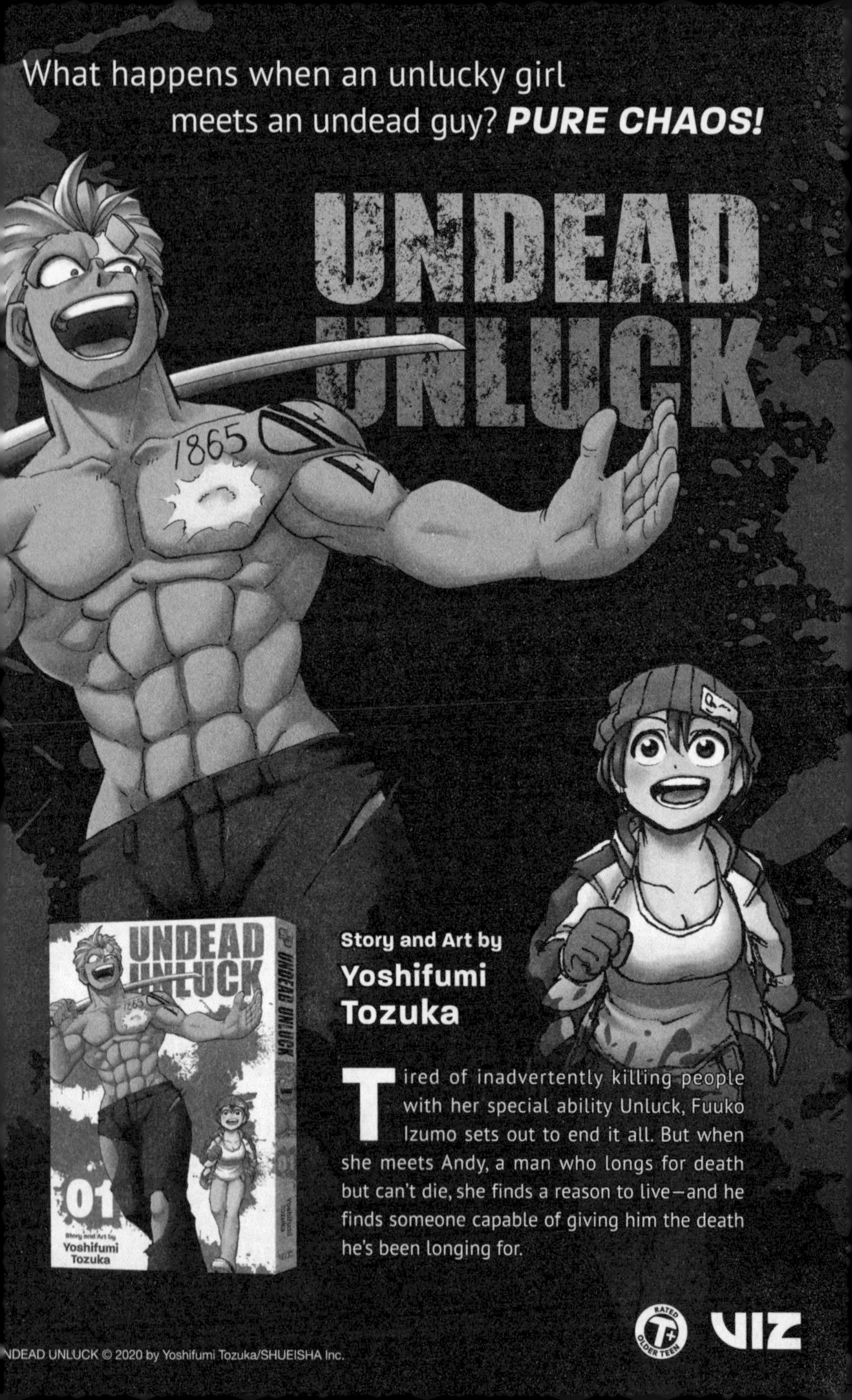

What happens when an unlucky girl
meets an undead guy? *PURE CHAOS!*

UNDEAD UNLUCK

Story and Art by
Yoshifumi
Tozuka

Tired of inadvertently killing people
with her special ability Unluck, Fuuko
Izumo sets out to end it all. But when
she meets Andy, a man who longs for death
but can't die, she finds a reason to live—and he
finds someone capable of giving him the death
he's been longing for.

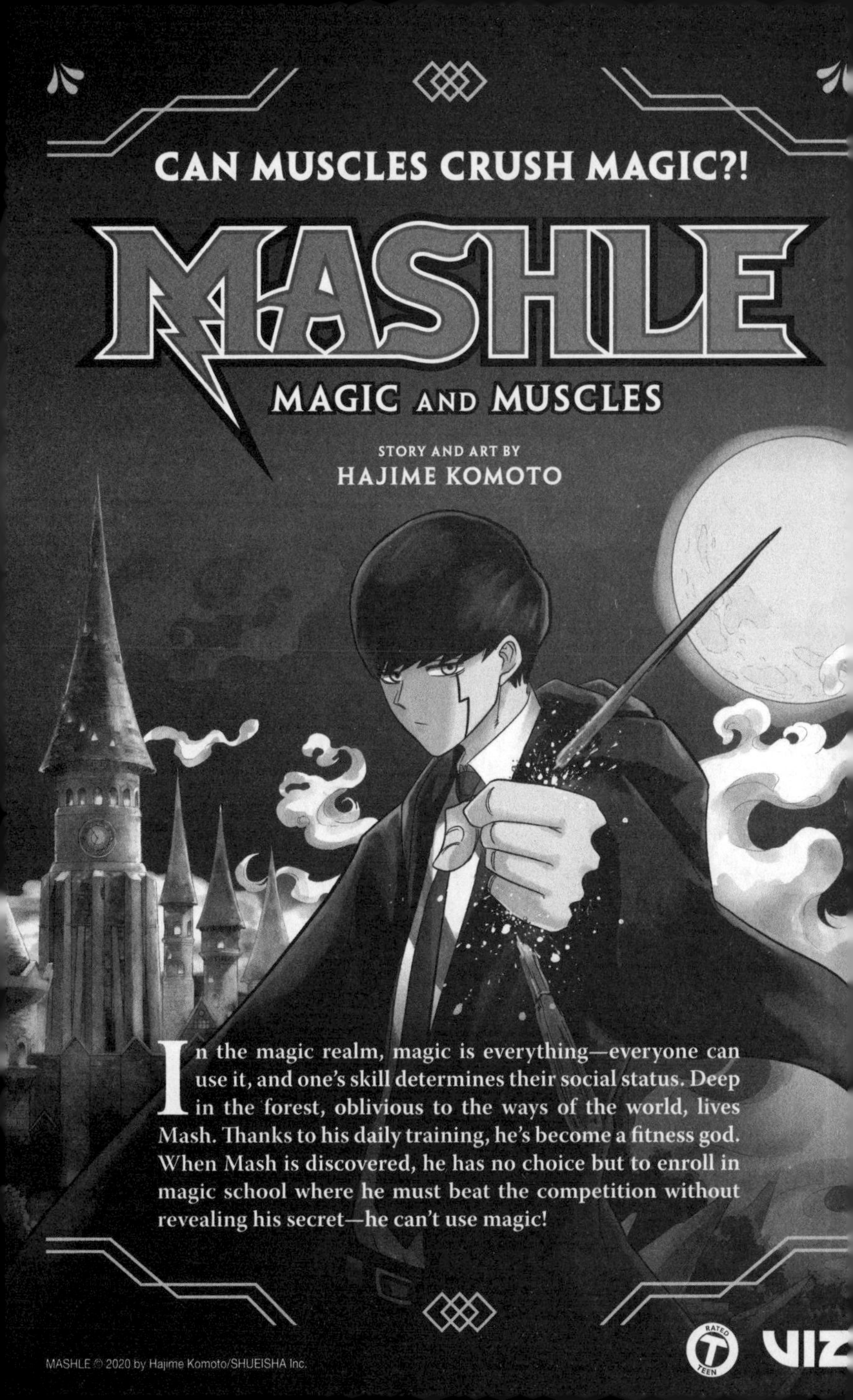

CAN MUSCLES CRUSH MAGIC?!
MASHLE
MAGIC AND MUSCLES
STORY AND ART BY
HAJIME KOMOTO
In the magic realm, magic is everything—everyone can use it, and one's skill determines their social status. Deep in the forest, oblivious to the ways of the world, lives Mash. Thanks to his daily training, he's become a fitness god. When Mash is discovered, he has no choice but to enroll in magic school where he must beat the competition without revealing his secret—he can't use magic!
RATED T TEEN
VIZ
MASHLE © 2020 by Hajime Komoto/SHUEISHA Inc.

STOP!

YOU MAY BE READING THE WRONG WAY!

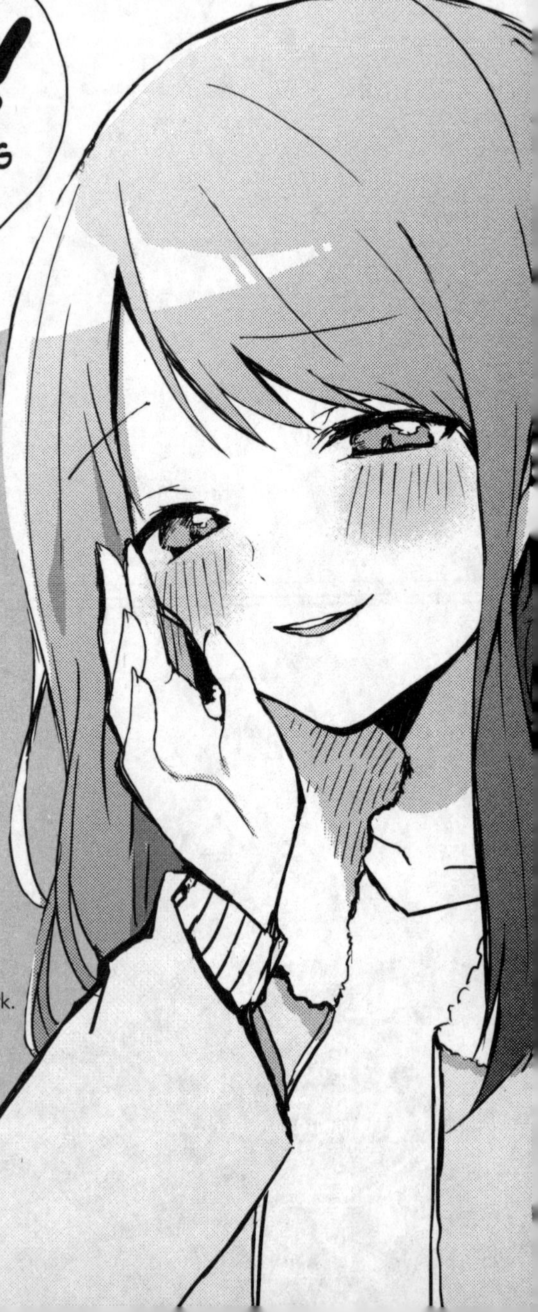

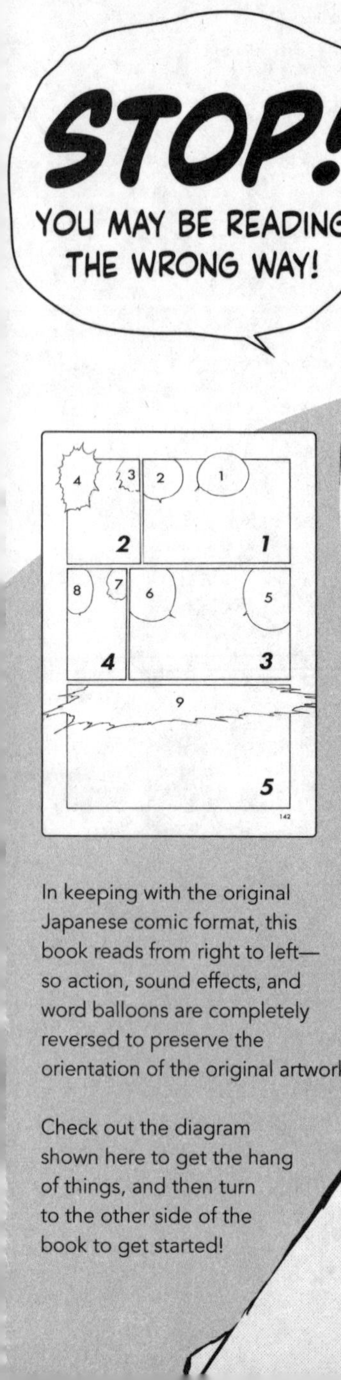

In keeping with the original Japanese comic format, this book reads from right to left—so action, sound effects, and word balloons are completely reversed to preserve the orientation of the original artwork.

Check out the diagram shown here to get the hang of things, and then turn to the other side of the book to get started!